TALES

of the

SEVEN SEAS

TALES

of the

SEVEN SEAS

The Escapades of

CAPTAIN DYNAMITE JOHNNY O'BRIEN

DENNIS M. POWERS

TAYLOR TRADE PUBLISHING
Lanham • New York • Boulder • Toronto • Plymouth, UK

Published by Taylor Trade Publishing
An imprint of The Rowman & Littlefield Publishing Group, Inc.
4501 Forbes Boulevard, Suite 200, Lanham, Maryland 20706
http://www.rlpgtrade.com

Estover Road, Plymouth PL6 7PY, United Kingdom

Distributed by National Book Network

British Library Cataloguing in Publication Information Available

Library of Congress Cataloging-in-Publication Data

Powers, Dennis M.
  Tales of the seven seas : the escapades of Captain Dynamite Johnny O'Brien / Dennis M. Powers.
      p. cm.
  Includes bibliographical references and index.
  ISBN 978-1-58979-447-4 (cloth : alk. paper) — ISBN 978-1-58979-448-1 (electronic)
  1. O'Brien, Johnny, 1851–1931. 2. Ship captains—Biography. 3. Seafaring life—History—19th century—Anecdotes. 4. Seafaring life—History—20th century—Anecdotes. I. Title.
  VK140.O2P69 2010
  387.5092—dc22
  [B]

                                                    2009049759

CONTENTS

PREFACE

As I reflected on the multitudes of files when writing my last book, *Taking the Sea*, I became curious about the seaman who single-handedly saved a three-thousand-ton steamship: Captain "Dynamite Johnny" O'Brien. While tracking down what was written about him, I became enamored with the tales of crude and refined men, their endurance, and their abilities to survive very difficult times on the dangerous ocean—some of their making, all of their choosing.

Reading about sailing on nineteenth-century full-sail ships and early-twentieth-century steamers engendered feelings of nostalgia and romance. The stories also had an underside, however, of cruelty, toughness, combat, and raw courage. I found myself traveling with Johnny O'Brien from the South Seas to Alaska on his sea ventures, and this book—*Tales of the Seven Seas*—was born when I came across Pierre Berton's masterful book *The Klondike Fever*, which contained this passage:

> O'Brien, perhaps the most colorful sea captain on the Pacific Coast, had a history so garish that it tended to read like one of the more florid sea novels popular at the time. He had narrowly missed being eaten by cannibals; had fought off Chinese pirates with cannon fire; had supped with the Royal Family of Hawaii; had made love to a Tahitian princess; had been offered a partnership by King O'Keefe, the famous white emperor of the island of Yap; and had shipped with the hairy and villainous Robert O'Malley, prototype for Jack London's Sea Wolf.

My research made extensive use of old maritime journals, historical society journals, personal interviews with sea historians, and worn newspaper clippings detailing these and other sagas. When I finally tracked down O'Brien's original letters and journals and reviewed them at length, I had the basis for this book and its stories.

Captain O'Brien sailed the seven seas for more than sixty years, starting in the late 1860s in India and ending in the early 1930s on the U.S. West Coast. He sailed every type of ship imaginable, but this book is intended to be more than just the story of this incredible captain.

Tales of the Seven Seas is about what sailing over the oceans was really like from the nineteenth to the twentieth centuries, when danger and adventure coexisted every day. With this book, I hope the reader will smell the salt in the air and hear the ocean's rush as a ship sails with hardened men, leaking seams, and shrieking winds. Sailing the seas then was not for the faint of heart, whether one was a passenger or crewmember, and this was the time before legalities and lawyers began to rule the maritime world.

O'Brien was born in Ireland in 1851, and his first command was the American sailing bark *Alden Besse*. He was twenty-five years old, a very young age to obtain this rank. The nickname Dynamite Johnny came from his actions when he first sailed on the large steamer *Umatilla* in a storm off the Pacific Northwest. He was able to save the ship by "subduing" a rolling safe that was battering a case of dynamite—hence the nickname. This was during a horrendous gale, when just being inside the hold was an act of courage.

Among his more notable accomplishments was a second saving of the *Umatilla* after she struck a reef near British Columbia that's now known as Umatilla Reef. With the vessel being crushed from "stem to collision bulkhead," the captain and crew abandoned ship. Believing the ship was still seaworthy, Chief Mate O'Brien stayed around until the vessel drifted off. He succeeded with others he commandeered in getting her sails up and safely brought the ship to British Columbia. The ship sank in shallow water, but her proximity to shore allowed the vessel to be raised. He was lauded from coast to coast for this feat.

During these times O'Brien was well known in Alaska because he was the one captain who didn't lose a ship, and he brought thousands of prospectors into the region along the Inside Passage. Along the way he became friends with Jack London when the budding writer was making his way to the Klondike gold fields. O'Brien was a confidant of the builder of the Alaskan and Canadian railways, Michael J. Heney, who willed a monthly stipend to the captain, and of the famous—or infamous—outlaw Soapy Smith.

I wrote this book to illustrate the world that O'Brien's adventures reflect: sometimes violent, always risky, at times lawless, when shipping out was a feat of rugged individualism—before the judgmental filter that today's world applies.

O'Brien's time was one that was raw and real in its underbelly—and he lived his way in an age when one could.

His shipmates and friends called him "the Nestor of the Pacific," one who feared God but defied everything and everyone else with hard fists and spirit. O'Brien commanded a ship in 1924 on its gala excursion to the South Seas and Tahiti, where the island princess—the granddaughter of the "slim beauty" that O'Brien had met nearly fifty years before—came onboard to welcome him. Back in San Francisco, a motion-picture studio chartered the vessel for the filming of Buster Keaton's *The Navigator*, and Dynamite Johnny regaled the actor and others with his experiences. When O'Brien died in August 1931 at the age of eighty, he was mourned throughout the West Coast and nationally.

I applaud O'Brien and these men of the sea. The stories are about the sea, courage, failures, and overcoming incredible odds—which are so applicable today. I truly enjoyed working on this book.

ACKNOWLEDGMENTS

I wish to thank everyone connected with this project for their generous suggestions, information, and assistance. The writing of *Tales of the Seven Seas* required a mixture of librarians, researchers, maritime museum curators, and experts to sort through the myriad facts—some in total conflict—to write the stories about Captain "Dynamite Johnny" O'Brien, and others, that spanned from the late 1800s into the twentieth century.

Maritime museums and historical societies always receive deserved recognition for their assistance in tracking down information about vessels, their captains, and maritime life. The San Francisco Maritime Museum, especially Bill Kooiman of its Porter Shaw Library, provided help again with their old pictures and files on maritime life during these periods. Carole Marnet of the Puget Sound Maritime Historical Society was especially helpful in checking universities and libraries that could shed further light on O'Brien. Dave Pearson and Jeff Smith of the widely respected Columbia River Maritime Museum helped in answering my questions on Oregon's connection. The highly regarded maritime author Jim Gibbs gave much-needed background on the old sail ships and steamers of the times.

Experienced librarians are always a key to successful research. Elizabeth Walsh of the Seattle Public Library provided needed copies of newspaper articles, including old ones of the *Seattle Times*, which contributed to this understanding.

Gladi Kulp, the head of Historical Collections for the Alaska State Library in Juneau, also assisted.

Anna Beauchamp is the coordinator of interlibrary loans for Southern Oregon University and was instrumental in arranging the review of Captain O'Brien's microfiched memoirs and letters. Kevin Knapp assisted in finding excellent articles in the same respect. Dr. Clarice Stasz, emerita professor of history from Sonoma State University—and an expert historian, including on Charmian London—gave helpful leads, as did Jay Williams, the senior managing editor of *Critical Inquiry*, a University of Chicago Press humanities journal, who later helped me weave my way through Captain O'Brien's memoirs regarding Jack London's character of Wolf Larsen in *The Sea-Wolf*.

In historical research, pictures are important in supporting the personal accounts. Reviewing the old pictures of wrecks, cities, and the times gave much accuracy to this story. In this regard, the previously mentioned maritime museums were very helpful, as was the Royal British Columbia Museum in Vancouver, British Columbia.

Special thanks also go to Dainan Skeem, the archivist in Collections Management for the Hawaii State Archives located on the Iolani Palace Grounds in Honolulu, Hawaii; he was especially supportive in reviewing the pictures of old Honolulu, its harbor, King David Kalakaua, and Queen Liliuokalani. As well, Stuart Ching, who is the curator of the Iolani Palace in Honolulu, gave appreciated input as to King Kalakaua's royal residences for entertainment during O'Brien's visits.

Rose Speranza of the Alaska and Polar Regions Collections, Elmer E. Rasmuson Library at the University of Alaska-Fairbanks, graciously allowed me to review the entire memoirs of Captain O'Brien through an interlibrary loan (ILL) exchange with Southern Oregon University's Hannon Library. These very extensive written works were in hundreds of microfiched pages and in three sets: O'Brien's Journal I (1851–1889), Journal II (1889–1909), and Journal III (1909–1930). Reviewing O'Brien's notes against old newspaper, magazine, and book accounts about his life—especially Milton Dalby's *The Sea Saga of Dynamite Johnny O'Brien* (1933) and Horace Smith's *A Captain Unafraid: The Strange Adventures of Dynamite Johnny O'Brien* (1912)—gave the support and accuracy needed to write these accounts. The partial bibliography also exemplifies what had to come together for this book.

Continuing in this regard, I wish to give my special appreciation to Sandy Clunies, who provided very valuable historical and genealogical research. And no thanks could be complete without my specially mentioning my literary agent, Jeanne Fredericks, who has been a constant friend, agent, and adviser throughout the years.

To my wife, Judy: I am so fortunate to have you in my life and to be able to do what I truly enjoy. Thank you.

1

EARLY SEA DAYS

"**A**loft with ye, Paddy, and clew that fore royal!" Kicked hard in the ribs with that order, sixteen-year-old Johnny O'Brien awoke with a start. Half-starved and sore, he had tried to sleep on the deck that night with the crown of the starboard anchor as a pillow. When he jumped to his feet, the youth was now shoeless and didn't know if he had misplaced them or if they had been stolen.

O'Brien stared up the soaring foremast of the *Marlborough*, a square-rigged tall-sail ship. He couldn't put his hands around the trunk of this thick pole, the high mast closest to the ship's bow, and it seemed to disappear through the stretched, moonlit sails into the stars. He hesitated at first, knowing that climbing up the tallest sail by the clew rope to its yardarm under these conditions was difficult at best. The seaman yelled, "Get going, boy!" and the disapproving look of the bulky, whiskered mate drove him into action.

O'Brien grabbed the weblike rope shrouds to the massive pole and began pulling himself up. He climbed into the silhouetted darkness on the crossed ratlines, while the taut sails about him pulled or noisily flapped with the ever-changing winds. The higher he went, the more he became aware of the surrounding noises from the ship's creaking, ropes pulling tighter, and the vessel's rolls into the sea. Before he was halfway up the rigging, the lad found he was holding on tighter as he neared a cross-tree, the short bars across the mast that spread the rigging—all used to support the heavy pole, canvas sails, and yardarms.

1

Continuing upward, past more yardarms and sails, he finally stopped in front of the highest sail and clung to the ropes while the royal flapped in front. The wind gusted stronger with the rising sea, while the large sail ship heeled over sickeningly toward the rolling, white-capped ocean. He now looked straight down at the churning sea stories below, and O'Brien felt the mast bend from the strain.

When the vessel righted, he tried to pull the sail up and then to smother the wind from the shaking canvas. A roll to windward and the ship's pitch forward threw the sail full of wind; the vessel's rise on the next wave tossed the sail around his head as he clung with clenched fists to the ropes. The next roll carried the sail back, slapping it coarsely against his head and scraping his face.

O'Brien tried to use his weight, feet, and legs against the sail. By pulling and hauling blindly, he nearly succeeded in spilling the wind from it when a big sea carried him high in the air. The tall ship dove forward again, and a gust of wind caught the sail and tore it from his grasp, at the same time ripping off a fingernail. The deck seemed chasms below, and the *Marlborough* threw noisy spray high over the bow as the ship plowed through the frothing water. Everything about the vessel was streaked with white foam. When he glanced below, the wet decks seemed to shimmer in the moonlight with a surrealistic look that he didn't understand.

This was his first windstorm on top of the sails, and he was high in the skies trying to take in an unheeding one. With the wind came the first spatters of rain, making the sail even more difficult to handle and the rigging harder to hold onto. While he struggled to control the royal, a strange vibration of the sail shook his arms, frightening him.

Another dip to the leeward and he understood. The wheelman was keeping the schooner into the wind; and the foresail, or lowest sail, flapped back and forth when too near the wind, shaking the foremast from trunk to keel. While the ship bounded through harsh waves, he tried his best to pull up the clew lines, the ropes attached to the free corner of the high sail. With turns of the mooring lines, he gradually smothered the wind and secured the sail fast to the masthead.

O'Brien slowly inched down the slippery mast, clinging fretfully to the rigging. It was always easier to climb up than down. Johnny didn't know how long he had been aloft, but no sooner was he back on the safety of the wet deck when the mate called Lawrence cursed, "Get aloft again and loosen it!" He again crept up the mast and this time put his feet on the yard and began letting the heavy sheet of canvas down. The work was hard, the windy and wet conditions precarious, the night suffocating, and the sea stories below. O'Brien finally loosened the sail from its bindings to the yard, with the wind blasting into his face.

The short, lithe teenager worked his way carefully down to the pitching deck. His feet had barely touched the planks when the mate yelled for him to go aloft once more to "clew and furl it." Without shoes, Johnny's bare feet and shins were cut up and bleeding by now as he again inched his way up the ratlines. The skin was chafed from his shins.

After completing again what he had done on his first climb, O'Brien began the dangerous descent down. Exhausted and losing focus, he slipped halfway down, skidding into the dark abyss. He felt a crack to the back of his head and lost consciousness. Later, a bucket of saltwater splashed over his face, and he looked up into the face of another seaman. He was alive—bruised and hurting, but alive. The cross-trees of a lower sail had broken his fall.

The year was 1866, the location somewhere in the Pacific, and the English ship's final destination was India. Lawrence was the chief mate and did what he could to break down the young man in the manner of the times. A "boy" started out friendless and could be unmercifully picked on. He did the dirtiest work, even at times the most dangerous. This brutality was calculated to "put the fear of God into us," as one survivor said, and "to strengthen discipline, to add snap and vigor to our movements."

These "boys" weren't the cabin boys, who worked inside the ship and attended to the needs of the captain, passengers, and crew. They would do the duties everyone else avoided and as directed by the chief mate. The relative youngsters were the ones who brought the food to the seamen's quarters and then brought the dirty dishes back. If the food wasn't plentiful or mainly poor—as on this voyage—the boys ate the least. These "green hands" had to learn fast, whether the task was pulling up sails with a myriad of ropes, scaling to the top, or furling sails. Their labors were tortured until their "outraged" muscles finally adjusted to the unaccustomed work.

Like all initiates, O'Brien's hands on his first voyage were raw, red, and bloody from working the ropes. A time-honored approach was to hold your raw hands in saltwater. If you could stand the pain, the hands seemed to heal faster—or at least, the pain was less afterwards. Over time, a seaman's hands could become so calloused, scarred, and ugly that men would look for gloves to wear when they left on shore leave.

Chief mate Lawrence, the seamen, and O'Brien lived together in the small fo'c'sle (or forecastle) at the forward part of the deck. The high break of the fo'c'sle head sheltered this billet from sea and wind. Running fore and aft, a bulkhead could divide the quarters to separate the different watches. Plain wooden bunks lined the sides, and above a few bunks were rough calendars marked on the woodwork, some from past voyages. Small shelves rigged above the bunks held tobacco, matches, ditty bags, well-thumbed books, old newspapers, and assorted bric-a-brac. Small lines were stretched above the bunks for drying clothes, and hooks for hanging clothes, sea boots, and oil skins were screwed into the wall planks.

The fo'c'sles were bitterly cold in winter and uncomfortable no matter when. Crewmen usually didn't have the luxury of a small stove; it was nearly impossible to read inside, even though the men would have a flickering "slush" lamp—made from an old tin can half filled with slush (fat from salt beef or pork) or oil, with a floating wick made from a bit of rag. The furniture was sparse, if at all: a long narrow table with hard, crude benches on each side. Small lockers were sometimes present where each man could stow a horse blanket, spare clothing, and his mess gear of a mug, plate, knife, fork, and spoon.

The short half deck forming the fo'c'sle head was not high enough for a man to stand upright, and the bosun's lockers, if there, were arranged along the sides into the bow—along with the paint locker and oil stores. In the very nose of the fo'c'sle were the crew's toilets, which were very wet and uncomfortable during storms, noxious in all weather. Large oil tanks with leaking seal or whale oil were put above these and fitted with small copper tubes for discharge.

Whether he was taunting the lad in the fo'c'sle or on deck, Lawrence seemed to live his life every hour of the day with a hatred of O'Brien. He seemed infuriated at his inability to break the lad down. When it was Johnny's morning watch and the weather fine, Lawrence ordered him to clean up the pigsty under the deck. The mate would wait until O'Brien was working there and then lock him inside the smelly, rotten enclosure for two hours with its three large pigs. Johnny was not afraid of this and didn't mind the time when he could leisurely clean the area, although he was careful not to let Lawrence know. At night, the sadistic bosun forced him during the watch to walk the quarterdeck with a heavy capstan bar on his shoulder, shouting that he was going to make a soldier of O'Brien yet. "I suppose he thought I would throw down the capstan bar and that would be the reason for more humiliation," O'Brien wrote later. "Oh, how I love the memory of that. Some brute was that Lawrence and I despised him." But he would later exact his revenge.

* * *

Johnny O'Brien was born in Cork, Ireland, on January 29, 1851. He wrote in his memoirs:

It seems our family, especially on my father's side, was always in trouble with the British Government. I may say also on my mother's side, as her father had to flee Ireland for the United States in the 1820s, landing in Baltimore, Maryland and eventually making his home in Washington, where he became a businessman. My grandmother remained in Ireland and her daughter, my mother, became engaged to General Thomas Francis Meagher until he—with John Mitchell, Smith O'Brien, Dorsey McGee, and others—were arrested in 1848 for high treason and sentenced to be hung, drawn, and quartered.

Afterwards, their sentence was commuted to life imprisonment; a few years later, he escaped with others from a South Pacific prison island and sailed to the U.S. on a New Bedford whaler. During the Civil War General Meagher was in command of the famous Irish Brigade.

[Note: Meagher escaped from Tasmania, Australia, to the United States and arrived in New York City. Once in the U.S., he studied law, pursued journalism, and traveled on lecture tours. An opponent of slavery, he joined the Union Army when the Civil War started and rose to the rank of brigadier general, most notably forming and leading the Irish Brigade during that conflict. After the war, Meagher was designated the acting governor of the Territory of Montana.]

After becoming completely convinced there was no possibility of her imprisoned lover ever receiving a pardon from the English government and giving up on his return, she married my father, who at the age of thirty-three, also fled his country in the cause of Irish freedom. My mother followed him a year later.

His Irish family had "some means" and sent Johnny across the Atlantic Ocean and English Channel to a boarding school at St. Leonards-on-Sea in Sussex, England. After four years, they arranged a post for him in London with the offices of Sir Wally Cugin, a well-known architect and engineer. Although barely fifteen, after a short visit home O'Brien journeyed back to England and the position. However, he never arrived to meet Sir Cugin.

While in a jolting railway car, he noticed a bearded man who was sitting on the long seat across the aisle. The man smiled and asked him if he had ever been to sea. Johnny responded that he had loved his time spent sailing about Cork Harbor on a "catboat," a wide-beamed sailboat with a centerboard and single sail.

The stranger he had happened to meet was an English sea captain on his way to join his ship, which was to sail to the East Indies. Johnny O'Brien showed the quick decision-making ability that he carried to his death. He penned:

> The wonderful stories he told of the sea and the prospect of some day being in command, as he was, impressed me so that I at once decided that a sailor's life was the life for me. This was late in the year 1866. On our arrival in London, I went to the shipping office and the shipping mate was very kind. He told me to do my best as a "boy"—and that someday—I may sail up the Thames River in command of a ship. The day after arriving in London, I signed on the ship *Marlborough*. Twelve years later, I came to London from British Columbia with the first full cargo of salmon just that way—on the *Alice Dickerman*.

* * *

O'Brien knew what he wanted to do with his life, and this decision meant he could avoid working in a boring, closeted office, day in, day out, toiling over a drawing board—the future post that troubled the adventure-minded lad. He also had made another commitment. Instilled when young, his staunch and unquestioning Catholicism played a vital part in his life. Simple yet powerful, this commitment fulfilled a need for religious expression with a daily regimen of worship first nurtured in his Irish home. This faith also made him quick to conclude divine intervention in the near calamities that seemed to constantly occur around him.

One incident during this first voyage served to strengthen his sturdy belief in God. The *Marlborough* was surging through bad weather when rounding the Cape of Good Hope, and the captain ordered the seamen to bring down the royal and t'gallant yards, which due to the vessel's rolling and wild plunges would be dangerous. A grizzled sailor named Bass, who was "some sixty years old," was the first man aloft and, while securing the gantlines on the highest yardarm, fell a dizzying distance.

O'Brien was on deck and saw Bass's body hurtle down, crash through the longboat lashed bottom up, and land on the hatch. He had fallen wildly more than one hundred feet. When sailors hurried to pick up what must have been a corpse, however, the old man shook his head weakly and protested: "Let me be, boys. Soon's I get my wind, I'll get up."

He gravely informed the shaken O'Brien that Providence didn't intend for him to die aboard a ship—and not be buried on holy ground. A few minutes later, Bass picked himself off the deck and slowly walked away. Bass's survival was the exception to the rule on high-wire falls to the deck.

The work was constant and hard, but Johnny was equal to the job. An important task was to continually wash the ship down, since this kept the decks tight and the ship sanitary. The men worked the "pump brakes" back and forth to draw up water from the suction hose thrown down into the sea and then washed down the decks. Canvas water buckets filled with seawater, brooms made of coir (hard, dried coconut fiber), wooden buckets, and "much slopping about in bare feet" were used. Being the lowest person on the totem pole, O'Brien, as with other new recruits, would have to swab and clean all of the white paintwork, railings, and cabin moldings.

The work of "holystoning" also began. The seamen worked in gangs, sawing away at the deck planks with different stones to wear away the scum. In holystoning, the men used two sizes of stones, the larger ones called "bibles" and the small pieces—useful for getting into the corners and along the edges of paintwork—were known as "prayer books." Cushions to kneel on were built by nailing three cleats to pieces of board and stretching a piece of old canvas over that.

While scrubbing, seamen used two buckets: one of water and another half full of beach sand. A piece of old canvas was used as a cloth to wash the painted sections. Since this was not very soft, rust stains and blotches of tar on posts and railings couldn't be removed as easily; dipping the canvas into the bucket of beach sand helped, but if the sand failed, the mate threw a handful of lye into the water. This usually removed the stains—as well as the skin from the man's fingers.

Due to washing through heavy seas for several weeks, the long hard sweep of the main deck became slippery with a deposit of white saltwater slime, making the footing precarious. The sheen of this scum under the moonlight and a film of running water gave the decks a ghastly *Flying Dutchman*-like appearance, which

O'Brien had seen from the top of the royal sail. The seamen then brought out the "bear": a heavy box with a thick thrum (unspun fleece) mat lashed on the bottom and heavily loaded with broken holy stones and wet sand. Four stout rope lanyards were rigged to the corners and used to haul the box back and forth as sand filtered through the mat, providing the necessary scouring agent. It took a day or two, night included, before the bear worked to scour off the deck.

During a voyage, the ship's timbers kept her bilge "sweet" by allowing quantities of cool seawater to seep in. When "heavy" (or bad) weather happened, sailors needed to continually man the bilge pumps—and this was back-breaking work. Four men were on each crank, two to a side, and while facing each other, their tired arms and backs needed to be synchronized to the rotation, like toy figures on an antique clock. When the low, raucous wheezing of the valves informed the men that the hoses were sucking air, the mate in the darkness yelled, "Belay the pump!" And Lawrence had ordered O'Brien onto one of the cranks.

After a voyage of four months and "lousy food," the ship arrived off Calcutta, and Johnny had made up his mind that he would never again ship "before the mast on an English vessel, not if he had to rot in that heat-moldy, dirty town off the bow [the fo'c'sle]."

In those months of hard work and harsh treatment, O'Brien had to learn the rules of surviving long trips over the sea as a boy. He had to quickly obey any order to the letter, especially when he lived and worked so closely with his chief antagonist. O'Brien learned that a savage attack was the best way to survive fights on board—with bad accidents being only a heartbeat away—and that only tough bodies with calloused fists could survive a fight. His hands had become strong from the constant around-the-clock work. His body was now muscular from the constant walking on watch, washing down decks, cleaning the unthinkable, pulling on heavy ropes, and climbing tall masts. Although short at five-feet, five-inches and a lad of 135 pounds, he was now strong and quick as a cat.

The ship had anchored near the docks when O'Brien heard a loud crash behind him. Looking around, he was startled to find the sadistic Lawrence—whom he had named "the Devil Mate of the Ship Marlborough" in his memoirs—lumbering toward him. O'Brien knew that with the ship's reaching its destination, Lawrence felt all bets were off. He didn't have to observe the smallest of rules on the treatment of a lowly "boy."

O'Brien saw murder in the man's eyes and grabbed the first object that was around. He took the sharp-edged binnacle light and put it behind his back. When the screaming man's hands were closing on his throat, O'Brien swung the brass object around with all his might. He heard the crash of the lantern against flesh and saw the mate's hulk crumple to the deck, blood spilling from his face.

Shortly thereafter, O'Brien was sullen and a bit apprehensive as he eased out onto the yard to furl his last sail on this ship. He wondered which of the "great buildings yonder" would be his jail, for he expected to be punished for his insubordination in striking the mate. But it felt good to look at the disfigured man with the badly swollen and bandaged face. "Some Calcutta doctor will have a good job coming to him," he thought, still burning from the thoughts of the man's bullying during those long weeks. Even with his act of retribution, O'Brien would remember that man's face for as long as he lived. Whenever he met a man named Lawrence, he would find out if there was any kinship between that person and the "brute." "The man's face is as plain in my memory," he inked, "as when the day I disfigured it."

When the crew was departing, O'Brien walked straight to the ship's captain. He stopped and simply requested that he be put in jail due to his act of injuring the mate. True to his character, he didn't make excuses—O'Brien was ready to pay the price. But the captain did not blame him and paid him off with about sixteen rupees, or four dollars, for the voyage. The boy had received one dollar for each month of his hard labor.

The "tanned and hardy, if half angry" youth was too eager to leave the ship to worry over what to do when his slender earnings were gone. He quickly lowered his bag of clothes onto the lazily rolling shore boat. O'Brien could only wonder if the "evil-countenanced mate" had seen him spit on the shining deck of the *Marlborough* just before he slid down the hand rope for land.

* * *

He wandered lazily through the crowded, noisy, strange streets of the great Indian city of Calcutta (now named Kolkata). Located in eastern India on the east bank of the River Hooghly that emptied into the Bay of Bengal, the British East India Company and then the British Empire had developed the colonial city as its Indian capital. Johnny ambled through one congested, dusty alleyway after another and listened to the strange mumble of different tongues. He found himself very much alone, but he felt optimistic in that he was now "a sailor, in a sailor's proper setting—a faraway port." After asking a seaman who carried a similar duffel bag under his arm, O'Brien was led to a boarding house. And a Catholic church.

He attended church every morning, and soon he was hurrying along to get there on time. As he passed a gentleman who was dressed in an expensive-looking suit, the man turned and said, "My boy, why hurry? You have plenty of time." The two talked as they walked together. When at the church, the man invited him to his home that afternoon and handed Johnny a card: "J. Cutto—19 Chilpore Road."

O'Brien kept that card for many years until it was yellowed with age and nearly illegible from being kept inside his leather wallet. He carried it as a "memoir of a care-free youth, and of a time when a slight Irish lad of sixteen chatted in a sun-splashed Indian garden with a teasing girl of fifteen."

Passing through a "most beautiful garden" and by a dozen native gardeners fast at work, he came across an equally exquisite home and an awaiting Mr. Cutto. After exchanging greetings, the man called for his daughter, who smiled back from a French window and left to come onto the veranda. She seemed to flow toward him with her hand extended, and that "vision of loveliness" said, "Papa has been telling me lots of nice things about you, and I am glad to know you." They talked for hours as if they were longtime friends. He learned that she was half Irish and Portuguese. Her brother was an engineer and was building the railroad from Calcutta to Delhi.

Her father invited him to stay for dinner, and afterward she "charmingly" played the piano and sang for him. The two spent time together on more occasions in the colorful, manicured gardens and drew closer. On their last meeting, she told him when her brother returned, she'd make him take Johnny along to be an engineer and that India was the "most lovely country." He wouldn't have to go to sea again. Although he treasured those "last hours of pleasure," especially after the hardships he had endured on the *Marlborough*, O'Brien wasn't sure what to say in return.

The answer came when a "horde of mosquitoes" attacked him that night in his boarding house room. When he awoke the following morning, his face, body, and hands were covered with swollen, red blotches. Thinking that it would not do to have the girl that "he almost worshipped" see him this way, he shipped out that day on the vessel *Eliza*, bound for various ports, including Singapore and Hong Kong.

Johnny reasoned he would return to Calcutta to see his lovely lady as soon as his face and hands were in better shape. However, the "fates had thought otherwise," and he never returned. Mr. Cutto answered his note about his leaving, but then the family and O'Brien never communicated again. Even after the horrible Mr. Lawrence, Johnny O'Brien had used the excuse of the mosquitoes to not end his sailing over the seas.

He "blew some wind" and was accepted on this voyage as a seaman. The sail ship *Eliza* was now his home, and this voyage was in sharp contrast to his first one. The weather was ideal with clear nights under the Southern Cross and easy gales as the ship sailed past the Malay Peninsula, Ceylon, and the East Indies. The chin-whiskered Captain Sedgley and his wife invited Johnny to attend church with them when the boat finally came to port, although the tropical islands they passed seemed to be as far away as the dim clouds on the horizon. When his work was done onboard, O'Brien could spend idle moments reading and watching the magnificent sunsets—and the good food was in marked contrast to his first experiences.

Food and water were the great variables on these voyages. The quality depended on the captain's disposition, the owner's budget, the cook's temperament, and how long the voyage was. The amount of food carried was large and depended on the crew's size. A small sailing vessel for a round-trip between San Francisco and Australia carried the following provisions: 2,500 pounds of flour, 800 pounds of biscuits, 1,800 pounds of salt beef, 900 pounds of salt pork, 200 pounds of salt fish, and 600 pounds of canned meats—plus oatmeal, beans, split peas, rice, barley, buckwheat, sago and tapioca, canned fish, canned milk, canned fruit, canned vegetables, sugar (400 pounds), syrup, jam, coffee, and tea.

Although it depended on the ship's captain, coffee was typically served at 5:30 A.M.; at 8:00 A.M., three-quarters of an hour was allowed for a breakfast, for example, of hash or stew, bread, and coffee; from noon to 1:00 P.M. was a "dinner" of soup, meat, and vegetables; from 3:00 to 3:15 P.M., coffee; and at 6:00 P.M., a supper of cold corned beef or pork, bread, margarine, and tea. The coffee, however, was typically "more chicory than coffee and always muddy."

On a ship with a good menu and cook, breakfast would be combinations of porridge and milk, pork and beans, Boston brown bread, bread, and butter; lunch (called dinner) could be pea soup, corned beef, potatoes and vegetables, pie, biscuits, and cheese; supper might consist of corned-beef hash, cold corned beef, pickles, bread, and butter. On Sundays, the menus improved: breakfast (stewed prunes, hot cakes with syrup, bacon and eggs, bread and butter); dinner (vegetable soup, tinned roast beef, potatoes and vegetables, plum duff, and bread); and supper (meat stew, cold ham and beef, pickles, corn bread, tinned fruit, biscuits, and cheese).

On poorly provisioned vessels, seamen would complain about the continual use of salted beef and pork, salted fish, one pound of margarine (no butter), and one pound of sugar a week—all measured out—with only soft bread and hardtack (a small brown rye loaf, halved and rebaked, much like zwieback, only harder). And when the food was bad, it was a terrible situation. On one voyage off the Yucatan coast, the crew endured provisions of "Mexican black beans, a few bags of moldy worm-eaten biscuits, and a couple of barrels of half-rotten fish." Their supply of brackish water turned so bad it was almost undrinkable. Day after day, the scanty meals were "beans, stinking fish, and biscuits out of which the weevils crawled." When they finally reached Falmouth, England, the only provisions onboard were "five gallons of the putrid water and a few biscuits, or rather, just a few hundred dusty weevils."

A breakfast item for some seamen was "cracker hash": a mixture of broken pieces of hardtack soaked in water until it became soft and then mixed with pieces of salt beef, pork, and sliced onions for flavor. The coffee might need to be sweetened with molasses, especially if the water was drawn from a rusty iron tank. The cabin fare for officers and passengers was better than for the ordinary seamen—they could have sugar for their coffee, butter on their bread (soft-tack), and other delicacies thrown in. The crew would have salt beef and pork, but the cabins would be furnished with the choice cuts of meat.

The beef came in three-hundred-pound cakes and was soaked in brine "well saturated with saltpeter." When taken from the cask, the meat was "red as a flannel shirt." This was placed inside a wooden oval cask, holding about forty gallons, that was larger at the bottom to keep it from tipping over. The wood was usually scraped and oiled on the outside. Bound with brass hoops, polished brightly, and called a "harness cask," this container was used exclusively for soaking out the salt. The meat was allowed to soak for a day or so in freshwater before it was fresh enough to cook. The salt beef wasn't noted for its moisture and usually was as "dry as a chip." Sailors said it took a little time to get used to salt beef, and at the first eating it took the skin off the roof of the mouth—but as with his hands on the first voyage, as soon as a sailor's mouth became calloused enough, he could digest anything that he could swallow.

In *John Cameron's Odyssey*, the seaman told what meals were like when he first shipped out in 1867 as a "boy":

At four-thirty in the morning, coffee was served to the watch on deck. This was drunk, like many a better draft, straight, for few could bring themselves to also eat a fragment of biscuit from last night's allowance. At seven thirty, we had what was known as breakfast: another swill of bewitched hot water [tea], a hard biscuit, and (for the self-denying) a sample of beef or pork left over from yesterday's rations. At noon, dinner was graciously handed out by the cook in a greasy wooden mess tub from his pigsty of a galley. It consisted of a boulder of salt beef, or "salt horse," marked now and then, but full of bone and fat; a biscuit was added with more bog water. At five o'clock, something suggestive of tea was doled out. With this, a biscuit, and a small portion of beef or pork left over from dinner, we made our supper.

On Mondays, Wednesday, and Fridays, we fared a trifle better, for then we had pea soup, which we ate with gusto, if it was not burned and unpalatable—as it almost invariably was. On those days we also had salt pork, but I could not stomach the stuff. On Saturdays we had a mess of rice, and a mess it was, half cooked, or boiled to a mush, or scorched. "Duff Days" fell on Thursdays and Sundays. This was a mixture of cake and pudding, seasoned highly with spice, generally almost as dark as gingerbread, and served with hard sauce—which could be tasty if done right. But we had a duff pudding compounded of a little flour and a few anemic raisins and cooked in a canvas bag in the coppers wherein the beef and pork had been boiled. From this method of preparation, it derived a certain brassy weight. Some vessels (not our ship, the *Ida*) gave allowances of butter, potatoes, pickled and tinned meats occasionally, but then the other rations were materially reduced.

The longer the voyage between ports, the less fresh and more salted portions were used. In turn, the men traded food and anything else desired for what they liked: for example, a seaman would pass off his share of fish for another's share of meat. Short voyages would have fresh fruits and vegetables, cuts of meats on ice, and a variety of provisions.

Many ships carried cows and pigs for slaughter. However, catching the porkers, killing them, and then dressing them on a pitching ship could prove difficult. On one voyage, after sticking the pig, the men let the animal go. Instead of dying, he ran out of the pen and didn't stop until he jumped into the sea. A trailing shark quickly ate the pig just as it struck the water. The captain was so mad that he knocked the steward down and then jumped on him. The watching seamen thought that every rib in the steward's body had been broken, but the man was able to clean up the mess and get dinner.

Seamen hated sharks, as hunters hated snakes, and seldom lost an opportunity to kill one. After the sharks were hooked and dragged aboard, the men battered the heads to pieces with handspikes, seeing that they endured punishment before dying. If someone had lost a friend to a shark attack, he really took his time. Cutting off their tails was a quicker but dirty job, as streams of blood sprayed the deck for fifteen feet or more. Although shark meat is safe to cook and eat, the flesh has a high ammonia content unless soaked in milk, so the crew and passengers usually preferred to eat other caught fish, such as the delicacy of flying fish.

Flying fish are easily identified by their long pectoral fins and lopsided tails. They don't fly the same way as birds, because birds vibrate their wings during flight. This fish gains its power and speed from its tailfin, which it moves from side to side with powerful strokes. Flying fish can launch themselves from the water like rockets and can fly distances over five hundred feet at thirty miles per hour. They are attracted to light and would often strike against a ship's sails at night. If the ship's cook was friendly, he would fry this little delicacy (about one foot, or so, in length) for those fortunate enough to find them.

In light winds, the men could lie out on the bow and fish for bonito, albacore, and dolphin. Using a cod line baited with a small fish the size of a flying fish, the men straddled the boom of the forward sail. Leaning against the stay for support, a seaman skipped the hook at the end of the line on the surface. The fish would swim across the ship's bow and rise to the surface like a trout for a fly. Pulling a hooked fish hand-over-hand from under the ship's bow, the seaman would yell for a gunny sack. As he pulled up the fish, someone always rushed over to see if the man had fallen overboard—with or without the fish.

The most important provision was having sufficient quantities of potable water. As drinking water could become contaminated with salt during a storm, be undrinkable due to poor quality, or deteriorate over a long voyage, freshwater at sea could be scarcer and more valuable, as was said, than whiskey ashore. When a ship's water stores became low, drinkable water had to be rationed among the men.

In *John Cameron's Odyssey*, the writer observed:

When the weather turned favorable, the men should have been thankful. However, nearly all of our scanty allowance of three quarts of water a day for each man went for cooking our food. What remained was stingily doled out, and the tin dipper locked up to prevent us from pilfering a drink from the barrel. Now and then, when the good Lord sent rain, we caught what water we could from the cabin deck and from canvas spread down for that purpose. After a heavy shower, the barrels on deck were full; but the water turned rotten—I am no scientist to explain why—and the reek was as horrible as the taste was abominable. Both smell and taste vanished, however, after ten days; the water then was clear and sweet, although it reeked of tar from the spun yarn used in slinging the dipper. To this reek we were inured, for the odor of tar permeated the whole vessel: it was in our food; it was (incredible as that may seem) in our bodies. Since Heaven sent the rain and it cost the *Ida*'s owners nothing, the dipper at last was allowed to loll in the barrel.

Lack of drinking water was not our sole privation. More than once I saw eight men wash their hands and faces, one after the other, in a single quart. Economy could scarcely go farther. Small wonder that we prayed for rain, aye, importuned Heaven for a deluge, and when a tropical shower fell, we plugged the scuppers and turned the decks into a huge laundry and bath, all in which we washed our clothing and bodies and frolicked like school-boys.

At other times, a ship could be sailing under a bright sun with the tar starting to run from the deck seams, and then a rain squall would suddenly spring up to pass within a few feet of the ship without one drop falling on board. When the squalls passed over a ship, the crew would catch the water from the cabin top. If enough was captured, they could wash their clothes and blankets; however, some seamen would stay in the same clothes for the entire voyage with "smells and disgusting appearances."

When the rains came, the sailors used a variety of ways to catch the freshwater. Sometimes the harness cask was quickly scrubbed out and taken aft to catch the rainwater from cabin tops. A short piece of hose connected the downspout or scupper to the cask, from which men filled the empty water casks on the deck. The water in the first cask was usually very brackish, but the cooks could use this. The men also rigged an old sail over the main deck to catch rain, which was diverted through a canvas pipe to the main tank, a large upright iron cylinder standing on the blocks in the main hold. The men used anything they could to catch fresh rainwater—and this was precious indeed.

As for other seaman needs, the ships had slop chests. The men could buy clothing (underwear, shirts, dungaree pants and jumpers, socks, sea boots, slippers, and oilskins), matches, soap, pipes, tobacco, and threads and needles, but typically no cigarettes due to the fire danger. The owner supplied these items, and the charges were deducted from pay owed at the voyage's end. Although the articles were supposedly sold at low prices, or 10 percent over cost for American ships, arguments over the pricing were frequent. Thus, most men tried to acquire what they needed when their ship was in port.

* * *

The *Eliza* arrived at Hong Kong "without an incident" and anchored for six weeks while the crew readied the ship for a chartered voyage to San Francisco. During this time, the seamen were busy loading cargo into the lower holds and building quarters for a large number of Chinese laborers who were being brought to work on the West Coast. On every nonrainy day, however, the crew assembled on the stern and were drilled in the handling of muskets and clubs. When O'Brien asked about this, the captain told him that pirates were lying in wait off the neighboring islands.

The ship carried a crew of thirty-six able seamen and six ordinary seamen, including Johnny O'Brien. If the sailors showed experience (usually three years at sea) and skill, they were graded able-bodied seamen, or ABs. Men who weren't ABs were paid as ordinary seamen. Few sailors had obtained certificates, and there was often no way, other than actual trial, to prove that a man had the claimed proficiency. At the end of a voyage, most sailors were too eager to get ashore to take the time to ask for a "paper of experience."

Tattoos had some value in recognizing "professional" experience, as some of the old-timers were walking art displays. An old picture of one unidentified sailor showed large tattoos on his legs, body, and arms. These included a man-of-war, a huge green snake (its head extending down to the top of his foot, while its body encircled his leg twice and continued over his thigh), and a beautiful nude woman. His chest pictured a full-rigged ship with studded link chains running over each shoulder and down his spine. On his left forearm were the words "Sailor's Return," while the right displayed "Flags of All Nations." Bracelets were tattooed on each wrist; nude women were inked on his hands, the thumb and forefingers outlining their legs; and bands of rings were around his fingers. There was literally no room left on his body for any more tattoos. When questioned about the tattoos, he answered, "I was a damned fool for having it done, but being drunk at the time, I was in such a condition that anything suggested was just fine with me."

The men on the *Eliza* were a "formidable-looking collection of ruffians," usually wearing a beard or mustache, generally shoeless (unless it was winter or they were working under a hot sun with tar on the decks) and wearing dungarees. A scarf around the neck, long shirt (rolled sleeves in summertime), and a rough sweater when cold. These men—like all other crews—were rough-and-tumble, uneducated men. Seamen were rascals. Some were deserters, running from the law; others couldn't hold down any job, and policemen were always looking to "spot their troubles." There were turbulent, belligerent souls among the men; personality conflicts, cultural differences, and language barriers made flare-ups unavoidable—which also happened daily on the *Eliza*.

During the last two weeks of the stay in Hong Kong, the Chinese boatmen on the docks or gliding past the ship showed a "wave of restlessness." O'Brien had come to know one, who was especially adept at gracefully moving his junk through the waters with its long oar at the back. He told Johnny that six native boatmen had disappeared, and only their floating, water-filled, empty junks were later located in the harbor. The day before the *Eliza* sailed, the body of one of the missing sampan men was seen drifting by the ship.

O'Brien helped to bring up the body. His first taste of seeing death was unsettling, especially with the way the man's skull had been crushed. The body was still wrapped with a broken rope, which had ripped away from the weight used to sink the boatman. As it seemed the body hadn't drifted far, the harbor police questioned every man on the *Eliza*, but nothing of a suspicious nature was found.

Onboard, O'Brien had made the acquaintance of a strange seaman. He was a "magnificent brute, the strongest man on board" and apparently liked O'Brien. The man didn't talk much, and he observed the police and the dead man with a detachment like a researcher does with lab rats. They were making small talk while walking the deck on their watch. The man suddenly grabbed O'Brien by the elbow, stared at him intensely, and coolly said:

> Jack, you remember those Sampan coolies who were missing in the harbor. Well, I was the one who put them out of business. You know, my boy, these coolies are not human. When I used to come on board at night, I always took a sampan where there was only one of them working. Just before reaching the ship, I would crack him on the head, throw him overboard with a weight, and come up to the ship. Then, I would punch a hole through the boat's bottom and let her go adrift. Now, Jack, you tell anyone about this, and I find this out, it will be a sorry day for you. [Note: Seamen were often called "Jack Tar" in England and the colonies; the name "Jack" then came to be used interchangeably for "sailor" or "mariner."]

The seaman looked strangely at O'Brien and continued on the watch. There were no further conversations between them. As he thought it over, O'Brien had no proof other than the serial-killing statement of a crazed sailor. He decided to be quiet for the time being, and the man then disappeared after their watch. When Johnny asked about him, the mate said he had no idea where the seaman was and that he had probably jumped ship. When O'Brien returned years later to Hong Kong, he asked about the seaman, but no one had heard of him.

The work of hiring the new crew began, and this included a bosun, cook, steward, carpenter, and the mates. The first officer or chief mate was the ship's executive officer and reported directly to the captain; he had usually passed his examination for a master's license and was hopefully awaiting a change to obtain his first command. The lowest rank of the regularly certified officers was the second and third mates. They took the captain's and first mate's orders and carried them out with the bosun and crew. All ate in the officers' mess and had their own rooms.

The bosun was the link between the quarterdeck (officers) and fo'c'sle (seamen). He was the top sergeant in this army and supposed to be the best all-around sailor on the ship, barring the licensed officers. He led the way for his men in crisis; if he didn't, the captain or chief mate demoted him. The man then gave up his room and moved his sea chest into the fo'c'sle to take his place with the crew as an able-bodied seaman.

The cook prepared the meals for everyone; at mealtimes, each watch in turn sent someone to the galley to receive the food in a large wooden basket and which they ate in the fo'c'sle. The steward supervised the cook, kept the forward cabin and pantry in order, and served the officers.

Like the steward and cook, the carpenter was a specialist: He stood no watch, didn't work with the sailors, and worked at jobs assigned by the captain or first mate. In fair weather, he replaced the dry rot on the deck, spars, or railings. In foul weather, he worked making fancy gratings and adornments. The carpenter was the village blacksmith, if the ship had a portable forge, and typically watched over the vessel's freshwater supplies.

As to the captain, *John Cameron's Odyssey* described him best:

> The captain was king and his word was the only law; he exacted implicit and instant obedience from all, officers as well as men; he was the autocrat of a floating kingdom, nay, of an isolate universe; and I gained what comfort I could from the reflection that I was not his only serf. He could suspend his mates and send them to their rooms, or even could disrate them, reducing them to foremast hands, fellows of the men they had once commanded.
>
> Of greater immediate importance, he kept no watch. While we were at sea, the weather side of the poop was reserved for his sole use, in order, I assume, that the air he breathed should be contaminated by no lesser being. When he elected to grace the deck, the officer of the watch stepped quietly to leeward; and the seamen, in going aft to relieve the wheel, always went by the lee gangway, or if the vessel was running before the wind or was lying at anchor, by the port side. Ceremonial gone mad? Perhaps. But formality is the essence of discipline, as generations of sailors and soldiers have proved.

With its new crew and officers, the ship sailed for the Pacific Coast. Headed for American and Canadian railroad construction crews, 510 Chinese laborers were jammed into the b'tween deck, along with general cargo now loaded in the lower holds. In addition to the cargo, food, provisions, and water stores that this (or any) ship carried, the vessel also brought along a variety of materials for repairs and maintenance purposes: paints, brushes, linseed oil, tar, pitch, turpentine, varnish, kerosene, holystone, soap powder, brooms, assorted manila and wire lines, ropes, twine, sail needles, spikes, chipping hammers, scrapers, different-sized canvas (usually six hundred yards), carpenter materials, and a variety of other items.

The first few days at sea was always a period of shaking down and adjustment. If the mates were new to the ship, they had to learn the captain's ways and their vessel's seaworthiness and handling. The officers had to find out which sailors could best do their tasks. The seamen needed to adjust to the new mate, and this change could be difficult.

One of the cooks became ill, and the mate, a Mr. Farmby, told O'Brien to get in the galley and help out the cooks. There was no discussion, and O'Brien went. As he hated to work in the galley—but dared not refuse—he made up his mind after the mid-day meal that he wouldn't "last long." And he didn't.

O'Brien piled all the soiled dishes, lifted up as many as he could, and let them shatter with a loud crash onto the brick floor surrounding the iron oven. The mate gave him a "cuffing" and he was sent to the mainmast to climb up it and "whistle to the wind." After whistling for an hour with not much wind being called, Farmby ordered him down.

The same mate later ordered him up the mast to scrape and oil a heavy, sixteen-foot-long metal spar. From eight stories above the quarterdeck, O'Brien yelled down that it was loose and needed to be lashed down. The mate told him to do as he was told. Johnny finished the task, worked his way down the ropes, rigging, and ladder to the deck, and just as he landed, the spar plummeted down and crashed through the poop deck into the cabin. It narrowly missed him. "Why it didn't give way when I was working on it, Heaven only knows," he wrote later. These incidents seemed to happen all too regularly on these ships.

2

NEAR DEATH AND A PROMOTION

When O'Brien arrived in San Francisco in 1868, he worked with the rest of the crew to unload the ship's cargo. Then he impulsively headed off to seek his fortune in this "land of gold." Although the California Gold Rush was nearly twenty years before, the rumors of golden fortunes suddenly discovered still abounded, and so he packed up his duffel bag on "one dark night" to make his way past Oakland into the countryside. After a "twenty-four hour tramp," the teenager came upon a ranch in the golden hills and asked the owner if he had any work. From daylight to dusk, O'Brien labored for two days with a shovel and pick axe in digging a ditch. With the following day being Sunday, he thought he would have the day off.

He was mistaken. The man sent him for the entire day into the grain field, where O'Brien with yells and raised arms scared away the crows that swooped down for their meals. When darkness finally and mercifully came, the lad lay down in the barn where he was bunking "among the mice." At nine o'clock that night, the owner returned from town and promptly ordered O'Brien to wash down his buggy. At that command, Johnny knew he was not cut out for this type of life.

The following morning, he asked the owner to pay him for the three days of hard work. After the rancher cussed him for quitting, he threw a quarter at O'Brien in full payment. Johnny angrily picked the coin up and threw it back,

18

hitting him square on the forehead. When the enraged man lunged at O'Brien, the youth took off running and left behind both the rancher and any further ideas of ranching.

After "tramping around" for a week in search of any possible gold fields or strikes still undiscovered, he returned empty-handed to San Francisco, only to find that his old ship *Eliza* had already sailed away. Locating a beaten wooden boardinghouse by the docks, O'Brien befriended the owner—a man by the name of Bob Penny—whose acquaintance proved to be quite helpful. The old, wrinkled, and tattooed ex-sailor warned the youth about the nearby kidnapping of men, who were then pressed into working on a ship that quickly sailed away. Drugged, clubbed on the head, or unconscious from drinking too much whiskey, the "new" sailor was shanghaied onto a shorthanded vessel to awake hours later on the bounding ship. Whatever was left of the man's pay was either with his last drinking "buddies" or at the boardinghouse—and this usually happened one or two days after the poor soul had left his old ship on shore leave.

O'Brien spent the next two days on the waterfront checking out ships and destinations from leads provided by Penny. That night, the infamous, chilling San Francisco fog had swept in. O'Brien quietly walked back into the rundown boardinghouse and stopped by the doorway. As his eyes swept around the shadowy room of hewn timbers, a scarred counter, and rough tables and chairs, he heard a noise to one side. In the flickering light from a candle on the counter, he could just make out the outlines of two burly men carrying an unconscious body through a door down the corridor. With a grunt from one, the group then disappeared.

Johnny had assumed that all of the doors led to small, barely furnished rooms like the one he was in; but he was curious and inched his way to the open doorway. In near darkness, he saw what appeared to be stairs that led downward. O'Brien slowly walked down the open staircase and peered into the void. He heard the sound of scraping and an eerie noise like a rusty gate being opened. The youth then saw the shimmering of moving candlelight and watched as they lowered the body through the gloom and a trapdoor to what seemed to be a waiting rowboat below. The men disappeared into the boat. O'Brien next heard the low guttural singing of a sailor's ditty and turned in that direction. He saw Bob Penny walk from the other side toward the opening and quietly close the trapdoor.

O'Brien turned and quickly went up the steps—two at a time. He raced down the corridor and into his room. Once there, he didn't light the candle on the crude table by the small bed, as he didn't want Penny to see any light leaking out at this time from under his doorway. O'Brien never mentioned to Penny what he had seen, but now thought he ought to find a position a bit sooner than before.

He knew the best crewmen were not found this way. O'Brien now guessed that experienced seamen stayed away from these places, if they could, and asked for work only on the best ships. Unscrupulous sea captains without enough crew-men and soon set to sail away, however, wouldn't pay much attention to how their crews were brought onboard—if they knew that beforehand. Johnny didn't like that unconscious men were dumped that way through the trapdoor so close to his room, but he didn't worry that he could also be shanghaied. Although his confidence could have been misplaced, Penny apparently liked him, and probably just as important, O'Brien had promised to pay the gnarled owner a "referral fee" when he found a ship he liked.

Johnny decided to accept a seaman's position on a small sailing bark with three masts, all square rigged (except for the stern), named the *Cambridge*. He liked the captain of this coastal lumber ship that was heading up the Pacific Coast and decided to join the crew. He didn't know that the heavyset, unkempt mate by the name of Hegg would take offense to him—which mates seemed to do with the young—and decide that O'Brien needed "convincing in discipline." Physical and verbal hazing of men by mates and officers was commonplace, and it would be decades before this would be controlled by the strict enforcement of seamen's laws.

O'Brien was on the lookout watch on the forecastle during a windstorm and was staring intently out to sea for any signs of reefs, ships, or land. Standing with his back to the forward capstan (anchor winch), he was knocked completely over from behind and landed on his face and stomach. Turning over painfully, he looked up into the sneering face of the large Hegg, who was standing over him. A quick kick in his ribs turned O'Brien over, and the mate walked away, yelling over his shoulder, "Watch out for surprises, Limey!"

The enraged Johnny jumped to his feet and without thinking grabbed a nearby handspike from the rack. Waving the heavy iron crowbar over his head, O'Brien charged Hegg with a blood-curdling yell. The large man ran over another sea-man as he lumbered toward the stern, with Johnny and his raised spike closing the gap. Before the mate could crash down to the presumed safety of the officers' quarters, O'Brien threw the spike at the man. It ran true and thudded into Hegg in the small of his back. He fell down to the planks as if cut down by a scythe. The captain and another seaman took the moaning Hegg to his cabin, and he stayed there for a few days before being able to return to duty. O'Brien commented later, "He didn't trouble me or the crew again."

O'Brien had learned on the *Marlborough* that there was a point where rough seamen had to be met, quickly and with full force. Whether in social situations or hostile ones, however, he was considered "impulsive" by some, "thoughtfully" spontaneous by others. He had a quick temper that lasted his life, but he was also showing another trait of trying to control whatever situation he found himself in. O'Brien had a natural instinct to lead that clashed with authority. This was coupled with a curiosity to learn more about what interested him at the time.

A few days after his run-in with Hegg, the ship docked in Eureka, California, a small logging town about two-thirds of the way to Oregon from San Francisco. Having been warned that the mate would wait until the best time to attack and kill him, O'Brien jumped ship. He never saw the ship, captain, or mate again—including what wages he had earned—and it sailed away with its cargo of lumber.

Eureka was a small, bustling port due to its unending supply of redwood lumber, which was needed—even in current times—for building houses and structures in San Francisco and Portland. The harbor was constantly filled with sailing ships, and the now eighteen-year-old O'Brien decided to stay there and learn more about sails and ship rigging. He found a job with an elderly ship rigger and sailmaker, John Fox, who had for years been a mate on deepwater ships. The much-younger Johnny learned about the heavy gear of large ships, knowledge that would be very helpful for him in the years to come. Although not growing taller, his body was maturing; the hard labors with stout cables and tarred ropes had thickened his arms and strengthened his shoulders. He stayed for several months in Fox's home, learning more about the sea, ships, rigging, and sails than he could have ever learned from any school.

After a stint of "a few months" with a lumber mill interspaced between his time with the sailmaker, O'Brien one year later joined a sail ship, the *Washington Libbey*, which sailed from Eureka to Peru hauling a large cargo of redwood lumber. The seamen onboard were mainly hardworking, fairly collected men, but there were exceptions—and every voyage seemed to have a few.

The muscular cook on the *Libbey* had gone mad when the ship under heavy sail was crossing the equator. He had rushed from the galley, shrieking curses and manhandling one stricken sailor with "maniacal strength." O'Brien and other seamen ran after the cook, who was lifting the screaming man over the railing to throw him into the white-capped sea. The seamen were just able to grab the sailor by his legs before he was tossed overboard. With contorted twists and snaps of his massive shoulders, the cook at first easily shrugged O'Brien and another sailor away. Both seamen then rushed the crazed man and rammed him to the deck. When another sailor joined in, the men were finally able to subdue the thrashing cook.

The captain gave the order to put him in irons, and seamen snapped wrist and leg irons onto the screaming man. He was so violent that to put the leg irons on, the carpenter had to bore two holes into the bulkhead and lash him "close up" to the wood. Whether it was orders, curses, promises of help, or liquor placed to the man's lips, nothing could calm the deranged cook. The man struggled to the very last. Striking his irons again—and again—against himself, the bed, and the wall, the insane cook died the next day.

The captain asked O'Brien to recite the services at the burial, and he thought this was because he owned the only prayer book on board. Johnny read a few passages, gave a prayer for the man's soul, and put the book down. The day was ironically calm, with little wind or clouds and a warming sun. The captain gave the signal for crewmen to lift the canvas-wrapped body over the poop rail, and the dead man slid away into the blue seas. With iron spikes placed at the bottom of the canvas, the shroud quickly disappeared into a splash of white.

Although Hong Kong had initiated Johnny into what death looked like, the way in which this man died was tragic. He had seemed normal enough, but then suddenly lost all control. One could not assume anything on a voyage, Johnny concluded, because danger and death seemed to coexist with safety and life.

Without further incident, the ship made Callao, Peru, the port of entry for landlocked Lima. The lad traveled to Lima for a couple of days, and as Milton Dalby wrote in his book *The Sea Saga of Dynamite Johnny O'Brien*, this was a city where "empty-eyed Indians drifted by with a shuffling of shapeless feet and a few listless carriages rolled over the rutted paving." After discharging its cargo of lumber, the vessel returned to San Francisco with a cargo of textiles, cotton, and sugar.

Along the way, O'Brien began studying navigation when off watch and in the forecastle. The mate liked the hardworking young man and lent him books and charts. Answering the questions that poured out from Johnny, the mate showed him the stars and how to navigate by them.

By the time the ship anchored in San Francisco Bay, O'Brien knew how to calculate a ship's position by estimating where it had traveled from the last point, known as dead reckoning, as well as how to "shoot the sun" for latitude and take star sightings for longitude. The ship's officers had also discovered that the promise of a half hour with an old sextant was the best way to get O'Brien to do extra duty. He would have to rely on these skills in dangerous times—sooner than he would have thought.

* * *

He shipped out from San Francisco on the small 256-ton three-masted bark *Samuel Merritt*. O'Brien worked on this vessel for one year as it made runs between San Francisco and Eureka, hauling shoes, clothing, and manufactured goods north and redwood lumber back. This vessel was another ship that came as close to any to bringing about his demise. The *Merritt* had sailed directly into a screaming nor'wester off Cape Mendocino—the jut of land thirty miles south of Eureka that is the furthest U.S. western point. The captain quickly ordered Johnny and a Dane to climb aloft and furl the topsails to keep them from being shredded by the gale. They reached the stories-high topsail and began their work while bracing themselves against the winds and the ship's violent lurching.

To have freedom in working on the out-of-control sail, O'Brien decided not to pass his arm through a nearby "safety" rope becket (looped at its end). They had hauled half of the heaving canvas to the yard when the ship, dominated by the huge rollers, crashed heavily into the sea. The sail suddenly bellied out, and the ship's movement pitched Johnny over and into the air. His freefall to the deck and thrashing ocean was thwarted by a quick bone-jarring jerk when the footrope attached "fast to his ankle" became taut.

Dangling upside down by the short rope, he was swinging uncontrollably with the wind gusts and bouncing motions of the vessel. The Dane climbed down the mast and tried to grab the spinning seaman but was unsuccessful. Arms outstretched toward the heavy pole, O'Brien tried to reach safety. When he was tantalizingly close, the ship lurched away and he swung out again.

The crashing seas and surf seemed to reach toward him, and Johnny was becoming anxious as to whether he would reach the mast—or whether the rope around his ankle would break first. He began to swing again toward the heavy wooden pole, and when the vessel pitched forward, O'Brien reached mightily for the mast. The Dane stretched his foot out, which Johnny gratefully snatched, and he was shortly back on the yard. With his arm now inside the becket, the two men finally succeeded in furling the sail.

Once back in San Francisco, O'Brien traveled to Portland "on a lark," interested in seeing the city. Once there, he soon ended up with the boatswain's position on the *Roswell Sprague* out of Boston. Sailors usually worked on different ships in short periods, but it wasn't that typical for a young man to work himself up the ladder this fast. By "blowing more wind" as to his work experience and qualifications, the twenty-year-old O'Brien succeeded in jumping to being both an able-bodied seaman and boatswain (or bosun) at the same time. Depending on the size of the ship and its crew, the bosun could be the chief mate or even a third or fourth mate. The bosun was the deck crew's foreman and had to be highly skilled in all matters of seamanship, from supervising repairs and operating the anchor windlass to overseeing cargo storage and changing rigging. The boatswain assigned and supervised work, whether it was changing the sails in a gale or repairing them afterward.

The trade-off from his quick "promotions" was that this ship was so old and severely overloaded that others passed it by. The *Sprague* was loaded with "many more" tons of grain inside her holds than the law allowed. The creaking, deeply laden vessel shipped heavy amounts of water, and even in an ordinary sea, the men had to constantly man the pumps. Despite this, the three-masted tall-sail ship eventually crossed the dangerous Columbia River Bar and "squared away" south for South America and eventually Cape Horn.

While running down the northeast trade winds, the mate, Mr. Hatfield, who was a "fine, handsome, young man," came forward while O'Brien was setting up the rigging on the foremast. He asked if Johnny was superstitious. When the boatswain answered in the negative, the mate replied:

> Neither am I. But during my four to eight watch below this morning, I had such a vivid vision, or dream, of seeing this ship in a terrible gale. I saw myself and a great number of the crew washed overboard, while the ship left us to drown. I awoke covered with sweat, and mark my words, Jack, this ship will never round Cape Horn. I and others will drown.

O'Brien laughed at the man's seriousness about such a tale, but then he felt a strange anxiety over whether it might come true. A few days later the ship sailed into a bad northward gale, which increased to near hurricane force. The *Roswell Sprague* was running under only its lower mainsails, and the captain ordered all hands to be "mustered aft." Several crew members were lashed to the pumps amidships, where they struggled to man the pumps but still breathe through the crashing floods of seawater that cascaded down. The pumps then stopped. With the sea surging inside the holds, the sailors knew that they and their ship were in great danger.

Since Johnny was muscular but slender, he told the seamen to lower him down by ropes into the dark pump well. Once inside the stinking hold, he discovered that the sea had washed in grain that now clogged the pump valves. He began to grope around the machinery to clear the equipment at the leaky, watery ship's bottom. Thrown by the vessel's bucking into the slimy, grainy water, O'Brien choked when he went face-first into the filthy saltwater. The smells were torturous, the labors excruciating, and the conditions risky, but he finally cleared the pumps so they could continue their vital work of pouring out the ocean through the hoses.

The storm blasted winds and waves, and the ship rolled sickeningly in the frothy seas. One seaman kept chanting nervously, "Lordy, I'm going to be washed overboard," and ran forward to try to hide, but the ship's bucking threw him back. When the sodden ship's staggering and pressure on the large rudder became too much for one man to handle, O'Brien left the deck by the pump well to help the overwhelmed helmsman. The second officer ordered two sailors, who had been standing by the forward hatch, to find thick line and secure the clew (corner) of the bow's upper topsail, which was now noisily snapping back and forth like a whip. The men, however, slunk away to find a safer place.

With the savage shaking of the heavy canvas, it was only a matter of time before the sail ripped completely from the yard. O'Brien told two others to take over the helm and grabbed the helmsman. Trying to yell over the din of the shrieking winds, he told the man that both of them needed to get up to the upper topsail and tie down the corner. The two men grabbed the mainmast to keep from being washed overboard by the savage green rivers of ocean that crashed over the railings. They began climbing up the humming, vibrating rigging in the teeth of the gale. Trying to keep their balance over fifty feet high in those winds was a hard task, but they finally got to the yard and successfully secured the sail.

When they were ready to descend, O'Brien noticed that the winds had begun acting strangely in striking him on one side of the cheek, only to whip back and hit him on the other side. He knew that something serious had happened on the deck. After O'Brien told his companion to get down and go aft as soon as possible, the bosun then "hastened" to get off the thick pole. He made his way down the mast, jumped aft to the yard of a lower sail, and then peered through the raging darkness to where the two quarter boats had been lashed. They had disappeared. "No men, no boats, no hatch, no bulwarks," were visible, O'Brien penned later, "and a big gaping hole appeared in the forward part of the poop [the exposed stern deck]." A spare topmast that had once been securely lashed to one side was now adrift, and the surging seas smashed it against the ship's sides and railing.

Even with the strong winds, a strange sound began to be heard. It was human—but not human. Listening closer, O'Brien realized it was the moaning of someone injured, and it seemed to be coming from the floating wreckage on the deck. When the ship surged on its port side, he leaped onto the deck from the lower yard and pushed his way through the debris toward the sound, nearly masked by the shrieks of the gale. He struggled against the constantly moving water and wreckage, sometimes knocked off his feet, always groping through the cold seawater, and when the ship went into a deep, near-death roll, he slid through the water to grab the aft mast's rigging. When the heavy sloshing washed him toward the wreckage, O'Brien frantically thrashed his hands around the ever-present ocean to find and save the man, with the knowledge that time was against his efforts. The helmsman joined him, and the two finally dragged up the unconscious body of a seaman.

They carried the man to the fo'c'sle and laid him down on the first bunk. They then saw that the man's eyes were lifeless. He was dead. The man was Smitz, a middle-aged German, who had told O'Brien that this would be his last voyage: His wife was running a small store in Hamburg and wanted him to help her. If the ship was lucky enough to survive, she would have his casket instead.

Turning their attention back to their deadly circumstances, they hurried aft through the maelstrom of white death, only to stare at a tremendous combing sea rolling up over the stern. With other crewmembers joining them, the seamen leaped to the mizzenmast for their safety, just out of the reach of the roaring ocean tsunami.

The towering, green rogue wave smashed over the *Sprague* and swept Hatfield and two other men over the side. The heavy tons of seawater crashed against the steering wheel and the replacement helmsman; there he remained, head drooped, his body still lashed in place with every rib broken. The crest had carried the captain, Mr. Sawyer, down the ship's deck and washed him over the side past the mainmast rigging, but when the heavy ship rolled deeply into the sea, he had frantically grabbed the mizzen rigging as he swept by. The crashing weight of the ocean had split a topmast, splintered cabins, and washed most of the ship's provisions overboard.

Trying to come to his senses, Captain Sawyer told the second mate to secure the yards with braces, or ropes, to prevent their destruction. This officer quickly passed the order down to O'Brien, ostensibly because he was the boatswain, but more than likely due to the danger of this work. O'Brien agreed. He made his way down the sloshing passageway to the storeroom with two other sailors. They brought back manila-hemp ropes with which to secure the yards; when O'Brien told them to take the ropes aloft and fasten them to the topsail yardarm, however, they responded, "We might as well be killed on deck than be killed aloft," and begged off.

O'Brien knew instinctively this wasn't the time to try to enforce discipline—just wasting such valuable time would ensure disaster. Making the heavy line fast over his shoulder, he waded through the washing seas, climbed up the rigging, and worked his way to the topsail yard. "Then the struggle began." The ripping winds slashed at him, and the weight of the swinging rope over his shoulder became dangerous. It tugged and pulled to rip him away to a stories-long fall. Seeing this, the carpenter climbed partway up and grabbed the rope to try to lighten its weight.

Out on the yardarm in the whipping gale, O'Brien strained against the incessant pull of the rope's weight back to the hard decks far below, but—foot by foot—he worked to the yard's end and brought the line fast. When that happened, O'Brien heard a faint cheer echo up from the deck and realized that the crew had been watching the entire time. He then thought about the four year's of savings he had accumulated—a total of $950—that had been in a canvas bag pinned to his undershirt. Immediately grabbing at his chest, he felt relief at finding his money bag still there.

When he reached the deck, the captain slogged through the saltwater and debris to thank him for his actions; the ocean continued in its quest, however, to overtake the ship and destroy it like the mythical kraken. But over time, the gale thankfully lessened, although it continued to pummel the vessel. Had these conditions not slackened, the tales of this ship and Johnny O'Brien would have never been heard.

The ship's railings were just above the sea. Its stern was nearly destroyed, bulkheads and partitions made useless, nautical instruments lost, sails shredded, riggings ripped away, and decks cratered. The after hatch had caved in, with tons of water cascading into the hold; six feet of ocean slurped back and forth inside the ship as it rolled into the swells. Since the waterlogged ship had no maneuverability, it was a sitting duck for any new storm, which would surely destroy the remains. Although four crewmembers continually took turns in laboring over the pump, two days would elapse before the ocean was finally pumped out of the hold.

The men were saddened by the loss of the mate and two other seamen. With the first mate now lost, O'Brien was promoted to second mate, taking the man's place who had been elevated to take over for the lost man, Hatfield. His vision— or nightmare—had become a reality, when the great wave crashed and washed him and others overboard to their deaths. There was no time to give poor Smitz a ceremonial burial. The carpenter stitched canvas around the man's crushed body, loaded heavy amounts of coal at his feet, and dropped the bundle into the sea. With the ship's condition, no lifeboats, little provisions, and a skeleton crew, the prospects even for those alive weren't good.

The old, leaking ship was battered and rode low in the water, with the ocean swells still crashing down on it. The *Sprague* didn't have the buoyancy to handle even gentle waves. Seawater leaked into the ship from all sections, and the pumps had to be constantly manned.

Shocked by what had happened to his ship and his near-death immersion, Captain Sawyer stayed inside his cabin, appearing only for short times to smoke his pipe, look around again at the ship's condition, and then walk slowly back to his quarters. O'Brien handled the night watches with "little word" from the captain, but he didn't care because this meant he was the one in charge. Johnny had been promoted from able-bodied seaman to bosun at the beginning of this voyage, then to second mate, and now with the chief mate's deferral and Sawyer's absence, he was the captain by default. At a young twenty years of age, he already had under his belt four years of experiences at sea. And he had survived them—so far.

* * *

On the third evening after the storm's fury had abated, the captain "broke the dimness" of the quarterdeck with a feebly glowing bull's-eye lantern. He looked worn, and his eyes were bloodshot. The man looked old and had obviously had little sleep. He thrust the lantern into Johnny's hand.

"O'Brien," he said quietly. "I want you to go forward and down into the forepeak [the ship's hold within the angle made by the bow] and see what kind of shape things are. I'm afraid the ship has been straining even worse than I first thought."

When O'Brien went to investigate, he struggled to remain on his feet when the sea crashed over the railing. Holding the flickering lantern high in one hand, he worked his way into the dark forepeak. O'Brien continually needed to steady himself as the ship bounced and rolled in its passage through the sea. It was clear, however, the captain was right. Seawater streamed in when the ship simply slid into a wave on its bow. The storm's pounding had not only shaken the timbers and opened leaks but also forced a gap of one inch between the bow plates, and the ocean spurted in every time the ship hit a roller.

The situation had obviously worsened over the last few days. During this time the *Roswell Sprague* continued on a general southerly passage. O'Brien felt it was foolhardy to continue in this direction, since this path would bring the vessel into even worse southern seas. He believed the ship should turn eastward to reach the closest harbor on the west coast of South America and felt the captain had no choice but to change the course of the *Sprague*.

O'Brien approached Captain Sawyer, who was standing on the edge of the poop deck, and told him that the sea would splash with each plunge through the bow's gap and flood more of the ship. The captain "impressed upon" his second mate not to tell a soul about what he had found. "I'll take the ship to the Falklands for repairs," he said.

Johnny was aghast at this. "Capt'n, if we get another blow like we had before—and from what I saw this morning—the ship will not be able to weather it. With our crew loss and provisions so short, wouldn't it be better to put into some port on the west coast?"

Sawyer became angry, the veins on his neck bulging. "Shut up, O'Brien! Shut up!" he shouted in a "strange way" and then turned around to disappear down the passageway leading to his cabin. O'Brien had picked up a feeling of despair, wrapped with fear, in the captain's voice.

Johnny found a young English sailor that he felt was trustworthy and told the youth to go below and confirm the bow's bad condition. The seaman did. He also talked to the crew and later told O'Brien they were going to give the captain a "round robin" to take the ship to the closest port—and as soon as possible. (A round robin is a seamen's petition that's signed by the crew, but the names form a circle so that a provoked captain can't single out the first signer for punishment as being the instigator.) The petition was a protest against Captain Sawyer's actions in continuing on the present course, given the lack of supplies, lifeboats, crewmembers, and the *Sprague*'s seaworthiness. He was directed to put to the nearest port, and the crew signed this in a circle of scrawled signatures.

Shortly after daybreak, the captain read the directive on the poop deck in the gray light. As the crippled vessel slammed into one roller after another, chilling seawater rushing over the bow and railing in hissing currents, the crew tried to maintain their position by the officers. Sawyer looked around the circle of signatures and immediately glared at O'Brien. Pointing an accusing finger at him, the captain yelled:

> This is your work, mister. You are directed to report before the mast. You are disrated to the rank of seaman. If I could, I would hang all of you from the highest

yardarm. You are nothing more than a damn lot of mutineers. This ship is not going to put back, you understand! But it will continue on around the Horn and we will put into the Falkland Islands.

O'Brien answered, "Captain, we refuse to follow your order, as that is foolish and will end up in all of our deaths." The rest of the crew muttered their approval with the second mate.

"Well, damn you, then!" spat Sawyer. "This ship goes around Cape Horn!" He and the mate then turned on their heels and disappeared below. The crew had another "consultation" and turned to the second mate. "Johnny, you know enough navigation to get her into some port on the West Coast. We will back you up in taking charge of the ship." They didn't like mutiny, but they feared even more a bad death by drowning in trying to round Cape Horn with this leaking sieve of a ship.

O'Brien thought over what he had been asked to do. This was mutiny, and he was the second mate, regardless of what the captain had said. The only navigational instruments he had onboard were an "ancient quadrant and a faded epitome [a book on navigation]." A wide grin spread over his face as he said loudly, "Boys, let's get going! We have a ship to save!" He might be a mutineer, but he was also going to be a navigator. He looked over a small world chart in the epitome, which gave him the idea of making the latitude of Valparaiso, Chile, and then running down that parallel to the port.

"Change course to the nor'east," he commanded the wheelman. The sailor grinned broadly back and showed the recognition that a new commander had just taken over. O'Brien with his youth and love of command felt on top of the world, regardless that if things turned out poorly, he would be guilty of mutiny and spend a long time in jail, if he was that lucky.

The heavy, waterlogged ship plunged into the waves like a drunken sailor staggering and reeling through a crowd of onlookers. It shuddered and creaked and rumbled throughout. O'Brien stayed aft all morning, anxiously watching the lofting—and then expanding—as the stretching canvas worked with the winds. The captain and the mate had not reappeared since the crew's round-robin conference. O'Brien grabbed his old quadrant and waited for the sun to "dip at noon" so he could determine the ship's latitude. He was so intent on this finding that he didn't pick up the sounds of running feet behind him.

Without warning, he was kicked from behind and knocked over the poop rail. O'Brien sailed down onto his face and hands, his quadrant smashing noisily into metallic pieces on the hardwood deck. As he scrambled to his feet, he heard Captain Sawyer's irate words, "You damn mutineer—forward you go!" Johnny doubled his fists in hot anger and ran toward the captain, but before he could get to the man, two crewmen jumped in and restrained him.

The captain stood at the head of the ladder swearing at the crew about the evils of mutiny, and as O'Brien's temper cooled, he laughed to himself that he was so intent on being captain, he had the "shortest spell of being one." Accepting the command and reluctantly his fate, O'Brien walked slowly to the fo'c'sle where the mate locked him in.

Although Sawyer and the mate took back command, the captain strangely didn't change O'Brien's set course or navigation. The *Sprague* continued its struggle through the ocean toward Valparaiso, Chile, the decrepit vessel's pumps barely able to keep ahead of the quickly filling sea. Later that night, the captain reinstated O'Brien. He simply told his bosun to get out and keep that "miserable crew in tow." Whatever problems the mate had run into with the others was kept to him and the captain. Johnny gave the orders and worked with the other seamen on the ship's ripped sails, rigging, repair problems, and on the previously set course.

The ship sailed into cold, rainy weather, but there were no damaging winds or huge rollers. As salt spray continued to fly over the ship, the crew unfortunately couldn't catch any fresh rainwater to augment their scarce supplies. The ferocious storm had washed overboard all but one of the water casks. The water left in that cask was too salty to drink, so the men were forced to use what was left in the iron tank on the between decks. This water with its strange metallic taste was used sparingly.

Eatable food was also scarce. What wasn't destroyed or scattered about by the storm was mildewed or salty. It seemed impossible for the stores to deteriorate further, but they grew worse as the ship continued on its course. Weevils and maggots infested the bread, and if a biscuit wasn't tied down, men drily said it would crawl away. "What are you growling about?" demanded one sailor. "You're getting fresh meat, when you're not entitled to it. Shut your eyes and go to it blind." Yet hunger drove the men to eat what was there: salt beef and broken pieces of soaked, hard bread from which they picked out, or tried to, what was moving inside. Small cubes of lean salt pork fried in deep fat—or pork scraps— were served floating in its clear liquid. The fat, or nearly all of the meat, went to the slush barrel, which was used in their lamps in the forecastle. It was possible to read there, but the stench of the smoke was nearly unendurable.

After several more days, the *Sprague* finally and mercifully approached the longed-after port. O'Brien took aboard a pilot who directed the vessel to its dock. As the longshoremen yelled and took the thrown-down ropes, Johnny knew his moment of truth was fast at hand. Followed by the mate, the captain marched sternly past him and disappeared down the gangplank. Neither had said a word. O'Brien wondered why the officers had continued on with their course, but he waited somewhat nervously for the response to his leading that "band of mutineers."

Two surveyors—who inspected ships for the insurers and reported why voyages weren't completed or a ship was found in disrepair—marched that day onto the *Sprague*. They looked over every part of the ship and also left without comment. O'Brien heard later that Captain Sawyer had bribed the surveyors. Whether he did or didn't, their report concluded the captain was fully justified in aborting the original destination and putting into Valparaiso for repairs, especially given the ship's severely damaged condition. O'Brien suspected that Sawyer wanted a "mutiny" argument if the owner and underwriters didn't buy his reasons for why the *Sprague* didn't reach its final destination.

The inspectors had wholeheartedly accepted Sawyer's "decision" to head to its present port. With its disastrous condition, the crew was not needed to repair or maintain the vessel for its next voyage. Everyone was discharged. When the captain and O'Brien met later, Sawyer was "most gracious" to him and gave him three months extra pay, the customary reward for the crews of vessels forced to lay over in foreign ports for a lengthy time. He later discovered that he was the only one so rewarded.

After the *Sprague* was condemned as being unseaworthy, the insurers auctioned the ship for scrap and what was left of the cargo. The twenty-one-year-old O'Brien remembered the mate, Mr. Hatfield, whose vision of drowning and disaster had become an unfortunate reality. Hatfield was right in worrying that this vessel would never get around the Horn. It didn't.

3

LEAVING ONE HOMELAND FOR ANOTHER

Three months later, O'Brien secured a sailor's berth on an English bark bound for Liverpool with grain. Although he still hated the English due to his experiences on the *Marlborough*, which would change over time, he wanted to see his homeland again. He visited with a sister who was living in a convent in the south of England and learned that his Valparaiso letters recounting the gale had arrived weeks earlier. Her superior was taken by his accounts written during the severe storm, and she had led the sisters in a prayer for his safe return—which he ascribed to why he was now safely inside the convent.

In that spring of 1873, O'Brien traveled to the south of Ireland and Cork where he had been born. He "plucked up the courage" to climb to the top of Blarney Castle and kissed the Blarney Stone, the mythical block of bluestone set in the fifteenth century into a castle tower located five miles from Cork. According to legend, kissing the stone endows the kisser with the gift of great eloquence or skill at flattery, which is what the word *blarney* has come to mean. Within two weeks, he found two sweethearts, one met at his first cousin's home in the town of Youghal, County Cork, and the other at a friend's home in the same region—which he attributed to the Blarney Stone. O'Brien didn't seem generally to be at any loss for words, however, and the good-looking lad with the "gift of gab" had become confident in his social relationships with people.

The lovely girl met at the friend's home became his one love, and her name was Mary. They were together for several weeks. O'Brien wrote later:

> We made hurricane love. One Sunday while we were walking along the banks of the river Lee, I said to her, "Mary, I am going to leave in a few days. . . . I love you very much and I think you love me, but let's try not to let our love get the better of our judgment. You see, I'm not in a position to marry. I want to be in command of a ship first, and when I am so, if I find your heart still free when I return, I will. And I will then be your loving slave as long as life lasts."
>
> She looked at me and her large blue eyes filled with tears and she sobbed, "You don't love me—you don't love me." We sat down and after she had her cry out, we walked home and didn't again refer to the subject. I was also upset over what had happened.
>
> A few hours after dinner that evening, she said to me, "I am going to sing you a song that whenever or wherever you hear it, you will think of me." She went to the piano, sat down, and with a voice that seemed to come from Heaven, played and sang the old song, "Sweet Spirit Hear My Prayer." As she sang the last verse, I could hardly keep from rushing to her and holding her in my arms and then asking her to marry me—but all I had was about seven hundred dollars and no bright prospects of advancement in my profession, so I held in my feelings and just gave her a strong embrace. I left and the parting was sad.

The next day, O'Brien sailed for New York on a passenger ship, the SS *Baltic*. He felt he couldn't stay there another day. Again intending to return when he was a ship's officer, he never heard from her again, although he wrote Mary when in New York. By now it was clear: O'Brien was attracted to women who were refined, came from a good family, and would benefit (and benefit from) his sought-after station in life.

He enrolled in Doctor Thom's Navigation School in New York, studied hard, passed the examination, and received his mate certificate from the American Shipmasters' Association of New York, number 6331, issued October 26, 1873. He kept that license with him for nearly fifty years until it was stolen from his room on the SS *Dellwood*, when he was in charge of the U.S. Shipping Board fleet at Benicia, California.

While deciding where he would ship next, O'Brien took his sextant to a nautical store for cleaning. An hour after leaving the shop, he felt for his wallet, but it was missing from his pocket. Also gone was the $600 inside—nearly $25,000 now—which was a $400 check on a San Francisco bank with the rest in cash. He hustled back to the store and asked if they had his wallet, but he was told he hadn't left it there. O'Brien felt "pretty bad," not only about the loss but also because he had met a "charming young Welsh girl" on the Atlantic crossing and had invited her with her cousin to go out to dinner and attend a theater party that evening.

When Johnny told them about his loss, the women tried to console him and asked him instead to be their guest for the evening. Being "flat broke," he politely declined. His next step was to pawn his watch and advertise a reward in the New York newspapers for the finder who would return his wallet. After waiting a few days with no response, he rethought his steps and concluded that his wallet had to have been left at the nautical store.

Quickly returning there, he asked another clerk about the wallet. The man eyed him silently, and this look told O'Brien all that he needed. They had it. He asked once more, and the clerk answered by asking what the wallet contained. After Johnny told him, the man left the counter and walked inside an adjacent office. He returned with the missing item.

Inspecting it thoroughly, O'Brien was pleased to learn that none of its contents was missing. Fast to attack bad behavior and quick to reward good, he divided the cash and offered the clerk half, or about one hundred dollars. The honest clerk turned down the offer. O'Brien was so happy about this turn of events—and in finding an honest man—that he insisted the clerk go with him to a tailor. Johnny paid for the "best ready-made suit that he ever could have received, including overcoat, hat, and shoes, and made him accept it." He rewarded good behavior as strongly as he punished bad.

Preferring the West Coast with its dark fogs and redwoods, the newly licensed mate decided to take the train back and see the countryside along the way. With the returned money, O'Brien purchased a second-class ticket on the railroad train to San Francisco, redeemed his watch from the pawnshop, and paid the repairs to get his sextant back. He left that night.

The train ride was "without incident" until it stopped in Wyoming. When the train was sidetracked at Fort Laramie, a lanky, well-dressed man came onboard and began talking amiably with O'Brien and the other passengers. He asked about the number of times the folks had been back East and told them about the "wonderful" gold discoveries made just a few miles from where they now stood. He spoke of how the successful men were throwing their money around Fort Laramie and then asked if anyone wanted to leave the train to have a drink on him. Since the train wasn't to leave for another hour, ten passengers—including Johnny—took up the kind stranger's offer.

The men walked into a scarred, beaten saloon by the railroad depot. The dark room was smoke filled; noisy from a tinny piano being played to one side; and dominated by a large, polished bar counter and a huge ornate mirror—half-empty liquor bottles lining the back wall—with several tables close by. The stranger introduced Johnny and the others to the clean-shaven gamblers, who were in marked contrast to the dusty, nonshaven men congregated around O'Brien. At one table, a whiskered man sat with a mound of rich quartz gold nuggets in front of him; he seemed to be talking to himself and at the same time playing with three cards. Johnny's new acquaintance commented, "There's one of the fools who sold a mine and in the last two days dropped ten thousand dollars. He has a mania to gamble with those fool cards."

Once their drinks were in hand, the passengers sat down at the tables. Content to watch, most at first didn't start playing. O'Brien never hesitated to try anything for the first time and started right away by asking what the game was. The tall stranger told him it was "three-card Monte." O'Brien learned the game was outwardly simple.

To play, a dealer places three cards facedown on the table. He shows that one of the cards is the target, or bet card (e.g., the queen of spades), and then quickly rearranges the cards to confuse the player about which card is which. The player is then asked to select one of the three cards as the right one. If the player correctly identifies the target card, he wins an amount equal to the bet; otherwise, he loses his stake. Any agreed card can be the money card.

O'Brien played against the "so called miner" with the stack of quartz gold, called the right card of the three being moved around, and quickly won twenty dollars. On returning to the bar for another drink, the grizzled miner slurred, "If any one of you fellows want a little easy money, now's your time to get it." Half of the crowd immediately left where they were sitting and crowded around the table with the gold quartz.

One of the passengers made a bet of ten dollars against the miner and won. He again won another ten dollars by identifying the right card being switched around by the miner. The dealer at the table then looked up at the winner and said, "Pretty lucky, young fellow, but I bet you an even one-hundred dollars, you can't find the joker on this deck in the three cards I put down." While he was talking, the gambler slowly lifted the playing cards, one over another.

Johnny could catch a glimpse of the joker once in a while, and the three cards with their backs up were then quickly placed on the table. The dealer said, "Now, lucky men, make your bet." The bet was made. As soon as the money was on the table, the dealer said evenly, "Pick your card, at once." A young passenger close in age to O'Brien, by the name of Sam, pulled a large knife from his belt and slammed it through the middle card to the table; at the same time, his friend drew out a revolver. Sam then moved to turn up the two side cards, saying, "If one is the joker, I lose; if not, then I must have it under this knife."

The dealer slowly looked at both men, half smiled, and without turning over any of the cards said, "You win." Sam turned up the two side cards, which were blank. He pulled up the knife from the table, turned over that card, and it also was blank. There were no jokers in this setup.

The "lucky" man pocketed his bet and the winnings, ordered drinks for everyone, and his friend put his revolver back. Most of the passengers felt good by now, either from the drinks or knowing that one of them had beaten the crooks.

One day later, however, O'Brien and several others had a different experience on the train and lost the ready cash they had. A couple of "fairly respectable looking men" started playing another game of monte. Shortly one of the passengers joined in and won. Seeing this, Johnny, Sam, and another passenger began playing, believing there was easy money to be made. They started to lose. On one deal O'Brien grabbed all three cards, but the money card was there—and not one of the selected cards. After more rounds, the three men as well as other playing passengers had lost all their cash.

It dawned on them that they were being conned, and this game was made for the sleight-of-hand crook. If a mark happened to pick the joker as the right card, the dealer could substitute a losing card. Picking up a bad card, the dealer holds it by a corner between the thumb and forefinger, and then slides it under the chosen card, ostensibly to turn over the selected one. In fact, as the two cards become vertical, the dealer shifts his grip from the nonchosen card to the chosen one, takes the good card away, and leaves the losing one to fall face up on the table. Like other throws, a properly executed turnover could be virtually undetectable.

The fleeced men began to realize that both the dealers and first player were crooks, and the victims soon collected together to make the "sharpies" give back their money. The confidence men were one jump ahead, however, and while the crowd was searching for them during the night, the train came to a sudden, shrieking halt with squealing wheels and brakes. The gang jumped off, but as they leaped away, those on the train fired several revolver shots at the fast-moving men. The gamblers returned fire, the metallic splats and pings echoing as the bullets hit the car's side. Nobody on the train was struck, and the passengers couldn't see in the darkness if any of the gamblers had been hit. But they made their getaway.

Johnny and Sam had lost all their cash, including their "small change." Although O'Brien still had his four-hundred-dollar bank check, neither one could buy any food or water—and O'Brien had learned a lesson, or so he thought. Sam then said they'd need to figure out how to get some food. He proposed, "I'll tell you what we'll do: The next station we come to, as the crowd floods out into the eating house, you and I will go with the bunch. You grab a big bologna sausage, and I'll take a couple of loaves of bread." They did this. When O'Brien walked from the place, however, he felt as if "every eye" in the house had been on him and he would surely be arrested. They did get away with their act of larceny.

O'Brien never felt comfortable about his part, even if they were hungry and broke. When they needed to eat the next day, he sold his watch—the one "bailed" out from the New York City pawnshop—so they would have no excuse to steal bread and sausages for the rest of the trip. Once in San Francisco, he cashed his check and found a decent sailor's boardinghouse. The owner asked him a few days later if he'd like to "go before the mast" [work as a sailor] on a fine little schooner to the South Seas."

Although the trip had appeal, O'Brien didn't want to do this at first because he held a certificate showing he was a licensed ship officer, or sailing ship's mate. Since he didn't want to loaf and spend his remaining cash while waiting for an officer's berth, Johnny banked the rest of his money and shipped for the South Seas.

* * *

The ship's name remained a secret even after Johnny O'Brien's death. The vessel's master was newly married, and his young wife was onboard the ship on this voyage. As he wrote: "After what happened on board, we the crew promised to never mention her name or that of the master, who was also the owner."

A "big Negro" had been hired as the cook and steward. After the ship was midway into her voyage, the captain was fishing on the stern for bonito. During that time—as O'Brien was told later—the cook attacked the captain's young wife; during the assault he choked "off her voice," after which he told her that if she ever told a word about this to the captain, he would instantly kill him and the rest of the crew and keep her for himself. He then grabbed the revolvers the captain had stowed in the after cabin.

After the cook freed the wife, her husband later found her. On the deck the men heard continued moaning. At three o'clock the next morning, O'Brien was at the wheel and noticed that the crying had stopped. Soon afterward, the captain came on deck, called the mate to one side, and the two had a brief conversation that he couldn't hear. At four A.M., O'Brien's watch came to an end, and he was relieved from the wheel. He was turning in when he heard the "most fearful cursing and yelling" and then a heavy fall.

Johnny later learned that when the cook came out of the galley, he had seen the mate standing some distance away lighting his pipe. Upon seeing the man leave the galley, the mate told others he had said, "Good morning, doctor [the sea name for a cook]," and the cook had answered a surly, "Good morning, Mr. Wilson." The cook next flung a canvas draw-bucket over the ship's rail and was starting to haul it up when the mate jumped on the man's shoulders; the two fell to the deck, thrashing madly about.

Before the cook could regain his feet, the captain rushed forward and struck the struggling man on his head with a belaying pin. Hearing the commotion outside, the crew and O'Brien rushed from the forecastle. They saw that the big man was still struggling, but the captain and mate soon had his legs and arms lashed. After subduing the cook, the captain yelled, "Hang him!" and the crew was driven to a fury.

O'Brien wrote in his memoirs:

The gaff topsail was lowered, and the halyard block was dropped to the deck. Then the men dragged him to the break of the after house. Lashing the halyard block around his ankles, the men hoisted him up to within a few feet of the topmast head, and there let him swing. The thud of the body as it struck the mast at each roll of the schooner remains with me to this day. He must have been dead before the seamen hoisted him aloft.

When daylight came, the captain came on deck, and in short order had a couple of boards secured to the vessel's rail and the combing of the poop. The men lowered the body, rolled it over and over to the planks where the boards were secured, then with the roll of the vessel and a venomous curse, a final kick, and over went the body. It floated astern, the last we saw of it.

A few days later, the schooner came upon an island where there was a settlement. The captain paid the crew off, secured their passage on a trading schooner bound for Tahiti, and shipped away with a native crew. Years later, O'Brien accidentally came across the mate on the San Francisco waterfront. He told Johnny that the captain had paid him and the second mate off before leaving for Australia, and while he remained onboard, no one ever saw the captain's wife again. Once in Australia, the master sold the vessel and disappeared. O'Brien wrote, "I have never seen or heard of any of the vessel's crew except for the mate for the last fifty-eight years, but that horrible scene on that early morning is as fresh in my mind as when it occurred."

After arriving in Tahiti, he quickly shipped out on a sailing brig that was bound for California.

* * *

Soon after the ship docked in San Francisco, O'Brien secured a berth as the quartermaster on the *Prince Alfred*, a small freight and passenger steamer that ran northward along the coast. On its second trip to Victoria, British Columbia, O'Brien met two bearded prospectors, Abbott and Steele, who were on their way back to the newly discovered gold strikes in the Cariboo Country area of British Columbia. After talking with him, the two concluded Johnny would be a good partner in this gold venture—undoubtedly because he had $450 that would go a long way in outfitting the venture. Abbott and Steele had been quite successful before in taking a fortune of gold out of that country, but their high living, partying, and gambling had soon emptied their pockets.

Struck by visions of finding a golden fortune, O'Brien wrote about his two newfound friends:

> They lost their money by a wild way of living. They were the men known to old timers in Victoria, who used to fill their pockets with twenty-dollar gold pieces, and go from saloon to saloon, inviting all hands to drink with them. They would haul out their gold pieces and throw them at the large mirrors behind the bar, telling the bar-keeper they guessed that the thrown money would be enough to pay for the damages.

O'Brien left the ship in Victoria, bought provisions and an outfit, and took passage with the two men on the tiny steamer *California* to Fort Wrangell, Alaska, and the trail to the gold fields. Wrangell is located on the northern tip of Wrangell Island, an island in the Alaska Panhandle, some 150 miles south of the Alaskan capital of Juneau. Years before the Alaskan Gold Rush in 1897, men grouped together in teams to find the gold, this time in the newly discovered fields of the Stikine and Dease Creek regions, northwest of Wrangell. One day after arriving in Wrangell, the threesome discovered that the camp was full, so they directly headed out for the gold fields. Two other prospectors, who were friends of Abbott and Steele, joined the men, and they hired four Indians and two canoes to help them port their provisions.

When the group began moving up the Stickine River, they found the traveling to be very strenuous. The men had to paddle against the fast-moving currents of three to five miles per hour, navigate around bad rapids, and tow their rafted supplies with heavy ropes over their shoulders. The riverbanks were steep and covered with dense underbrush, and their work was described as "pull, plod, and every so often fall." They stopped at the small, rustic outpost of Telegraph Creek, where the men paid off their canoe men, made their packs, and hired more Indians to help move their stores. O'Brien found the terrain to be nearly inaccessible, the weather daunting, and the work tiring. His part was to carry two fifty-pound bags of flour and a shovel up and then down the treacherous mountain passes.

A few days after starting out, the group came to a towering mountain, whose side skirted the Stickine River, and where for two hundred yards, a zig-zag trail was cut into the rock sides. The path was two feet wide through a slope that angled precipitously down to the turbulent river that coursed five hundred feet below. Each step had to be made very carefully, as one slip meant certain death. The Indians flatly told them, "Plenty white men fall to river."

Keeping their eyes on the trail, the men worked to safely trek over the course, dark pebbles and rocks that littered the way. They had to be wary that their packs and supplies didn't catch on the close rocks. The only sounds heard were feet tramping against the trail and an occasional rock tumbling over the side, followed by the shattering noise of others. The skies were gray and the setting bleak. Slowly, anxiously, and breathing hard, the men angled over the narrow path. Finally—and to their great relief—they safely passed around the mountain.

When the group came to the mines at Dease Creek, they discovered that all of the available land and claims were already staked out. This was an unfortunate but common finding after a grueling trip into the interior during a gold rush. After a few days of rest and searching around the area, the men decided to return to Telegraph Creek and follow the blazer trail made by the Western Union Telegraph Company in the "late sixties"; they would head into the Yukon River region, where the accompanying Indians reported that gold had been found. This would be a march of more than 250 miles, but the group by now could care less. With the time being late June, they felt there was ample time to find a claim and mine it before the savage winter crashed in.

While on the new route and camping by a lake, the men one evening decided to swim in the waters. After frolicking in the lake, they were putting their clothes back on when one man showed off pearls gathered from the nearby mussels. Everyone immediately began hunting for pearls. After opening hundreds of the shells, however, they found only the "small pearls good for sewing," which they considered to be of little value. The next evening they camped alongside an immense ledge of marble—"blood red with milk-white streaks"—but they were so distant from any shipping point that this discovery also had no value.

Continuing on, the group came to a stretch of forty miles of soft tundra. The brownish green setting was interspaced with colorful wild flowers, grasses, and groves of spruce and conifers, but the going quickly became onerous and depressing. Their feet sank down past their ankles with every step, and with each man carrying one hundred pounds on his back, this slogging was tough and back breaking. The passage was made worse by the "millions of mosquitoes" that viciously attacked them in the bogs. The men had no choice but to keep going; within a few days, there was no turning back.

One day when O'Brien was in the lead, he heard a faint, strange cry to one side. The sound seemed to be human, and it came from a grove of trees a quarter of a mile away. As they quietly approached the area, Johnny saw a young Indian boy, about eighteen years old, stretched out on mounds of brush. His eyes were closed, and he was gasping through a wide-open mouth; what had to be his Indian mother was kneeling beside him and moaning the sounds they had heard.

"I tried to soothe her," he wrote, "but she was inconsolable." When the woman looked up into a nearby tree and her voice sounded as if she was calling someone, O'Brien walked over to the point. He found a bundle in the lower crutch of a limb, but it didn't move or answer the mother's calls. O'Brien knew that the woman was all alone in the wilderness with her dead and dying children. They left her what food they could and sorrowfully continued on their journey. Their Indian packers told them it was their custom to place the dead wrapped in leaves and fiber in a tree, so the wolves and other wild animals couldn't eat the bodies.

After a "long, weary journey," the group arrived at a river, and they discharged their Indian workers. The men constructed two rafts from felled timbers, loaded their possessions onboard, and poled downstream until they came upon the mighty Yukon River. They set up camp and immediately began to prospect. Although the men found black sand and flakes of gold in every pan swirled in the river's water, as well as by digging down to bedrock in a few places, they didn't find any type of "paying prospect." The prospectors spent six weeks without finding a significant claim, so they held a "council." They decided to give up and return, as the men didn't have enough provisions or ammunition to last through the fast-approaching savage winter into the following spring.

They packed what stores they had left and "started back to civilization, our hopes for a fortune blasted, and our spirits low." The group arrived back in Wrangell in September and took passage on the old sidewheeler *Beaver*. This little steamer was said to have been the first to turn a paddlewheel on the Pacific Ocean; it had been built in England more than thirty-five years before and was still in use. Fifteen years later, O'Brien would be the captain of a ship steaming across the Puget Sound. He would see from his wheelhouse window the same paddlewheeler now impaled on a rock—and where the "grand old ship" had finally met her demise.

Finally arriving back in Victoria, O'Brien met a captain whom he had sailed with before. The man asked him to "go mate" on a new sail ship named the *Discovery*. Since the ship would soon sail to San Francisco, he gladly accepted the work and one week later arrived in that port, his dreams of finding gold on land at an end.

Although the captain asked him to continue on the *Discovery*'s coastal trips, O'Brien declined because he wanted to find a similar position on a deepwater ship. He wanted to get back on the ocean-bound sail ships, to again be in the "white path of the sea winds." He would try to find his fortune on the sea.

4

A TOUGH
FIRST CREW

After a few days, O'Brien heard about a mate's berth on a ship named the *Edwin James* and "fresh in" from Australia. He understood that "No Irish need apply," as the captain told his friend, and without any further explanation, the master said he wanted only an American or German mate. The undaunted O'Brien immediately found the long San Francisco wharf where the ship was docked. He saw that it was another three-masted bark, square rigged on the first two with the third (aft) mast rigged "fore and aft" (sails jutting at an angle and perpendicular to the keel). The bark (or barque) was a popular rig on the seas, and more ships of this type were built than all other square rigs combined.

O'Brien marched up the gangplank, asked around, and was led to the master, who was leaning against the forecastle. Although older, the man was similar in size and build to Johnny, and after their introduction, he learned the man's name was Walter Moffett. When he told the captain he was interested in the position, the master leaned back, looked him over, and said succinctly, "You look too young." O'Brien told him about his years of experience on the different ships.

When Moffett asked where Johnny hailed from, O'Brien answered that he had passed his officer's examination the year before and received his shipmaster's license in New York. He felt his answer was justified since he had received his citizenship papers prior to passing the examination to become an officer on sailing ships. Although his license was for these vessels, it did not encompass every type of ship, size, or geography. His Irish descent, for the moment, had been passed over—and it didn't come up again. There were other hurdles, however, that he had to pass.

"Young man, you look pretty light to be handling a mate's berth," replied the older man. O'Brien answered that although his stature was smaller and lighter than the average mate, he was confident of being equal to the task.

"Captain, if you give me a chance," he said looking the captain straight in the eye, "I feel sure that I will give you satisfaction. If I do not come up to that satisfaction, I am ready to leave your ship at any moment you say the word."

The master looked him over again and gave a slight nod. "Just like that," O'Brien said, "I was hired as chief mate, but knowing I had to work out or be left off at the next port." Johnny gathered his belongings, paid his bill at the seamen's boarding hotel, and walked onto the *Edwin James* at noon that day. He felt a strong pride in walking onto a ship for the first time as an officer. The ship was hauled "into the stream" that day, and the task of bending (knotting) the sails on the long yards began. His first scrap as a mate happened that afternoon.

The twenty-four-year-old O'Brien had shouted an order to a "big, burly fellow" to lay out on the yard and haul up the head earing (attaching line) of the foresail. The sailor stared down resentfully from his high perch and told the new mate to go to a "place which is supposed to be warmer than San Francisco Bay." O'Brien yelled at the man to get down on the deck, and the quickness with which he descended gave no doubt that this seaman intended to beat up O'Brien—and badly.

The grinning man couldn't wait to get his hands on the new mate, but as soon as he landed on the deck, O'Brien took a quick step forward, feinted with one hand, and cracked him straight on the jaw with a pistonlike shot from the other. The man crumpled down, and the fight was over in a few seconds. The steward ran over to the fallen seaman and began "giving repairs." O'Brien didn't have another major problem with that man, nor any other crewmember on the initial voyage to Portland. He knew, however, that he would be further tested in the continual rituals of the sea.

The next day the ship left the dock and sailed out through the heads into the ocean. The captain told him to come below and get dinner. O'Brien would eat for the first time in the dining room with the other officers. They had just taken their seats at the table, with the attentive steward waiting by, when muffled shouts were heard from above.

O'Brien was on the deck "in a flash." He quickly realized that the sails weren't properly trimmed, and two sailors were arguing over what next to do. He gave the order, and the men began doing the work. As he looked around the ship, however, he saw the seaman he had clashed with the day before, now stripped to the waist and "stargazing in the waist of the ship." O'Brien yelled, "What in the hell are you looking at! Get to work!" When he didn't move, O'Brien "made a run for him." When the seaman saw the mate racing toward him, he turned around, raced up the closest mast, and quickly began to work. Looking down, he said with a grin, "Mr. O'Brien, you'll have no more trouble with me." And he didn't.

During the voyage up the West Coast, Johnny learned that Walter Moffett was also the owner of the *Edwin James*. When the ship arrived in Portland, Moffett discharged the entire crew but kept on O'Brien. Although the owner said he liked how the young mate had taken charge, Johnny knew that results were what would keep him his job. Moffett next hired a new captain, a chin-whiskered man named Jefferson Forbes who came from "down East." The ship's destination was chartered to China to haul general goods, such as liquor, axes, shovels, and nails. A few weeks later, new seamen had been hired before the mast, and at that time O'Brien thought they were a "tough lot."

When the loading was done and the ship cleared for Hong Kong via Honolulu, a chugging steam tug towed the ship down the Willamette River from Portland to the Columbia River and ran the short westerly distance toward Astoria and the ocean. (Note: The Willamette River passes through Portland, Oregon, and is a tributary of the Columbia River; the two rivers lie close to one another, with Astoria being fifty miles from Portland—and a short ten miles west to the Columbia River bar and Pacific Ocean.)

* * *

When the vessel anchored in the late morning at Astoria, the crew left the ship to buy what they needed until reaching Hawaii, such as underwear, shirts, pipes, tobacco, and matches. O'Brien took his time and strolled around the bark. The *Edwin James* was a deepwater ship, an aristocrat of the sea, which allowed the ship to sail the seven seas. The vessel had three decks: a main deck, quarterdeck, and forecastle deck. Since sailors never pronounced the word *forecastle* as it's spelled, they called their quarters the "fo'c'sle," just as they pronounced it. The main deck ran the vessel's full length; the quarterdeck ran forward from the stern and was raised about five feet above the main deck's level; the fo'c'sle deck ran aft from the bow and was raised above the main deck. The space under the quarterdeck was enclosed and called the lazaret.

Two deckhouses were on the main deck. The forward house was located toward the bow, and the forward third of it contained the crew's quarters, the "fo'c'sle proper." This space was divided lengthwise into two compartments: the port watch living in one, the starboard watch in the other. The rooms were unfinished except for two tiers of built-in bunks; there were typically no lockers for stowing away personal belongings. Some sailors brought their sea chests, others made do with canvas bags, and the sea chests could take the place of chairs or benches.

In larger ships, after the fo'c'sle quarters would be the carpenter shop, equipped with a long workbench, tool racks, the carpenter's room, and a locker for storing paints and oils. Next to the carpenter's quarters could be the galley with its big coal-burning iron range, freshwater reservoir, and utensils; the cook, like the carpenter, rated a room of his own. The boatswain (or bosun) had his room in the starboard after corner of the forward house; the room had an upper and lower bunk, and when a boy was onboard, he took the upper. These quarters could also be on the after house located on the stern. A small steam engine, called a donkey engine, used for loading and unloading cargo could be housed here or on the deck. With a complicated system of rope belts and pulleys, the engine was used to power the windlass and heave up the anchor or even work the pumps.

The after house was reserved for the captain, his family, the mates, and steward, and this stern area was divided typically into forward and after cabins. The forward cabin was the dining room where they ate. The first mate typically joined the captain and his family for the first meal served by the steward. After that meal, the steward reset the table and served the second mate and the carpenter. Or, if the captain didn't have a family, they all ate together. If the cook and steward were congenial, they ate together in the galley after the rest of the ship's company had eaten. The other cabins were off the dining area.

On the quarterdeck at the stern was the wheelhouse, which housed the steering gear and sheltered the helmsman. It was divided into two sections: the forward part had the steering wheel and tall brass compass; the after room housed the tiller and the blocks and tackles that moved it. A small hatchway led from the wheelhouse down to the lazaret, a dark, eerie place where canned goods, bulk provisions, coils of rope and "other interesting things" were stored.

The captain could enter his room from the main deck through the forward cabin or from the quarterdeck by descending a companionway. These quarters could be dark, small, and dreary, or as one was described, "An elegant little apartment with walls of bird's eye maple with panels of mahogany embellished with delicate scrolls and border designs done in gold. Pilasters of cherry divided the panels. A settee was built into each sidewall and these were upholstered in dark-red plush." Bedrooms and a bathroom for family members could be located off the captain's room.

After his stroll around the ship, Johnny went to his room below deck, a small but comfortable cabin underneath the quarterdeck. His transom berth had several large drawers underneath for his clothes, razor, and other possessions. The steward polished the brass oil lamp that swung over the space where a desk folded down from the wall. His brass port window opened to the sea through the bulkhead. Tinted matting covered the floor, and everyday clothes hung in one corner.

Jefferson Forbes came down and told him to get the ship fully ready for sea by the afternoon. Saying he was going to find a tug for the tow to the Pacific, Forbes then left for shore. Johnny told the second mate to have the men "turn to," but the officer soon returned and said he had given the orders to one of the new men, but that seaman had refused to work. He also told the mate that crewmen had returned from shore with bottles of whiskey bought from a dockside bar, adding they had broken the whiskey out to others, were drinking heavily, and were in an "ugly mood."

O'Brien briskly walked to the dark, odorous forecastle and saw the men drinking shots of whiskey. He ordered them to the deck to start work. The men refused with "floods of insults." Johnny believed there was a time for war and a time for strategy, and he saw the futility of driving topside this crowd of unruly seamen. He left and sent the second mate to find the captain on shore, tell him the problem, and await further orders. Captain Forbes soon sent back word that the "lot of them" should be locked in the forecastle, and he'd bring back a new crew.

Hearing this, O'Brien stomped back to the forecastle and ordered the men once more to start working. When they laughed back, he simply clicked the padlock on the door. The men had no idea they were locked in until one drunk decided to report for work. The cries of the enraged men then sounded over the ship. The captain soon returned to the ship, however, with the new crew, "all brawny Negroes, apparently smart seamen," and just one man short.

When the new seamen came over the rail, O'Brien ordered them forward to man the windlass and get the ship under way. While the new men worked, the angry, drunken cries continued to pour out from the fo'c'sle. The dripping anchor was then raised, the tug's stout hawser brought onboard and secured, and the tug began its tow of the heavy vessel for the bar. Forbes then told Johnny that since the old crew had received a month's wages in advance—which he would never again do as it went too fast for booze—that he would release the fo'c'sle prisoners on Clatsop Spit, a small projection of sand covered by the sea at high tide.

Clatsop Spit is a very unpredictable place on the Columbia River's entrance from the Pacific Ocean, and one where the channel by itself is a highly dangerous and "mean" crossing. During flood currents and slack water, this spit may be calm with only a gentle swell breaking far in. Yet five or ten minutes later, when the current has started to ebb, it can become extremely hazardous, with large breakers extending far out toward the channel. Although the tide was turning now and the sweep of the sea was imminent, there appeared to be enough time to put the drunks on the spit. And the tug skipper had agreed to then take them off.

"Get the yawl ready to take those mutineers, mate," the captain ordered O'Brien. "Take away every stitch of clothing except enough to cover them, like old underwear or dungarees. Tell them what you want, but, one by one, get them on that boat."

"It was much against my will that I had to carry out the captain's orders in this case," O'Brien said later. "Although the men were a drunken, unruly crew—and had refused duty—I tried to persuade the captain to put them ashore at Astoria, but he had made up his mind to punish them by taking everything they had and in a rising tide, especially since they had pocketed the month's advance pay."

When the tug's pulling stopped, O'Brien followed his orders and told the drunks to come out of the deckhouse, one by one, shirtless, shoeless, and near naked. He and the second mate had "quite a job," but with drawn revolvers, they managed to coax, threaten, or force all but one of the cursing men over the side into the boat.

One "German, quieter than the rest," stayed in the fo'c'sle when he agreed to complete the crew, although O'Brien later regretted this decision. Although the flooding tide would soon be racing in, the angry Forbes wouldn't hear anything to the contrary. O'Brien jumped into the boat, and four of the Negro crewmembers rowed the drunken mutineers to the spit. Brandishing his revolver with his new crew in support, he forced the cursing ex-crewmembers to the spit as the tide began setting in. He wrote, "After landing the nine, and hearing nine-hundred-and-ninety-nine curses back, we left them. Fortunately for them, it was in the late day. The sun was out, bright, and warm. Had it been otherwise, I think the captain would have allowed them more clothing."

The ship then took its tow to the ocean. The Columbia River bar can be very dangerous due to its sudden and unpredictable current changes with large breakers and quickly rising winds. The ebb currents on the bar's north entrance can reach over five miles per hour, not to mention that the crashing of the river's flow with the ocean waves can create a maelstrom of rogue waves. This time, the crossing was uneventful.

When the *James* was outside the bar, the tug chugged its way to the spit. While the new crew and its officers watched intently, the tug picked the men out of the water as they swam silently in the currents, the ocean to their necks. By then they had undoubtedly sobered up. "We would be gone for over two years," penned O'Brien, "so the incident apparently would be forgotten on the ship's return and we left for Hawaii and eventually China."

* * *

The captain had brought his young wife along so they could call on friends in Honolulu, but Moffett stayed behind with his family in Portland. When the ship was a few days off the Hawaiian Islands, the northeast trade winds became light and eventually died out. The listless sail ship took days to go what before took hours and like other vessels began to drift about aimlessly. Sailors disliked having no winds nearly as much as they disliked violent windstorms. When winds abandoned ships, the sails slatted against the spars, and the vessel rolled and pitched with the ocean's undulations. The crew had to "clew them up" to prevent the sails from chafing to pieces. The men on the yards had to be careful because without the wind keeping them jammed against the rigging, as if glued there, they could fall from the shrouds. A fast voyage had now become nearly interminable, and tempers flared.

The winds finally picked up, and the ship headed into the islands. When the winds again died off Molokai at sundown, however, the ship without any available anchorage began to drift dangerously and uncontrollably toward the breakers. O'Brien told the second mate to get the boats ready to abandon ship, and when they were ready, the captain with his wife, second mate, and half the crew crowded into one. O'Brien had orders to take the remaining crew in the other boat, but he suggested to the captain they ought to be absolutely sure "she would fetch up in the breakers" before abandoning ship.

The captain was taking no chances, and he ordered that his boat be lowered as the rolling sea began driving the listless ship closer to the breakers. "We can always come back if the ship doesn't break up," he told O'Brien loudly. When his yawl was rowing away, the captain yelled back, "O'Brien, I want you and your crew to get off now!"

"All right, captain, but in a little while," Johnny answered. "I have room to wait and we ought to have a land breeze soon." He always seemed to accept danger as a risk worthy of solving, even though the *James*'s sails were flapping heavily against the mast on every deep wave. The faint but deep-sounding booms of the surf were becoming more noticeable. When the ship was four hundred yards from the breakers, O'Brien was about to lower the boat when he thankfully felt the breeze from land "whip up." He ordered his men to immediately trim the yards. Once the sails were adjusted to properly receive the wind, the ship was soon pointed to the sea—and away from the breakers. He picked up those in the captain's boat, who boarded "without greeting," and set the ship's course for Honolulu.

The "old ship" needed a twenty-minute "spell" at the pumps every four hours, which was not done when the currents were driving the *Edwin James* toward land. O'Brien ordered the men to start pumping her out as soon as the captain came onboard. Obviously upset over the turn of events after he had abandoned the ship, the captain called O'Brien down before the crew for not properly pumping the ship out during the day.

"Sir, all hands were busy on the sails then," Johnny retorted, "as we expected the ship to go ashore."

"You are not paid to forget, Mister!" the captain shouted.

"Sir, I will report at Honolulu that the captain's boat took off and left others onboard."

"No boats left the ship," Forbes insisted.

Knowing that any further conversation was useless, the chief mate turned to go to his quarters. As O'Brien passed Forbes, the captain kicked at him. Watching from the corner of his eye, Johnny reacted quickly, caught the kicking leg, and tossed Captain Forbes onto his back. O'Brien continued to his quarters and locked himself in, as he expected to be punished for what had just happened. Since he meted out discipline, he would accept that in return if he disobeyed an order.

About two in the morning, the captain came to his door and called him. Asking what he wanted, Forbes answered evenly, "I want you, Mr. O'Brien, to forget what has passed and return to your duty."

The chief mate opened his door and replied, "I will do so with the understanding that you'll find a new mate in Honolulu to relieve me." Captain Forbes agreed.

Guided by a native pilot in the morning, the *Edwin James* arrived safely in the harbor. The pilot's boat came by and took the Hawaiian away, while Captain Forbes and his wife were going ashore in the ship's boat. As the captain was walking over the gangway, O'Brien reminded him about getting a mate. He nodded his head and ordered, "Keep the ship going underway between Diamond Head and the mouth of the harbor until I return." O'Brien nodded back.

In the late afternoon, the captain's boat returned but without another mate— and without his wife. After coming onboard, the captain noted O'Brien's already packed sea bag and looked at him. He smiled and then said, "Trim the yards and set our course for Hong Kong." O'Brien then understood that Forbes had already made up his mind for him to stay: He had no way of getting to shore while the ship sailed back and forth and not at anchor. He never knew why the wife stayed behind.

* * *

This captain was also "fussy" about having the bobstays painted, a job that O'Brien wanted to do when the ship was first heading to port. These cables ran from the bowsprit to the stem, near the waterline, and counteracted the upward pull of the lines that supported the mast. He ordered Johnny to send a man over the bow to paint the cables. At noon under a hot sun and light blue skies, the mate told the young German sailor, whom he had convinced to stay on the ship at Astoria, to get a boatswain's chair, rig a hoist line over the bow, and do the job. The sailor did as he was told.

Seeing that everything was shipshape before leaving the forecastle, the mate was walking to the main rigging when he heard the sharp cry of "Man overboard!" O'Brien ran to the rail and saw the struggling German sailor sweeping past the ship. A rope had given away or the young man had slipped off. Another crewman threw down a cork life preserver that snapped on a wave close to the thrashing seaman. The German splashed to the preserver and grabbed onto it. O'Brien ordered the crew to quickly back the main yard, ease up on the sheets, and get ready to launch the lifeboat as the vessel slowed.

Five minutes later, the boat was in the ocean, and he and the crew quickly pulled on its oars in the direction of the hapless sailor. Fifteen minutes later, the men on the yawl could barely see the ship's mast, now a quarter-mile away, but they saw that the German youth was still gripping the life preserver. "Running with all our might," the men rowed and were within twenty-five yards of the seaman. Rescue seemed imminent.

Suddenly the "devilish fin" of a huge shark cut through a large roller and slashed toward the swimmer. The men yelled for him to kick and splash, but when the seaman saw what was coming, his face showed a "frightful look of fear." An instant later, the sea boiled around the life preserver and the helpless lad, as both disappeared under a sea inked with red. The small boat "followed in the wake for a moment or two," when chunks of cork bobbed to the surface—but the young German was never seen again. The crew stayed fifteen minutes while they waited in silent horror for some development, but they saw only the blood-red color of the ocean dissipate with its contractions.

By this time, the *James* had turned around and was approaching the yawl. As the crewmen hailed them, the seamen were silently rowing back to the ship. Once onboard, another crewmember told O'Brien that the German youth had picked up a deck of playing cards, pulled out the queen of diamonds, and said, "I'm going to have good luck today." He did until he undertook the dangerous job of working over the bow.

The *Edwin James* made Hong Kong harbor, but during the voyage a foremast had snapped during a windstorm. Once the ship docked, the work on installing another thick mast was taking place. The second mate was aloft on the foremast yard, as he was driving down the eyes of the rigging onto the new mast. When his mallet handle accidentally broke away, the heavy oak handle flew down and smacked O'Brien squarely on his head. The next thing he remembered was that he was holding a tumbler of Holland gin and readying to drink it. A few minutes later, he and the men were busy setting the rigging. A bump as large as an egg swelled from his head, and years later, he could still feel the area where the wood handle had hit. Accidents happened these days almost regularly to the men.

In September 1875, the *James* was lying in the Kowloon Dry Dock in Hong Kong harbor when O'Brien experienced one of the most severe typhoons that ever passed. He was a "few hundred yards" from the ship when the storm fully struck. When the winds made it impossible to stand up, Johnny was forced to crawl on his hands and knees to travel the distance and finally get onboard. The storm holocaust became worse with lightning, thunder, and torrents of rain. As he entered his cabin, he heard the loud thud of the mizzen topmast crashing down when the winds blasted away the rope backstays that supported the huge mast.

When he later looked out, the night was as black as pitch. The lightning briefly lit up the scene with surrealistic shapes, and the direct flashes just as quickly become blinding. The sea seemed to be running at all angles, and the crew believed that nothing could withstand the shrieks of the wind and the crashes from what was now airborne.

When daylight finally came and the typhoon's force was mercifully diminishing, hundreds of capsized sampans, junks, and damaged ships with snapped masts littered the harbor or floated aimlessly about the waters among the broken bodies of countless victims. The wooden sheds and buildings surrounding the *James* were shredded, and their debris littered its decks. Two moored ships had sunk at their anchor, while many others were ripped and spun away from moorings. One of the sunken vessels had entered the harbor with 250 coolies onboard just as the typhoon struck: Everyone onboard, including the ship's crew, had been lost.

Once the damage of the storm and the sea was repaired, the ship was towed from the dry dock and soon sailed for Foochow. At the mouth of the Min River, a Chinese river pilot with sixteen native seamen boarded the *James*. The pilot smiled and bowed, then took command. His group of sailors divided into two groups on the ship's sides. As the sail ship slowly worked up the river against winds and current, the channel twisting abruptly at different angles, the pilot skillfully tacked in one course, then quickly changed direction to the other. He barked numerous crisp orders in an incomprehensible language to which his crew set the sails so the vessel could head swiftly, or slowly, in different directions.

O'Brien was struck by the skill of this pilot. Years later, he wrote, "In my long experience at sea, I have never seen such splendid handling of a big square-rigged vessel as I did in the beating against the wind and currents going against it, as with this river man." The ship eventually came to the Pagoda anchorage some miles from Foochow. The captain complimented the pilot deservedly and offered him extra money for his obvious skill. The man "smilingly, but politely," refused, saying that the usual pilot fee was all that he would need. O'Brien always carried a high respect for that man, not only for his values but also for the competence shown in navigating that dangerous river.

The ship's cargo was teak logs destined for the government navy yard where French naval shipbuilders were in charge. While unloading this load at anchor, O'Brien had a run-in with one of the Chinese workers. The laborers were pushing the large logs into the river through a porthole, and a large number of Chinese soldiers were taking the timbers from there and binding them into rafts to float to shore. He noticed that one of the native workers was loafing on a raft. Regardless of who was on or around Johnny's ship, if there was a task to be done, this mate wanted everyone working as hard as the other; otherwise the work would get sloppy and morale head down.

O'Brien ordered the goldbricker to get going. The man paid no heed. O'Brien yelled "some lurid language," but the native was still unmoved. Knowing these men had some understanding of English commands and language, the furious mate yelled that he would cut "somebody's damn head" off if there wasn't action. The man looked up curiously, shrugged his shoulders, and motioned indifferently for O'Brien to come on down.

That was enough. O'Brien raced toward the man and grabbed a hatchet along the way. He raced into the ship's hold, through the forward port, and onto the raft of bound crude logs. When the worker saw the mate coming, the man came right up to O'Brien. He pulled his shirt open and said in pidgin English, "You cut 'em head off!" and bent his neck for O'Brien to strike. With his hatchet raised, Johnny was so astonished by this move that he stopped, looked the man over, and threw the axe into the river. O'Brien laughed admiringly and said, "You are some crazy man. Come with me and have some samshu [gin]."

The two went to his quarters, where Johnny produced a square bottle of gin, poured a large portion into a larger metal cup, and handed it to the worker. The man drank the liquid in one long gulp and then looked back with surprise but contentment at the strange American. O'Brien then gave the startled Chinaman an American silver dollar. He had admired the "pluck" of the man. The native worked hard from then on and gave O'Brien a little Chinese metal god in return, which he kept for a long time. This episode also showed how O'Brien—and other successful officers—lived instinctively through common sense and fast decisions to alleviate problems. They had to, otherwise they would wind up as shark bait.

The workmen on the *James* loaded mast poles back into its now empty hold for a new destination to Taku on the gulf of the Yellow Sea on the coast of northeastern China. Just before departing on an early morning during a heavy fog, the crew heard the most "weird sing-song chantey" off the bow against the background sounds of oars slapping on the sea. A few minutes later, a large sampan appeared, seventy feet in length and loaded with freight and men. Ten men on each side were rowing the vessel, and they passed close to the ship's stern in the heavy mists with their fast rowing pace, strange echoing chants, and dips of oars. O'Brien recalled this surrealistic experience for years when he spoke about this voyage.

Although Johnny O'Brien and the captain had their differences, their relationship was professional, if not comfortable. The chief mate spent his off hours reading different subjects or studying seamanship in his small but comfortable cabin, complete with berth and drawers. When his ship was anchored at a port, he searched on land for books on politics, economics, and history as well as "notable" ones to read. He wanted to learn as much as he could, and he had seen that captains needed to have a seemingly "educated" knowledge.

As seen with the Chinese native and the samshu, O'Brien also kept a bottle or two in the drawers. He strongly controlled drinking while on the ship, however, keeping an eye out as an example for his men. That is, unless there was an occasion when he wanted to be cordial to a guest, to an honored worker, or for some other good reason to him.

After unloading their cargo ten miles off shore, binding it onto rafts, and floating it to shore, the men on the *James* sailed away from Taku, China, and took on a cargo of coal at Nagasaki, Japan, that was consigned to Shanghai. The loading of this cargo was also entirely by hand, and numerous Japanese coolies loaded wicker baskets from a lighter moored by the ship. They passed the baskets from hand to hand into the hold, where the contents were manually poured into a large mountain of coal. The work was dirty and grimy, hard and tough underneath a hot sun.

Two days before sailing back to Portland, O'Brien found himself challenged again in this gladiatorial world of sailing on the high seas. Captain Forbes shipped two large sailors, who had already served several years in a prison in Shanghai for mutiny. They were brought to the ship by sampan, and O'Brien took their names as they came onboard: Heavyset Murry was from Mauritius, and gangling Walling hailed from the West Indies. They also had enough sake in them to be troublesome, which boiled up when O'Brien confiscated a bottle of liquor from each one and threw the bottles overboard. They cursed and complained at his actions, to which he yelled back, "Shut up! Go forward or I'll lick both of you!"

This was all that they wanted to hear. The men smiled down on the smaller O'Brien and laughed raucously. Murry lifted his elbow and jabbed Walling, saying, "Get this! You can tie one hand behind my back and I'll still push this little runt to Kingdom come!" He again laughed heartily. Murry was flexing his left arm when O'Brien dove between the man's legs and upended him. The sailor flew into the air, and his head snapped against a railing with a loud thud. He was unconscious before he hit the deck.

Walling incredulously watched his friend crumple to the hard planks. His attention drawn to the fallen friend, O'Brien stepped close to Walling and landed two hard blows to the man's jaw. The man dropped to the deck next to Murry. The fight was over in less than thirty seconds, and this was O'Brien's best. He wouldn't be so lucky in other ones, but this was one he savored because he stopped two large, drunk crewmen before they caused more trouble. He had learned well in his early years.

When Murry and Walling sobered up, they apologized on their own to O'Brien and were considered on the voyage back to be good, hard workers with fun and humor. Unfortunately in the tradition of sailors on leave, they hit the Portland bars, became drunk and disorderly again, wandered through the Chinatown section, threw some of the merchants from their shops onto the streets, and were arrested by six of Portland's finest. After that, O'Brien lost track of the two seamen, although he was quite curious about their exploits from then on.

* * *

In May 1876, Walter Moffett appointed Johnny O'Brien to be the master of the *Edwin James*. Captain O'Brien, or now Captain John, was twenty-five, sharp-eyed, alert, and cocky. When on land, his manner on the ship came through: a rolling stride, a smiling swagger, and a seemingly educated knowledge about many subjects spent from his months of reading at sea. Despite the tough voyages for months with hardened men, once in port he was drawn to the musical, theatrical, and social events of society, especially those of Portland. He didn't have much time at this anchorage after his appointment, however, to mingle with the "gentile" class, who seemed to be drawn to his youthful authority and colorful tales. O'Brien soon shipped out as the master of the *James*.

The captain reigned at the head of the ship's economic and social structure, and if his family was along, his wife and children were the royal family. There would be no questioning of his decisions. The lives of everyone aboard depended on his ability and knowledge. For the voyage's duration, he was not only the captain but also the police chief, chief justice, purchasing agent, food inspector, treasurer, and undertaker for the onboard community. O'Brien knew this from his ten years on the sea, was ready to assume this command, and understood he would be called upon daily to exercise this authority.

His first trip westward was back to Hong Kong, and after a "fine" crossing to Hawaii, O'Brien stopped at Honolulu for freshwater and provisions for his Chinese passengers who were returning to their homeland. While the *James* was in port, a sharp scream echoed from the forerigging of an American ship docked at a nearby wharf. Although O'Brien was in the middle of his dinner, he rushed out and at the railing saw a seaman, obviously injured and high in the nearby ship's rigging, still yelling and shouting curses. He watched as the crew rushed up to the stricken sailor and helped him down to the deck. Captain O'Brien learned later that the second mate had become so enraged at some aspect of the sailor's conduct that he chased the man up the rigging and slashed part of his buttocks off. The sailor was now dying in a Honolulu hospital. The police searched the nearby ships, including the *James* on the morning of its departure, but the brutal officer had disappeared.

The vessel was two days out on its way to China when the chief mate brought a husky man to the captain. The man's name was Jimmy Franklin, and O'Brien later learned he had been the knife wielder on that American ship. Discovered among the Chinese passengers, Franklin told O'Brien that he was broke and couldn't find a boat heading out. He had heard the *James* had a full crew and didn't approach O'Brien for that reason. Thinking he could get to Hong Kong, the sailor believed he would have no problems finding work in that port.

"If you give me a chance, captain, I'll show you I'm a good sailor." After looking the man over, Johnny decided he had the look of a sailor and told the mate to "turn him to" on the deck. A week later, the Scottish steward came to the captain and excitedly told him Franklin was so angry at O'Brien that he said he would "cut out your heart out, slice it, fry it, and then eat it before the crew the next morning for breakfast." The steward heard Franklin say this through a crack in the galley bulkhead and said other sailors had to have heard it from the fo'c'sle.

The steward swore he was telling the truth and hadn't told anyone else about it. Knowing the steward was trustworthy, Captain O'Brien found out that Franklin had the lookout on the forecastle head from midnight to two o'clock in the morning. He took his revolver and a double-edged knife and waited in his bunk until midnight. A "fine slashing" northeast trade wind was blowing over, and the *Edwin James* was skimming over the calm sea at speeds approaching fifteen miles per hour. The night was a "beautiful, moonlit" one, and neither the man at the wheel nor on watch saw O'Brien steal through the ship's shadows to the bow. There were no sounds except for the straining rigging, creaking planks, and whistling winds.

Under the bath of moonlight and glimmering shadow edges, O'Brien watched Franklin pace back and forth over the fo'c'sle head for several minutes. When the man turned to pace away on his lookout, the captain leaped to the deck, holding the sharp knife in his right hand. He touched Franklin lightly on the side of his face with the handle.

"I'm informed you're the man who's going to cut my heart out and eat it before all hands for breakfast tomorrow morning," he said. "Now is your chance, and no one knows I'm here. Take the knife and start carving."

The captain was ready. He had his revolver in his pocket, "cocked and ready for firing the moment Franklin made a move to take the offered knife." The surprised sailor stepped back one pace and said, "I'll fry the man who told you." He began muttering curses at the captain.

Set to shoot the man now for that insolence alone, O'Brien stepped toward Franklin and said loudly, "I know you were the man who carved that sailor in the ship's rigging in Honolulu. Take the knife and get busy."

Franklin hesitated, held up one hand, and nervously replied: "Captain, hold on a minute. I made the threats you stated, but I didn't mean them. You as a man must know that if a sailor means a threat of that kind, he's not going to let the hands know it. He'll keep it to himself."

"Really," O'Brien interrupted sarcastically.

"Yes, I was mad at the time," he continued, "but this was because our dinner had been just vile. You keep all hands on deck every afternoon working hard, and when I saw that supper, I just had to give vent to my temper. If you'll overlook this break of mine, I promise you in the future that you'll have no cause to find any fault with me."

Knowing Franklin had no idea how close he was to death, O'Brien asked why the sailor didn't tell him about the bad food. The man answered he didn't believe the captain would give any "satisfaction" if he had gone "aft" with it.

"Sailor, that was your mistake," spat O'Brien. "If ever I learn that you make any remarks such as you have, I'll throw you in irons and take you into Hong

Kong tied up by your wrists and your feet just touching the deck. I'll report you to the police as the man who sliced up that sailor in Honolulu."

Franklin said he understood and worked hard and quietly from then on. O'Brien knew the food was just adequate for the officers, but he didn't know how bad it might be for the crew. Although he had told the cook to "equal out the food" quality between officers and crew, he knew that no cook would give the worst meat to the officers. Since no one onboard could cook, he decided to wait until the *James* reached Hong Kong or the crew made a formal complaint. The ship's cook was not someone to rile up unless you had a ready replacement.

As one sailor observed:

> It doesn't do any good to pick a fight with the cook. If he wants to be dirty, he can fix all of us up. One time a cook pissed in the soup, and the skipper caught him and put him in irons. However, the cook had to be let out because he was the only one who could do the work, and everyone afterwards was very careful not to rile that one.

The cook of the ship was called "Doctor," but whether the name was given due to his creating something eatable from the salt beef and briny pork, or in rationing out lime juice in hot climates to prevent scurvy, no one could say. Be this as it may, sailors used the term "Doctor," just as they sometimes called the mate "Mister" or the carpenter "Chips"—a part of the tradition of the sea.

When the ship docked at Hong Kong and passengers disembarked, the crew began offloading the cargo. O'Brien started the crucial task of finding a paying cargo to haul back to Portland. One morning, the crew approached him after their breakfast and asked him if he thought the food was fit for men to eat. He went below to the crew's mess and tasted the food. The hash was sour, the coffee like water, and "the whole makeup" was bad. He strolled to the galley and told the cook, "Doctor, the breakfast you have given these men this morning isn't fit for a dog to eat. I want you to cook for the men just the same as you would for the officers—and as I told you before."

The cook's fingers quickly wrapped around the handle of a nearby butcher knife. The anger flared up in his eyes, and he raised the knife over O'Brien's head. "Drop that knife," O'Brien ordered. "Drop it, or I'll have you swinging from the yardarm inside two minutes."

The captain's eyes blazed at the cook's. Then O'Brien heard a swish through the air by his shoulder, and he watched the cook drop to the deck, groaning and holding one arm as blood spurted out from a deep gash. The mate, Mr. Wilson, had grabbed the carpenter's broad axe and swung it down on the cook. While one sailor bandaged the cook's arm, another raised the flag signaling an emergency from the masthead. The harbor police were soon out in their steam tug and took the cook into custody. He was tried, convicted, and sentenced to one month in prison.

The problems didn't end there. One night while on his way to board the sampan for the off-anchored *James*, O'Brien took a shortcut through the fish market. As he was passing a particularly dark area, he heard a sharp curse and in the shadows spotted the large cook, who had obviously been released from jail. O'Brien saw "the glint of the heavy, sharp knife and like a shot," he was running away with the ex-cook in hot pursuit. Johnny was too fast for the man—he had to be. The man threw the heavy knife at him, and it went through the shoulder of his coat. The attack ended when two of the large, bearded Sikhs who policed the town suddenly appeared around the corner. The cook saw them and turned on his heels to escape into the darkness. The captain never saw the man again, and his knife wound healed.

* * *

With chartered freight finally secured in the lower holds and passengers in the b'tween deck, the *James* after three months headed back to Portland, Oregon. Everything went well until the ship sailed into the Bashi Channel, south of Formosa. When the winds died, the Japanese currents took hold and carried the ship toward the dangerous, rocky shoreline. The undercurrents and tidal rips were so fierce that Captain John's seamen were constantly flying over the ship's sails to try to gain some traction and stay away from the seething, bleak rocks.

Before darkness set in, O'Brien raised his spyglass and spotted a "crowd of fifty savages" trotting along the shore with raised arms, waiting for the ship to strike bottom. He could see the long spears that they held high, and their threatening gestures gave no doubt as to what they would do if the ship beached. The captain ordered the crew to arm themselves with whatever weapons they could find. The same orders were given to the Chinese interpreters to relay to the coolie passengers who were sailing with them to Portland.

That night the *James* drifted from a quarter to a half mile from the shore, moving at a four-knot clip in the strong, captive currents. O'Brien watched the abrupt movements of the savages as they danced with flaring torches held high, outlining the dancers' rhythms. He knew in the black darkness surrounding the ship that they were readying for an attack if the chance was given. When the mate said out loud, "Those fellows are cannibals," the words added to everyone's discomfort.

As if directed by a supreme power, the current surprisingly and gradually changed directions to take the *Edwin James* away from shore toward the ocean, and their "cannibalistic friends gave up the chase a little while before midnight." At daybreak, however, an island loomed up, while the ship drifted closer to it. Soundings taken indicated that the waters were deep, and O'Brien thought the movements of the currents were sweeping around the island's eastern end. He took the chance of being swept clear—and the *James* did.

The winds picked up on the fifth day, and the attitude of the crew and passengers changed to one of optimism. The ship's sails tightened, and the vessel started on a faster pace toward home. The next day, however, their fair weather abruptly changed. The sky suddenly darkened, and the wind changed to a harder blow. The sea became choppy, and the men knew that a storm was approaching. O'Brien had the crew reduce the canvas to small sail as the *James* pushed through higher waves.

When a black ridge appeared over the horizon, the men headed into the fo'c'sle to put on their oilskins. As the winds shifted from the southwest, the sails whipped back and forth with the change. Large seas picked up and began to crash over the ship, while everyone onboard knew that a typhoon had unexpectedly reared its ugly head. With the raging seas and winds suddenly upon the *James*, O'Brien grabbed the wheel and ordered the crew to trim the sails.

While the rest of the crew was carrying out his orders, he noticed that one seaman was loafing. O'Brien yelled at the slacker to get going, but the sailor known as Gibbons didn't move to help out. The captain angrily yelled, "What are you looking at? Haul away on that spanker boom." When the man cursed back, he sprang for the sailor. As Johnny approached, the man made a run at him. Gibbons struck O'Brien first with a strong fist on the forehead, knocking him over the deck. In an instant, the captain was up and grabbed a belaying pin from the rail. He struck Gibbons repeatedly with the heavy object. The man fell to the deck, and the captain went about saving the ship while two shipmates dragged Gibbons to his quarters.

The *Edwin James* survived the typhoon, as did Gibbons. O'Brien's attack was so savage that the sailor needed twenty-seven stitches to close the deep gashes on his head. The ship was nearing port two weeks later when the captain needed someone to climb the masts and oil the metal hinges, which were at the highest part of the full-sail ship, twelve stories up. O'Brien told the mate to send Gibbons to the top.

The bandaged sailor refused. "You can take the signal halyards and the oil pot and go aloft yourself. I won't do it."

The captain snapped back, "Fly aloft there, Gibbons! You fly!" Remembering the last time he hadn't followed orders, the sailor took the gear and went up the rigging. When he was on the lower shrouds, he yelled down, "I want all to bear witness that I hold the captain for sending me aloft. I told him I couldn't climb up to the mizzen trunk, and if I slip, my death'll be on that devil's hands!" Gibbons continued climbing up the swaying rigging.

This was enough for O'Brien. In that state of mind, the sailor would not only do a poor job but would probably end up hurting himself as well. The captain ordered the man to stop and yelled, "Come down here! I'll show you what a Yankee sailor can do!"

As Gibbons was climbing down, O'Brien scooted up the rigging. When he reached the highest point of the mast—and the ship—Johnny discovered that the end of the line would not go through the grooved wheel over which the halyard runs, since it was too badly frayed. The captain waited patiently while the mate climbed up and trimmed the end so it could be passed through the wheel. The mast meanwhile whipped back and forth with each roll of the ship, office-building stories above the ocean. With the task completed, the captain climbed back down the rigging to the deck.

In the spring of 1876, the ship arrived off the Columbia River bar. The wind was blowing, and no pilot was in sight. O'Brien pointed the ship in, took it over the seething bar, and brought the *Edwin James* into Astoria. The voyage from Hong Kong had taken thirty-eight days. The captain secured the permit to sail to Portland and found a tug and river pilot to take the ship up the Columbia into the Willamette River, twelve miles from Portland.

When the *James* entered Portland, the ship was "spic and span." The decks were spotless and the brass glittered brightly in the sun. O'Brien in the old tradition had his men chip, paint, wash, and clean the ship "like new" for its entry. At that time, the city of Portland was clustered on the east bank of the Willamette, and its businesses—as with many port cities—were nestled around its waterfront. Its dirt streets led up the hill into the heavily timbered areas at the city's edge.

The captain noticed that a spare topmast on the ship's starboard side wasn't set properly in its bed. He pointed this out to the mate, who told him that the crew had refused to do any more work. Captain John yelled into the fo'c'sle for the men to come out and get that job done. At first there was no response. Then a deep voice yelled back, "You can go to hell and get it done yourself!"

O'Brien recognized the voice and headed down into the smelly, dank quarters. He saw the flash of a knife through the glare of an oil lamp. Feeling that he had been cut, the captain left the forecastle "much quicker than I got in." He discovered that the knife, however, had only cut through his clothes and not into his arm. The captain called down, "If you men will come out—one at a time—I will lick every damn one of you." When no one ventured out, O'Brien forgot about the matter.

He wrote:

> As soon as the ship was off Portland, the newspapers let it be known that the barque *Edwin James* was due that evening. Some two-thousand people lined the docks, seeing the home ship with the first load of Chinese laborers, numbering two-hundred-and-thirty-one of them, arrive for the canneries. As the anchor was let go, I heard a roar of voices from the shore and looking over the side saw my sailor Gibbons, who had jumped overboard, now swimming for shore.

The troublemaker—still bandaged and acting injured—was helped fifty yards from shore onto a passing rowboat. When Gibbons landed, he told his story about being beaten but left out that he had refused orders, avoided helping his crewmates in a perilous storm, and struck the captain first. "Indignation prevailed," and a warrant for O'Brien's arrest was soon sworn out. When he landed on shore, he was met by the U.S. Marshal, who asked, "Is your name O'Brien and are you the master of the vessel called the *Edwin James*, now lying in the stream?"

As soon as he said "Yes," the marshal served him with the warrant for his arrest for "cruel and unusual ill treatment on the high seas on the person of a Mr. Gibbons." O'Brien accompanied the officer to the city courthouse. At the time, the owner of the *James* was out of town and couldn't call in his attorney or any other connections. The trial took four days, and the captain's best witness was Franklin, ironically the same one who swore before several crewmembers that he'd eat O'Brien's heart in front of everyone. The judge found the captain guilty of the charge and fined him $500 and court costs. Franklin's testimony, however, spared him from spending time in jail.

O'Brien's bank account was virtually wiped out, and he worried over losing his command. When Walter Moffett heard about what had happened, the owner assured him that the trial wasn't important. In fact, Moffett said he would be on the next trip with the *James*, one that O'Brien would still captain. He liked the brash, young man who got things done and took command, regardless of the consequences. O'Brien's world quickly brightened up, not to mention that a wealthy Portland resident soon approached him with a money-making proposition.

5

"THE SEA WOLF"

After the publicized arrest, trial, and large fine, a "prominent" merchant soon came into his life. O'Brien was strolling along the busy waterfront one day when a Chinese sailor approached and asked him to join the man for tea. While sitting down and sipping green tea, the merchant said, "Would you, Mr. Brien, like to take a chance to make big money?" He cut off the full pronunciation of his name, but the man obviously had heard about the captain's financial reversals.

"Certainly, just show me how. I'll consider everything outside of murder."

"Good, very good," the merchant responded. "I understand you take risks, but make good decisions, and have been to Honolulu and China before. I know that you are a man of honor in your commitments but don't worry about the details, let's say, of the law." He paused.

"Go on."

"In our business arrangement I will send on your ship from two-hundred to two-hundred-and-fifty pounds of opium in half-pound tins," he said and waited for a response.

After O'Brien gave a slight nod, the Chinese merchant continued:

This is to be taken charge by you personally. It is worth from seventy-five to eighty dollars per pound in Honolulu and it costs six dollars a pound here. After you agree to take it, I will send a man to San Francisco, who will take passage from

61

there to Honolulu. He will make the arrangements for sale, which I guarantee will not be less than seventy-five-dollars per pound. Upon your delivery to my men in Honolulu, you will receive one-half the profits upon the sale.

"There is much risk, here," the captain replied slowly. The amount of money to be earned, O'Brien quickly calculated, would be fifteen to twenty times what his fine had been.

"Your discretion, of course, is most important."

"I understand," O'Brien said. "I'll give you my answer by tomorrow noon." He thought about this very carefully and knew he was risking the confiscation of the ship. There was the chance of jail and a fine that would be very high. He inquired around the docks and learned that while he was away the government had confiscated the bark *Mary Belle Roberts* over such an "arrangement" that had gone bad. The captain was convicted of dealing in heroin, sent to prison for several years, and fined $5,000. On the other hand, the business was thriving with the trade between the countries, and most of these transactions were completed "without interference." He confirmed that the price of opium delivered in Honolulu was eighty dollars a pound—and the rewards for success were very substantial.

The captain didn't know how such a transaction was handled, and caution dictated a different approach. He decided to try a small-scale delivery first to see how everything had to fall into place. He needed to see how closely the ships were watched, land the opium ashore safely, set the actual price, and size up those in the deal. If everything went well on his return trip, he could go with the merchant on the large deal. Even more important, his contacts on the dock swore that the Chinese businessman who approached him was one who "hated" the government. (The merchant's actual name was never identified in any of O'Brien's written letters or memoirs.)

The captain set up another meeting the next day and told the man that they should first try "a little sample, let's assume, of five pounds and see how that goes." The merchant smiled and said he would have suggested that approach. Later in the week, as he prepared the *Edwin James* to sail to Hawaii, the merchant's delivery boy brought O'Brien ten tins of opium, each with one-half pound inside and wrapped in oil paper. He hid the small black tins away in his cabin.

On the same morning that he received the tin bundles, O'Brien noticed a "remarkable looking man" standing on the forecastle deck. The man stood out with his "big square shoulders, swarthy face, and piercing black eyes." He was perhaps forty years old and strongly built. The man's meaty hand immediately went in a half-salute to the captain, and his T-shirt revealed muscular arms covered with thick black hair that coursed down to his second finger joints.

"I presume I'm talking to the captain," the man said in a deep, harsh voice. After John responded, he continued, "I understand you want a mate, and if so,

I would like to get that berth." When O'Brien asked about his experience, the large man said, "I shipped last on the *Edwin H. Kingsman* and my papers should be in order."

After looking over the papers of recommendation, the captain inquired, "What's your name?"

"Robert O'Malley, sir."

The captain looked down at the papers and back up to the man standing in front. He liked what he saw, and most hiring decisions were made by quick assessments. "Okay, O'Malley, you're hired as mate on this ship. Your wages will be fifty-five dollars a month. I would like you to turn to at one o'clock this afternoon, as we clear for the sea at five."

This was the man O'Brien later said was the character, or part of, that Jack London used for the malevolent captain Wolf Larsen in his book *The Sea-Wolf*. Years would pass before the young Jack London would be sitting in Captain O'Brien's cabin during the Klondike Gold Rush and hear his colorful stories about Wolf O'Malley's voyages on the *James*.

O'Brien came on deck at the appointed time and watched the new mate in his same shirtsleeves "mentally taking notes of the ship and its gear." After introducing the second mate, Captain John told them that the boarding master, James Turk, would have the crew onboard at two o'clock. Soon afterwards, ten sailors came along the ship with their sea chests and bags. The men were from thirty to seventy years old, hair cut short, and a variety of different sizes and weights. Some had tattoos and others didn't; most wore beards or mustaches. They stepped onto the deck one by one, as O'Malley took their names, entered these in the log book, and examined their packed belongings for any bottles of liquor.

O'Malley knew what he was doing and found four bottles of whiskey in the men's bags. He confiscated the bottles, saying in a deceptively quiet way, "They'll be times at sea when you men will enjoy a swig of this more than now." But they knew they would never get the liquor back. The new mate also inspected their sheath knives, packed away or not, and when he found one with "points on," he put the blade in the seam of a pin rail, snapped the point off, and handed the remnant back. He said to the first sailor, "A little out of order to have pointed knives in your sheath, don't you think." He said it in a soft, deep voice as a statement, not as a question. O'Brien looked on approvingly, as this was standard practice: Fists were to be used for fighting—not knives.

After his inspections, O'Malley told the men to go forward and "have a smoke." He would call each man when he wanted him. O'Brien was also looking over the crew. They were a tough-looking bunch, all "hard looking cases," and each gave the mate a sidewise look as they passed to the forecastle. With a "swaggering step," they headed to the fo'c'sle.

"What do you think about the men?" said the captain.

"Jim Turk, the boarding master as you said, picked them for this ship. They are supposed to all be good sailors, not bad men." O'Malley stopped and gave for the first time what seemed to be a sinister smile. Something then told O'Brien that this voyage would not be all smooth sailing.

The ship departed from Portland that evening and crossed the Columbia River bar the next forenoon after leaving Astoria. The captain gave the orders to the mate to take off the gaskets, or ropes, used to hold the stowed sails in place, as well as then letting the sails hang on the ropes, ready to sheet home when the tug's hawser was thrown off. The tug gave the signal to let go, and a minute later O'Brien gave the order, "Sheet home the tops'ls!"

Captain John was amazed at how suddenly O'Malley's demeanor changed when they were in the Pacific Ocean. As soon as he gave the order, the mate's voice changed from an easy voice to a "demon's" in roaring to the crew, "Aloft there, two of you hounds! Yes! You at the main and you at the fore!"

The last one spoken to stood looking at the mate for a moment and then slowly started for the fore rigging. O'Malley yelled at him, "Fly!—Fly there, damn you, fly!"

"Oh, go to hell," the seaman nonchalantly answered. The large mate, his large arms flying in the air, started running for the man. The seaman took one look at the enraged mate and jumped for the rigging, with O'Malley right behind him, and O'Brien had never seen any man going aloft as fast as these two men were. Regardless of the head start, however, the mate caught the seaman by his shirt collar just as he was about to crawl out onto the highest yard. O'Malley jerked him from the foot rope and let the screaming seaman drop 140 feet to the deck below. The falling man struck the ratlines of the rigging, breaking several and then abruptly being caught by one. When this rope also gave way, the seaman tumbled down, struck other yards and sails, and then smacked onto the deck. Arms and legs sprawled out, the man lay still and semi-conscious.

O'Malley "flew" down the rigging, nearly as fast as the seaman bounced off one sail and then the other. Seeing this, O'Brien jumped to the deck and ran toward the motionless sailor. He thought his new mate was crazy and would either kill the seaman, "if any life was left in him," or throw him overboard. The men stood around the deck as if "they were petrified." They didn't want to draw O'Malley's attention and found it hard to believe what they had just seen.

By this time, the mate had grabbed the sailor by the stomach and was lifting him up, no doubt intending to throw the man overboard. The captain ran with "all the force in me" into the new mate, and everyone fell in a crash onto the deck. Scrambling to his feet, O'Brien yelled, "You black murderer, don't you lay your hands on that man again. Get sail on this ship and be smart about it!"

"Captain, no man can tell me to go to hell," O'Malley snarled, "without him getting there first." The large man turned to stare back at the crew. O'Brien wrote later that of all his decades at sea, he had never seen sails go on a ship so quickly. With the sails spreading out to catch the wind, O'Brien and another crewmember took the injured man to his cabin, where he dressed the sailor's injuries. The steward gave him the usual remedy—a tumbler of whiskey to drink—given the deep bruises and rope burns that covered the seaman's body. He would stay in his berth for one week before being able to return to duty.

With the *Edwin James* splashing through the waves on her course, the captain ordered O'Malley to his cabin. He told his mate that he would have to write up what had happened in the log as an "attempt at murder." Staring directly at him, he said, "What do you have to say about that, O'Malley?"

"Captain, these sailors on board shipped out with the intention of doing just as they pleased once she was at sea. I happened to be in Turk's barroom [also the boardinghouse owner] one day, and heard a group of them telling about how they were going to run the ship after they'd crossed the river bar. They said there was a boy skipper on board and that he would be just so much mush in their hands. I thought I'd get the mate's berth and just drill them."

"I feel perfectly capable of handling this ship and crew, O'Malley, and so far I've done so. I'll maintain discipline, as long as I am in charge—so no more dropping men from aloft. That's all, Mister!" As the mate lumbered away, O'Brien had to admit he was "somewhat" placated by this answer.

The owner, his wife, and five passengers were also onboard. When O'Brien and Walter Moffett conferred about the mate's action, Walters (how O'Brien referred to Moffett) wanted him to signal the tug and have the mate put ashore. The captain argued that he could handle the case and keep the ship going. O'Malley stayed.

The following day, O'Brien noticed the mate standing in the waist of the ship, leaning against the mainmast. The shirtsleeved, muscular O'Malley was overseeing the men as they overhauled the rigging. He suddenly stiffened and hollered at one sailor, "Come here, damn you!" The sailor walked stiffly and obviously apprehensively to the mate.

"Pass it out, you hound!" O'Malley jabbed a finger at the man's wide leather belt, and the fumbling sailor drew out a cord with long rope yarns that were knotted at their ends. This was a "teaser," or small cat-o'-nine-tails. The mate grabbed this from him and quickly struck the sailor hard over the nose with it. He handed it back and hissed an order, "Fly, you hound, fly up the fore t'gallant and royal yards and tie up the buntlines [ropes to the sails]!"

The sailor started to run, gained speed, and came to the mast with "feet flying." He jumped on the pole and without hesitation began climbing up the rigging. Not one moment later, O'Malley hollered at another seaman to come over. This sailor ran to the mate, who with "an oath and a threatening manner," reached out his hand. This sailor handed over another teaser, or small "cat," that the mate had spotted. He also struck this man across the face with the cord and ordered the sailor to "Fly!" Watching a second man climb up the rigging as punishment, O'Brien had had enough. It was time to stop this "devilish work."

"Mr. O'Malley!" he shouted. "Come aft with me!" When they reached the stern and were by themselves, the captain said angrily, "When I shipped you, you told me you'd just left the *Edwin Kingsman* in San Francisco. Did you not make a mistake? Was it not San Quentin State Prison, or even possibly the insane asylum? And the papers were phony? I want an answer!"

"You guessed it the first time, Captain." The two men stared at each other, while the crew and a few passengers stood far away but closely watching them. "I hate a sailor. I hate sailor boarding house masters and runners. I killed a runner in San Francisco three years ago." Runners were paid men who didn't hesitate to use force, drink, or "knock-out drops" to get their quota of sailors. O'Brien had seen runners taking a knocked-out sailor into Penny's boardinghouse; Penny, like other boardinghouse owners, was complicit in this shanghaiing of sailors. It wasn't until 1906 that Congress finally outlawed this practice.

O'Malley continued, "I was just pardoned through the efforts of some friends I have in Washington, who were in the navy during the Civil War." O'Malley went on to tell the captain that he had been a warrant officer with a Lieutenant Cushing on the raft that blew up the Confederate gunboat *Albemarle*, and he had helped save Cushing's life. The man later interceded to have him released sooner from prison.

(In one of the more daring exploits of the Civil War, Lieutenant William B. Cushing rammed the ironclad *CSS Albemarle* on the Roanoke River and caused the gunboat to sink. Of his crew, only Cushing and one other escaped; two seamen drowned, and five others were captured. There is no evidence that O'Malley was ever involved, and historians credit Cushing with escaping dramatically on his own.)

On hearing O'Malley's story, O'Brien believed that his mate had been in prison, but everything else said was immaterial. The captain rebuked him again. He warned O'Malley that any more brutality would result in his arriving at the next port in irons. The rest of the trip passed smoothly, however, and O'Brien said he had never seen a "more thorough" seaman in a gale. O'Malley could give the "longest command in the fewest words," and a seaman would be fast aloft to furl a sail. His men would get to tasks on the mate's command "as if lightning had struck them."

O'Malley showed genuine respect for O'Brien: He would always salute when the captain came to the deck. He never spoke to the captain, unless spoken to, and just said "good morning" or "good night"—but when he slept, his eyes were always half open. At the slightest call or touch, he jumped out of his berth. O'Brien thought he either had a very guilty conscience or was always expecting a violent death. During the voyage, the two men built up a mutual respect—especially since O'Malley was no longer beating up the captain's crew.

When the *Edwin James* reached Honolulu, O'Brien paid off several of the crewmembers who he felt weren't as good as the others. He gave O'Malley some money so the mate could leave Honolulu and avoid being arrested for tossing the sailor from the mast. His strong "executive" abilities and apparent respect for O'Brien caused the captain to be lenient with him. After a couple of weeks, the swarthy seaman returned. The owner, Walters, also liked him. Partly due to this, they gave O'Malley another chance as mate.

* * *

The captain's attention centered now on the opium tins stowed inside his cabin. During the voyage, he had become friends with an elderly passenger on the *James* by the name of Peacock, who had made the trip to Hawaii to start anew. (This was the name Captain O'Brien called the passenger, but it isn't known if this was the real one.) The man was down on his luck, and the two spent long hours during the voyage chatting on deck or in O'Brien's quarters. When the ship docked, Peacock told him that he "hoped the good Lord would let him live long enough to repay O'Brien for his kindness on the trip" and invited him to share a drink and a cigar when on shore.

O'Brien quickly understood how close the native Hawaiians or customs officers watched the ship captains "in their doings on land." Everyone assumed that as commanders of their ship communities in the harbor, they knew what was going on—legal or not—off the boats. He couldn't see any way to personally find the buyers and handle the transaction by himself without being tied into the deal. The captain decided to share with Peacock his secret about the opium tins and selling them. He had decided this gentleman was trustworthy, especially since Peacock was broke and they had become friends.

Taking up Peacock's offer, he met the man in an upscale bar in Honolulu. O'Brien took a rickshaw through this city of "coral roads, beautiful and fragrant flowers, and mixture of small white houses and stately mansions" before coming to the impressive structure. Over drinks the captain broached the subject by saying, "How would you like to make some money, about two-hundred dollars for starters?" O'Brien explained he was to receive one-half of the opium tin sales, and the captain would split his share if Peacock found the buyer.

"Captain O'Brien," the man replied, "I'm glad you trusted me with this. I appreciate what you have done for me, and I guarantee I'll be able to dispose of the tins." The deal was sealed with a long handshake.

When Peacock returned the next day to the *Edwin James*, he explained he had looked discretely and found an interested buyer in the "dens of iniquity" John had suggested. O'Brien explained he would be happy to meet the man, but this would have to be away from the ship. Peacock would handle the transfer. Hearing this, the elderly man shook his head and explained that "this would never do." The contact needed to verify O'Brien's story on the vessel and not on land. The captain reluctantly agreed and felt more anxious than ever before about how to get the tins off his ship.

A couple of days later, Peacock came aboard the *James* with a smaller, thin man, whom he introduced as being in the business. The man was called Freddy and said he would pay eighty dollars per pound. O'Brien "instantly sized" up the man as being no fool, and his instincts were not to trust this new acquaintance. The regular customhouse officer, an old shipmaster named Captain Burrill, was standing at the time on the quarterdeck, and O'Brien thought he saw Burrill giving him some kind of a signal. Excusing himself, Johnny went aft thru the cabin to the after companionway. Captain Burrill met him there and said, "Look out for that man your passenger is with."

O'Brien had the warning but didn't heed it. He wanted the tins off his ship and thought Burrill was concerned about his being involved with the wrong people— well, he was. The captain returned to the two men, and after further "dickering" about the opium's price—and refusing to do any business during daylight—he said if Freddy showed him where he lived, O'Brien would bring the tins that night for the money. The house was two blocks from the dock, and Freddy said he had bought it with the money from past opium dealings. Although O'Brien still felt uneasy, he decided to go through with the deal.

About 10:30 P.M., he retrieved the tins from their hiding place and was stuffing them into his Wellington boots when the night watchman knocked on the door. As O'Brien hid the tins under the center table with its low-hanging tablecloth, the sailor told him that a man wanted to see him. Captain John walked onto the deck and saw Freddy. O'Brien immediately said, "Why are you here? I told you not to draw any attention to my ship!"

"I've been on the lookout for an hour," the man replied quickly, "and there isn't a soul around. I have come to pay you your hundred-dollars a pound for the opium. There isn't an ounce of the stuff in the kingdom, and my clients need it now. I thought you weren't coming."

O'Brien eyed him suspiciously. "My friend, your clients will not get any opium from this ship tonight. Less than an hour ago, I saw two men watching over here from the lumber pile on the wharf."

Freddy put his hand on O'Brien's shoulder and said louder than normal, "Get the stuff out. Here's the five-hundred dollars for the five pounds. I need it now."

O'Brien realized at once he had somehow been set up. The insistence of Freddy, if that was his name, to complete the sale on the ship just didn't ring right. If a search was made now, the opium would be found in his cabin, the ship would be seized, and a heavy fine and jail would follow. He instantly decided on another course of action, quietly saying, "Don't speak so loud, someone may be watching us. Now keep a careful watch, and if you see or hear anyone, then hail them in a loud voice as a warning. I'll be back in a few moments."

O'Brien took different passageways to his cabin, loaded the tins in his jacket pockets, and hid a short-barreled revolver. When he came back on deck, Freddy asked for the opium. The captain told him, "You're a married man and I'm single. If we're caught, I'll be the one to take the full blame, so let's get a move over to the house." Freddy seemed to hesitate, looked back at shore, and then followed the captain off the ship.

Once off the dock, O'Brien took a different route that ten minutes later ended in a dark alley. When Freddy complained the captain was moving too fast, O'Brien let the revolver—hidden in his coat sleeve—slip down into his right hand. Raising the weapon, he showed the gun and gave a "reminding light dig" with it on the man's cheek, saying, "Damn you, you're betraying me. If you're guilty, you'll never live to see daylight. If you're square, which I very much doubt, you'll have it later on. Let's get away from here."

With the gun swaying with each movement of his arm, the captain headed briskly away with the man. As quick as a snake, Freddy made a surprisingly fast grab for the gun, snatched it, threw the revolver away, and loudly yelled out for help. It seemed to O'Brien as if the whole customhouse force suddenly had appeared, as twelve or more shouting men, including the chief of police and two of his policemen ran toward him. The men formed a semicircle in front of the captain and began closing in. As John stepped back from the approaching law officers, he knew he didn't have a chance to outrun them into town. Somehow he had to get to the ocean and dump the opium, the problem being how to do that with all of these lawmen in the way.

A "big fellow" with a long, swinging nightstick came within fifteen feet and said, "Give up, young fellow!" O'Brien instinctively grabbed an opium tin from his pocket and pointed it in the darkness with a "donnybrook" yell, shouting, "Lie down, damn you, or I'll blow holes through your head." Screaming like a crazed man, he waved the tin while he ran right at the group. When two lawmen threw themselves down on the ground to avoid the apparent gunfire, he "flew over them" with a jump and raced away. Having been able to sprint "one-hundred yards in eleven seconds" before, the captain had to do just that as he raced to a nearby beach in front of what were "old docks." In a few minutes, he was running over the soft sand.

He sped onto the old wooden docks with the customs men close behind. While racing to the wharf's end, he grabbed the tins from his pockets and threw them into the sea. Although by now he had a one-hundred-yard lead on the puffing, out-of-shape lawmen, O'Brien lost his lead when he slowed down to throw the opium tins away.

Continuing down the long dock, he found an opening in the wharf planks with the ocean below and dropped down into the shallow water. Seeing the weaving beams of the pursuing men's bull's-eye lanterns, he waded out to deeper water. The briny ocean tasted foul but warm when he first submerged, but he tried to swim underwater as far as possible. When he surfaced, he looked back and saw the lights sweeping around the wharf.

Hearing the men's yells to one another, O'Brien took another breath and swam underwater toward a nearby offshore reef. He would swim under the sea for a minute or two, surface, take a breath, and continue on again. When sufficiently away, he swam quietly through the gentle wave rolls to the reef. Moving between two stands of coral, he stayed under the surface and breathed through his mouth just above the lapping ocean. When O'Brien heard the angry curses of the searching men, who said they had seen him in nearly every place—climbing on a coal pile, running back on the beach, and crouching by the dock—he decided to stay there.

He treaded water as long as possible, while the light beams continued sweeping around the area, including dangerously close to where he was hiding. As one light became brighter, he realized the lawmen had taken to their boats. He dropped under the water toward the bottom with his eyes open and waited. When the filtered lantern's light seemed to circle away, he came up for a fresh breath of air and dropped down again. The light zigzagged back and forth. It seemed to come even closer, and O'Brien was forced to stay down longer than he thought possible. The light passed close by. When he surfaced, the captain took "the most glorious breath of fresh air" he ever had.

After being in the water for an hour or so, he heard one of the men say loudly, "The poor devil must have drowned. Three of you remain here until daylight." With most of the group giving up the search, O'Brien decided to swim to an ancient, wrecked steamer about a quarter-mile away and try to get onboard without being seen. Looking back, he saw the three men sitting on a lumber pile and smoking. They were a "fair distance" from where he was. He stripped off his clothing, made a wet bundle, and sank it with a large piece of coral. He began to swim on his back for the steamer.

After leaving the coral reef's safety, O'Brien began to feel nervous. The phosphorus trail made when swimming through the water seemed to light up a path that led directly to him. He swam slower. Remembering now that a twelve-foot shark had been caught in the harbor the other day, O'Brien's imagination ran wild when he thought another shark was trailing behind him, its long tail slowly moving in the sea. He could feel it close by and shuddered. Deciding he didn't have the energy to make the wreck, O'Brien turned back. He was tired and had to get back on land.

He swam to where he had buried his clothes and dove down to find them. It took time to put most of his clothes back on—and only after having a "tussle."

O'Brien then started working his way over the reef toward land and away from the dock. He swam and waded in the darkness.

Finally reaching shore, he decided to find the ship's agent, R. W. Laine, who lived on Punch Bowl Hill. After squeezing as much saltwater from his clothes as possible, O'Brien started angling away in that direction. He decided to walk on the dirt road and not try to cause suspicion by evasive movements. After fifteen minutes, he started to feel comfortable that he would make his destination. The night was warm, the smells of fragrant flowers were in the air, people were in their houses, and he breathed a sigh of relief.

This was short lived when he saw one of Honolulu's night patrolmen walking toward him. He wanted to run away but didn't feel he had the energy. O'Brien knew he was suspicious enough and impulsively decided to act like a sailor would when on leave. He started quietly singing a "little sea chantey" with a dance jig. When the policeman stopped him underneath a gas lantern, the large man asked, "Here there, now where do you think you're going?"

Saying as civilly but drunkenly as he could, O'Brien slurred, "My sailors—the whole ship—got a little too much whiskey. I fell overboard. I now need to find a sailor's boarding house."

The policeman cocked his head and looked at him oddly. Taking two silver dollars from his pocket, O'Brien offered them to the man, saying, "I give one dollar to you and the other dollar I give for a drink of whiskey. Could you kindly tell me where I can get it . . . and a place to stay?" The man took the silver and gave him directions to a house further on.

As the captain walked along the dirt road in the darkness, he came upon a butcher's wagon. Asking for where he might find Mr. Laine, the driver told him and pointed down a different street. In a few minutes, O'Brien was pulling the doorknob of the stately residence with gardens and tropical trees, and a man called down from an upper veranda, "Who's there?"

O'Brien answered with his name and said, "I got into an opium scrape."

"Oh Lord," came the instant reply. Despite his wet, rumpled appearance, O'Brien was let in. The captain's first words were to ask for a drink. Over a large shot of whiskey he told what had happened, and Laine simply listened. Afterward, the agent was not sure what to do. He told O'Brien to get some sleep and he would think about it. After a hot bath, the captain went to bed, only to wake up in the morning to learn that most of Honolulu was talking about what had happened the previous night.

The newspaper headlines and front-page pieces read that O'Brien had drowned, nine of the opium tins had been found floating in the harbor, and the harbor police were now dragging for his body. The captain read further that his second mate, Mr. Boyce, had come ashore to see what the commotion was all about. When Boyce heard Mr. Peacock telling the reporters he was the one who had set up the captain, Boyce promptly coldcocked the informant with a wild haymaker. The second mate was now in jail for his assault.

Not to be outdone, O'Malley nearly killed the Chinese steward for disobeying his orders when the captain wasn't around. He was arrested and also locked up in jail with Boyce. The *Edwin James* now didn't have a captain or its first and second mates, and the flag was at half-mast because the owner, Walter Moffett, and his wife thought their beloved captain had drowned on some "fool expedition."

When Laine told him that Walters and his wife were actually grieving over his supposed death, O'Brien told Laine to tell them he was all right and would join the ship—by "being taken onboard in a barrel as freight." When they received the news, the couple came directly over to the agent's home. "You young scamp," said a miffed Walter Moffett, "why didn't you let me know you had opium onboard? I would have helped you get rid of it." After O'Brien went through the entire story, leaving no details out, the owner told him to "lay low." For three days, O'Brien hid out at the agent's home.

As it turned out, the D.A. prosecutor and Moffett were old poker-playing buddies and soon met. Walters told how the "rascal" passenger had been treated so well on the passage over, including Peacock's telling O'Brien that he hoped to live long enough to repay him for his kindness—and this was the way he had repaid everyone. The prosecutor thought everything over and told Walters that if O'Brien gave himself up, he would not press the case "hard against the captain."

The same day, Walters accompanied O'Brien to the police station, where he was arrested, taken to court, and then allowed out on $2,500 bail. The trial took place two days later, since justice then was swiftly administered, especially when the D.A. and shipowner knew each other. Everyone came as witnesses, including Peacock, Walters, crewmembers, customs officials, and the police.

During these proceedings the details of Peacock's informant days came out. During Peacock's search for an opium buyer, he also learned that informers received one-half of the fine assessed by the government when prosecuting opium dealers. The ship's owner paid a large fine rather than having the more valuable ship confiscated. Unfortunately, this was serious money, since Peacock could receive $2,000 or more from turning O'Brien in, ten times as much as the $200 at best he could get from his half of the small sale. His sale for O'Brien was that of information to the customs office.

Peacock testified during the trial that he had never seen the opium, but he swore he had seen O'Brien with the same recovered revolver, then being used before the incident to shoot at sharks. The "spy" swore he had seen the captain with several tins in his pocket on the ship that looked like opium to him, including ten of them on the deck. Peacock did everything he could to work up the fine and increase the agreed half of the fine he would receive.

O'Brien told the judge about his meeting Peacock, his bringing the customhouse's spy onboard, and how through all of this, he found himself in trouble. The young captain in his own words "threw himself on the mercy of the court." After the judge considered all the evidence and the prosecutor's recommendation, he first delivered a "rather severe lecture" to the captain on his bringing opium into the Kingdom of Hawaii. On account of his youth and Walters's otherwise good character references, the judge fined O'Brien $500 with a thirty-day jail sentence. When Walters paid the fine, the jail sentence was suspended and O'Brien was free to go. The next day, Walters arranged for his chief mate and second mate to be released from jail when he paid their fines. The understanding was the seamen would then quickly leave Hawaii, which was the typical deal for bailed-out sailors.

The ship sailed for Portland with four hundred tons of valuable Hawaiian sugar in its holds. Shore carpenters first built a lining inside the ship, one foot from the sides and two feet from the bilge, made of rough pine and spruce; the men wrapped extra thicknesses of gunny sacks around the bolt heads. This wood lining would keep any sweat or leaking water from running inside and destroying the precious cargo. Hawaiian sugar was only partly refined and a dull golden color when the sun struck it. The sugar was largely granular, and the particles were almost the size of a small pea; it was said to be "about twice as sweet as the white granulated sugar." The names of the various plantations—Ewa, Laie, Halawa, Holualoa, Kilauea, Wailuku, and a dozen others—were stamped on the 150-pound gunny sacks of sugar.

In addition to bulk cargoes such as grain, guano, sugar, and coal—which moved endlessly around the world—ships like the *Edwin James* also hauled "general cargo." This term included goods as varied as what a department store would carry and encompassed machinery, canned goods, barbed wire, liquor, lawn mowers, baby carriages, and even wheelbarrows. With a general cargo, seamen had the essentials in the holds to set up a small colony on some "forsaken island." Ships would take these goods from manufacturing countries such as the United States and Great Britain to those that were rich in commodities and raw materials.

Return cargoes included raw sugar from the Hawaiian Islands or the East Indies, hemp from Manila, tea and labor from China, flax and tallow from Australia, rice and jute from India, silks and matting from Japan, and nitrates from the deserts of Chile. A considerable portion of the oil (kerosene) exported from the United States went halfway around the world to India, China, Japan, the East Indies, Australia, and other countries, packed in wooden cases, each with two five-gallon metal cans. The case-oil trade with the Orient began around 1870 and grew rapidly; by the early 1890s, three to four million barrels of kerosene were being exported annually to Asia and the Pacific.

* * *

This voyage was going "fairly well" until the *Edwin James* ran into rough trade winds and a squall. The crashing around of different objects when the ship heeled over awoke the captain during the night. When he appeared on deck in his oilskin rain gear (cotton fabric made waterproof with oil), he found that the howling winds had ripped away a number of the ship's light sails. The winds were whistling without any smaller sails to channel them, and the ship was out of control. O'Brien called for the mainsail to be let and the others adjusted so that the winds could be used to their advantage. He ordered the sailors to climb to the lower yards and set smaller sails. Once the ship was under control, the captain called down the mate for not easing off the sails before the winds came. O'Malley protested loudly, however, that he had them off well before the winds, but when he went to square the main yard, the helmsman came into the wind, and this caused the loss.

Soon afterward, O'Malley relieved the man from the wheel, and the two had a "clash." When O'Brien arrived on the scene, O'Malley had beaten the seaman—one of the "biggest and best" seamen on his ship—"into insensibility." The captain carried the sailor to his berth, and after dressing the wounds, waited for the man to regain consciousness. He then went after the mate and berated him again for his abusive treatment. Again, this seemed to work for the rest of the voyage; the mate consciously tried to check his out-of-control temper. It was as if he knew that every dog was allowed "one bite" on a voyage, especially if he showed respect to the captain and worked hard to keep the vessel shipshape.

When storms and Wolf O'Malley weren't rearing their ugly heads, O'Brien found that life onboard the *Edwin James* was pleasing. The cheerful presence of and camaraderie with the owner, Walters, was a definite plus, especially in how he handled his captain's past scrapes with the law. He seemed to be more upset over O'Brien's not bringing him in on the venture than on the fact it cost him $500, not to mention the fines he had paid for the mates. Paying fines for loyal seamen was this owner's responsibility, especially when he had the costs deducted monthly from their wages.

Walters's wife and the other passengers were amicable and played cards together, read, walked on the deck, watched the birds and sea life, and talked. The small staterooms for the passengers opened off the dining salon under the quarterdeck. Captain O'Brien always wore his coat for meals and sat at the anchored swivel chair at the head of the captain's table; the passengers were also invited in selected numbers to eat and mingle with the officers. John liked interacting with the guests. He liked answering their questions, especially when they began with "Captain, would you tell us about your time in . . ." By all accounts, O'Brien had an "engaging frankness and cordiality" in social situations that attracted people. He had a quick mind and worked so his passengers would have an enjoyable voyage.

The days passed, and the *James* soon was approaching the Columbia River and its infamous bar. Riding high through another gale, the full-sail ship crashed through the ocean toward the dark loom of Cape Disappointment on the Washington state side. The vessel was under short sail in the strong winds, and the captain felt they had no choice that day but to go through the bar.

Walters was standing on the quarterdeck in his oilskins when O'Brien told him about his decision to head straight in, but the owner called his attention to what looked like a tug that was already inside the bar. The *James* stood off for one mile, and everyone onboard saw the violent, white-tipped breakers that were rolling completely across the wide channel entrance. The tug approached to see what the sail ship's situation was, but the violent, crashing seas and pummeling winds forced its crew to turn around and run for the safe harbor of Astoria.

A deckhand took soundings with a knotted leaded line and yelled out that the depth was twenty-two fathoms (or 132 feet) deep, then twenty fathoms, and then increasingly shallower. Walters's wife and the passengers huddled in their cabins with their life preservers on. The squall became worse, with the rains splattering down so heavily that visibility was limited to less than two hundred yards. With the ship smashing and careening in the heavy seas, O'Brien gave the order to set the mainsail and head back out to sea. The nearly out-of-control vessel, however, couldn't be turned around.

Time passed as the crew fought to keep the ship under control, but when the next sounding was taken, a seaman yelled out, "Three-and-one-half fathoms!" The water depth was just twenty-one feet now, and the vessel had only eight feet of clearance from the rocky bottom with its thirteen-foot draft. At that moment a "tremendous sea" caught the ship on the port beams and filled her fore and aft decks with tons of green water, washing away everything that wasn't tied down. The seas burst though the bulwarks and stove in the forward-house bulkheads. Although the aft cabins were flooded, the passengers and crew were not injured. Just before the huge roller hit, everyone on deck had to jump for the safety of the rigging, as the ship heeled over and the men stared down into the raging ocean. Then the *Edwin James* agonizingly and slowly rolled back.

The constant pounding of the wind and sea cracked the fore t'gallant mast, which crashed down and carried the jib boom down with it. The deck suddenly became a snake pit of writhing cables, rigging, canvas, splintered poles, and seawater. When O'Brien saw how close Cape Disappointment now was, he knew these dangerous conditions had carried his ship too close to land. He loudly ordered the helm "hard to port" and the sails squared, and the ship slowly heeled away from the seething shoreline. The ship passed closely by Peacock Spit. A few minutes later, the mate yelled out, "Black buoy on the port bow!" The helmsmen put the steering wheel hard to starboard and swung back into the channel to keep again from grounding.

When the owner, passengers, and crew recognized the outline of the large steamer *City of New York* ahead, everyone cheered, including those who now were crowding that ship's railings. As the vessels passed, the captain of the *New York* "sang out" to the captain, "How did you find the bar, O'Brien?"

"Hell!" he yelled back.

Badly damaged and low in the water, but still moving, the *James* had cleared the vicious bar in a bad gale with near-hurricane-force winds. When the ship finally anchored in Astoria, the captain and owner stared at the extensive repairs that were now needed. Bulwarks, masts, and the forward house were nearly destroyed; in addition to needing new canvas, yards, and rigging, the ship's windows and skylights were broken, and everything inside was flooded with stagnant seawater. Although most of the stacked bags of sugar in the special hold were spoiled, the owner had decided at the last moment to carry insurance. Captain O'Brien fretted about these damages and again keeping his job, but Walters instead gave him a chronometer and told him to stay aboard the vessel on full pay until it was again chartered. The owner told him that his seamanship had kept the ship from going down with all lives lost—as so many ships had before—when making that dangerous bar crossing. And Walters had seen the storm's fury firsthand.

6

CATTLE, BEARS, AND CATS

After the *Edwin James* cleared the Columbia River bar and was nearing Astoria, the sailors in the winds and rains were aloft and furling the sails still left. O'Malley approached O'Brien and said, "Captain, I know I'll be arrested if I get off at Portland. Would you give me a few dollars of what's owed me and let me go ashore now? There is a boat alongside, and I would like to leave while the crewmen are aloft."

O'Brien thought about his request. O'Malley ran tough crews with fine seamanship. He supported the captain and respected his orders, except those involving the handling of crewmen. O'Malley had done fine work with the sails when crossing the bar, and, as the owner had done with him, seamen who did their jobs could have some imperfections overlooked. He told the mate to go below with him, and in his cabin, the captain gave O'Malley "every cent" that was owed. After O'Brien told the mate to go quietly, the large swarthy man replied, "Someday, Captain, I'll do you a good turn." He turned and abruptly left.

As O'Brien watched him go, the men came sliding down the slippery masts and rigging. Knowing what they wanted, he stayed below to stall them so the mate could get a decent enough start. Hearing the crew call for him, the captain slowly walked back to the deck. He looked up and asked why they hadn't finished furling the sails.

"Captain, we saw the mate go over the side with his bag," said one sailor. "And we want him arrested. We want our revenge—let us launch one of the boats," added another emotionally. Shrugging his shoulders, O'Brien told them to go ahead. He watched as the boat was launched and crewmen jumped in, but by the time they could push away from the *James*, O'Malley was already ashore and disappearing into the gray, overcast waterfront. The men rowed away anyway. One hour later, they returned empty-handed as O'Brien had expected. The "black mate" had disappeared while in Astoria.

The Columbia River salmon canning industry is said to have started at Astoria when the Hudson's Bay Company began packing salmon there in 1823 for export. The small town was a mixture of Chinese, Scandinavians, Indians, and others who worked as fishermen, salmon packers or cannery workers, lumbermen, and sailors. With a reputation of being a rough town, it wasn't uncommon for men to be kidnapped late at night from there onto the fishing boats. In Astoria at this time, men more likely had salmon than cash to exchange, and at times one could serve for the other. This place would have been perfect for O'Malley—if he had stayed.

O'Brien later learned he had stowed away on the bark *Mattie MacLay*. Hiding by a wharf, the cunning Wolf slipped onto the vessel when it sailed away that same night bound for Honolulu. He had no intentions of remaining in the United States, and O'Brien wondered whether he had been pardoned at all from prison— or whatever place he had really been before finding O'Brien and the *James*.

Continuing to Portland for its major repairs, the *Edwin James* remained in port for weeks while the owner searched for profitable overseas charters. One year before while in the city, the youthful O'Brien was walking to church on a Sunday evening and stared as two girls passed him on the way. The younger one glanced at him, and O'Brien was instantly struck by her beauty and winsome smile. He headed to the same church the next evening, hoping he'd be fortunate enough to see them again. O'Brien waited by the entrance and closely watched every person who was entering, but with disappointment didn't find any sign of the "girl of his dreams."

One year later during the same church services while his ship was being repaired, he was greatly impressed by a young lady's singing of a hymn with a "beautiful contralto voice." This was her, he thought—it had to be the same girl. O'Brien felt that if the woman in person was as good and lovely as her voice, then "happy and fortunate would be the man who wins her for his wife." After the services he asked the choir leader, John Van Burden, who the singer was. The man pointed toward a wooden staircase and said, "Do you see the young lady walking down the stairs from the choir loft? She's with her sister and her name is Emily Showers."

He found himself staring at the dark-haired, fine-featured, beautiful woman who was gracefully walking, almost gliding, down the stairway. Van Burden gently tapped the captain to get his attention. He asked if John would like to be introduced, but the captain declined, saying he would introduce himself later. O'Brien stood by the stone-block church's high wooden doors and waited during the "dark and drizzly night." When the girls passed, he smiled broadly at them, but they didn't even look at him as they walked away. He quickly followed and after a few blocks, his dream girl whirled around and said, "You're following us."

"I beg your pardon," he answered quickly, "if I'm doing anything wrong, but I wanted to see you, even on this dark night. Mr. Van Burden gave me your name and said I might introduce myself. Over a year ago, I saw you both going into that same church and I wanted to meet you. Allow me to introduce myself." He told them his name and added, "I am in command of the bark, *Edwin James*, and I would be honored if I could see you safely home."

The girl demurred, however, saying they were perfectly able to reach home by themselves and added, "So please leave us." O'Brien drew closer and blurted out, "No doubt you've read the daily papers about my arrest for cruelty on the high seas, but I can assure you that these reports are exaggerated." He quickly mentioned he had an invitation to a reception at the armory for three U.S. Senators—Mr. Morton, Mr. Salisbury, and Mr. McMillian and their wives—who were visiting the city for a fact finding on a presidential (Tilden–Hayes) election controversy. O'Brien concluded by saying they would honor him by attending the reception with him that following evening, especially since his card included guests.

She answered, "Sir, please leave at once." O'Brien apologized, saying if he had offended them that they should make some allowance for a sailor on leave. By that time, the girls were at the gate to their home. John told them the invitation still stood and he would like to come by the following day "to make his peace." Emily's sister said "good night" for both, and they disappeared up the walkway and into their home.

He called the next day on Mrs. Showers, the "good, kind soul who received him coldly but kindly." He told his story of seeing her daughter twice over the ensuing year, about last night, and the senatorial invitation. The mother pursed her lips in deliberation and then responded that she didn't have any objections to her daughters going with him, but they would have to be the ones to decide.

O'Brien waited one-half hour before the smiling mother came down the stairs and said that her daughter Emily would go with him. And she added, "Captain O'Brien, you are the most persevering young man that I have ever met."

They arrived just in time to the large hall inside the building. When Miss Showers and Captain O'Brien arrived, a general in the National Guard introduced them as "Captain and Mrs. O'Brien." He, of course, felt joy at the mistake, but Emily's face flushed a deep scarlet. As they moved away to join those already in the large room, she indignantly whispered, "Stupid, stupid remark!"

After an embarrassing silence, he replied, "Barkis is willing!"

"Contain yourself, sir," she answered. Emily had never read *David Copperfield*, so she didn't know that Barkis was the coachman in this Charles Dickens novel who declared his intentions to marry a woman (and was successful) by saying, "Tell her, Barkis is willing!" When she pressed Captain O'Brien to explain his remark, he told her, as well as his admiration for her and that he hoped to marry her. In an attempt at gallantry, he offered his arm to Emily—who didn't accept it.

After the reception, Johnny didn't help his ardent pursuit with what happened later that evening. The two were saying good-bye at the garden gate outside Emily's family home. They were on opposite sides, and he reached over the low gate to clumsily embrace her. She pushed him away furiously after he kissed her, saying sharply, "You brute, you beast, you beast!" They left one another on that fine, downward note.

O'Brien tried to meet Emily again, but there were "more difficulties," and he was confused since these problems had never arisen before with other women. Many men in his position would have given up if they had looked closer at the situation. Emily Showers was from one of the oldest pioneer families on the West Coast, and her father was the treasurer of Portland. She didn't like seamen, and the question was whether the smooth-talking, handsome O'Brien could overcome her objections. The long social absences he had on his voyages didn't help, not to mention she had already known about the young, brawling captain's arraignment in federal court for abusing sailors. These were substantial impediments.

* * *

The maritime cargo market in 1877 was slow due to a widespread economic slow-down. The *James* was still anchored in the Willamette River opposite the city. One evening the crew was ashore for dinner and the captain alone on the ship. He then noticed smoke pouring from the main hatch. O'Brien sounded the alarm by banging sharply on the ship's bell, and it wasn't long before two fire engines were on the ferry boat making its way across the river to the ship.

The fire had made considerable headway before the men started the steam-engine-driven "washer" going, with two water streams ripping into the main hatch and a third angling into the after hatch. After pumping for fifteen minutes, the dense smoke pouring out completely masked the fire's location. O'Brien told the fire chief he had an idea where the fire was. He proposed being lowered into the hold with a hose so he could put water directly on the fire. When the chief approved, a rope was fastened around O'Brien's body and signals agreed to, such as when to start the hoses and "get me up now!"

When the men on deck lowered him and another fireman, Joe Day, into the hatch by ropes with their hoses, dense smoke and waves of heat greeted them. The captain could just see a "red glow" through the black smoke, as both kept their faces down near the floating crates of goods. When the heat became too intense to go farther, he gave the signal to start the water engines. The hoses stiffened with torrents of seawater leaping out, and hissing clouds of steam and more smoke billowed out when the saltwater streams were directed on the red glow. They kept the water trained on the area.

Shortly O'Brien saw the redness become fainter with the volumes of water crashing down, but the hose nozzle suddenly broke away from his hands and the snaking canvas tube writhed into his face. The heavy nozzle crashed across his head as he gave the signal to stop the water. O'Brien regained consciousness in his berth. He learned that the firemen on top had pulled him out unconscious, the fire was out, but he would have to stay in bed for another day.

His partner, John Day, was hauled up "insensible" and immediately taken to a hospital. Although he was still comatose, the doctors told the fire chief that he would eventually recover from the intense smoke inhalation. The captain felt he was lucky, both for himself and the ship. Fires are deadly on any ship, but at least this one was when his vessel was tied to a dock—not in the middle of the ocean. And accidents on ships seemed to routinely occur.

Whether recuperating or walking later on deck, the captain still couldn't get Emily out of his mind, especially with the way the two had last parted. He decided he would try to see her, even if she wouldn't speak to him. He showered and shaved, put on his best white captain's uniform and cap, rowed ashore, and walked to the Portland Bazaar on a Saturday night. He remembered Emily saying she liked going there at that time. When he walked into the festive carnival atmosphere, he didn't see anyone he knew. After he wandered around for an hour, O'Brien heard someone exclaim behind his back, "Why there he is!"

Turning around, he saw a group of young men and ladies, including Emily Showers. A young man approached him and said, "Captain, it was reported you were seriously injured during the fire on your ship. We all wanted to see that you were all right, and now you are here looking as if nothing had happened." O'Brien thanked the group for their concern and then glanced toward Emily.

He could tell by her reserved look that she still remembered their time at the Showers's garden gate. He was able to find the opportunity to apologize once more, and they "made their peace." Emily graciously allowed him to accompany her home. They parted friendly, but "not as friendly as he wanted."

After several weeks of trying to find a paying consignment without success, Walters decided to ship goods on his own account and sell them overseas. He discussed this with O'Brien, who felt that Hawaii was a market they knew and with good contacts—that is, assuming the officials had forgotten his little episode with the authorities. Walters agreed. He thought they could bring and sell "food stuff, cattle, and different products" throughout the Pacific.

Walters spoke with a representative of King David Kalakaua about what his interests might be. After gaining this feedback, Walters bought quantities of different items. The manifest indicated the ship's holds contained cases of preserved fruits, condiments, flour, and dried meats, along with twenty-five head of cattle, two bears, and more than one hundred tabby cats. The cattle were bound for Tahiti, the bears for a Hawaiian zoo, and the numerous cats for one of the islands of the Society Group, whose native king had a standing order for cats due to an overabundance of island rats.

* * *

As soon as the *James* cleared the Columbia River bar, the low gray-black clouds and heavy raindrops quickly turned into a "terrific squall." The vessel "hove to for hours" while heading deep into the Pacific under short sail, this time with only a lower main topsail. The captain fought to keep the ship from foundering, as green-white seas began washing over the rails. When a huge wave broke over the *James* and filled the decks, the additional weight caused the vessel to stagger and tremble as it shook to try to clear itself of the added weight. When the sea-water rushed forward, the stern settled and the *James* righted again, only to have the heavy mass rush to starboard with a list to that side. First to port and then to starboard, the ship wallowed with the direction of every inundating, heavy wave. The men needed to tie their oilskin jackets around their waists with a piece of rope just to keep them from blowing over their heads.

O'Brien had lifelines stretched fore and aft for handholds to keep the sailors from being washed or blown overboard. The helmsman and other seamen were lashed to their stations. He ordered four sailors to man the pumps. Working the pump brakes up and down wasn't considered to be hard work at first, but to keep the handles moving for hours tired even the strongest. Dressed in oilskins with rain and spray flying into their faces, these men kept on with the knowledge they were working to save their own lives. Wet as drowned rats while manning the pumps, they tried to avoid the sea's wash by quickly letting go of the hand brakes and jumping for anything to hold onto—otherwise the surges forcibly washed them into the scuppers.

The heavy seas eventually taxed the minds and souls of the hardest men. Frightened sailors finally grabbed axes to chop away the spidery network of ropes and nets that held the large heavy crates of goods to the deck. They wanted to jettison them and reduce the weight on the laden ship. When these men ignored O'Brien's orders to "stand fast," he raced down the narrow, swaying dark corridors to his quarters and brought up a Winchester rifle. Once back on the deck, he found himself in swirling, hissing seawater to his knees. Looking up through the wind-driven rain, he saw the seamen clinging to the rigging where the huge waves surging down the deck had forced them. When the ocean poured off the decks, the seamen jumped down. O'Brien pointed the rifle at the men, ordering, "Avast there! I'll put a bullet through the first man's head that touches those lashings."

A young, frightened sailor chattered back from above, "Captain, she's top heavy and we don't want to drown."

"You chumps!" he yelled through the din. "If you only knew it, but this deck load is our salvation. Its weight makes the ship carry easier in this rotten sea." When the *James* stormed down another ocean valley, the sailors dropped down, threw away their axes, and followed his orders. The rifle had its desired effect.

When the waves destroyed the fo'c'sle door, the men had an unusually hard time since their bedding and mattresses were totally wet. Sailors nailed canvas over the opening to keep out the whipping winds. When their shift was over, the men turned in, wrapped up in the wet blankets, but were glad to be away from the flooded decks.

Despite the deck wash rolling through the galley, the cook had managed so far to keep the fire going in the iron stove. Any food was relegated, however, to soup and coffee, and eating anything was difficult at best. It was near impossible to eat soup and crackers while holding a cup of coffee or to put anything down safely. There was no such thing as eating from a plate on the table with a knife and fork. Unless the sailor held the plate in his hands, it would slide across the table with every ship roll. Spilled food and coffee over the wooden planks and seamen became commonplace.

The galley fire continued until one great wash flooded through the vessel. Eating "cold salt junk" or being hungry became the choice until the stove could be relit. The men's "salvation," however, was the constant struggle to save the ship and their lives. Accidents occurred, and one sailor was forced to his bunk with a bandaged, broken arm when he slipped over the wet deck.

After more hours of terrible weather, the crew succeeded in safely controlling the vessel, but only after the winds had dissipated. The horrid conditions had enveloped all ships sailing those seas, and seventeen ships had disappeared forever. In passing another bark, the *Grace Darling*, the crew of the *James* were the last ones to sight that foundering vessel: It was lost with all onboard. The captain's barometer dropped to 28.15, the lowest reading he had ever seen, evidencing a very bad typhoon. Even the *Edwin James* was reported as being lost; splintered away by the horrific winds and waves, the ship lost its lower yards and most of its heavy sails. Among those with injuries, one mate was so severely injured by a falling yardarm that he required immediate hospitalization when in port.

The storm conditions were so fierce that it was impossible for two days to care for or feed the numerous cattle, bears, and cats. When the storm's crashing abated, the seamen heard the bears' grunt from under the cabin deck, where they had stored the hay and cattle feed. After the men lifted the main hatch, they expected to find most of the animals dead from lack of food, the ship's crashing, and flooding seawater from the leaks inside the cargo space.

Although they found a yearling calf with a broken leg, all the cattle had apparently survived. However, the cages holding the cats were all unfortunately smashed. All of the tabby cats had disappeared, but for a few now huddled in one corner next to the livestock. The bears had fed on the cats that had wandered into their domain. Holding their lanterns high, the seamen poked around inside the huge, shadowy hold. When they heard a bear's growl from the nearby hold— followed by a loud crash—the sailors decided there was no need for further investigation. The men quickly scrambled up the ladder to report their findings.

O'Brien worried that if the bears were loose they would eventually find their way into the compartment with the longhorn cattle. To prevent this disaster, the captain strapped on two revolvers, grabbed a large knife, took a bull's-eye lantern, and headed down into the cargo space with the bears. O'Brien crawled into the b'tween deck (below the main deck) where Walters had constructed a bulkhead to separate the bear cages from the livestock.

He shone the lantern in the dark, foul-smelling place, the light creating shadows and different illuminations of the wet planks and dripping timbers. Holding the lantern out with one arm, he worked his way toward the bear cages. Once there, he found broken wood planks and kindling scattered about. The bears were out.

O'Brien froze and listened intently. At first he heard only the creaking and pounding of the bark as it slogged its way through the waves. Seawater was up to his ankles and sloshing back and forth. Something quickly splashed by and startled him. He thought it was a cat.

Hearing a snakelike hiss and deep snort to one side, he looked in that direction and saw "Mr. Bears" crawling between the beams toward him and a separating five-foot-high bulkhead. When they were close, the captain put down the lantern, jerked the revolvers from his belt, and repeatedly fired through the space. As the bellowing animals crashed against the barrier to get over the space, they came within eighteen inches of his face.

When O'Brien pulled himself over the barrier, the wounded bears were still reaching toward him with outstretched claws. Despite the bullets taken, they were nevertheless trying to kill again. Out of ammunition, John slashed at the two bears. Finally they "slunk away" to disappear at the back of the second bulkhead between them and the cattle. He later found their bodies among the hay, and when the ship docked, O'Brien brought out two bearskins to the dock.

The terrible winds and monstrous waves continued for days at a time, and then after dissipating, another storm roared in its place. When they had decent weather for a day or two, all the sails were set and the decks dried off. At the same time, the sailors dried out their mattresses, blankets, and clothing, all soaked thoroughly with saltwater. When they had the chance, the crew started on the ship's repairs.

The carpenter and sailmakers were quite important—especially now. The *James* carried a few spare spars, but with the different ones lost, Chips needed to carve some that could be substituted. With seamen assigned to work with him, the carpenter had them sawing wood, hammering nails, and sanding molding as they built and repaired doors, railings, decking, and beams. The canvas sails needed constant repairing during any voyage, and after a severe storm, large patches and new canvas sails needed to be made. The old salts on most crews were expert sailmakers. With large sail needles threaded with heavy waxed twine, they ran seams through the thick, tough canvas supplied from below. This valued skill now translated into sewing all day, allowing them the gift that all sailors valued most: a full night's sleep without needing to be on watch.

The ship meanwhile continued on its lonely course. There were no communications with shore, loved ones, or anyone for months. Ship-to-shore radio and telephone did not exist, and the sailing ships seemed to follow lonely lanes, with few ships passing close enough to communicate by signal flags. The *James* needed fifty-nine days to complete this stormy run—a much longer time than usual—and other ships took even more time, including one nearly destroyed bark that sailed for three months before finally limping into Honolulu Bay's safety.

O'Brien enjoyed seeing these beautiful islands again with their tropical forests, coconut trees, white-sand beaches, and thatched huts that stretched into the jungle. The city of Honolulu rose from the dilapidated waterfront, its beautiful homes on long avenues lined by royal palms and "flaming red" hibiscus hedges. Houses of different sizes were built of adobe, straw, coral, cement, and wood, and fresh flowers glowed with rich colors that seemed always to be in bloom. The streets were narrow and formed of coral, leaving no room for streetcars, and nearly everyone walked, rode on horseback, or took a carriage. Trees of coconut, papaya, orange, banana, guava, and mango mixed with fields of sugar cane, pineapple, fig trees, date trees, and cinnamon.

He loved the people. The native Polynesians worshipped tikis and Christianity, liked to trade, and were among the most friendly and kindly people that O'Brien had met. Doors were seldom or never locked; money and valuables could be left lying about a house in perfect security. A seat at a table was always available for a guest, and one who declined such an invitation was considered impolite.

While they were in Hawaii, Walters became a friend of King David Kalakaua, a well-spoken, easy-going, massively built man of over six feet. In appreciation of the gifts the shipowner presented, the king invited him and Captain O'Brien to his royal residence for their final evening. Prior to Iolani Palace's construction, this was a stately three-story structure with sweeping grounds, a throne room, reception room, and large state dining room, as well as a conservatory and other houses for sleeping. (Kalakaua started construction of the massive Iolani Palace the next year and completed it three years later in 1882.)

Once they were there, the forty-one-year-old Kalakaua certainly lived up to his nickname, "the Merry Monarch." He had a passion for music, dancing, parties, and the finest of food and drinks. He was dressed in full regalia with a huge white sash and rows of glittering medals pinned to his dark uniform. Gold braids adorned the top, and gold insignias were sewn into his long black boots. Kalakaua was known as being "easy to approach and difficult to leave." During a visit to Honolulu, Robert Louis Stevenson described the king as a "capital fellow but a trifle too convivial."

Fluent in English and Hawaiian, Kalakaua had been elected as king four years earlier by the legislature. He believed in trade and quickly sailed to the United States to negotiate a treaty; in January 1875 this agreement was signed, and it eliminated the tariff on sugar and other Hawaiian products. As a result of Kalakaua's treaty, Hawaii's sugar industry boomed, the kingdom enjoyed economic prosperity, and ships such as the *James* had a very good business, especially in 1878.

During the evening, O'Brien was seated next to a "very charming, young native lady" who had cream-colored skin, long black hair, and an exotic look. Her name was Liliu. Although the princess Liliu was a guest of Kalakaua, she and John had a greater interest in one another than in the gala luau festivities. (Liliu was not related to King Kalakaua or the later successor to the throne, his sister Queen Liliuokalani; although O'Brien refers to his new acquaintance as a "princess," the only officially entitled one was Kalakaua's sister.)

The king had given the luau in honor of the *Edwin James* owner, his captain O'Brien, and their impending departure. As his great voice boomed out to the assembled guests, these men had traveled from across the ocean to bring him what he wanted; of course, Kalakaua had paid well for these services, he laughed loudly and genially, but money wasn't all that important. On this trip, the *Edwin James* had hauled for him flour, dried meats, and seasonings, along with two bears for his zoo. Of course, he joked, he never thought he would receive two bearskin rugs instead of live animals.

Everyone enjoyed these occasions with the king and especially the luau. The young, tender leaves of the taro plant were mixed with chicken and baked in coconut milk; this delicious dish was called luau. Eating the traditional luau feast on the floor, natives and Westerners alike ate while sitting on the lauhala mats. The traditional three-foot-wide centerpiece of ti leaves with ferns and flowers was laid the length of the mat. Gentlemen were dressed in white linen clothing and decked with flower leis; the women and children wore "head dresses" with mingled colors of green, red, pink, and yellow.

Bowls filled with poi from pounded taro roots and platters of meat, sweet potatoes, dried fish or meat covered in leaves, fruits, and other specialties were placed on the clean ti leaves. Roast pig, fish (raw and cooked), crayfish, turtle, breadfruit, taro, and "likely enough" dog were spread out. Coconut juice drank from the husks joined the ever-present gin and beer.

Much to the consternation of proper Victorian visitors—although O'Brien didn't have the problem—everything was eaten with the fingers. Poi of different consistencies received its name from the number of fingers needed to eat it: three-finger, two-finger, or the thickest, one-finger poi. A guest at King Kalakaua's coronation luau described the lavish decorations typical of the traditional luau:

> Tables were draped with white, but the entire tops were covered with ferns and leaves massed together to almost form a tablecloth of themselves; quantities of beautiful wild flowers were placed about mingling with the ferns. The natives had turned out in great numbers, and the scent of their leis of flowers and maile leaves was almost overpowering.

Even when the king's speeches had come to an end and the food was nearly consumed, the drinking and gala atmosphere continued. Liliu soon turned to quietly ask the captain if he would like to walk over and see the palace grounds. O'Brien whispered back, "With you as my guardian angel, I feel I'll be walking into Heaven." She smiled in a gentle, almost embarrassed way. Liliu was the first to make her excuses and left him with the uproarious dancers, festive drinking, hula girls, songs, and the "Merry Monarch." O'Brien left later when the king's eyes seemed to be as blurry as Walters's were. They had to be quite discrete, for with all of Kalakaua's gentleness, even he would have his limits, especially with white men and cream-colored princesses that he had invited to his palace.

The princess met him outside and immediately led him into the gardens, with its coconut trees, ponds of water lilies, and perfumes of orchids, hibiscus, jasmine, and gardenia. The princess picked a fragrant white gardenia and placed it in the lapel of his coat, her fingers trembling, his heart "thumping." The moment was magical in the silvery moonlight as O'Brien placed a gentle hand around her thin waist and drew her closer. Their lips were on one another, a "quivering, lingering kiss and then silence." She shyly took him by the hands, and the two wandered through the palace gardens, stopping to embrace and kiss again in the scented, beautiful setting.

The captain impulsively whispered, "What a beautiful night for a horseback ride to Waikiki."

She looked up into his eyes and kissed him, softly saying, "Delightful, how I would love to go."

"It is not impossible," he said, picking up on her reluctance.

"Oh, yes, it is. I am a guest at the palace and you . . . you are almost a stranger."

O'Brien laughed lightly. "One o'clock this night, I'll have two horses ready under those palm trees," he said, pointing to the clump of trees. "I will be under your window, ready to assist."

"But . . ."

"I'll take all precautions as to the guards. No one will know." She smiled, her eyes seeming to sparkle, and squeezed his hand in response. They walked back to the palace, and after a cordial handshake of farewell for the benefit of the two sentries, they strolled away in different directions. The captain found Walters and chatted amicably. When the drunk owner headed back to the hotel, O'Brien found the palace livery and arranged for two of their best riding horses.

At a quarter to one, he secured the horses under nearby palm trees, and at precisely one o'clock he was under the woman's window. He waited quietly for a moment or two, and hearing no sounds, he threw sand against the low window. Shortly afterwards, the striking Liliu appeared and whispered, "Please go away. It could be dangerous—remember the guards. The king won't like it."

But adventure was what he loved. He whispered back, "Please come. I have the horses and everything is ready. It will only be for an hour and this is such a heavenly night. On my honor, I will bring you back safely."

She was silent at first but then whispered, "Wait a moment, I'll be there." In a few minutes, she was by his side and they were one in a soft but sensuous embrace. Soon they were riding under the tropical moonlight, the hooves of each horse clattering over the coral road in near unison, each other's hands rising and falling together. They rode over the hard sands of the beach, into the gentle surf, and then allowed their horses to splash softly over the foamy seawater in the silvery night.

They traveled in tandem down the distant shoreline and through gentle waves to an isolated beach. Looking into each other's eyes, they dismounted. Liliu gently took his hand and led him to a secluded grove of swaying trees, where they lay down in the sands overlooking a bright moonlit bay. The gentle trade winds murmured through the palm and coconut trees, as the outlines of the overhead fronds trembled above. The perfumed smells of jasmine mixed with the gentle salt air, and they couldn't hear the muffled booms of the surf on the outside reefs as they made love.

7

SAILING THE SOUTH PACIFIC

The barefoot seamen in dungarees scrambled over the bark's rigging as they readied the three-masted *James* for its departure. Furled in the Hawaiian bay for anchorage, the magnificent square sails were now spreading out with the prevailing winds on each tall spar and the lower triangular fore-and-aft stern yard. The ship swayed rhythmically with the lapping waves, and the heat waves of the afternoon sun shimmered over the turquoise waters.

One hundred head of cattle bound for Papeete jammed the ship's holds, and the thumps of their hooves and their bellows echoed from below. In sharp contrast to the crewmen in their jeans and cotton shirts, loinclothed natives were manhandling the last of the hay bales onboard. They would stay and watch the cattle while the ship sailed to its new destination.

A French food contractor had arrived in Honolulu a few days before, and Walters had negotiated with him over the delivery of livestock to Tahiti for sixty U.S. dollars per head. This would be tidy profit, since the cattle could be bought in Hawaii for twenty dollars each, not to mention the ones brought from the West Coast. A French army regiment was stationed in Tahiti, as well as several small naval vessels, and fresh beef on the hoof was at a premium.

From the gunnels of the creaking wooden ship, Captain O'Brien saw a seaman pulling roaches from an oilskin—the insects had burrowed into the weather gear when in Hawaii—and then rubbing it with the traditional raw oil and melted

89

beeswax from the sailmaker's stores. He told the man to put the gear down and help out, and then he motioned to another sailor to work with the loading.

O'Brien took his duties seriously as captain and had learned to be watchful. The twenty-seven-year-old man felt fortunate at being his own shipmaster at this young age, but he had been able to learn from his mistakes—and still keep his captaincy. Still lean looking, the short-statured O'Brien was physically and mentally strong—and absolutely fearless. The sea, adventure, and commanding men as this ship's master were now what his life was about.

Since John began sailing on the *Edwin James*, he had become friends with the owner, and on this voyage, he came to know Walters well. The Englishman Walter Moffett was older, was married, came from a moneyed family, and was a fellow seafarer at heart. In 1860 Walters had married an eighteen-year-old Portland, Oregon, woman who came from a pioneering family. Before settling down and raising their own family, he and his wife, Charlotte Terwilliger Moffett, traveled for two years to Europe, France, and the British Isles, spending much of the time at Moffett's family home in England, where his mother still lived. Over the years, their family grew to six children, one daughter and five sons, and they lived in a large Portland home. Despite Moffett's initial long absences at sea as the shipmaster—before he appointed O'Brien—he looked forward to being home. However, he had been drinking heavily on this voyage to "while away the hours."

As the *James* was loaded, O'Brien found his concentration drifting back to Liliu. He remembered the sweetness of the previous night and the romantic setting of sand, surf, and trade winds. King Kalakaua was ever the large, jolly, well-mannered ruler who loved life. And Liliu had a gentle sensuousness about her that showed in her manners and caresses.

He savored those moments with her, but his thoughts were suddenly interrupted when a large, swarthy man appeared over the railing. It was Robert "Wolf" O'Malley. The man seemed to be on a mission as he walked with long steps toward the captain, stopped, and requested to be taken to Tahiti. O'Brien hesitated, remembering the problems this man had brought about before. He had never seen so fine a sailor, a man of "bone and iron," but Wolf O'Malley was also a sadistic man of extreme brutality and "hard-boiled" character.

The six-foot, three-inch man pleaded with O'Brien, who was ten inches shorter. The man's huge, hairy frame dominated two sailors who stood to one side, and his body showed the scars of past fights. His massive head and black hair were a perfect match for the "black devil," as he was nicknamed. O'Malley told the captain he'd been working last as a foreman on a sugar plantation on Kauai, but a mob of coolies had attacked him because he had punished one for insolence. The captain smiled wryly to himself, as he could imagine what the punishment must have been, but didn't find it amusing when Wolf O'Malley said he'd been forced to shoot his way "out of the damn mess." He had said this like a polite Englishman would ask his friend to pass the sugar.

O'Malley then offered to pay the captain sixty dollars, saying that would be fair to buy a job as either the mate or a sailor and without pay, especially since he wanted to leave so quickly. "I don't want any trouble from you on this ship," responded O'Brien. "If you do, I'm locking you up. Understand!"

"Yes, Captain. Yes!" Despite their difference in size, O'Brien knew that the large man realized he meant every word and would follow through. John told him he could be a passenger, but he wanted first to talk with the owner about this. O'Malley smiled thinly, nodded, and turned quickly to leave.

O'Brien asked a few sailors if they had heard from either the mate or the owner. They hadn't. He had assumed his chief mate would have shown up by now. It wasn't like the man to be late, especially since the ship was to leave that day. O'Brien didn't appreciate this absence, and he could always appoint someone else from the crew or head to the docks for another one. He surely wasn't going to give O'Malley another chance at the position. His crew was now two men short, including the mate, but O'Brien decided to wait and see who might show up. He had to get the vessel ready for its departure.

Turning his attention to the *James*, he oversaw the last stowing of the cargo and enough food and water for the long sail to Tahiti. He watched over the loading of a boatload of provisions, including fresh vegetables, onions, bananas, pineapples, joints of clean red meat, and, as one sailor wrote then, "a big basket of real baker's bread, the loaves rich and mellow in the sunlight, like bricks of gold." Remembering the hardships of long sea crossings with weevil-infested food, tepid water, and hardtack, the seaman ended, "Have you ever been without potatoes for three months? If you have, you will know how it feels to crave them, not to mention fresh bread and delicious ripe bananas."

A few hours passed before the captain heard a commotion by the wharf. Walters was stumbling from the carriage that had brought him to the dock. His pace was erratic. Small, powerfully built, and determined, Walters could hardly keep his balance. The owner was drunk—and O'Malley was by his side.

O'Brien's lips tightened when the two men rowed out to the ship, and Wolf O'Malley's "iron hand" aided Walters up the gangway from the small boat. He knew that the owner liked his strong drinks and apparently the "swarthy adventurer" as well. Johnny also liked O'Malley; he just didn't want to always be "on the jump" to keep some poor sailor from being kicked to hell and back.

Despite his befuddled condition, Walters tried to stay dignified as the ship's owner. He told the captain that their chief mate was in the hospital with jungle fever and that O'Malley would be a good substitute. Apparently the swarthy devil had seen the poor man being taken away and just had to track down the owner and tell him the news. Regardless of O'Brien's arguments that Wolf would be trouble as the crew's supervisor, the owner had his way.

After giving O'Malley a curt order to prepare the ship to sail, Captain O'Brien went ashore to find one more crewmember. He wandered around the docks for a short time before finding one that was available, a "bleary-eyed New England whaler" who had the usual story of woe. The man's name was James Barry. Barry told O'Brien he had left a New Bedford whaleship in Honolulu one week before with a $1,000 check, his share of a three-year South Pacific voyage. The money hadn't lasted long. Barry went on a "glorious spree," carousing with women, buying drinks for everyone, and purchasing everything in sight. When he finally sobered up, he found himself stretched out inside another ship readying to sail to the Puget Sound. Barry had only the clothes he wore and a few dollars left inside his pocket, a not rare tale of woe.

After jumping off the ship before it left the harbor, the new crewman ran into O'Brien, who talked him into a warm cruise through the South Seas to earn more money. He accompanied the captain back to the *James*. The two had just stepped on the deck when Barry turned around and looked up into the glaring eyes of O'Malley. The new recruit dropped his sea bag and backed away as if he had seen a terrifying ghost, while O'Malley took a quick step toward the shaking man. Face white as a sheet, Barry jumped onto the ship's railing and leaped overboard. As soon as he surfaced, men coming aboard from a gig next to the *James* and its gangplank hauled up the dripping man.

O'Brien took the shivering seaman by the shoulder and walked him to his cabin. Barry then disclosed more about the life of one Robert O'Malley. The seaman had shipped a few years before with O'Malley on a seal-poaching voyage to the Bering Sea. Once there, Wolf showed cunning that was beyond anything seeming to appear human. He captured schooners by calling for aid and then taking both the ship and sealskins when the vessel's crew stopped to render help. After confiscating what was valuable, he usually let the sealers and ship go. O'Malley at times did switch ships, sail the newer or larger vessel to Japan, and quickly sell it and its cargo to whoever wanted the bargain. The Russians heard about his escapades and sent soldiers after the pirate. They trapped the men on-board a ship and captured the sailors, but O'Malley shot his way out and killed several of the soldiers. Barry feared the black devil more than any man, but he never told O'Brien the complete reason why. After the captain gave him a shot of whiskey with assurances that all would be fine, the still nervous Barry went back on deck to take the first wheel-watch.

When Captain O'Brien later met up with Jack London, he told him the stories about Robert "Wolf" O'Malley—and more were to come. The character of Wolf Larsen and his equally sadistic brother in *The Sea-Wolf* bear a striking resemblance to the notorious seaman. The author wrote in that book:

> "You are a man utterly without what the world calls morals?"
> "That's it."
> "A man of whom to be always afraid . . ."
> "That's the way to put it."

"As one is afraid of a snake, or a tiger, or a shark?"

"Now you know me," he said. "And you know me as I am generally known. Other men call me 'Wolf.'"

—Jack London, *The Sea-Wolf*

* * *

The sail from Honolulu on the coast east of Waikiki and past Diamond Head was beautiful and uneventful. British sailors had so named this high formation because at a distance the crystals in the lava rock appeared to glimmer like diamonds. Felix Riesenberg wrote in *Under Sail* as his ship sailed away:

> As I looked back, I saw a mere blur of bluish green across our wake. I wished to have another look at that fair city of dreams, but it was already a thing of the hazy past; a figment of memory; the port of phantasmagoria [a constantly changing medley of real or imagined images as in a dream]; a jumble of many colored people, smells, and music; of green and restful flowers; of feverish energy and indolence; days of dirty, sweaty labor, and nights of romantic adventures.

Onboard the *James*, the men held onto the rigging when ordered, slacked the sails when needed, and quickly followed every command that O'Malley gave. The quiet nature of the sail, however, soon changed.

O'Brien happened to look through a cabin window and see the apparently drunk O'Malley smack Barry across the face with a resounding whack from an open hand. Racing over to the two, John yelled, "Mr. O'Malley. I told you to keep your damn paws off the crew! You're disrated and I don't want any mate that can't obey orders. Go below to your room until I send for you!"

O'Malley didn't move, as he seemed to be pondering what the captain had just said and what he should do. The ship continued surging through the ocean with the prevailing winds, the sails and rigging full but tight. A few sailors stared at O'Malley, who finally shrugged his shoulders, and the heavy figure disappeared down a hatchway.

O'Brien told another seaman to relieve Barry and walked over to the stricken man. The seaman seemed to be "violently ill," and his hands and face twitched uncontrollably. The ashen man walked toward the quarterdeck as if hypnotized. He walked directly to the railing, jumped up, balanced for an instant on its top, and then leaped again without a sound into the sea.

"Man overboard!" sounded the immediate cry. A sailor threw a life ring out into the ocean and its rippling blues. At the gunnels, O'Brien watched the vessel move past the man as he floated in the swells. However, the captain was curious about what was happening: This sailor wasn't trying to get back to the ship. He was avoiding it.

"Back the main yard! Clear away the gig!" shouted O'Brien. The sailors jumped into action and pulled on the lines to bring the mainsail into the wind. The breeze filled the sail on the other side and pushed the *Edwin James* into a slow turn. Two crewmembers lowered the lifeboat into the ocean, and it trailed by its rope against the ship's weathered hull.

O'Malley appeared back on the deck. He didn't seem drunk as when O'Brien had stripped his position and banished him below. His T-shirt was off and his scarred body showed the marks of different fights, knife wounds, and abuse. "Captain," he said in a deep voice that got everyone's attention, "Since I caused the man to jump, I'll pick him up."

The much smaller O'Brien stared angrily at him. "Then do it!" he yelled, adding four-letter words for emphasis. O'Malley walked slowly to the railing, grabbed the rope, and easily dropped over. He used the rope to walk down the ship's side into the bobbing gig. Several of the sailors watched this, along with poor Mr. Barry who was now a distance from the ship.

Another crewman scrambled over the vessel's side for the small boat, but he landed instead on O'Malley. The large man cursed and threw the sailor down against the lifeboat's side. Quick as a cat, he was on the surprised seaman with powerful hands around the man's throat. The small boat rocked precariously while O'Malley throttled the man and dragged his neck toward the water. He was going to drown him.

O'Brien shouted down that he'd shoot O'Malley if the seaman wasn't released. "Go ahead, captain, and shoot. I'll have this one in hell first!" Captain John looked quickly around, untied the attached rope, and picked up a heavy iron belaying pin. He raised the weapon, took aim, and quickly threw it at O'Malley. The swarthy man twisted around, and the iron just missed his head. The abrupt movement caused the gig to overturn, and he was forced to let go of the seaman's throat. Although another sailor leaped into the ocean to save his comrade, no one made any similar motion toward O'Malley, who was thrashing his way back to the small boat. Barry meanwhile floated farther away from the *James* while the ship completed its turn and slowly began to work its way back toward the hapless crewman.

O'Malley managed to right the gig, however, and pull himself into it. He called up calmly for someone to throw him a bailing bucket. A large, daring seaman slid his arm through two buckets and grabbed another iron belaying pin. He slid down the ship's side to join O'Malley inside the surfboat. When O'Malley asked suspiciously why the sailor was carrying the pin, the other answered back, "In case you try something funny."

Nothing this day seemed to satisfy the out-of-control man. O'Malley quickly grabbed this iron from the sailor's hand and held it over the rolling ocean. Making a point, he looked at the man, dropped the pin into the sea, and then grinned back. When the seaman relaxed, O'Malley jumped over and pinned him against the boat with his strong hands. His ruse had worked. He looked up at O'Brien, who was seething at this latest infraction. Seeing the captain's face, the large man relaxed his hands and let the seaman go.

The captain turned on his heels and stared severely at the sailors who were watching from the railing. Pointing toward two of the men and calling them by name, he barked an order for them to get into the boat with O'Malley. The men at first hesitated. One of them looked down at the gig, while the other stared at O'Brien.

The captain simply pointed again at the two and motioned them toward the lifeboat. They dropped quietly over the side and joined the two in the small boat. The men untied the line, pulled hard on the oars, and headed in Barry's direction. After fifteen minutes of continued rowing, they were able to pick up the exhausted seaman.

Although Barry hesitated when first seeing O'Malley, the other three reached over, grabbed the man, and hauled him inside. Shivering and never looking up, Barry huddled inside the gig in a fetal position. When the boat returned to the *James*, the men dragged Barry physically back onboard. He didn't make an effort to help, but he staggered below upon O'Brien's command. O'Malley wore the same sick grin on his face the entire time, looking as if he would grab the pitiable man as soon as he had the chance.

Crewmembers approached O'Brien at the stern and told him they wouldn't work anymore unless O'Malley was locked up. The captain quickly answered, "I've already got a new mate, men. Mr. Boyce, the second mate, is promoted, and Nelson, the carpenter, will take Boyce's place. Now go about your work as usual and I'll handle O'Malley."

He marched over to two men and told them to take O'Malley to the brig. "I've gone with you as far as I can, O'Malley," he roared. "Now go to your quarters and stay there!" The sailors were hushed, and the only sounds heard were of the sea smacking against the ship's sides. O'Malley looked indifferently at the captain, as if he was again trying to decide his alternatives. He gave a slight smile and again headed down. Once he was inside his small room, O'Brien had the room padlocked. The door was opened only when four sailors came down to bring food and water in a large bottle.

The captain brought Barry back to the deck. With O'Malley now locked up, O'Brien felt that the seaman would resume his duties. Still demonized by his fears, however, Barry soon leaped into the hold of cattle, and the longhorns were probably as surprised as the crew at this latest act. O'Brien locked the man in an unused cabin for two weeks, hoping this would give Barry some needed rest. As strange as his behavior had been, when Barry left the cabin he was rational and hard working from that time on. He stayed with the captain for two years.

* * *

Meanwhile O'Brien realized that Walters had become a "sick, sick" man. He had been drinking nonstop during the Hawaiian layover and told John he would take the first vessel back home from Tahiti. He would leave the *James* in the complete hands of his good friend. Walters had already shown signs of dementia. Running down the narrow hallway inside the ship, his arms spread wide, with "horrid, blazing" eyes, he had continually screamed in a high-pitched, eerie voice, "Stop the ship—get the angels aboard! Get the angels!" O'Brien had grabbed him and pulled him back into his cabin.

Walters had been breathing hard with glazed eyes. He kept screaming about getting the angels aboard. The captain decided he had come down with "the DTs," or the irrationality of delirium tremens. The owner then raced up to the deck with O'Brien in hot pursuit, and the captain caught him by the railing as Walters peered out over the ocean. Although O'Brien didn't think his friend would jump, the mere fact of his running to the gunnels caused concern. As John led Walters back to his cabin, the owner began talking to imaginary spirits from heaven and hell. The distraught man bowed to them and asked O'Brien to have the cook immediately bring the finest of foods for his friends. He wanted wine to be served and one of the cattle slaughtered for fresh meat.

Walters now hadn't eaten for days, and John had to physically restrain him from again racing away. He snapped wrist irons on the man. Looking confusedly down at the irons on his wrists, Walters snapped his strong arms and wrenched them apart. He threw the manacles at O'Brien, and one sharp edge cut his lips. "Wonderful, my friend, wonderful," Walters commented. "Show me how you do that again." Holding out his hands, he playfully egged O'Brien on. The captain once more snapped the irons on, but this time he reinforced them with strong tarred rope. That did the trick.

When the owner couldn't break these binds, he stopped struggling and lay limp on his cabin sofa. He alternated between bouts of unconsciousness and maniacal behavior when he regained his senses. When he became rational for a time, O'Brien took the irons off and brought food and drink to Walters. The owner didn't eat, however, and barely sipped the ale.

As the *Edwin James* sailed southward under a cloudless sky, the northeast trade winds picked up and blew the ship along. Walters soon fell asleep—but he never awoke. With froth oozing out of his mouth, he died a little before noon on that day. O'Brien was saddened over the death of his friend, and especially the manner of the death. He called the passengers and crew in for one last respectful look at Walters, who was now finally at peace.

Captain John knew that the body would quickly decompose in the hot, sticky climate of the tropics. After asking people how to best preserve the corpse, he made his decision. He remembered what he had learned in school about the Egyptian mummies. O'Brien told a sailor to bring him blankets, tar, and an empty hogshead or wood barrel. He had the seaman cut the blankets into strips that were four inches wide.

After washing and drying the body, the men wrapped it with the blanket strips, which had been heavily covered with the tar used on the rigging. A layer of clean strips was next bound over the tarred cloth. Although the following step was difficult—and all of them were unpleasant enough—two crewmen stuffed the body into the tall keg in a kneeling position. Then they covered all the cracks in the barrel with tar. Sailors took the hogshead to the deck, lashed it to the mizzenmast, and stretched an awning over the barrel to ward off the sun's heat.

Weeks later when back in Honolulu, O'Brien had to smuggle the body onboard a steamer bound for San Francisco. He accompanied the remains to Portland, where the body was discovered to be in good condition. A number of Portland's leading citizens attended the services, and Walter Moffett was finally laid to rest in the Lone Fir cemetery where his sons and daughter would also be buried.

* * *

The vessel meanwhile continued sailing on to Tahiti. The sails were tight most of the way with a decent wind, and the ship fairly skimmed through the easy seas. It took less than two weeks to cover the 2,500-mile journey from Hawaii to the French Polynesian island. Although O'Brien's compass, maps, and sextant were true, the glare of a burning ship in the lagoon became a navigational beacon for the crew. The burning vessel was the bark *Ira Iredale* out of Liverpool. When her cargo of coal caught fire off the coast of Chile, the crew was forced to abandon her. She had drifted across the South Pacific, and the day before the *James* arrived, the ship floated close to the outer reef of the island. The crew of a French warship managed to attach a hawser to the mangled bow and towed the hulk into the bay.

When the *Edwin James* anchored off Papeete, O'Brien ordered O'Malley to be released and called him to his cabin. "I'm sorry, O'Malley, to tell you to get off this ship," he said, "but, by God, I don't want any murders on this vessel while we're in port."

The large man responded, "It's all right, captain. You've treated me squarely— I'm not complaining." Once Wolf left, the next problem O'Brien had to solve was selling the longhorn cattle. The owner was dead, and he couldn't find the original sales contract.

As he pondered what to do, O'Brien stepped onto the deck and admired the beautiful scenery that was Tahiti. A gentle wind blew over the island. The ever-present white-sand beaches, aquamarine and light blues of the bay, palm trees, and thick jungle growth blended together like a painting by the gods. Most days included some type of light wind, often picking up toward the latter part of the day. For the most part, these breezes were considered a blessing. The cool feeling from a gentle Pacific wind could somewhat offset a very hot day.

These Polynesian islands had numerous bird species and a magical array of marine creatures. From sea turtles, dozens of shark species, and dolphins to manta rays, numerous fish, and humpback whales, the islands thrived with marine life. However, there wasn't a lot of natural wildlife. When these islands of volcanoes rose up, they were far from surrounding land masses where other land creatures could migrate from. The only mammals on the islands were those that humans had brought: horses, sheep, pigs, dogs, cats, rats, and—of course—cattle.

The tough-minded cattle buyers soon came onboard the ship. The three men were French and well dressed in white trousers, colorful short-sleeved shirts, and straw hats; for this occasion, the captain was in his white uniform. Once in O'Brien's cabin, they laughed at his price of sixty dollars per head for the cattle, even though this was the price agreed in Honolulu. They told him they had all the cattle they needed, but since they liked the young man, they would buy his "worthless" animals at forty dollars a head.

O'Brien didn't say a word. He understood when to bark a command and when to figure out another way to handle a situation. "Sorry, gentlemen," he said in an even voice, "but we had a deal in Hawaii at sixty dollars each. And I'm holding you to that."

The smallest man of the three approached and lightly held his elbow. "Captain, we don't have any papers showing that. I can't remember what was agreed to, but, as we said, we'll pay you forty U.S. dollars for each one."

"I can't go along with that. Sixty was the price." The meeting was concluded on that note. The buyers gave a bow and left, leaving the captain to watch the shirtless natives paddle them away in canoes toward the lapping waves on another white-sand shore.

O'Brien thought over what to do. First, the longhorn cattle couldn't stay onboard the ship until they were sold. He had no idea how long it would take to sell them, and feeding the animals would become a problem. Deciding to find a place on land for the cattle, he left for Tahiti. O'Brien searched through the tropical island and finally found an owner willing to rent land for the cattle's use. The Hawaiians who had taken care of the cattle onboard the ship then left for the ranch to watch over them.

A Captain Chapman, who worked as a trader, came onboard the ship later and told O'Brien he was the agent for King Tapoa of Bora Bora. This beautiful island was located 450 miles northeast of Tahiti. Chapman told him the king had a "great quantity" of wood that he wanted to sell, and he had heard the captain traveled throughout the seas and might be interested in buying this.

Captain John knew he could sell the lumber in Honolulu for another tidy profit. Since the owner Walters was now dead, this would be his first trading venture, and the thought of this excited him. Before he could sail away, however, he had to dispose of the cattle—and for a decent price.

O'Brien then thought out his plan. He would sell them at the public market. If he sold them at the normal price, the cattle would bring a slightly higher price than the buyers had offered. It would take time to sell all the animals this way, however, and he would be competing with the buyers who had just been to see him. So he decided to sell the longhorns at half of the price the buyers had offered.

After two days of selling two cattle each day at that low price, the buyers came back to him. He knew they hadn't sold any of their cattle, given the low price that he was offering his cattle. They offered to buy his stock for fifty dollars per head. O'Brien didn't have to think it over. He said crisply, "The deal was sixty dollars. If I can't get the price you agreed to, then I'll sell them at any price I want."

The next day he brought two more cattle to the public auction. They quickly sold for the low price of twenty dollars each. The buyers again weren't able to sell any of their livestock. On the fourth day, O'Brien brought all his cattle to the market. He knew he had to make a deal that day: The *James* was soon bound to sail for Bora Bora. Although he had decided to accept fifty dollars a head, O'Brien's instinct was that the buyers might come up with their price. They did. He sold the remaining ninety-four cattle at the agreed sixty dollars each, and the captain would give Walters's widow all of the money her husband would have been entitled to.

The next day, the crew was busily raising the sails and taking on supplies. Kegs of freshwater, crates of chickens, boxes of vegetables, and other provisions were taken onboard. The captain was getting ready to give the order to raise anchor when he saw O'Malley's huge shape appear over the rail.

"Mister, you're not sailing on my ship. I made that clear." Despite his warning, the large man crept closer.

"Captain, I hear you're sailing to Bora Bora. Look, I'll give you the money for the fare. I don't think I'll be welcomed here."

O'Brien quickly gave his answer. "Take your things to steerage, O'Malley. You'll eat as a passenger at normal hours and not with the crew. You'll be treated with respect—but no talking. If you do, I'll throw you overboard. And you know I'll do that."

O'Malley smiled broadly and thanked O'Brien. This was probably the first time the man had ever honestly thanked anyone. While on the five-day passage, the captain learned more about the man. O'Malley told about his naval service during the Civil War, his long years sailing, and his times spent sealing in Russian waters off Siberia. Upon O'Brien's prodding, he responded, "Yes, captain, I was poaching. Only their ships were supposed to seal there."

O'Malley told him how he took schooners "faster in the winds" than his own by calling for help and then taking those ships by guns and brute force. When the Russians caught him sealing and jailed him, he did escape, although he had to knife a man and shoot others in the process. And, yes, his last job was in that penitentiary.

The captain listened closely and noted that Barry's stories had been right; however, O'Brien didn't judge what others had done, as long as it wasn't onboard his ship. Their world was savage at times, and he had an odd affinity for the man.

Perhaps it was that if he hadn't been given this command, he might have ended up like O'Malley. More than likely, it was because they were both strong men, and O'Brien thought he was a good sailor. He could run a good ship and was equally a strong disciplinarian. However, the captain couldn't countenance the man's brutality, his arrogance, his appearance of not caring one whit about others. Wolf was a beast in one way but charismatic in another. And O'Brien would tell the tales about this man as he sailed over the seas.

> "Then you are an individualist, a materialist, and, logically, a hedonist."
> "Big words," he smiled. "But what is a hedonist?"
> He nodded agreement when I had given the definition. "And you are also," I continued, "a man one could not trust in the least thing where it was possible for selfish interest to intervene?"
> "Now you're beginning to understand," he said, brightening.
>
> —Jack London, *The Sea-Wolf*

* * *

After the sail ship anchored at Bora Bora, O'Malley left the longboat to wade ashore. Wearing only a red bandana loincloth and holding high a case of gin, the hairy and scary man disappeared into the jungles. O'Brien later met in the largest thatched hut in the clearing with King Tapoa, who was a jolly, heavyset man and accompanied by his two wives. He had acquired "some" education, spoke reasonable French, and always appreciated gifts. During their discussions about business, the sea, and women, the two men eventually agreed on a price for the lumber. The king told O'Brien that his timber could be loaded on the ship in two days. The captain paid the king from what he had earned by selling the cattle—and John was showing that "horse trading" on the oceans was a business he understood.

After O'Brien left, he stopped outside to watch O'Malley stride up to the king's hut, singing a ditty and swinging a bottle of gin. When O'Malley looked at him with a broad grin, the captain acknowledged the large man with a nod and both continued on their way.

O'Brien then oversaw the loading of the timber. His longboats hauled the wood for two days to the *James*, and sweating men with pulleys and swaying poles swung the timber onboard into the hold. As the captain readied his vessel to leave the following day, a crewman alerted him that two canoes were quickly approaching. He watched the rhythmic slaps of the paddles into the calm turquoise waters as the slim boats glided toward the *Edwin James*. The crafts nosed quietly up to the hull, and three Polynesians boarded by a rope ladder.

One native began pleading with O'Brien in broken English to please take O'Malley along. The king had been drunk for two days, and both of his wives had run away. John tried his best to maintain his composure, but he could only laugh heavily in response. The next day, however, he had to obtain the king's signature for his ship's clearance papers. He finally located the king and O'Malley in the green hills above the village and its cluster of huts. Their arms were draped over each other's shoulders while they sung together an "odd" French song that was definitely out of tune. The two were propped against one side of a stick shelter, each wearing only a loincloth and swinging gin bottles in rough cadence to the words. An empty bottle lay off to the side.

O'Brien managed to get the drunken king to sign the papers, but his price was that the captain had to sing a song with them and take a strong belt from the gin bottle. The two drunks continued to rant and poke at one another with gales of laughter; O'Malley seemed to have found his place. He turned to O'Brien as the captain left. "Go on back to your hardtack, bully boy," he said with a lecherous grin. "I'm staying here. I'm going to be the King of Bora Bora." That was the last time the captain ever saw the man. He heard later that O'Malley had entered the pirate trade off the Russian coast and then disappeared from the face of the earth.

* * *

Months later in that year, O'Brien was back in Tahiti. He still commanded the same stout bark, but her name was now the *Liliu*, after the Hawaiian princess that he had ridden wildly with across the Waikiki sands. He had brought another boatload of cattle to sell and knew the price this time would be as agreed.

He was understandably happy because he owned a "good part" of the ship. Walters's widow had tired of the ship's problems and outright gave a half interest to O'Brien. She sold the remaining half to Henry Cornwall, a planter and cattle grower in Hawaii. O'Brien then sold part of his interest to Sam Parker, the owner and operator of the extensive Parker Cattle Ranch on the Island of Hawaii. The name of the ship was changed, and the former *Edwin James* became the *Liliu* and sailed under the flag of the Kingdom of Hawaii.

O'Brien came to Tahiti to trade, and he found himself watching a Tahitian fire dance as the chief's guest. He was sitting cross-legged in front of the roaring flames, and the moon was high over the surrounding thickets of jungle. When the large pile of fiery hardwood burned down to glowing red embers, "lithe warriors" suddenly appeared and danced wildly around the coals and pit. The fire's glow reflected off their glistening bodies, as shadowy images from the moonlight mixed with the radiating heat waves and shimmering coals.

The Tahitian dancers swept closer and closer to the red heat, pirouetting, spinning, and sweeping their arms and legs. Then the young men jumped into the fire pit. Their bare feet swept through the red-hot coals, scattering the embers about in showers of glittering sparks, which brought the "tom-tom" beats of the drummers and singers into faster beats of excitement.

O'Brien was captivated by the barefoot men and sizzling coals. He looked closely but couldn't see any pain on their faces. The natives would spiral close to him and pause for an instant as he looked up with amazement. Seeing his reaction, the dancers laughed or boasted of their prowess and leaped away. When the dance was over, he looked closely at their hardened feet, but he couldn't find any sign of blisters or redness.

During the time he spent with the chief, the captain saw a comely, lithe young woman who smiled shyly at him. He smiled back and was instantly attracted to her. He ended up spending his free time with the beautiful "barely" eighteen-year-old Tahitian princess, who fell in love with the ten-years-older O'Brien. He became enamored with the "soft-skinned" daughter of the chief.

During the day they walked through the lush jungle and its luxurious tropical flowers, rich orchids, flowering water lilies, and tall palm trees. The colors duplicated the rainbow, with flat coastal jungles ringed by a rugged coral coastline and sparkling, greenish-blue bays. The fragrance of jasmine, white gardenia, and hibiscus filled the air. The sunsets exploded in the sky with differing hues of light yellows, oranges, and blue streaks, while the reddish-yellow sun reflected onto the clear turquoise waters of the lagoon.

They were together on soft beaches with warm nights, gentle breezes, and swaying coconut palms. Johnny taught her a few words of "gurgling English" because he couldn't understand her patois picked up from the French who lived on the island. Her laugh was as soft as her manner and her touch like an ocean breeze. She learned the strange way that white men showed affection by placing their lips together and found it pleasant. They loved as "lightly as the foamy fingers of the night surf ran up the sands of the beach."

One starlit night, the two paddled a tiny outrigger canoe to the outer coral reef and fished with crude hooks. When the princess was the first to catch a small tropical fish, she slipped the six-inch fish off the barb. To his horror, she bit off the head of the wriggling fish with "strong, small" teeth, spat it out, and swallowed the rest whole. As she chattered with excitement at the fine delicacy, he could only gulp and stare. He never had acquired the taste for raw fish, and his goodnight kiss that night "lacked its usual fervor," not to mention he had lost his interest in love.

O'Brien sailed the next day for Honolulu. With an escort of decorated catamarans and canoes, the *Liliu* left the harbor and sailed through the narrow opening in the surrounding reef. The long canoe in front of the procession carried the chief and his daughter. As the ship sailed into the deeper waters, the princess happily held up her hand to show off the gaudy bracelet that he had given her as a parting gift. He reached his hand to the sky and acknowledged her wave.

The chief had already shown off his prized gilt-covered clock that struck each hour with a metallic gong. Captain O'Brien had given the present as part of the final ceremonies in the ruler's huge thatched hut. In front of the protective tiki gods and with a Tahitian temple offering, the chief in return had bestowed on him the luck of the gods on his voyage.

O'Brien appreciated the gesture, knowing that danger always lurked on the seas.

8

ON THE ATLANTIC

He never met the "dear girl" again, but O'Brien a year afterward learned the princess had married one of the French officers stationed at Papeete. He also heard that his sweet Liliu had also met someone else and married. On arriving in Honolulu, the captain decided to take the bark on the run between San Francisco and the Sandwich Islands, which turned out to be another very profitable venture. During these times, John wrote to the young lady in Portland, Emily Showers, and his first two letters didn't even merit a reply.

On his return to the West Coast from the Sandwich Islands, O'Brien committed to Emily as the woman he truly loved, and they were married on January 21, 1879. What caused her to change her mind—"the attractive, haughty Portland miss who shunned rough sailormen"—is not known. Whether she broke up with someone else, or she realized she had to marry the handsome captain or somehow figure out how to stop this man's persistence is also not known. Whatever the reasons, they kept this to themselves. His memoirs had one mention: "The third letter got a rather formal brief note, and it was not long before we became engaged—and married in San Francisco."

After a brief honeymoon, they sailed together on the *Liliu* to Hawaii. On the first night out from Honolulu Bay, the bark sailed straight into a southwest gale. Its deck was loaded with three tiers of stalls filled with mules bound for a plantation in the Sandwich Islands. The ship was rolling and pitching so badly in the heavy seas that the terrified mules were screaming "fearfully." Their brays were so pitiful that O'Brien headed below to see how his bride was handling this. He found her lying on her back in their berth and staring up with her "big, dark blue eyes."

He asked if she was frightened, to which she replied, "Are you?" John replied, "Of course not."

"Well," she said, "I don't know anything about the old ship, so if you get scared, then I suppose I'll also get scared." They both laughed.

When daylight came, they discovered that a number of the mules had their tails bitten off by the ones caged behind them. After the ship arrived in the Sandwich Islands, the plantation owner refused to pay the freight on the dozen or more tail-less animals and threatened a lawsuit. The captain settled with the owner by agreeing to a lower payment owing to the delivery of "damaged merchandise."

While in Honolulu, O'Brien had purchased a half interest in what later became known as the California Hay, Grain, and Feed Company, and he also operated the *Liliu* between San Francisco and the Hawaiian islands on business. Upon his return to San Francisco, he brought a full cargo of "everything" pertaining to the enterprise, while his partner, Mr. R. W. Laine (the ship's agent who helped him in Hawaii), purchased land and built an office and warehouse. In a few years, the company's sales began mounting. From a financial standpoint, the venture was excellent, so much so that his partner soon offered to buy out O'Brien's interest at a substantial profit. They agreed on a price, and Laine bought out the captain's participation. John now had a nice amount of money; however, he wrote later, "That was my big mistake, as they got rich and retired with enough money to live on, while I'm still going to sea. I am better off in one way, however, as all of them, including the later partners, have all passed away."

Another opportunity presented itself one evening when he was dining in the "old Hawaiian Hotel" with Sam Parker, who now owned part interest in the *Liliu*, and John D. Spreckles, the son of the wealthy "Sugar King of California." After dinner, the young Spreckles said, "Captain O'Brien, I'm going to put in a line of fine ships between San Francisco and Honolulu. How would you like to be in command of the first one? I'd strongly advise you to leave that old bark you're in and come with us."

O'Brien graciously refused, telling them he had a business with the *Liliu* that was making five times what the average sea captain earned. Later, he discovered that Spreckles's vessels were "fast sailers, well equipped, and carried full passenger loads." Spreckles invested large sums of money in the plantations, and his vessels carried so much of the trade that his agent advised O'Brien "to lay" his ship up. The *Liliu* sailed with empty holds owing to the competition until he finally sold the ship. During this time the captain used much of the money from his partnership sale to cover the ship's operating expenses. He never seemed to let too much money, or not enough, get in the way of what he wanted to do at the time.

A few days after he regretfully left his old vessel, he received a telegram offering him the command of a Boston-owned vessel named the *Alice Dickerman*. It was to sail from Victoria, British Columbia, with the first full cargo of canned salmon bound for London, and the agent, who was also a large investor in the cargo, offered him a bonus of $500 if he made the passage to London within ninety-six days, equaling the time made by the noted clipper ship *Thermopholae*. He accepted and quickly was on a Pacific Mail steamer to Victoria.

The *Dickerman* was a stout-looking ship, but she sailed so low in the water that two full crews, even though they signed contracts, refused to go to sea when they boarded her. Her large holds were filled with canned salmon from Alaska and British Columbia as well as a seven-foot-high load of pine and fir spars for ship masts. O'Brien sailed away and on the twenty-second day passed the equator, where King Neptune made his usual visit.

The equator is the imaginary line around the earth's center that divides it into equal parts between the northern and southern hemispheres. When approaching the equator, a longtime maritime tradition is to hold a ceremony that "initiates" seamen who were crossing the equator for the first time. The ritual starts with seamen heralding King Neptune's approach by savagely beating on pots and pans, while the costumed sailor walks to and stops at the break of the fo'c'sle deck.

Wearing usually a navy blue blanket as a robe, fastened under his chin and trailing behind, the seaman strutted like King Neptune toward the others. His robe's edges were trimmed with seaweed or "bunches of rope-yarn," painted green to look like eelgrass pulled from the sea's bottom. He wore a red-painted crown and a canvas mask with holes cut for the eyes and nose. Around his mouth and chin was a fringe of rope-yarn for whiskers. In his right hand, the sailor carried a five-pronged iron as a trident, from which dangled more pieces of rope-yarn to look like seaweed, and his left hand held a "speaking trumpet" or megaphone. His sea boots could be much too large, but in keeping with the overall effect.

He yelled through his trumpet, "Why in the hell didn't you lower a boat when I hailed you? There must be someone aboard this ship who hasn't yet joined the Order of the Sons of Neptune, or you would have done as I commanded. If there are any such people, they must pay the price and I want their names. Give them to me!"

As the names were announced, the initiates would bow in ungainly ways to Neptune. A crewman would yell that the new recruits needed a shave: This would be a painful streaking of one's face with tar, then razoring it off with a dull blade. Sometimes cook's flour was thrown over the face or a new sailor was wrapped in a small piece of canvas like a straitjacket. At times, the seaman was sitting on a board on a tub of water, and then, after being admitted to the order, someone jerked the board away.

After the ceremonies, the ship continued on its way with a full crew. On the forty-fifth day the *Dickerman* rounded the Horn in moderate weather. O'Brien had good weather, was making excellent time, and felt confident that the bonus was as "good as won." On the sixty-eighth day, they crossed the equator on the Atlantic Ocean side. Since everyone who hadn't crossed the equator had already been initiated, the captain ordered a holiday for his crew with "full portions" of grog passed out and the best food that the cook could muster.

Soon after passing the island of Fernando de Noronha, the Brazilian convict station, the captain's luck changed. The wind died down and the ship became becalmed for several days. The *Dickerman* drifted within a mile of an American ship, the *Harvey Mills*, whose sails on its tall masts were clewed up to keep them from chafing. The master of the ship, Captain Mills, rowed over to the *Dickerman*, and the two captains chatted. Mills thought O'Brien's ship was waterlogged due to its deep draft, but John told him this was due to its heavy load.

Mills invited O'Brien over to his ship for dinner. When a strong breeze suddenly blew in during the meal, John felt he needed to be onboard the *Dickerman* and headed back in a small dinghy. When halfway there, he heard a seaman from the *Mills* yell a warning, and on looking back, he saw a large fin cutting through the water with speed. The immense shark quickly sidled up alongside the tiny boat, and the sailor who was rowing turned "livid white" as he unshipped the oars. The predator lunged for one oar when it was pulled up, just missed it, circled underwater, and surfaced noisily under the stern.

The sailor meanwhile had put the oars back and was madly rowing for the *Dickerman* while the shark trailed closely by. O'Brien yelled to the onboard mate to throw meat or bread overboard to distract the predator. Before his crew could do this, the dinghy and its two passengers were alongside the ship's Jacob's ladder. The rowing sailor sprung up the side with the demon seemingly after him. As he leaped on the rope ladder, his feet pushed the boat away, and for an instant O'Brien was stranded by himself. The shark rushed closely by with a small white trail, giving time for the crew to throw a rope down to him and pull the boat back.

The captain leaped for the ladder and lifted himself out. He had hardly left the longboat when the shark crashed into the small rowboat and rolled it away from O'Brien's feet. When they brought the dinghy back onto the ship, the crew discovered that the shark had broken the rowboat's keel. With the shark cruising around, the captain told his men to forget about trying to get the oars back—and to trim the sails for the wind.

One week later, the watchman sighted the American ship *H. L. Richardson*, whose masthead flew a signal that it was short of provisions. When O'Brien boarded the ship, he learned the vessel had been out for 149 days bound for Queenstown with a cargo of guano from the "bird islands" off Chile. For the last ten days, the men had been trying to survive on one biscuit a day. O'Brien divided his ship's provisions in half and gave them to the captain, while the mate on the *Richardson* signed a receipt. He also delivered fifteen cases of salmon and fifteen sacks of wheat for the crew.

As soon as the provisioned ship left, his sailors squared the *Dickerson*'s sails, and the vessel headed away. When the *Richardson* arrived in Southampton, England, the ship's captain traveled to London and completely paid for all the provisions he had thankfully received. A week before O'Brien arrived off the chop of the English Channel, however, he discovered that his own ship didn't have enough drinkable water. The carpenter had discovered that the main freshwater tank was badly salted, caused by a loose brass cover over the tank.

With no more than fifty gallons of water onboard, O'Brien cut the daily allowance to one quart per man, and just two days later, this was further reduced to a pint. He constructed an improvised still from a five-gallon pot, filled two-thirds high with saltwater and kept constantly boiling. A small hose passed the steam through the middle of a ten-gallon keg filled with cold seawater at a downward angle leading into a smaller pot. The keg's coldness caused the steam to condense into freshwater that dropped into the smaller receptacle. This homemade device made four gallons of freshwater every twenty-four hours. After several days of this, he intercepted an English ship and traded a case of salmon for two barrels of water. A day after the trade, the needed rains came, which allowed them to trap as much freshwater as they needed.

When the *Dickerman* approached Plymouth, a channel pilot boarded to chart the path to the port city. The ship had been out for more than one hundred days, and O'Brien had lost the bonus. Still the vessel had made decent time, considering it had sailed into a week of no wind, met heavy easterly gales that blew her off course, stopped to render assistance, and ran out of freshwater.

When approaching the Southampton lighthouse a hard wind suddenly arose, and O'Brien called the half-awake pilot to the deck. The captain had noticed another vessel's lights close by and told the pilot that his ship couldn't clear her. The Englishman said there wasn't a problem. When O'Brien realized the pilot didn't understand the gravity of the situation, he knocked the pilot from the wheel, and with the helmsman's assistance, swung the helm hard and away from the other ship. The maneuver caused O'Brien's ship to slowly swing from the other, which began to loom larger in the darkness. Its lights outlining a large silhouette, the huge ship cut toward them. At the last moment the *Dickerson*'s bow just cleared the other vessel, and as the ship passed, a voice cut through the darkness, yelling, "What in the hell are you trying to do?" O'Brien didn't answer.

The pilot was now standing and said, "My heavens, Captain O'Brien, I did not think she was so close." He asked John to please not report the incident; hearing the man's apologies and understanding the error, the captain decided not to press the matter. O'Brien learned later that several seamen had drowned the same night due to a collision twenty miles from their close call.

Injuries, death, collisions, and close calls were part of this business. Another captain's near collision was so close that the adjacent ship's wash boiled over the stern in a mighty wave; the force threw the master against the wheel box, causing him injuries, and hurled a seaman against the mast, cutting his cheek open. In another incident, the "large black side" of a steamer passed so close to windward, the vessel took the wind from the smaller ship's sails. With a gale blowing and the steamer moving on, the winds then caught the sail ship directly across its beam. The wind blasts heeled the ship into the ocean, and its railings were underwater. Somehow the bark surfaced and continued on.

The *Dickerman*'s heavy cargo of salmon and masts was safely landed in London, and Captain John took the precaution of loading a ballast of 250 tons of chalk into the holds. He learned later that dock officials wouldn't have let him leave without this ballast. Ships with empty holds needed to sail with such weight, whether they were of goods or stones. Heavy gusts of winds or large waves otherwise could too easily capsize the vessels.

The journey back to the East Coast was uneventful, and O'Brien looked forward to when the *Dickerman* would be sailing proudly into Boston Harbor. Like other masters, he wanted the ship to look her best when docking at a berth, especially since the owners would be there watching. From trunk to deck during the voyage, O'Brien had the crew scraping, varnishing, and painting the ship. Brightly polished copper was secured to her yards, and all of the rigging was "gone over." He even fitted a snowy white canvas cover over the steering gear by the wheel.

When only a few days from the harbor, the captain found a "dirty stain" of tobacco juice running down the ship's lowest sails. O'Brien discovered the next morning that the sail needles through the canvas on the yard had been broken off, and yellowy chewing tobacco stains were splattered on the white steering gear cover. Even though he had warned the crew, the disgusting stains appeared again the next day. O'Brien waited by the helm during the night to find out who the culprit was. Sure enough, in the late-night darkness, he saw a big "Russian-Finn" sailor breaking the just-replaced sail needles. When he confronted the guilty sailor, a furious fight ensued. Although the man was a "heavy-shouldered," hulking man, O'Brien swarmed over him, "fists and feet flying." The man was taken to his bunk with injuries and then later to a Boston hospital. A week would pass by before the man could be discharged.

The owner's brother tracked down O'Brien in Boston and warned him that a detective and policeman were waiting for him on the dock. He was told it would be wiser to return quickly to the Pacific Coast, as an arrest warrant was going to be quickly served. His clothes and personal effects on board would be shipped to him in San Francisco. O'Brien did just that and jumped on the first train to Montreal, as he thought the police might be watching for any trains traveling across country. Once in Canada, he took another train to San Francisco, arriving safely and finding his promised personal belongings.

* * *

Back in San Francisco, Captain O'Brien headed immediately into the Merchants Exchange, where sea captains, owners, and shippers met regarding trade, and happened to meet Captain Cyrus Noyes of the bark *Coloma*. The two had become acquainted during their long stays in Hong Kong when John was master of the *Edwin James*. Noyes told O'Brien that his present company was interested in the China trade and was buying another vessel. He asked if O'Brien would be interested in being the chief mate on his ship. The incentive was if John sailed on the *Coloma*, he would be guaranteed the captain's job on the new vessel.

O'Brien accepted but told Noyes he needed time in Portland. He was "anxious" to be there with his young wife and baby boy, born while he was sailing off Cape Horn. This also proved agreeable, as the ship wouldn't leave for another two weeks—and would sail to Portland where he could then board the ship. His time spent with Emily and his baby was joyful, but this ended way too soon. Before he knew it, the *Coloma* had a new mate and was sailing past the Columbia River bar.

The ship was loaded with cargo and 450 Chinese workers who were looking forward to their return home. The *Coloma* unfortunately sailed immediately into a heavy sou'wester with high seas and winds. O'Brien thought the anchors were well secured by strong straps to rings in the deck. Once he had the sails set, however, the ship slid into another deep dive, and the port anchor ripped through its straps to crash into the sea. One hundred and twenty fathoms, or over 700 feet, of new chain ripped over the side and hung at the end of the windlass. Noyes ordered O'Brien to slip the shackles and let the anchor go, but O'Brien felt this was his fault and wanted the chance to save the valuable equipment. The master agreed but cautioned John about the danger of the anchor's flukes smashing through the ship's bow, if he was even able to raise it above the waterline.

Such a task would be Herculean, given the heavy weight that needed to be lifted, and O'Brien knew his crew wasn't up to this task. He decided to use the Chinese coolies and selected forty of the strongest, toughest ones. O'Brien headed below and brought up six large bottles of gin, giving each of the Chinese men a "big drink" of the raw alcohol. John called for a "chantey man" to sit on the capstan, take some strong belts from the gin bottle, and start singing out an old square-rig chantey.

With a rope end in one hand and an uncorked bottle of the gin in the other, O'Brien exhorted the men to turn the windlass and haul up the weight. He urged them on, pouring gin from the opened bottle into his own throat as well as into the grinning mouths of the coolies while he lightly swung the rope against their sweating bodies. He would swipe the rope against one back and then pour gin down the appreciating mouth of the same man.

Slowly the men turned the windlass, and the incredible weight of anchor and long chain began coming up from the depths. Meanwhile the heavy seas were crashing over the bounding ship and washing down the decks. The chantey man sang drunkenly, the coolies put their muscle to the windlass, and Johnny kept pouring out gin and incentives. In an hour, the anchor was "safe and snug" on the bow. No one had believed that any windlass on any windjammer could raise an anchor with that much heavy chain out—but the Chinese workers did it. Although O'Brien wasn't outwardly tipsy, he kept to himself whether he was.

Seamen sang chanteys while they were hard at work, whether bringing up the sails or an anchor. They would pull on the accented notes, singing songs such as "Whiskey," "Drunken Sailor," and "Heave Away Cheerily," although the last was usually sung at the pumps. Seamen would typically sing "Hanging Johnny" when setting the mainsails. Felix Riesenberg wrote in *Under Sail*:

"A chantey, boys!" shouted the mate. "Come on now, run her up, lads. Up! Up!" And the heavy yard commenced to creep along the mast with creaking sounds, some of the sailors complaining, but all in time to the haunting deep sea tune of "Blow the Man Down," the greatest of all the haul chanteys.

Another time the men were pulling hard on the sails. On the yard, we were holding—by our stomachs, chests, and elbows—all of the sail we had gathered in, and we were loath to let go our hands for a fresh hold, fearing we'd lose what we had gained. But with Jerry starting, "To me way-a-hey (the song of 'Paddy Doyle and His Boots')," our feet were thrown high in the air, regardless, while our heads went down, with bodies hanging over the yard, as we reached below in another attempt; and with the pause, "O," drawed out, everybody on the yard began the chorus in unison, holding all he had, knowing full well that it required a pull of all together, as we sang, "Paddy can't dive for his boots!"

On the word "boots," down came our feet under the yard, every man pulling as one, and up rolled the sail, little by little, with the help of the song. Cursing was forgotten and a broad smile broke over the faces of the sailors, who, a moment before, hated themselves.

One afternoon before another strong wind, the main royal sail ripped and the winds blew it through the buntlines, or the ropes at the bottom of a square sail. O'Brien ordered two men to go aloft and furl it. When the men were halfway up the rigging, they stopped and didn't climb further due to the heavy slatting, or flapping, of the sails. The mate shouted up orders for one man to climb up to the royal masthead and shin down the lift to the yardarm and furl the sail.

"O'Brien, that's too dangerous for the men," Noyes shouted back.

"Captain, I don't give any orders to the men where I cannot go." John quickly climbed up the rigging, and when he reached the men, yelled, "What in the hell are you afraid of?" The sailors answered they were worried about being knocked off the yard if they tried to carry out his orders.

O'Brien shinned up the pole, came down on the lift, and "won the tug of war" to hold on while working on the yardarm and finally furling the sail. Once the mate landed on the deck with a definite satisfied look, Noyes said loudly, "Mr. O'Brien, I would rather lose the sail, than have you take such a risk. Do not do that again."

The top of another high sail carried away just before the change of watches at 4:00 A.M. O'Brien again ordered two men to go aloft, but after lowering the yard partway, they also feared straddling the yardarm. Disregarding his master's orders, O'Brien decided that he again had to go aloft. He worked astride the yard, but one of the men became insulting. O'Brien thought to himself that if the sailor opened his mouth once more, he would kick him off the yard, just as O'Malley did. But the sailor kept quiet, and the mate put his mind back on the task. Later when on deck, the religious O'Brien felt that the Lord was smiling over him. One little shove by that sailor and he would have sailed off into eternity. Noyes didn't say a word about O'Brien's next scaling of the mast, as he realized that this wouldn't make a difference.

By now John had become a skilled and careful navigator. The mate and captain had amicable disagreements over the relative merits of star observations when navigating, which O'Brien strongly championed. The ship was eighty miles from Pedro Blanco, a small island not too distant from Hong Kong. O'Brien had taken a star sighting for the longitude and latitude early in the morning, and this indicated that the ship would sail by Pedro Blanco at about 3:00 A.M. He was confident of navigating this way at night—over using a sextant and chart during the day—as he had sailed the *Edwin James* completely from Portland to Hong Kong by star sighting.

Since Captain Noyes always made his sightings during the sunlight, he disagreed with O'Brien's conclusion that the *Coloma* would pass by the island at that time, including that the land mass would be "two points on the starboard bow." Noyes asked his mate to stay on deck and see how his calculations came out, concluding, "For my part, I don't think we'll see Pedro Blanco." It was a dark night with passing rain squalls, and the time was one o'clock in the morning.

O'Brien decided this would be the time to "work" a drink from the captain's three-star Hennessy brandy, one of the few bottles kept in Noyes's quarters, and he hatched a plan to do so. O'Brien started by leaning over the railing, holding his stomach, and groaning as if in great pain. When Noyes asked what the matter was, O'Brien said he had terrible cramps.

"What can you take for this?" asked the captain solicitously. The mate replied that "something hot" would do.

"Do you think that a little brandy would help you?" After O'Brien's quick nods, the captain told him to stay on deck and watch for the island while he got the brandy. Noyes soon returned and said he had left the brandy in the pantry, but that O'Brien could go below and take some. Holding his stomach and groaning as if his "last hour had come," John limped away.

As soon as he left the captain's view, he straightened up and was shortly pouring a "dandy" portion of the finest brandy. O'Brien was soon on deck without any signs of cramps and a smile on his face.

An hour later at about 2:00 A.M. he had another attack of the cramps, as he figured this was the only way he'd get another tumbler full of the smooth-tasting brandy. He again went through the acts of groaning and moaning. Noyes looked at him suspiciously. "Mr. O'Brien, I don't believe there's anything wrong with you, but if you want another drink, I'll go below and get the bottle, put it in your room, and you can keep the damn stuff. But before you have another drink, I want you to pick up the sight of Pedro Blanco and show me if your star observations are worth such a continuation."

Twenty minutes later the sky cleared up and the lookout reported a sail two points on the starboard bow. O'Brien turned to the captain, pointed starboard, and observed, "There's your island, just as I said." When Noyes was sure that Pedro Blanco was behind the ship's sail, he replied, "That is fine; now go below, have your drink, and turn in. I will call you after a couple of hours of sleep to bring me up on the use of star observations." O'Brien did as he said, but now couldn't sip the brandy. He had drunk enough and couldn't do more—as Noyes had figured out.

Navigating correctly was, of course, extremely important. Had O'Brien been wrong, the ship could have sailed directly onto the island's reefs. Or missed completely and headed to the China coast. By the following afternoon, however, the *Coloma* was in Hong Kong harbor. The vessel had encountered "thick, nasty weather" in going through the Bashi Channel (which divides the China Sea from the North Pacific Ocean); despite the weather encountered, the ship docked five days ahead of the *Alden Besse*, which left San Francisco about the same time.

This brought about conflict, because the two ships were owned by the very competitive Noyes "brothers." When he arrived later in port, the chin-whiskered Allen Noyes was angered to find that his half brother's ship was already discharging its cargo. To make matters worse, the crews of both ships catcalled one another about the other vessel's seaworthiness and sailors. Further, the *Besse* had beaten the *Coloma* by three to six days on the last four passages to the port.

O'Brien approached his captain, Cyrus Noyes, one day. "If you will give me a set of studding sails [light sails set on the sides of a vessel's mainsails that increase speed], inexpensively purchased here, you need not pay me one cent of my wages if we don't beat the *Alden Besse* back to San Francisco." O'Brien was still mad at the half brother over an argument they had a few years ago. Cyrus quickly gave his approval for the studding sails.

The Noyes brothers agreed to sail for Portland on the same day. Both captains drove their crews to repair the heavy canvas sails, bend them to the best shape for the winds, and inspect all of the ship's rigging, masts, and equipment. While getting the sails ready for the "grand hoist," the Chinese stevedores on the *Coloma* began stowing cargo. When they were in the way of the crew, O'Brien "gave way to my impetuous nature" and swore at them to get a move on it. When Captain Noyes heard this, he pursed his lips and shook his head but said nothing to O'Brien because he wanted to win so badly.

The two ships sailed away, but on the first night they lost sight of one another. Eight days later, the *Besse* sailed into Astoria after O'Brien's *Coloma*. No doubt, the new set of studding sails—or "kites"—were a good reason for the difference. These light squares of canvas are tucked out on the yardarms, and the lightest puff of wind gets them working. Why Allen Noyes didn't think about this wasn't known.

O'Brien couldn't wait to board the *Alden Besse* and kid the chief mate over what had happened, especially since they were friends. He asked the second mate, whom he was not on friendly terms with, where the mate was. The man's response was, "If we had those same 'lime juice' kites, we would have beaten you across."

Not wanting a fight this time, O'Brien "rather quietly" replied, "I guess we were fortunate in getting a better slant of wind than you." This did not appease the second mate, who spat out, "Get over the side. We don't want any lime juicers here." Various four-letter curse words, including some about O'Brien's mother, then came out. The second mate was larger, beefier, and said to be meaner than O'Brien. The inevitable fight occurred, and the other man outweighed Johnny by fifty pounds with a five-inch height advantage.

O'Brien didn't wait and landed the first blow, as usual, but when this fight was over, both men looked as if they were the losers. Trying to stop the blood flowing from nasty cuts over his eyes, John spent the night holding slabs of raw meat against his face. The next morning when Captain Noyes saw O'Brien's battered, bruised face and half-shut eyes, he wanted to know what had happened. Worried about what punishment he would receive for this latest infraction, O'Brien first said that he had slipped and struck his face on an iron railing.

Noyes replied he would find a doctor, but first the captain wanted to see his brother, since the *Besse* was moored nearby. In a half hour, he was back and knocking excitedly on O'Brien's door. Cyrus Noyes was "all smiles" and said loudly, "I'm proud of you, my boy. You should see the other fellow's face. A doctor is now trying to straighten out his broken nose."

O'Brien was relieved that it didn't appear the captain was going to dock part of his wages. "In fact," Captain Noyes continued, "I'm going to give you a raise for licking that big bully of a second mate. From this day on, your wages are seventy-five dollars a month, not twenty-five dollars, and you are to go ashore to the Occidental Hotel and eat right. I'll send a doctor over to tend to you, but don't return until you've healed."

Although O'Brien won the battle, he had lost the war. Allen Noyes was furious at what had happened. He refused to recommend that John be given the command, as promised, of the company's new vessel. At the request of Cyrus Noyes, Johnny sailed the *Coloma* back to Hong Kong with goods and passengers, but while there, he learned how upset Allen was. The step brother had told Captain J. E. Ainsworth, the principal owner of the company, that O'Brien was an alcoholic and untrustworthy. O'Brien gained some measure of revenge, however, when he again beat the *Besse*—the promised "new" ship—back to Portland.

When the vessel anchored, O'Brien went onboard to see Allen. He confronted the man, saying he had lied to Ainsworth about O'Brien's using liquor to excess. John said strongly:

> I defy you, or any other man, on this earth to prove—or say—that they have ever seen me partly or in any way under the influence of liquor. All I have in this world is my reputation. You have been the reason why I wasn't given the captaincy of the *Kate Davenport*. [Although these details are not given, this incident comes up again.] I insist that you either write me a satisfaction at once, or accompany me to Captain Ainsworth and tell him that you were wrong in what you said.

Allen Noyes rose and stood in silence. He then surprisingly, but showing his character, apologized to O'Brien.

> I am very sorry, as I have since found out that I was mistaken. The second mate, who you beat up, was my source. I need to make one more voyage in the *Besse*, which will complete my sixtieth year at sea. I would like you to make another voyage with my brother as mate, and upon your return, this ship will be at your service. Also, if you would like, you may take your wife with you.

Although Allen Noyes would make good on his offer, all of this had to wait until O'Brien had another ship venture under his belt—and this one turned out to be more dangerous than the others.

9

SAVING THE
UMATILLA

One of the most successful and skilled large-ship builders, John Roach & Sons in Chester, Pennsylvania, built in 1881 the two-masted, two-decked passenger and cargo steamer *Umatilla*. The 3,069-ton iron-hulled ship was 310 feet long with a 41-foot beam and 22-foot depth. Quickly becoming one of the best-known ships on the Pacific and international fleets, it carried different sails on its two masts, including "fore-and-aft canvas with squares forward." At that time, it was believed that the engines of these ships weren't completely reliable and that fuel wasn't readily available. Able to transport four hundred passengers along with heavy cargo, the *Umatilla* joined other prestigious steamers, such as the *Queen of the Pacific* and the *Congress* (the largest coastal passenger ship then under the American flag), as well-known flagships of the great Pacific Coast Steamship fleet.

Two years later, O'Brien joined the *Umatilla*'s crew as chief mate. Although having been the captain of his own sail ship, his desire to locate on the Pacific Northwest and be closer to his family—plus to learn new skills so that he could become the master of a steamer—brought about his acceptance of the position. He knew that steamships would dominate the sea over the tall-sail ships, and the decision showed his ability to put his advancement as a mariner over pride. O'Brien told Captain Noyes that "he'd be back," but he wanted to learn on the steamers.

116

Acknowledged as one of the finest ships of her type, the *Umatilla*'s first voyage from the West Coast and San Francisco also proved to be one of the most dangerous—and O'Brien received his nickname of Dynamite Johnny on this voyage. Several hundred carboys of muriatic acid and a cargo of railroad flatbed cars were lashed to the deck. This was a heavy load and dangerous, since muriatic acid is highly corrosive hydrochloric acid, which causes severe irritation or burns to skin and eyes as well as being quite toxic if inhaled. It is used to remove rust, to wash dried masonry from stone, and in various manufacturing processes. Looking like an office water-cooler bottle, each carboy was a large globular container made of glass (now plastic) and encased in a protective wood crate.

While sailing off Cape Blanco in southern Oregon, a powerful storm swept in. Large, sweeping rollers soon swelled over her decks with loud, foaming crashes and broke loose the large crates and heavy railroad cars. With whistling winds in their ears and slippery decks under their feet, the seamen found these conditions perilous at best, but O'Brien led the crew toward the huge railroad cars. Lassoing the sliding steel cars with thick hawsers, the men tied the stock temporarily down to the gunnels. The floating containers of acid were splitting open from the collisions, however, and spilling out their dangerous contents. The captain ordered his men to grab the carboys so they could be thrown overboard.

With the rising breakers slamming into the *Umatilla*, the ship staggered from side to side, and the wood cases and bottles were washing over the deck with the waves. O'Brien yelled at his crew to form a line leading to the rails, and the drenched seamen began passing down the containers. When the closest man grabbed a crate or bottle, the mate shifted his grasp from the shifting gunnels, gingerly accepted it, and then heaved it overboard. Although sailors pitched to the deck with the ship's sudden movements and ocean wash, the men kept at what they had to do. Finally they were finished. "Braced against the lee deck" and soaked by the ocean's waves, O'Brien, "of course, got most of the flying acid" but faced down the dangers of frothing sea and bubbling acid. Their clothing was in shreds, but they were fortunate that none of the acid splashed into their eyes, although the sea-filled deck was littered with broken crates and shattered carboys.

The gale winds and sea surges continued into the next morning, when O'Brien heard the muted sounds of crashing from below the decks where the "powder in cases" was stowed. Directing two seamen to open the hatch, he peered down into the dark hole. The colliding sounds were loud with heavy thuds, but he couldn't see anything. O'Brien climbed down the ladder with one hand, while the other held his lantern high. Once down on the wet floorboards, he discovered a large safe had broken loose and was battering the dynamite cases stored inside. Calling for more men, he and the others threw mattresses in front of the sliding safe to slow its progress and shield the cases of "explosive powder." The sailors finally were able to lash down the safe. For O'Brien's heroics in this situation, he earned the nickname Dynamite Johnny, which he carried for the rest of his life.

Upon the ship's arrival in Seattle, the company's stevedore began unloading the dynamite by hoisting the cases out in slings. O'Brien called the man's attention to the danger of a load falling out. The seaman countered that this was the way they always did it. Dynamite Johnny went straight to Captain Worth to ask about changing from this method to handling the dynamite in stages, with men passing the cases ashore. As they were talking, the men heard the hoisting winch scream wildly, and an instant later the sling load fell into the main hatch, but "wonders of wonders" there wasn't an explosion. From then on, the unloading was done by hand.

After unloading the dynamite, railroad cars, and other cargo, the ship steamed through Puget Sound on its way back to California. However, early that February 8, 1884, the *Umatilla* sailed into a cruel northerly gale as it passed Cape Flattery, the farthest northwest point where the Strait of Juan de Fuca empties into the Pacific Ocean. The intense winds whipped the gray seas into a churning maelstrom of foaming breakers, while blinding snow flurries coated the lurching vessel and its masts, spars, and rigging with sheets of crusted snow and ice. No one could see more than a "blurry mist" ahead.

O'Brien had the bridge watch from 4:00 to 8:00 A.M., and about 7:30 he noticed a few "yellow beaked divers or saltwater ducks" occasionally skimming across the bow. He called the captain's attention to this, noting that these birds were only seen when close to shore. Worth said, "Okay, but we're still twenty miles from Flattery Rocks."

The wind-driven snows continued to beat viciously against the vessel and its crew. Duty tours were shortened as even hardy seamen were forced to leave due to their uncontrollable shaking. The men on deck shivered from the bone-chilling gale blasts, and Captain Frank Worth stayed on the bridge deck. Visibility was at a minimum, and the ship crept blindly through the cold murkiness.

At eight o'clock in the morning, O'Brien left his watch and went to his room. After washing and stepping through the snow to walk aft to the dining saloon, O'Brien heard over the din the lookout's muffled cry, "Rocks and breakers ahead!" He felt that the ship "couldn't be more than two ship lengths" away.

Hideous white-specked bleak rocks with crowns of spray noisily arose from the gloom. A jarring, terrifying crash suddenly ripped through the ship as it slammed "dead head on" into the uncharted reef. A wild clanging sounded sharply from the engine room's telegraph, while the wrenching jolt threw everyone to the decks. The ship shuddered from stem to stern, and frightened men heard the sounds of the ocean pouring inside through what had to be a gaping hole in the ship.

O'Brien ran for the bridge after he heard the lookout's cry, but the collision's force hurled him "head over heels" against a hatch. Quickly regaining his footing, he raced to the bridge where he shouted at the second officer, "Why in the hell didn't you port and go inside the reef? You had plenty of room."

Captain Worth stood silently by, frozen by the sudden crashing of his vessel. O'Brien quickly gave the order to "haul down the forestaysail, lift the number one and two hatches." Since most of the ship's canvas had been set before the collision, seamen now ran forward to lower the forestaysail (a triangular sail set on rigging that braces a mast), which was flapping heavily in the winds. They moved to open the hatches. When the chief mate stared down into the number two hatch, he saw cargo floating from side to side inside both holds.

Awakening from his stupor, Worth gave the order to reverse engines at full speed astern. The ship began slowly sliding with a grating sound from the reef. Her bow then started to slam "mightily" against the rocks, and each vibration shattered throughout the vessel. All hands—forty men (including the steward and his wife)—had raced up, some half-dressed, and now milled around the deck. Some were clearly afraid. The captain next ordered the engine room to start the ship's pumps, but even with their operation, the vessel sank lower into the stormy seas.

Seeing that the vessel was in danger of going under, O'Brien shouted from the forward deck to the bridge, "Shove her nose onto the reef again—before she sinks." And the captain deferred to the mate's order. The engine-room telegraph clanged noisily once more with the directive to move her forward. During the time that the gears reversed, the propeller's thumping stopped momentarily, but it quickly started up again as the *Umatilla* scraped eerily back onto the reef. "Straining the rigging with a fury," the blasts of wind whipped the ship's overhead sails out of control. The vessel carried several sails: forestaysail, hoisting fore-square sail, large fore-and-aft foresail, main topmast staysail, and fore-and-aft mainsail. When the *Umatilla*'s new position caught the winds differently, the sails swung sharply over and pulled the ship in a bad list toward one side.

The vessel angled further toward the writhing sea as the ocean rushed into the torn hull faster than the pumps could eject. Seeing this, Captain Worth gave the order to abandon ship, and sailors quickly readied the lifeboats for lowering. In response to the captain's direction, seamen passed the ship's chronometer (a precision timepiece used in direction finding) and other navigation equipment to his longboat, while others dropped the swinging, nearly filled boats into the ocean from their holding davits.

O'Brien was hungry, however, and when the captain told everyone to abandon ship, he raced away instead to eat in the officer's mess. He was the only one who hadn't had breakfast, and this was more important than following that order. O'Brien hailed the steward's wife, saying, "Is breakfast still available?" He was served. The steward's wife then joined the others who ran to the two large lifeboats now lowered safely on the lee side. The remaining seamen shimmied down a rope into the boats—all except one man, Dynamite Johnny O'Brien.

While he was eating, O'Brien kept thinking about this fine steamer with her bow on the rocks. But the wind was strong from the north, so perhaps that would keep her from broaching the rocks broadside. He then had a "wild thought" that she might drift off after the steam had expended itself from the forward 800-ton ballast tank. The engineer had told him they had the steam pump working, and this would use up the water stored in the ballast tank. He thought the ship could possibly stay afloat as long as the pumps sucked the sea out nearly as fast as it poured in.

Staying onboard also seemed to be a better decision, since it was nearly "zero weather" out on the ocean. The snow was still falling severely, and O'Brien thought it made more sense to stay onboard until they knew the ship couldn't make it. To directly go against a captain's order was a serious offense, so he decided to drop a raft into the seething waters. A "junior engineer" who had scrambled back to retrieve money then assisted O'Brien in moving the ten-foot-long, six-foot-wide raft into the tossing ocean.

Buoyed by two airtight cylinders underneath it, the flat raft and the waiting lifeboats rose and fell with the rolling waves. When he spotted O'Brien at the railing, the captain yelled, "Get into the boat, Mister! The ship is sinking." The mate nodded and used a rope to climb down instead into the bobbing life raft. Clutching to its wooden-frame sides, he spread out inside it. Captain Worth again demanded that his first officer join the others, arguing, "The ship's going down, O'Brien. If you stay on that raft, you'll be sucked down when the ship goes down."

Dynamite Johnny didn't move, concluding that the hulking vessel above just might not sink and the better decision was to stay by it. The captain told two of his sailors to row to the raft and drag O'Brien into his lifeboat. When the seamen approached the raft, they leaned over to seize the mate. Surprising everyone, he sprang up, grabbed them instead by their wrists, and jerked the two men into his raft. Telling the two startled sailors that they were better off with him than drifting away into a blinding snowstorm, O'Brien shoved the lifeboat away. The seamen stayed, not knowing at first what to do. Shaking his head sternly, the captain ordered the boats to row away and leave the "damn fool where he was." Both boats were soon lost in the snow flurries as the seamen searched for a way through the rocks to shore.

Once the lifeboats had disappeared into the gloom, O'Brien told the men to go onboard and bring back all the provisions and blankets they could find. If the *Umatilla* began to sink, the sailors would have only minutes to get back to the raft, so O'Brien stayed there to stand watch. He told them, "I'll warn you in time—so now fly!" Using the rope to climb back on the vessel, the two men carefully made their way over the snow- and ice-covered steel deck to the galley. They foraged through the storeroom and grabbed canned goods, butter, and hardtack. Finding a dozen blankets as well, the sailors brought everything back to the raft.

Once the men were inside, O'Brien "slacked off the heavy line" that held the raft to the ship's railing. While the raft swept up and down with the long swells like a rollercoaster, the men wrapped themselves inside the blankets and huddled together for warmth. The thick snow continued hurtling down and eventually covered them with a wet layer. The large bulk of the *Umatilla* loomed above, and when the ship rolled with a large wave, a loose iron door banged and equipment slid noisily about. The men could hardly move, and the intense cold seeped through their clothing into their bones.

* * *

Losing track of time, the shivering sailors anxiously awaited their fate. A sharp metallic sound then sliced through the air, and when they looked up through the lessening snow flurries at the mass of iron above, the vessel seemed to move past. O'Brien yelled for the two seamen to give slack to the tying rope and start rowing away. The eerie sounds of metal over rock continued, and as the men stared upward, the vessel slid off the reef with a sharp list to the other side. Her head was low in the water, with the hub of the propeller shaft just at water level, and the *Umatilla* rose mightily and fell in the sea with her sails set, the sheets to windward giving her a twenty-five-degree list. She drifted bodily toward the Flattery rocks, which the seamen could just make out, since the snowstorm was thinning out for the time. When the tying rope tightened, the men allowed their raft to be pulled behind by the drifting ship.

Concerned about the ship's steep angle, O'Brien stared at the vessel before concluding that the wind-whipped sails were causing the problem. "We were wondering why she didn't go down," he said, "and we came to the conclusion the steam pumps had indeed pumped out enough water from the forward ballast tank to counteract the sea inside the forward holds."

Due to the force of the collision, the bow with its "busted nose" was low in the water; however, the *Umatilla* seemed to have stabilized in the ocean, and Dynamite Johnny decided that the ship was still seaworthy. He ordered the two seamen to "pull hard and tighten the dripping line" to the ship. When the raft was at the *Umatilla*'s side, the mate pulled hard on the line to bring himself to the hull. However, O'Brien's frozen hands couldn't pull him up the rope. One of the seamen handed him a small flask of whiskey. Dynamite Johnny took deep draughts of the sharp liquid, rubbed some on his stiffened hands, and then tossed the empty container into the ocean.

He grabbed the rope and swung off, only to be slammed painfully against the ship's hull when a large wave broke over them. Coated now with ice, his hands painfully inched up the rope, which was covered with icicles. His soaked clothing, its heavy weight, and the icy conditions sent a ripple of fear through his mind that he might not make it. But the anxiety and booze worked—he finally hauled himself up with a last effort, brought his legs over the railing, and collapsed to lie exhausted on the iced deck. Picking himself up, O'Brien slowly made his way through one foot of snow to a storeroom, grabbed a Jacob's ladder, and threw it down.

Once the two sailors were also onboard, the ship continued to veer out of control and close in on the reef. They knew they had to control the whipping sails—and fast. Hoisting the foretopmast sail, the men sheeted her to the windward and then let the main sheet swing also to the wind. Although pounding and slatting in the wind currents with crackling sounds, the large, iced sail was finally able to take hold. O'Brien headed to the bridge and shifted the steering gear from its inoperable steam control to hand steering. The men jibed the sails over so that the wind came over the *Umatilla*'s starboard quarter.

Staring out from their stations, the sailors saw their ship closing toward more bleak rocks and crashing seas. Shouting commands back and forth, O'Brien watched while the vessel slowly began to curve away from the reef. The whistling winds and strong northerly current pushed the steamer away broadside, and it just cleared the last rocks to drift toward the "graveyard coast" of Vancouver Island. At the same time, the men watched their safe-haven raft start falling behind. Racing to the railing, they discovered that somehow the connecting rope had been severed. With all of the lifeboats also gone, they were marooned on the *Umatilla*—to live or die.

O'Brien knew that although the ship was low in these choppy seas, the pumps were keeping the ship afloat. Staring into the engine room, they discovered the ocean had flowed up to the boiler platforms and had extinguished the fires. One of the men climbed down the iron ladder into the fore hold and watched the cargo washing around. Seeing a broken case with "straw sticking out" by the ladder, he reached for an object sticking out and gleefully grabbed a bottle of whiskey. He plucked another one from the swirling saltwater and brought both bottles to the deck. The first was passed around for a stiff shot each "to warm their innards," and the second was safely put away.

With the floods having doused the boilers in near-explosive clouds of steam, the dangerous winds now were the ship's only source of power. O'Brien estimated the vessel was moving about three knots, or a little over three miles per hour. The shifting, shrill winds pushed and pulled the *Umatilla* through the now increasing snowfall and heavy seas into the late afternoon.

The vessel rode lower in the ocean, while the seas continued to pour inside and the waves crashed higher over her gunnels. The situation worsened with each passing hour, and their prospects were dim. For three men to try to sail a 3,000-ton steamer was foolhardy at best, but O'Brien already had earned the reputation of trying to do what most would never dare—and probably shouldn't have tried. But he navigated to the nearest port, which was in Esquimalt, British Columbia, knowing that if Providence was on his side, he might just make it.

The ship slowly smacked through the heavy waves as the shaking, exhausted men tended to what sails they could. When the sailors saw their first vessel, they lowered the flag to half-mast with the Union Jack down, the signal for immediate help. A small sealing schooner approached, and a loud voice asked what they needed.

"All the men you can spare and one or two dories," O'Brien shouted back. Continuing to crash into the large gaps in the bow with heavy thuds, the massive rollers then drained away in hissing waterfalls. When the schooner's crew didn't answer while they stared at the ship's condition, Dynamite Johnny added, "And fifty dollars a day to whomever will come over and help." A sailor rowed two men through the white-capped sea to the rolling ship and returned to the bobbing schooner. With five men now working the vessel, they were able to set the square sail forward, and the ship gained another half knot. Night seemed to come too early, as the exhausted men traded watch duties on the "frigid cold" deck and then sought shelter from the winds "in the lee of the after deckhouse."

The crippled ship continued its low slog through the snarling seas while the winds kept the ocean lashed into jagged peaks. Then around midnight, the watchman picked up the faint lights of another vessel that was passing in the darkness. After firing a flare to attract the master's attention, the seamen watched the vessel's light become larger with its approach. Once it was closer, they could see that this was a large ship, and it identified itself as the steamer *Wellington*. Bound for San Francisco, the vessel anchored by the *Umatilla*, and the crew lowered a dory. The angry waves seemed to swallow the small boat, and the lantern's light swung with the swells as it came near. A man asked from below what their problem was. O'Brien answered and then shouted, "Can you give us a tow?"

The chief mate climbed up on a lowered rope ladder. "How much will you pay?" he asked. It was well-settled maritime law that a ship and its men that came to the rescue of another in "immediate peril" were entitled to be paid—and quite handsomely—for that aid. O'Brien and the *Wellington*'s mate wrangled over the price. When Dynamite Johnny simply concluded the rescuing ship and its crew would be "well paid" for its efforts, the mate agreed his crew would help out. O'Brien knew the seaman would agree, because the compensation for towing a ship as large as this one would be high indeed. However, John had been cagey in not giving in to a set price.

This wasn't, however, the end of the negotiations. Next was whether the tow would use the rope from the *Wellington* or the new four-inch hawser from the *Umatilla*. The steamer's chief mate argued, "Our orders are that you shall take our line—or we won't tow you."

"How in the hell can I haul your damn hawser on board with a handful of men? I may not have steam, but with this fair wind I can make the Columbia River by tomorrow. If you wish, you can report our location upon your arrival in port." O'Brien gave the orders to trim the sails and keep the ship on course.

The steamer's mate left but then came alongside in the longboat and shouted up, "I'll give you one more chance. If you want a tow, you'll take ours."

Dynamite Johnny again refused. He knew the drill: The *Wellington* would have a larger claim for salvage dollars if the *Umatilla* didn't even have a tow rope to use. As the men argued, it was all the dory's seamen could do to keep up with the *Umatilla* in their six-oared boat. As the huge ship "blew away from him," the steamer's chief mate finally yelled, "Heave to, we'll take your line."

O'Brien shouted his agreement. If the winds should change to a winter southwesterly storm, his ship would beach on the rocks, and "very likely" all of their lives would be lost. The steamer's crew positioned their boat under the *Umatilla*'s bow and took the hawser. The ship's "sluggish" helm was put hard over, and the bow-heavy *Umatilla* came around into the wind with her sails flapping. Within an hour, the *Wellington*'s captain changed his ship's course, came about, accepted the *Umatilla*'s line, and steamed away with its tow for the sheltered waters of the Juan de Fuca Strait and Esquimalt, British Columbia.

The rough northeast seas, snows, and winds beat against the vessels while they made their way. With the *Umatilla* down by the head and sinking lower by the hour, the mate onboard the *Wellington* kept a wary eye on the tow rope. He wouldn't hesitate to give the order to cut it immediately if the *Umatilla* began to sink. Battling the elements, including the tide, the tow ship and its captive struggled on.

Its crushed prow sliding deeper into the sea, the *Umatilla*'s low bow slowed their efforts to move through the ocean. At times, the ships seemed to inch their way through a bad spot, then nearly stop, and then start slowly up again. His vessel sailing as if it were a snowplow in worsening snows, O'Brien knew it was entirely possible the crippled ship wouldn't last long enough to find the sought-after safe waters. Seemingly waiting for one final moment to put the ship and its crew out of their misery, the bucking winds and high rollers smacked into the vessel without abatement.

The next thing Dynamite Johnny knew, a boatload of men came alongside in the dory and said they were boarding to help them make port. Knowing what this was about, he refused. The salvage claim would be higher if even more men came onboard to assist. "I don't want any further assistance," he shouted. "I have enough men now to take her into port. Your tow is all that I need."

"Can't I come on board?" said the *Wellington*'s chief mate from below.

O'Brien shouted down, "Aye! But only as a guest—and don't forget the word, 'guest'." The ship with all sails set and a northeast wind made "good weather of it." Feeling tired, O'Brien told the *Umatilla*'s two men to wake him if there was any change in the weather. He went below to his quarters for a nap.

An hour later, one of the seamen awoke O'Brien. He had seen the chief mate on deck and now "all of our sails, except one, had ripped away." O'Brien checked and saw where the ropes holding the foresails and mainsails had been cut away with a knife. It would take only a few minutes before those sails ripped themselves into pieces.

The *Wellington*'s chief mate had sabotaged the sails so the *Umatilla* couldn't discard the tow and sail by itself. O'Brien was furious. He marched to the man's room, awoke him, and clobbered him with a stick when the mate first attacked. When O'Brien worried that he might have killed the man in his anger, he poured whiskey down the man's throat. This brought the *Wellington*'s chief mate back to consciousness—and O'Brien knew he would live.

What was left of the sails began to rip away. Seeing this, O'Brien decided not to worry: His ship was under tow and working its way toward the safety of Esquimalt. As if made of crepe paper, the remaining canvas was soon shredded by the whistling winds. Keeping an intense watch over the tow, O'Brien waited out the night until the dim grays of an angry dawn worked over the horizon.

The ships had left the open sea at first light and were now by Cape Flattery. It was then that the worn-out O'Brien felt the pains of his efforts. A sharp throbbing seared through his side where he had smacked against the ship's iron hull, but he kept "working through this" with the knowledge that safety was near. The ships slowly continued on during the day.

Two miles from the harbor entrance, a chugging tug with a trail of dark smoke finally approached the vessels. The day had thankfully passed, and safety now seemed to be near. The craft approached the *Wellington*'s side, and a pilot scrambled up its ladder. The steamer's captain told O'Brien over a metallic-sounding megaphone, "Standby to anchor!" In turn, he pointed to a small wharf where he wanted his ship to be towed and shouted back through his speaker, "If you cannot go there, put me into a shoal in shallower waters."

Not feeling that his ship was yet safe, John ordered his helmsman to steer for the dock, and the two ships angled toward the wharfs. He was soon unpleasantly surprised to find the *Wellington* turn quickly around, swing the *Umatilla* out of position, and drop the towline. O'Brien was forced to anchor in the much deeper forty feet of water than where he wanted. Nightfall was quickly approaching.

Due to the towed ship's tight turn at the anchorage and an engineer's mistake on the pumps, the *Umatilla* began to take on more water. During the night, a seaman yelled that the ship was sinking—and O'Brien felt the extreme list. The vessel quickly sank and the sailors were just able to get off in time. Dynamite Johnny waited until the last minute before diving into the cold seawater from the sinking ship's bridge.

A passing lighter plucked him from the waters and brought him to shore. After borrowing dry clothing, O'Brien paid a livery stable owner fifteen dollars to drive him to nearby Victoria. Once there, he sent a telegraph message to the owners in Seattle about what had happened to their ship. He then returned to Esquimalt.

O'Brien worried about his shipmates as he began to realize what they had endured for the last forty-eight hours. "The loss of that magnificent ship, and thirty-seven of our shipmates," he fretted, "as I felt sure that blizzard of a snow-storm and rock-ribbed coast had doomed them."

After making housing arrangements for the men in Esquimalt, O'Brien felt a numbness creep over, and "all went dark." He came to in a hospital with a doctor hovering over him. The physician diagnosed that his kidney was in bad shape from the smash received against the ship's side. He was forced to stay there for two days while doctors tended to his hypothermia and internal injuries.

The *Umatilla*'s owners were understandably upset at the news of their ship's sinking, but this changed when they realized the vessel was close to shore in Esquimalt's harbor. Even during this era, however, lawyers and courts were used to resolve differences. The owners of the *Wellington* strongly pushed their claim for a $50,000 rescue fee, while the *Umatilla*'s owners argued the *Wellington*'s cutting of the tow in deep water had caused the loss and demanded $100,000 for the ship's sinking. The insurance company, Lloyd's, responded by filing its own lawsuit arguing that the *Umatilla*'s Captain Worth was the one who caused the loss. During this time, Dynamite Johnny O'Brien received wide publicity. But although wondering where he stood in all of the financial goings-on, John returned to enjoy time with his family.

*　*　*

The Oregon Improvement Company owned the sunken ship, and it had valued the vessel before the loss at $350,000. Any salvage operations would have been near impossible by Umatilla Reef—the name afterwards given to the rock—had the vessel sunk in those deep, foreboding waters. Although the ship lay peacefully in calmer harbor waters, the continuing storms and cold weather delayed any work being started until late spring.

The owners first requested that English salvagers come to Esquimalt to see if the ship could be saved, but they then decided it wasn't economically possible or timely to ship the necessary equipment to that faraway port. Learning about the challenge, Captain Thomas P. H. Whitelaw of San Francisco traveled there, inspected the site, and agreed to raise the vessel for $60,000 if he was successful. If he wasn't, then under his contract, Whitelaw wouldn't receive one dime for his efforts, including the costs of his equipment, men, and out-of-pocket expenses. The owners couldn't award him the bid fast enough.

The sunken ship was massive—as long as a football field—and had extensive damage to her bow. With the *Umatilla* sinking in deeper water and listing badly on the bottom, the task of raising this vessel was daunting. Whitelaw's men encased the vessel in a watertight cofferdam that was 321 feet long by 40 feet across, and his crews used 400,000 board feet of lumber with forty tons of iron in building the immense corral. The number of workers ranged from ninety to two hundred men, and he employed ten divers alone for the underwater work.

The salvage project included patching the gaping holes and building an artificial bow from concrete. The workers built support beams inside the ship to restrain the strong water pressure, and large water tanks were sunk on both sides to give additional buoyancy when the water was pumped out of the long containers. Divers laboriously worked chains underneath the hull and pontoons and then lashed the tanks to the ship. Storms raged, waves rose, and winds howled during the entire project.

When the work was finally completed, the huge steam-driven pumps threw out seawater at the rate of forty tons per minute—an awesome display like the release channels at a flooded dam—to suck the water from the cofferdam, hull, and pontoons. These actions made the ship lighter and caused the pontoons to lift powerfully from underneath the ocean. As Whitelaw noted, the construction took over five months to ready the ship to be raised, but it took only twenty minutes to bring the *Umatilla* successfully to the surface.

From time to time, Dynamite Johnny traveled to Esquimalt and watched the salvage operations taking place. He became acquainted with Captain Whitelaw, who was a highly regarded ship salvager, and the two became friends. O'Brien stated that in those operations, two men tragically died.

Among the divers employed during this time, Whitelaw had hired one by the name of McLaughlin. When workers onboard the sunken ship saw McLaughlin's alarm signal line being frantically pulled up and down, they tried to haul him up by his attached rope. This failed. Another diver headed down to "clear things below." When both divers were brought up, O'Brien saw that "poor McLaughlin's eye piece in his helmet was broken and his face almost as black as ink." Apparently a broken piece of the hull had pierced his helmet when the vessel shifted on the bottom.

The next fatality occurred when one of the heavy cofferdam planks fell twenty feet and struck a worker across his skull. "I was close by in a skiff," O'Brien wrote. "His brains were oozing out through his skull. To this day, I can see the poor fellow's lips and body quivering; after one look by the doctor, he quickly said, 'The man is dead.'"

During this time, the legal controversies swirled over the ultimate responsibility for the accident, the amount of salvor awards, and the rights to insurance proceeds. A maritime inquiry was convened in Seattle over the question of fault, and this investigation held that Captain Worth was blameless. The given testimony pointed to the presence of the strong northerly current during the snowstorm, and the board concluded the *Umatilla* would have grounded on that uncharted reef regardless of what the captain could have done. Although exonerated from all blame, Worth felt very uncomfortable that it was his chief mate, Dynamite

Johnny O'Brien, who brought the ship safely into port. The claims and lawsuits were quietly settled later.

The investigators and board of inquiry highly commended O'Brien for his acts of bravery, which gave Captain Worth even more disappointment, and not to be outdone, the British Admiralty decidedly congratulated Captain Whitelaw, saying that his work was the "most scientific piece of work most masterly handled that they had ever known." Both men received widespread acclaim for their actions, and the newspapers were "generous" in their coverage of what took place. The two men's careers became notable from this point on, and Whitelaw over time became the premier ship salvager on the West Coast. (T. P. H. Whitelaw's work on the *Umatilla* and other master "wreckers" is described in the book *Taking the Sea*, by this author.)

Neither man received a reasonable financial return for his actions. Although the company officers were happy to pay Whitelaw his agreed fee, it is apparent that owing to the high costs of that salvage operation, he didn't make a profit. O'Brien's experience was worse. The Lloyd's insurance agent and the owners praised Dynamite Johnny for his heroics, but they offered him only fifty dollars for his saving of the ship.

When the general manager of Lloyd's, one Mr. Howard, told him the reward was ten pounds, or then fifty dollars, O'Brien considered this to be an insult. He smiled at the man and said:

> If I had abandoned the ship, as our captain insisted I should, your company would have had to pay over three-hundred thousand dollars. I lost all my effects, including a sixty-seven dollar gold watch. You know I tried to put the ship alongside the dock or in shoal waters—and you have brought suit for $100,000 on that evidence. It will cost you $60,000 to raise her and $25,000 to put her in shape as she was before the accident, and you are offering me fifty dollars. I consider that an insult and I quit right now.
>
> I was a member of the crew that remained alone on a raft in a snowstorm. The captain gave orders to pull me in his boat and the result is you have your ship in port. Good bye, Mr. Howard. I'm going to Portland.

He turned in his resignation. The owners then offered him the command of the ship—and he turned that down. Their argument was that O'Brien, as a member of the crew, could not be rewarded as a salvor. According to the lawyers he consulted, a different legal conclusion stood out: Although a ship's master cannot save, or be a salvor, of his own ship, members of the crew may become so under "extraordinary circumstances"—and these were present.

With the two men he pulled onto the raft, O'Brien hired one of the best admiralty lawyers on the Pacific Coast. A week later, the attorney sued the owners in a San Francisco federal court over the owed salvor award. O'Brien arranged for the two sailors to remain in San Francisco, "ready for a call from the lawyers," and paid them "a certain amount" each month. There is no mention of Captain O'Brien receiving any settlement moneys, so it's assumed he had the satisfaction of receiving the accolades—but no money. With the way legal proceedings are drawn out, O'Brien more than likely let the matter lapse when he was away at sea. The result would have been quite different today—if anything due to the movie rights alone.

Once repaired, the *Umatilla* was placed by its owners back on West Coast runs. She had more misadventures during her long career—no different from any other ship during these times. She smashed into another uncharted reef in September 1896, this time while crossing from Victoria to Port Townsend, Washington, in a thick fog. Two nearby lighthouses weren't sounding their foghorns; owing to an exceptionally dry summer and heavy fog use, these sentinels didn't have any freshwater left to run their steam boilers. During the panic, the captain and crew forgot the *Umatilla* was equipped with watertight doors and didn't shut them. With water pouring in through a thirty-foot hole in her bottom, the captain beached the vessel close to, ironically, one of the lighthouses and its silent foghorn. After these repairs, the ship quickly came back into service.

Struck by gold fever like everyone else, novelist Jack London boarded the *Umatilla* in San Francisco Bay on July 25, 1897. Loaded down with heavy clothing and camping gear, would-be prospectors crowded the decks, hallways, and rooms. The *Umatilla* carried London to Port Townsend on the Puget Sound, where he boarded another steamer bound for Juneau, Alaska. He and others in his group then made the difficult, dangerous passage through mountains, passes, and river rapids to the Klondike goldfields. His experiences during this time and the Alaskan wilds became the subject of his most famous works. (This is further described in chapter 14, "Jack London and the Gold Rush.")

Five years later, the *Umatilla* steamed into Seattle harbor, and the pilot began directing the ship into her docking space. Due to his error, the huge vessel didn't slow down in its approach; the ship "sailed majestically" through docks and walkways, finally coming to a stop when her large iron nose became embedded in a street. Before tugs could pull her away with little damage, waterfront traffic had to detour around the huge ship that was now marooned on land.

An insane passenger later that year was certain he was the captain of the *Umatilla* and the only officer who could save the vessel from impending doom. As soon as he was on the bridge, he began ordering the crew to do what he felt would safeguard the vessel's trip, all to the astonishment of the real master, Captain Nopander. The passenger didn't pick up, however, that the crew disregarded those commands and went on about their business. Nopander decided to humor his deluded guest, who periodically yelled out orders from the bridge while the ship steamed down the coast. Once safely in San Francisco Harbor, the passenger turned over the ship's operations to Captain Nopander, all as agreed beforehand between the two men. Several attendants in white coats then took him away.

Steaming to the coal bunkers through a heavy fog in Tacoma three years later, the ship slammed into a lumber schooner and smashed in a large section of the schooner's hull. The *Umatilla* was relatively undamaged. Navigating the ship later through another dense fog, Captain Nopander sounded the ship's whistle every minute for a returning echo. When he heard an answering whistle that seemed to be very close, the captain slowed the ship down to listen if another vessel was nearby. Preparing for what seemed to be an imminent collision, anxious passengers and crewmembers crowded the decks. Suddenly a huge whale breached alongside and blew water from its blowhole over the people with a large gush. The "ship" then vanished underneath the sea.

The *Umatilla* cruised for a number of years over the Pacific on different routes. In 1918, the veteran steamship became stranded on one of its transpacific voyages off the coast of Japan. Although everyone onboard was saved, the old ship was abandoned when thought to be a total loss. But she still lived a charmed life. Over the months, the tides and storms gradually built up a large sandbar between the shore and the listing ship. The Japanese realized their workers could dismantle the ship and take the pieces over the sand and shallow waters. They obtained the plans of the ship from the original builders and then reassembled the *Umatilla* just as they had broken it up—plate by plate and section by section. The Japanese then operated this extraordinary and seemingly impervious vessel for many more years. After World War II, the ship was eventually sold for precious scrap, having outlived the men who had built her over six decades before.

10

THE PIRATES AND EMILY IN THE CHINA SEAS

Dynamite Johnny soon took command in Portland of the full-sail ship the *Alden Besse*. His old enemy and competitor, Captain Allen Noyes, was now his good friend, and true to his word, he allowed O'Brien to bring his wife. Emily joined him along with Ned, their five-year-old son, on this voyage into the China Seas. He had his needed experience on a steamer, but now he not only was the master of a ship but also would be with his family. The time was October 1884.

O'Brien looked forward to this voyage, and soon he was sailing over the warmer Pacific Ocean waters. He hadn't counted on a few changes that had taken place, however. For starters, Emily had redecorated his cabin with "turkey red" curtains and gilt-framed pictures, because this room would be their home for many months. She had the furniture polished and the carpets changed to a "brighter" color.

The captain's stateroom was "nice sized," and it took up the space of two ordinary staterooms. The connected bathroom had a large saltwater tank—filled each morning by the deckhands—and a spare stateroom opened into this space. A bulkhead divided these private quarters from Ned's small room and a dining room, off which were the pantry, storeroom, and the steward's room. The officers were berthed in two staterooms on either side with a separate entrance.

John and Emily's room was furnished with a large built-in double bed that had drawers underneath for clothes storage. The furniture included a great curved-back

131

armchair beside the bed, a chronometer case, and a marble-topped dresser with two wide drawers. Against the forward wall was a marble-topped cupboard called the "wine cabinet." This article of furniture didn't hold wine but did safeguard the bottles of whiskey and brandy. In the center of the captain's stateroom was a table solidly bolted through the carpet to the floor. A large kerosene lamp hung over it, tightly secured in an ornamental iron frame. The table had a marble top that was enclosed by a three-inch wooden rail when the ship was at sea.

Across one corner of the rail was a rack designed to hold an earthenware water cooler and glasses. Within the short enclosure, the couple kept their knicknacks, including a tobacco box, a tin of sulfur-tipped matches, his navigation books, and whatever reading they wanted. Next to the table was the large upholstered armchair, which was also securely anchored.

Under the captain's pillow was a coiled speaking tube that came down from the wheelhouse on the quarterdeck. The mates had standing orders that during their watches the captain was to be notified if anything unusual or drastic occurred. Across the cabin was the entrance to Ned's very narrow room. A large, coverless wooden box, about three feet high and three feet wide, stored his toys and clothing.

The medical center was in one corner of the bathroom. A cabinet had bottles and jars on its shelves containing colorful powders and liquids. A small counter provided workspace in front of the cabinet, and below it were drawers, one filled with medical books, the others with gruesome-looking surgical instruments and appliances. In the corner of the bathroom was a washbasin that had a faucet with a spring shutoff, which prevented "extravagance" with the scarce freshwater. Opening off the bathroom was a toilet that flushed with saltwater. The water for the washstand and toilet came from tanks that were periodically filled through fittings in the deck covering the after house.

Captain O'Brien would have breakfast at 7:30 A.M. with Emily, if possible, and then make his inspections, solve the inevitable maintenance problems, have dinner (usually midafternoon), and try to spend his evening time with his family. Depending on the weather, they could be on the poop deck (the decking over their rooms at the stern) or in their cabin. He could read by the light of a lantern or talk with Emily and the mate on watch. Emily was always busy talking with him, walking around the ship, reading, writing notes, embroidering, playing with Ned, enjoying the scenes, or doing any number of activities.

When the captain was tied up by an emergency or other problem, Emily could be served breakfast either in their stateroom or in the officers' dining room. Either way, Captain O'Brien usually ate with the officers in the dining room. This room was about fourteen feet long by twelve feet wide. The long dining table had a pewlike bench on both sides, and the backs were reversible for cleaning. The captain's wooden armchair was at the forward end, and its back and seat were

Vallejo Street Wharf in San Francisco in 1860s with moored full-sail vessels; O'Brien first came to the United States in 1868 and stayed for good. *San Francisco Maritime National Historical Park.*

The magnificent sail ships like the *E. B. Hutton* in this picture were commonplace into the 1900s. *San Francisco Maritime National Historical Park.*

This rare picture shows the *Edwin James,* the first ship that O'Brien was an officer on and captained in the 1870s.

Honolulu's harbor was a frequent destination in the late nineteenth century for South Seas ships, including that of O'Brien's *Edwin James. Hawaii State Archives.*

King David Kalakaua was the ruler of Hawaii from 1874 to 1891 and gave banquets in honor of the *Edwin James*'s owner and O'Brien. *Hawaii State Archives*.

Until the great Iolani Palace was built in 1882, Kalakaua entertained guests at his palatial residences. Although this picture is of the old Iolani Palace—and not used during this time—it shows what this structure would have been like. *Hawaii State Archives*.

Iolani Palace was the official residence of the Hawaiian Kingdom's last two monarchs—King Kalakaua, who built the palace in 1882, and his sister and successor, Queen Liliuokalani. *Hawaii State Archives.*

This is another rare picture of an O'Brien ship; this time it's the *Alden Besse.*

The *Alden Besse* with its sails furled while anchored at Puget Sound. Puget Sound Maritime Historical Society.

Two pirate ships from Nine Pin Rocks tried to capture the *Alden Besse* off Hong Kong but instead received a deadly surprise.

Gale winds were terrifying on these ships, and this picture is believed to be of the *Alden Besse*.

Dynamite Johnny received his nickname and national recognition for his efforts to save the *Umatilla*, not once but twice. *San Francisco Maritime National Historical Park*.

This undated picture, believed to be in the 1900s, is of Captain O'Brien.

The Klondike and Nome Gold Rushes brought about an unprecedented migration to Alaska and the Arctic. This picture is of a typical gold rush vessel, this time bound for Nome. *Anchorage Museum of History and Art*.

The lawless town of Skagway was at the head of the Lynn Canal, and from there, prospectors had to work their way over the Chilkoot Pass. *University of Alaska, Fairbanks, Walter and Lillian Phillips Collection.*

Chilkoot Pass was a tortuous climb for the would-be Klondike-headed prospectors in frigid cold with heavy packs; the human mule trains had hundreds of miles more to travel. *Alaska State Library, William Norton Photograph Collection.*

Soapy Smith and his gang ran Skagway until his untimely death some months later. *Alaska State Library, Wickersham State Historic Site Collection.*

The *Buford*—three decades later captained by O'Brien to the South Seas—is pictured at Skagway during gold rush days. *University of Alaska, Fairbanks, J. Bernard Moore Family Collection.*

Horse-drawn wagons and unloaded freight on the beach at Nome, Alaska, in late 1900; the lighters used to offload prospectors and their supplies from the anchored ships were typically large shallow-draft barges. *Anchorage Museum of History and Art.*

A storm strikes Nome, Alaska, during the same period. *Anchorage Museum of History and Art.*

In 1905 the 54-year-old O'Brien captained the new 4,000-ton *Seward* on different Arctic runs, including a near disaster with heavy railroad cars and rails being shipped to Katalla, but forced to a safer port at Cordova in the Prince William Sound. *Seward Community Library Collection*.

In his later years, Captain O'Brien and his *Victoria* were the most popular for years on the Arctic and Alaskan runs. Longer than a football field, this ship was usually the first to plow through the ice on the Nome run and usually the last one out in the late autumn. *University of Alaska, Fairbanks, John Zug Collection*.

Regardless of weather, O'Brien's *Victoria* made stops at numerous small coastal towns and cannery settlements in helping to pave that state's development. *University of Alaska, Fairbanks, Candace Waugaman Collection.*

This classic picture of O'Brien and Buster Keaton was taken when the silent-screen actor used the *Buford* to film *The Navigator*; Dynamite Johnny was a consultant and used in the public relations efforts. *Puget Sound Maritime Historical Society.*

upholstered in black leather. This chair, the table, and the benches were also screwed tightly to the floorboards. At the after end of the room, by the doorway that led to the captain's staterooms, was a paneled casing enclosing the mizzenmast (which went down to the keel) and to which an oil lamp was attached.

When the *Besse* first sailed away, Emily became seasick. The ship's motion didn't coordinate well with what her body was telling her, and it took a few days before she found her "sea legs." Once that happened, she was happy being with her husband on the voyage.

The crew and officers were polite and always accommodating to the family. When Emily came on deck, the men bowed slightly to her and would always say, "Good morning, Mrs. O'Brien." Cursing was nearly nonexistent on this voyage, for any offenders would have to contend with Captain O'Brien. Her mere presence muted the usual in-your-face conflicts and confrontations. The sailors would play with Ned and were ever watchful when he was on deck.

Ned loved the cats onboard. The seamen, however, loved them because a good "ratter" could kill a dozen or so rats every night. No matter what sail ship was traveling, rats seemed to abound. A time-honored trap was to half fill a barrel with water, bait the lid with cheese, and balance the lid on a pivot. When the rats scampered for the cheese, the lid would tilt and slide them into the barrel. The sides were well greased, and every morning there would be dozens of dead rodents in the barrel.

* * *

The voyage over was smooth and uneventful. The *Alden Besse* soon docked in the muddy waters of Hong Kong among the myriad sampans and junks. The owners had invested $5,000 in spars as part of the cargo, and once the ship docked, O'Brien sold them for $25,000 in gold. Most deals didn't go this well, but Noyes and O'Brien had seen the need for these large spare parts.

He did come close to meeting his Maker because of the spars, however. The captain told Emily he planned to get the poles over the side to the buyers. His wife pointed out that he should stay away and let the mate, Mr. Monroe, do this since he knew more about handling them. John felt that he needed to be sure no one was hurt in the process.

While walking forward, O'Brien noticed the ship had a slight starboard list. The crew was in the process of sliding a giant one-hundred-foot-long spar over the bow, and this large pole was resting on a shorter one that had been lashed down. Swinging on heavy tackle, a chain sling was wrapped around the spar and sliding it over. To start the heavy pole moving, a sailor on O'Brien's order jerked the wood piece with a large crow bar. Due to the starboard list, the giant spar rolled heavily toward that side, caught the tackle, and ripped the heavy line from the seaman's hands.

When O'Brien jumped back, one foot stepped into a loop of the flying line, and his legs flew up as his shoulders struck the deck. Dynamite Johnny was carried quickly upwards by his trapped foot, and he realized he had to get his foot clear before reaching the sharp edges of the sheave block, through which the rope was whipping. He would have been severely injured, if not killed, by the thirty-foot drop to the deck. By the time he cleared the line, he was unfortunately fifteen feet above the planks and fell straight down. He smashed down on the hard deck planks onto his head and back.

The mate and another sailor picked up the half-conscious, "livid gray" O'Brien. His five-year-old son saw him fall and ran crying to Emily. She ran frantically toward her husband but stopped when she saw he was alive, surrounded by sailors. "I told you not to do that!" she said loudly.

"Em', don't scold me now, please," he quietly replied. The mate took O'Brien to his cabin, his body aching "all over and throbbing." Emily gave him a half glass of brandy and rubbed lotion over his bruises. He lay there for two hours until he remembered he had to play the *Great Admiral*'s captain for the billiard championship at the Hong Kong Hotel. The American captains had been playing there for several days, and these two were the only undefeated ones left. There was no chance O'Brien would miss this.

Satisfied he didn't break any bones and—although the worse for wear—was going to live, Emily left the stateroom so that her husband could rest. He didn't. As soon as she left, Dynamite Johnny slowly arose, took a bath, dressed, and snuck away. He hailed a rickshaw and went to the hotel. Deciding this wasn't such a good idea due to the continuing strong spasms of pain and deep aches, O'Brien ordered a glass of whiskey and took a deep swallow. He played in front of twenty other captains—and won—although it isn't known how many "swallows" of liquor he took during the competition. When he returned to the *Besse* and showed Emily his hard-won prize, she simply said, "A friend that knows us says the only way you're going to die is by a hanging—and I think he's right."

Long stays in Hong Kong from two to three months were the rule. Captains were selling or unloading their cargo and then searching for more to take back. This time allowed for diversions such as the billiard's championship, luncheons, and even social balls.

At a luncheon given later by the American consul, Captain O'Brien and Emily met a Captain Bradford, then the executive officer of the U.S. frigate *Trenton*, and in later years, a rear admiral in the U.S. Navy. He invited them aboard his ship, along with a small group of naval officers and government officials, for a seven-course dinner. John was proud of his wife, seated to the right of an admiral, since the men gave her the "most deferential attention." He always thought he had married one of the loveliest women that Portland, Oregon, "gave to the world," and on this night he was sure of it. The admiral showed her around the ship and then asked to escort her off. Captain Bradford said smilingly, "Admiral, seniority is my only excuse for not having the honor of being Mrs. O'Brien's escort over our ship on this fine evening."

One week later, the governor of Hong Kong was to give his formal ball, and the men and women both needed to be in formal dress. Having received an engraved invitation, O'Brien bought what he thought was a beautiful lace evening gown for his wife to wear. When she tried on the expensive dress, however, she came out sadly and said she couldn't wear it. The totally confused husband asked why, and Emily quickly replied, "The dress is cut too low— it would be immodest."

John answered that all the ladies in the Orient wore low-necked dresses. He felt hurt, knowing she had a "wonderful" figure and feeling the dress was just right. Basically, the captain wanted to show off his wife socially and had the confidence to do this. When she refused once more, John angrily put on his coat and hat and left for shore. He took a rickshaw to the hotel, located two miles away, but when he entered the exquisite mahogany and mirrored bar, he knew he had made a mistake and immediately returned to his ship.

When the captain arrived by rickshaw on the dock, he ran into Emily who was hailing another one. Heading to the hotel, she was wearing the new dress. She had found a solution to the problem by placing "fluffy stuff" around the edge of her bosom, which satisfied her feelings for decorum. O'Brien immediately apologized.

Upon entering the grand ballroom, the couple found elegant young ladies with their escorts, a band in full-dress uniform from a nearby English battleship, and couples "grandly dressed" in combinations of fine ballroom gowns, pressed tuxedos, and shiny military regalia. The large room was complete with a glittering crystal chandelier, a large orchestra in front, red-clothed tables in the back, an open bar to one side, and huge Chinese pennants draped on the walls. This was the governor's annual "grand" affair for dignitaries, and that included the ship captains who were known in the port.

When John and Emily were dancing, however, he unfortunately stepped on her dress and she made a "slighting remark" about this lack of grace. O'Brien "flew off the handle" and told her that was the last time he would dance with her that night. He stomped off to guzzle champagne at the bar and left her for the rest of the evening with a group of naval officers. Occasionally he came out and watched Emily dancing with the uniformed men. He apparently wasn't jealous, with the knowledge that everyone would end up back at his ship.

The affair wasn't over until past three o'clock in the morning. He watched amusingly as his Emily left the ballroom with two escorts, one of whom was a "handsome devil," young Lieutenant Patrick "Pat" Hourigan of the *Trenton*. Emily looked over at her husband and nodded but didn't say anything. The two escorts placed her in a sedan chair and then called to have their wheeled chairs run up next to hers. They took off, with Johnny trailing behind in another rickshaw. The group made their way over the deserted, unpaved streets, past empty food stands, fish markets, and open-air restaurants. The night air was warm as the human taxis weaved their way to the damp, salty-smelling docks.

Once everyone arrived by the *Besse*, O'Brien invited the two men to have a "very late dinner" onboard—or depending on the view, an early breakfast—an invitation that delighted Hourigan. The naval officer afterwards bunked out from too much drinking in one of the officer quarters, and Johnny later took him back to the *Trenton*. Emily then told her husband about how the lieutenant's dance with her had cost him shore leave. When his stiff gold epaulet (the ornamental shoulder insignia showing rank) continued to uncomfortably touch her cheek, she asked him to remove it. Hourigan did even better: He took off both epaulets. When the admiral noticed this lack of dress, he sent over an aide, who told the officer to put them back on. For the infraction, Hourigan lost his shore leave.

For ten years on every New Year's Day, Hourigan wrote to O'Brien a brief, supposedly jocular note: "Old man, are you dead yet? I'm still waiting for your widow. Pat Hourigan." Dynamite Johnny's replies were equally brief but to the point, "I'm still in love with her and very much alive." This result could be expected when unattached young men came in contact with attractive women, married or not.

During this anchorage in Hong Kong, O'Brien met the legendary King O'Keefe, the white ruler of the island of Yap, located in the Micronesia islands of the Pacific. According to O'Brien, O'Keefe had deserted from an English ship that had anchored in the bay at Yap. The sailor married one of the native king's daughters, and when the king died, O'Keefe declared himself to be the successor.

At that time, Yap was noted for its stone money, known as Rai: large doughnut-shaped carved disks up to twelve feet in diameter, although most were much smaller. To quarry the stones, the Yapese sailed to distant islands and dealt with the sometimes hostile natives. The scarcity of the disks and the risks made them valuable. The enterprising Irishman David O'Keefe hit upon the idea in 1874 of hiring the Yapese to import more "money" in the form of shiploads of large stones. O'Keefe traded these stones with the islanders for other commodities such as sea cucumbers and copra—and called himself the king. (The U.S. dollar is the currency in use today.)

O'Keefe was fifty, bronzed by years in the sun, and tall. He was in Hong Kong for his annual copra-selling voyages, along with visiting ten of his children, whom he had placed in a private school. The other ten, he told Johnny, were in an Australian school. When O'Brien exclaimed that this was indeed a family, O'Keefe answered: "Well, I have what you would call a harem. One wife would be monotonous." He explained that when his first native wife died, he decided to adopt the local customs and take more than one.

The king owned five schooners that traded throughout the region, including the one now anchored in Hong Kong with its cargo of pearls, shells, copra, and coconuts. After this cargo was sold, he would enjoy the city and find other goods to bring to the various trading stations along the way home. By this time, his ventures were simply "coining money," as he told O'Brien. The two had met by the waterfront one day, and the gregarious O'Brien had invited King O'Keefe to come onboard the *Besse* and dine. He found the man to be one of the most interesting characters he had ever met. Savoring an after-dinner brandy and a fine cigar in the captain's stateroom, O'Keefe offered to set O'Brien up in business.

"Now, captain, should your dear wife ever die—which a kind God forbids— don't pine away in the states. Come to Yap and I will give you a half interest in all that I own, including my harem, and if I should pass on, I will have arrangements made for you to take my place as the King of Yap."

When O'Brien asked why he was making such a generous offer, King O'Keefe sighed and said, "I'm becoming an old man and perhaps this is the way of life. But I am a pretty good judge of character." He explained he needed a younger successor and wanted to spend less time traveling away from his wives. The copious amounts of liquor drunk could also have contributed, and O'Keefe later commented he was from the same town of Cork—and that his mother's maiden name was O'Brien.

When O'Keefe left, he gave the captain until noon the next day to give his decision. O'Brien thanked him, smiled, and escorted the king off his ship. Once he returned, Emily said dryly:

> That man must be crazy to make such a proposition to you in front of me. He may be King O'Keefe of the Island of Yap, but if I die first and you should ever go to that island, I will haunt you day and night, especially if you took over that old harem.

As O'Brien wrote later, "Needless to say, the next day I gratefully refused his more than generous offer."

* * *

After returning to the West Coast, the *Besse* sailed to Victoria, British Columbia, in October 1886, its lower holds heavy with cargo and carrying 450 Chinese passengers housed in the b'tween deck (the deck immediately below the main deck of a sailing ship). After discharging and taking on more cargo, the vessel headed back to Hong Kong. When the ship crossed the Pacific midway and stopped at Honolulu, 100 more returning Chinese boarded the ship, which left the crowded interior deck with 550 Chinese, all laborers and their families.

Ten days after leaving Hawaii, the chief mate ran into the captain's stateroom at three o'clock in the morning and woke everyone up with the sharp yell, "The ship is on fire!" O'Brien turned over to Emily and said quietly, "Don't worry, we'll have that out in a few minutes." He quickly dressed and dashed out. Along the way, he grabbed two fire grenades, at which his son Ned said, "Don't be afraid, mama, papa will put it out with his 'bottles'." (Containing a mixture of saltwater and chemicals, these handheld glass fire extinguishers were meant to be thrown at the base of a fire.)

Despite his outward coolness, O'Brien was very concerned because he had a cargo fire at sea. Nothing is dreaded more than being on a fiery ship with nowhere to go, except into the churning ocean with its sharks, typhoons, and drowning waters. He rushed onto the deck and fearfully saw the flickering light inside the hold and smelled the acrid smoke swirling about the vessel. Not only were all of his passengers at risk, so was his family. O'Brien shouted for his sailors to man the deck pump and throw the suction hose over the side. As others rushed topside, confusion reigned with more shouts, questions, and fears.

The captain ordered the sailors not needed to go below, but they didn't listen, being too worried about staying below. O'Brien couldn't maneuver where he wanted in the thicket of jostling crew and passengers, so he climbed on a lower yard with the two fire grenades, worked his way over the masses, and then leaped "as far as he could" to land among the frightened Chinese passengers on the other side.

He forced himself over the coolies, who were lying prone on the deck to avoid the heat and smoke blasting up. Making his way to the fiery hold, the captain threw both grenades into the fire, one exploding with a fierce "bang" and the other bursting with less noise. The fire seemed to subside, but the smoke was so thick that O'Brien stumbled and fell face-first onto the planks. His crew by now was hosing powerful streams of saltwater into the open hatch, which caused sharp sizzling sounds and hissing clouds of steam to rise.

The men fiercely battled the conflagration. Over the next hours, the dense smoke mercifully lightened and then became sharp vapors. The hold became filled with the sea, and the ship settled into the ocean, but the blaze was finally brought under control. The sailors opened the fore and after hatches, turned the ventilator system of openings to the wind, and brought up the overcome passengers from the b'tween deck. More than one hundred people were lying on the top deck, the trade winds and crew working to comfort them. Although several suffered from smoke inhalation, no one died.

The fire smoldered for another day before finally being extinguished, but the pungent smell of smoke came from every canvas sail, every rigging, and the ship's structure for the duration of the voyage. The seamen worked the pumps for another day to remove the massive volumes of saltwater inside the hold—equivalent to what happens after a major storm when the seas pound through an open hatch. Chips and others started the needed repairs of the charred wood and weakened joists—but they were lucky this time. They survived, and permanent repairs would be completed after reaching Hong Kong.

On its voyage back to Victoria, the *Besse* hauled a valuable load of hardwood, teak, and mahogany; $50,000 worth of raw silk in sheets piled into tight bales; and a consignment of $75,000 of prepared opium for "medicinal purposes," among other valuable goods. Temporary bulkheads were built to hold the contents in different locations, and old tarps were stretched over the walls and floors to keep moisture out. The opium was packaged in numerous "square, grey, firmly sealed tins," and these were locked away in the captain's cabin inside the cupboards. The shipment was listed on the manifest and legal; with his experiences before, O'Brien carefully saw that every legal requirement was met and every needed signature obtained. Onboard were four hundred Chinese laborers, bound again for construction work on the American and Canadian railway.

A smattering of English and American passengers were also onboard, including one Englishman who had finished a big-game hunt through Africa, India, and China. He brought along his trophies, as well as two large hunting guns. O'Brien still had his Winchester rifle, two hundred rounds of ammunition, and two five-pound brass cannons, a necessary precaution when sailing in these pirate-infested waters.

When the ship was cleared from Hong Kong, all of its fore and aft canvas sails were set. Most of the passengers were out of sight in the b'tween deck, their bulky rolls of bedding, boxes, and inadequate bundles of clothing scattered about in the forward deckhouse to be later brought down. Unfortunately, the pump hoses spraying jets of saltwater in cleaning the decks had also inadvertently splattered some of the passengers' belongings. The voyage was off to an inauspicious start.

Leaving behind the numerous smaller sampans, boat shanties, and junks plying their trades, the *Alden Besse* slowly headed out to the open sea through the shipping lanes. As the ship worked its way out, a sampan "came flying alongside." One Chinese crewman hooked onto the channels, climbed onboard, and ran to the quarterdeck, where O'Brien and several passengers were watching. The odd thing was the man kept his face turned away the entire time. He handed a letter to O'Brien. The sailor quickly turned around, ran back to the side, and disappeared over the railing. The sampan then dropped back to sail away.

O'Brien opened the envelope and read the letter. Written in crude lettering, the words were simple: "You look out. Pirate man will catch you outside." The captain thought about his next step; he decided not to tell the crew and instead went to see the English big-game hunter. The captain showed him the warning.

"What are you going to do about this?" the man asked.

O'Brien thought out loud:

> Like others, I know I should anchor, wait it out, try to flag down the harbormaster, and get a gunboat to accompany us. The problem is we could wait forever and you never know how long the gunboat would guard us. Or when it would pull away and leave us in the same danger. I also don't know if the warning is true. But they did go to a lot of effort to get this to us and we do have valuable cargo onboard.

The men talked about the best plan of defense. O'Brien had his two cannons, which had been used to give gun salutes when high-ranking military and other officials came onboard to visit. They had their guns and ammunition—and they were forewarned.

O'Brien brought his mate into the discussions, and he brought up a chilling story:

> Captain, remember a few months ago when a coastal steamer was on her way to Hong Kong and the pirates stopped her. A number of the passengers were part of the plan to capture the ship. All hands were killed, except for the engineer, whom they forced to keep the engines going to unload the cargo. Then they set the ship on fire, but the engineer lived to tell the tale.

The captain remembered that during the pirates' wild celebration, the engineer was able to steal away and hide. When they couldn't find him, the pirates set the ship afire after leaving with their loot, believing the man would burn to death. When the bandits left, the engineer made his escape through a ventilation port. He grabbed the wood grating, wrenched it away, and jumped overboard. Fishermen on a passing junk saw the bright fire during the night, and when the boat came to investigate, the sailors spotted the engineer by the blazing vessel and hauled him onboard.

When they asked him what had happened, the man was frightened and didn't want to tell about the pirates in case they were friendly with them. He told them his ship had caught fire and all hands had abandoned ship, except he was drunk and passed out on his bunk. A windstorm then drove the burned-out hulk to where it was found. Once in the safety of the harbormaster's office, the engineer told what had really happened, and a later investigation corroborated his story. Thinking it over, O'Brien believed the warning was legitimate.

The captain told the Chinese supervisors to get all of the passengers on deck. O'Brien wanted to find out if there were any stowaways. When they found some, they checked everyone back into the b'tween deck, and the Chinese officials agreed to watch closely over the stowaways. Hatches were battened down and windsails (open, funnel-like canvas rigs) secured to the ventilator tops on the b'tween deck so sufficient air would pass through for the passengers.

O'Brien next readied the cannons. His men removed the canvas covers and loaded the weapons with extra charges of powder. They crammed heavy spikes, nails, nuts, and washers down the barrels. While the captain stuffed wicks into the cannons, he had two poker sticks taken to the galley to be heated red-hot. With what he had available and now ready, O'Brien ordered the crew on deck. He told them about the warning and what each should do in case of an attack. "Keep behind the bulwarks," he ordered the second mate. "And be ready to trim sail." Then they waited.

The men didn't have to wait long. The *Besse* was twelve miles outside the harbor when the captain sighted two junks that had sailed from a hidden cove on nearby Nine Pin Rocks. Through his telescope, he saw the two pirate ships had a rope attached to each bow. The junks would sail around the side of the *Besse* and snare its bow. The boarding would be swift and simple, as their momentum would drive the boats against the ship's sides and the pirates would swarm aboard. Whoever resisted would have their throats cut or be thrown overboard; what happened next would depend on how bloodthirsty they were.

"What should we do, Captain?" worried one officer.

"Nothing. Just keep sailing straight at them."

"But then what do we do?"

O'Brien told the man to stay calm. He sailed his ship straight at the junks, and to the pirates, it must have looked as if the Yankee skipper didn't know what to do—or was too frightened to do anything. He seemed to be heading right into their trap. The junks and the full-sail ship sailed at one another with the distance between them closing fast. O'Brien could see the gun-waving, machete-wielding bandits, naked to their waists and ready to board. He watched the pirates shove three "old fashioned" cannons through the junk's false ports, ready to fire a deadly crescendo of shot when close to the *Besse*'s sides.

Watching the slower boats work to stretch their hawser up from the ocean's surface, O'Brien gave a sudden order to "put the wheel hard to starboard," and the ship veered toward one. With the guillotine rope less than one hundred feet away, the ship swung past the bow of the nearest junk, the other also being to that side. At the same time, the captain ordered the bearded Englishman to light the fuse on a five-pounder. The glowing poker touched the wick, and the cannon soon exploded with a shot of iron and metal debris that whistled into the closest junk. O'Brien watched as "ten or more" of the pirates crumbled to the deck or hurtled away from where they were standing.

Giving orders to the second mate and helmsman to keep their crews low, O'Brien and the Englishman blazed away with their weapons at both boats. The pirates were surprised by the ship's movements, the cannon fire, and the rapid firing of weapons, but they fired back with their rifles. Bullets whizzed into compartments with loud "smacks" and opened small holes in the sails. In response, O'Brien gave the order for his armed men—who had been given guns and revolvers from the ship's locked gunroom—to fire at the two junk-rigged sailboats.

The battle took half an hour as the full-sail ship with guns blazing sharply angled around to pursue the junks, which had been forced to drop the tying hawser. Rifles and pistols fired indiscriminately, their "cracks" interspaced around the louder "booms" from the cannons and hunter's guns. The ship's cannons fired time after time with deadly effect, since the *Besse*'s weapons had a longer range. Throughout it all, O'Brien continued to exhort his crew to keep firing and kill every last one of the bandits. Finally the galleys withdrew, with forty pirates who weren't moving and numerous men wounded. The *Besse* had two dead and two wounded, but the ship, its cargo, and many people were safe.

When he first saw the pirates coming, the captain had told Emily to keep their son in the cabin, saying he wasn't sure about the problems that could occur. Emily ducked up from their cabin afterwards. "John, John, what's the matter? What was all that shooting? I knew we were in danger but didn't need to tell you that."

"Oh, it's nothing, Em'," O'Brien said. "We were just giving a salute to a Chinese naval vessel." She smiled knowingly back.

With the danger at an end, O'Brien ordered the helmsmen to take the ship back on course and to the open sea. Many of the Chinese passengers came up, and their eyes and manner showed their understandable fear at what they might find. The deck was littered with spent cartridges, pools of blood, shrapnel from what landed on the ship, and multitudes of bullet holes. Their excited speech and motions created a "babble of talk" that the crew didn't understand, but with the threat now passed, they headed below to finish arranging their quarters.

A few days later, Emily became slightly ill and lost her appetite. The captain called for the head steward, Lee Wong, to kill a chicken and prepare a broth for his "Missi." The steward did as he was told. Lee Wong was usually in bad humor at the beginning of any trip, since he had to leave his family at their home in Canton to again work at sea. He dressed for the first few days in a brightly colored outfit of a rounded red cap, flowing blue silk gown, and embroidered trousers, but then he would change to his faded blue uniform for the rest of the voyage.

The steward had been with him for five years and, according to O'Brien, made more money than he did because the captain allowed Lee Wong to run a slop chest for the Chinese passengers. The steward would bring as much as he could haul of dried food, notions, sandals, raingear, and blankets and then mark them up for a tidy profit. Dynamite Johnny let him travel to see his "wife or wives" in

Canton and hire another "good steward" until he returned. After a month or two, Wong would join the crew before the *Besse* sailed from Hong Kong. It wasn't easy for the steward to again be part of the crew's discipline after having such unlimited freedom at home.

When the broth was brought to Emily, she said she couldn't "take it." O'Brien had the steward take the bowl back to the galley, telling him, "She would like the bowl a couple of hours later, if you please." When the captain had the bowl brought back, he looked in it and saw that it was nearly empty. The captain said angrily, "Where's the broth?" Lee Wong said, "Where do you think?" and swore at him.

O'Brien's temper flared. Seeing this, the steward ran away, with the captain in hot pursuit. The man fled through the companionway, and O'Brien caught him when they reached the main deck. He spun the steward around, who threw a fist at him, but O'Brien punched back with a sharp, hard shot to the nose. Lee fell down with a groan, and O'Brien left him and stomped away. A few minutes later, the captain heard a knock at his cabin door. When he opened it, an apologetic Lee Wong was standing there with blood all over his face.

Looking to see that he didn't have a knife up his sleeve, O'Brien then invited his steward in. When the captain washed the blood from Lee's face, he saw where his fist had flattened the man's nose. O'Brien felt guilty for one of the few times after an altercation. He called for the carpenter and asked him to make two pine cubes, sand them down, fit them for Lee Wong's nose, and then bring them to his cabin. When Chips brought the nose plugs, O'Brien rubbed them with olive oil and gently fitted them into the broken nose. He wrapped a lengthy bandage around the man's head, and O'Brien told him that he'd ring the steward's neck if he took the plugs out before the boat in five weeks reached Victoria. When the ship arrived, O'Brien took the plugs out and looked: The broken nose had healed.

Two days later as the crew was unloading the valuable cargo, a sailor brought a large package addressed to Captain O'Brien. When he opened it, he saw that it was a "fine, large pennant," sixteen feet long, gold fringed, and with Chinese characters embroidered throughout. The captain thought this was a token of appreciation by the Chinese passengers for his service to them during the voyage. O'Brien proudly flew the flag on the mainmast. With a fresh breeze blowing at the time, its "golden letters and fringe glistened in the sun to make a beautiful sight."

Before long, a number of Chinese were on deck, looking up at the flag and laughing hard. When he called one of the giggling men over and asked what was so funny, the man said, "The flag say 'This captain number one nose fixer'." O'Brien quickly took the flag down, but he heard the story repeated by his fellow captains for years, who laughed just as heartily in the bars as far away as San Francisco.

The high point of John's adventures on the China Seas was when his wife Emily gave birth to their second child. The *Besse* was skimming to the north of the Marianna Islands when his wife told him "the stork" was going to visit within the next twenty-four hours—and not when they were anchored in Hong Kong, as originally planned. The first sharp pains of labor were upon her. O'Brien thumbed frantically through all the worn medical books in his cabin for information. He also had twenty hours of anxiety to go.

He wrote:

> A sailing ship master is expected among his manifold duties to act as a doctor for his crew, fixing broken arms, legs, ribs, and other troubles that sailors are heirs to, but a midwife's job was new to me. A gale of wind with rain squalls then swept in, and I could see our mate's oilskin jacket flapping outside our cabin window.

O'Brien heated pans of water and kept them simmering on the wood-burning galley stove. Quantities of clean clothes and newly washed blankets were on hand, and he had morphine tablets nearby. O'Brien then helped as his wife went into labor on their bunk bed. The captain wiped her brow, gave her water, wiped her with towels, kept her warm, and then took the blankets off when she said she was too hot. But there was nothing else he could do. This was all about his beloved Em'.

To make matters worse, the rains smashed down hard on the deck over their room. He heard the pellets crashing down, the winds whistling outdoors, and the sails flapping. However, this time—but for a quick look outside at times to bark orders to the mate—he stayed inside the cabin.

The baby boy was born in the midst of the storm. His healthy cry sounded inside the room as O'Brien lifted the baby away and cut the umbilical cord. Once mother and baby were "attended to," he rapped on the window and shouted, "It's a boy!" The longtime mate, Mr. Monroe, heard the captain and ran to the poop deck to yell out the news with his "thunderous voice."

Sailors not on duty ran to their quarters, and O'Brien told the steward to open two bottles of whiskey and pass drinks out to the crew in celebration. Although muffled by the outside winds and waves, the cheers sounded throughout the ship. The squall seemed to be passing, and when the clouds later lifted, the tip of an island became visible, and the sun gave muted grays of sunshine through the boiling dark clouds.

Once the celebrations ended, the crew went back to work. Emily nursed the baby in the cabin and went out only infrequently until she had regained her strength. The fact of a baby born at sea brought a spring to the crew's steps. It was as if this newborn was one of theirs—or at least was part of their life on the ocean. But for O'Brien's fight with his longtime steward, physical confrontations were nonexistent. The men were softened by Emily's and Ned's presence; the baby brought out their thoughts of families back home, and they knew they would be there soon enough.

Two weeks after arriving in Victoria, the ship "without further incident" would sail to its berth in Portland. Emily decided she wouldn't join her husband on further voyages. Although both enjoyed having the companionship of the other, their children needed to have a home on land with playmates other than tattooed sailors, schools other than Emily could provide, and playgrounds that didn't involve typhoons, pirates, or sharks.

They named the infant Francis (Frank) William O'Brien.

11

CANADIAN VOYAGES

The captain made several more transpacific voyages in the *Alden Besse*, but the owners eventually told him to sell the ship due to the declining trade. The faster tramp steamers with their heavier cargo-carrying abilities took away part of the business, and when the Canadian Pacific Railway completed its tracks, this took away the labor traffic between China and the West that the *Besse* relied on.

Pleased with the "first rate" condition of the old full-sail ship, John D. Spreckles bought the *Alden Besse*. The son of Claus Spreckles, who had built up the Hawaiian sugar empire, now owned the sugar fleets that worked the trade between Hawaii and the West Coast. Eleven years had elapsed since O'Brien's meeting with John Spreckles and Sam Parker at the Hawaiian Hotel, and he still regretted not taking their offer. Spreckles told O'Brien he could remain as the ship's captain and gave him one day to make his decision.

O'Brien knew too well the declining future of wooden sail ships. Their dependency on winds and Spartan living conditions would have to give way to ships that steamed toward their destination every hour of the day and night. Travel time on steamers was cut dramatically; good food and drink became the norm for passengers and crew alike; sailors had more comfortable quarters; and crews avoided the constant risks of having to man sails in stormy weather. The steel or iron steamers were stronger and safer with their metal hulls, of course, than those of wood in collisions; steel plates were less likely to leak than planks; and wind blasts were less likely to cause these ship to severely roll. Steel allowed vessels to be built much larger than sail ships, increasing cargo capacity and allowing more amenities, such as larger dining halls, saloons, theaters, and even swimming pools.

Dynamite Johnny chose steam over sail, shorter voyages over longer transpacific ones, and a port where he could be closer to his family. He politely declined the offer. In response to a telegrammed offer from an old friend, Captain John Irving, O'Brien took the train to Seattle from Portland and then a ship to Victoria to take charge of a passenger and freight ship, the *Premier*. Its run was the close route from Seattle, Washington, where he and Emily had decided to make their home.

The *Premier* was a steel single-screw steamer with a wooden upper structure; the ship was two hundred feet long and had a wide beam of forty-three feet with only a ten-foot draft. The Union Iron Works in San Francisco had constructed the ship in 1887 for the Canadian Pacific Navigation Company and placed it in service under American registry between Vancouver, Victoria, and Puget Sound ports. Captain O'Brien was ironically succeeding Captain Frank Worth, the hapless master of the *Umatilla* when he had been chief mate.

The manager told him the *Premier* was their only ship registered under the American flag. He agreed that O'Brien had full charge of the ship and could hire or fire crewmen, settle claims on freight for damages up to $150, give passes to anyone in the company's interest, and see that discipline was kept. A prime reason for hiring O'Brien for his first steamer captaincy was his reputation as a strong and solid disciplinarian—and this ship needed a firm hand. Captain O'Brien had acquired the nickname "the Nestor of the Pacific," or one who feared God but defied everything and everyone else with hard fists and spirit. This ship would be a challenge. The crewmen on the *Premier* were so rowdy that not only were the passengers continually complaining, but Captain Worth had given up and left.

On taking command, O'Brien told the engineer and steward to tell him immediately if they found any crewmember causing trouble or not following an order. Two days after the *Premier* left Vancouver, British Columbia, on its southern passage, Dynamite Johnny was dressed in his new blue uniform for dinner. He heard what had to be a drunken brawl on the main deck. Hurrying over to the sounds of cursing and crashing, he found two men swinging wildly at each other. One man was the American customs inspector who traveled on the ship, and the other was a fireman from the boiler room.

The "big, husky, half-drunken bruiser" was using the foulest language he had ever heard—and was a crewmember. O'Brien walked straight over and stood between the two men. He ordered the sailor, "Go to your quarters at once!"

The man spat out, "Go to hell!" and called him a string of cusswords. In an instant, O'Brien sprang at the man with his hands stretched out. One strong hand grabbed the man's throat, while his leg swung behind the fireman's, and he pushed the two over, O'Brien landing on top. With both of O'Brien's hands now strangling the cursing fireman, the man's face began turning pale. Before the captain choked the man unconscious, the chief mate ran over with handcuffs. They cuffed the man, and the struggle was over. O'Brien's new uniform, however, was "torn beyond repair."

As the captain led the fireman to lockup, the angry man quickly turned and slammed his hands down O'Brien's face. The handcuffs tore a gash on his forehead to the bridge of his nose. Dynamite Johnny's first impulse was to take the handcuffs off and jump the man a second time, but he decided against this. He remembered a promise made to Em' that he would try to avoid all scrapes while on this ship. The captain instead locked the man up and tended to his wounded forehead.

When the ship arrived in Port Townsend on the Olympic Peninsula above Seattle, Johnny swore out an arrest warrant on the seaman as a mutineer. The U.S. Marshal boarded the ship to take the prisoner and asked O'Brien to bring the man up. As soon as the captain opened the door, the maddened ex-fireman ran at him from the back wall, his cuffed hands held high. O'Brien rushed in turn straight at the bully, struck him hard in the belly, and continued through with the tackle as if he were playing football. He drove the man straight to the metal floor and knocked him out. Two buckets of water were thrown over the man's head before he was revived. Once taken away to jail, the ex-crewmember was convicted of mutiny and sentenced to two years in prison with the added counts of assault and battery. He escaped after six months. The episode toned down the inappropriate behavior of the *Premier*'s crew—or so O'Brien thought.

On an ensuing trip, the captain walked over to the purser's office to ask what rates were being charged on several Indian war canoes and horses that were onboard. Looking over the copy of the reports sent to the main office, he didn't find any mention of the shipment or the money that was collected. When he asked the purser about this, the seaman said he would check and get back. O'Brien didn't accept this and headed immediately to the sailor who was in charge of the freight deck. Not finding him there, he walked into the man's room.

"What happened to the money collected on the horses and canoes?" he demanded. O'Brien moved toward the sailor. The seaman opened up his locker and pointed to a stack of silver dollars and apologetically replied, "There's the share the purser gave me." The captain would discipline him later, but first he marched over to the purser's office. John was disappointed because he knew the young man and his parents.

"I know you're a damned thief," he said when confronting the purser. "Open the safe and I'll give you a receipt for the contents. And what wages are due you will probably cover the freight you pocketed." When the safe was opened, O'Brien fired the man. "Now pack and I'll check what you've taken. Get off at the first port we make, keep on going, and leave the state, as I may change my mind not to have you jailed."

He wired the ship's manager in Victoria about what had happened. The answering wire read, "Have him arrested, prosecute to the full extent of the law, and am sending another purser." O'Brien decided he had more important duties to do than to arrest the young man and put him in jail. He was more concerned about controlling the crew, and kicking the man off at the next port seemed good enough.

The new purser came. He turned out to be from a very prominent family, well dressed, a "six-footer," but unfortunately thought he was a ladies man. He soon was making advances on the women passengers. The captain asked the night watchman to keep a good eye out on what was going on. The "old reliable salt" came to O'Brien's room one night and told him the new purser had taken a female to his room.

When O'Brien knocked on the purser's door, there was no answer. He rapped loudly a second time, and the purser slowly opened it up, wearing only his underwear. "What do you want?" he demanded as the captain put his foot inside the opening. O'Brien looked in and saw a half-naked woman on the bed. He pushed the door open, walked in, and told the woman to get dressed and leave.

While she excused herself, put on clothes, and ran hastily away, angry words rang out between the two men. In the inevitable fight, the captain was the winner, and the injured purser needed medical help when the ship docked. O'Brien then wired the manager, "Purser in hospital; please send one more."

* * *

Life on these steam-driven steel- or iron-hulled ships was pleasant to O'Brien over the ones he had been used to, what with quality food, freshwater, sufficient fuel, and even musicians onboard. Although people were traveling the only way possible then between many cities and ports, the distinction between what one could afford was continued, especially between first class and steerage (third class). First-class passengers enjoyed their own stateroom, ate in their own private dining room, and had service both inside their rooms and out. In steerage, the folks slept in bunks, three to a stand in quarters that resembled army barracks. They ate in shifts at a lower dining room, usually cafeteria style, or in steerage (depending on the vessel), and the food was never equal to what those on the upper decks were eating.

Due to the close quarters, traveling by ship also had its drawbacks. In early 1889 the vessel arrived in Vancouver, but the health officer discovered a case of smallpox onboard. The worried officials ordered the *Premier* to the quarantine facilities at Royal Roads off Victoria. The crew scrubbed down the interior of the ship with disinfectant, and the passengers were "thoroughly fumigated." They stayed in quarantine for fourteen "long boring" days, not able to receive any guests or leave the ship. The sick passenger was released from the hospital after those two weeks, recovering from a mild case of smallpox.

Since no other passengers or crewmembers had come down with the dreaded disease, the health officer allowed the ship to leave Royal Roads for Vancouver. Upon the ship's arrival that evening at the dock, however, the mayor, city council members, and prominent citizens were waiting there. They told O'Brien that his ship had been in quarantine for only fourteen of the twenty-one days prescribed by law; hence, the *Premier* couldn't dock and had to turn back. O'Brien answered the group that the lifting of the quarantine by the appropriate officials was sufficient. The ship and everyone onboard had been fumigated, and the one person with a mild case of the deadly disease had recovered and been left behind.

The manager wired O'Brien that he would send another ship, the SS *Islander*, to take the passengers off the *Premier*. The mayor and his people, however, wouldn't allow the second ship to take anyone away. Firemen on the wharf used pressurized fire hoses to drive back the *Islander*'s captain and prevent him from even coming down the gangplank. The captains decided to transfer the passengers from ship to ship and take everyone to nearby Port Moody for their departure, which was then outside Vancouver's jurisdiction and about fifteen miles east.

Showing the rampant fear of smallpox, hundreds of police headed to Port Moody and arrived as the passengers were disembarking. They arrested a number of happy people that were on the dock making plans for their ultimate destinations. The police chief ordered his men to take the arrested passengers back onboard the *Premier*. O'Brien countered by telling his crew to take up handspikes and lumps of coal. He warned that if the police captain marched on his ship, he would be doing so "at his own peril." The captain knew O'Brien and that he could take him at his word. The captain backed off. The situation was finally defused when the Ottawa government intervened and ordered the local authorities to let the passengers depart in Vancouver.

These complications and conflicts were balanced out by the interesting people O'Brien met. Able to make several trips with different passengers in the same time it had taken him to cross the Pacific to Honk Kong and back, the captain enjoyed a variety of experiences with different personalities. From various Canadian ministers and officials to the builder of the great railroads, Mr. James M. Hill, leaders ate at the captain's table and sat in his cabin talking politics, religion, and business. Even those in steerage added to O'Brien's world.

Danger, of course, was always lurking on the seas. In the summer of 1889, a dense fog swept in and made navigating the Puget Sound and British Columbia waters very dangerous. The *Premier* sailed from Tacoma and Seattle in this fog with 510 passengers bound for Port Townsend and then Vancouver. The fog lifted. O'Brien told the pilot since the visibility had improved, he didn't need to call him when the purser returned from the customhouse, but to get the ship under way. The captain went to his quarters to finally get some sleep.

Although he could hear the propeller throbbing, O'Brien felt uneasy in his cabin. He came on deck and found the ship plowing full speed ahead through a thick fog bank. O'Brien asked the pilot why he wasn't blowing the foghorn, and the man simply said, "I forgot about that, sir." The captain ordered the engines stopped and asked the pilot where the ship was. He said the *Premier* was off Smith Island, but Dynamite Johnny didn't think the facts were adding up. The man couldn't have a clue where they were, since the ship was in dense fog, steaming at full speed, and with no position sightings taken.

O'Brien immediately sounded long blasts of the fog whistle. Not hearing an echo coming back, the captain ordered the engines at half-speed ahead. Decades before the development of radar, sonar, GPS, or other warning technologies, masters had to rely on these cruder techniques when sailing. While the foghorn eerily sounded out in the gloom, the ship slowly continued on. When he thought he heard a faint echo after hitting the foghorn, O'Brien ordered the vessel brought to a full stop. As the ship began slowing down, dead ahead loomed a mass of rocks in the gray mists.

There was no time to reverse the engines, and the captain ordered the helm put hard to starboard—but full-speed ahead. When the ship's head swung clear of the rocks by some twenty feet, he then ordered the helm hard to port, so that her stern wouldn't strike the spires, and rung the engineer to back the ship in full reverse. He knew from past trips that there was a reef with five feet of water on it only two hundred yards ahead, once they passed the first dangerous obstacle.

The ship responded "beautifully," and when he heard a four-second echo from the next island, he knew the ship was out of danger. O'Brien walked to the ship's rail and "fed both the birds and fishes with the contents of my stomach." If the ship had struck any part of the reef, he knew that her bottom would have been ripped out, fore and aft, and hundreds of people would have drowned or died from hypothermia.

O'Brien now knew his pilot was over eight miles off from the location he first gave. The "old sailor" and wheelman must have fallen asleep. Once in command of large steamers in the Orient, the old man was in the last stage of his career—and on his last voyage. O'Brien fired him as soon as the ship docked.

* * *

These were good times for the Puget Sound shipping companies, as thousands of people journeyed every month through the wide northern expanse. Among them, gamblers, thieves, and con men were also well represented. The gamblers would travel on the ships, gain the confidence of honest passengers, buy them a drink with a friendly pat on the shoulder, and invite them in for a "friendly" game of cards. Drunks and the naive were easily conned out of their cash. When the victims realized they had been fleeced, they complained to the captain. O'Brien would work to get the money back—if it had truly been a con—by telling the crooks he'd lock the gamblers up and turn them over to the police at the next port. The captain had a "decent success rate" due to his reputation of carrying out on any promise, and to stay in business it was certainly easier for the crooks to refund their ill-gotten gains.

A Canadian farmer with his wife and four young children were sailing to Puget Sound to start a new life. An honest, trusting man, he soon was ripped off and lost all of his savings. The farmer stoically took his loss, blaming himself for being so gullible, and told only a fellow passenger. He didn't have the money now to buy a farm and worried about what he could do for his family. The man didn't even have the money to buy a railroad ticket to ask faraway relatives for a loan.

When O'Brien learned this, he sent word for the farmer to come to his cabin. The man said, "It was my fault. I thought I could increase my little store of money and they took all of it instead." Asked to describe who was involved, O'Brien headed down to the stateroom and opened the door.

He found three men laughing in a smoke-filled room. One of the men, known as Peg Leg, was as dishonest as they came. O'Brien demanded the gamblers return the savings to the farmer, arguing that the man had nothing left to care for his family. Peg Leg said loudly that he ran an honest game of cards. He then sneered back, "And what business is this of yours?"

Dynamite Johnny's quick temper flared. His right hand grabbed the man's throat and pushed him from his chair to the deck. When O'Brien saw Peg Leg reach for his revolver, the captain grabbed the gun with his left hand and wrenched it away. He pointed the weapon at the three men. "I told you to give back the money. Do it now!" he bellowed. "All of it, or by heaven, you'll be in hell within ten seconds. And lose your good leg!"

The money was quickly thrown to the table. Leaving the room, O'Brien said evenly, "The money is for the farmer, but I'll keep the revolver as a little memento of this time. Don't forget that if you travel on this ship, don't try to swindle any of my passengers. You'll get a ride that you will never forget!"

A few weeks later in Seattle, a "prominent saloon keeper" hailed O'Brien while he was walking by. He said he had an offer to make and hoped the captain wouldn't be offended. "A third party will leave you three-hundred dollars in gold on the first of each month," he said. "All you have to do is overlook any little gambling done by these folks on your ship. We don't have any problems with most of the other captains, as they've decided to look the other way. And it doesn't really do any harm."

O'Brien replied angrily, "How long have we known each other?" When the man said, "A long time," the captain responded, "I can't believe you have the gall to ask me to assist others in the robbing of my passengers. They are placed in my care—and no one else's. Had I not known you this long, I'd figure some way to punish you. Now go tell your friends what I said."

A month later O'Brien was on the *Premier* watching the ship leave its Seattle dock with hundreds of passengers. He spotted two gamblers talking on deck with another Canadian traveler. Two hours later, the same Canadian came to his stateroom and complained he'd been robbed of four hundred dollars. He told a story that the two men had met him yesterday at his hotel, and they had even said, "Seattle isn't a safe town for a stranger, as it's full of thieves." They were in the hotel lobby, and the men invited him for a drink, which turned into several more. Feeling they were friends, the man ended up in their cabin on this voyage and was fleeced of his money. With his wallet on the line, he ended up playing the shell game of picking the right card.

When the man pointed out one of the gamblers, the captain strolled over. Pointing to the victim, he said, "A serious accusation has been made by this man against you," and went into the details. The gambler denied everything, and when an argument started with the passenger, a second man sauntered over and asked what the problem was about. The captain quickly sized up that this was the confederate, and the Canadian confirmed the same.

Asking his chief mate and another sailor to come along, O'Brien ordered the men to a spare stateroom and searched them. When he didn't find the money, he knew they had already passed it to someone else. The captain locked them up in the brig until the next port. When the men were led away by the police, one of the gamblers said he would "get" O'Brien one day, but the captain laughed this off. The man's name was Jimmy White.

Two years later, a stockbroker invited O'Brien after a dinner party to a Seattle poker game. He said he was from New York on a world tour with other New Yorkers and showed a letter of introduction from a New York bank. Once on land, gambling to O'Brien was like everything else: Life was to be lived, instinctively and without hesitation. While in this game, the captain lost $250 before he figured out he was with some "sharp card players." He decided to call it quits before he really lost money. When O'Brien was leaving, Jimmy White entered the room and laughingly said, "My only regret, Captain O'Brien, is that you caught on too soon." Feeling this was his fault for having been caught so easily, the captain let it go as another learning experience. O'Brien later learned that Jimmy White had been arrested for his illegal activities and spent ten years in jail.

Meanwhile, passengers on the *Premier* came and went. The authorities received information that drug traffickers regularly used the train stop at the Puget Sound dock. The customs collector and O'Brien left the ship to meet the train at the dock entrance and size up the passengers. They noticed a beautiful young woman leaving the train, but struggling to carry a large box of planted flowers.

The gallant customs official strolled up and said, "Young lady, may I help you carry the box?" When the well-dressed lady gratefully accepted his offer, the woman handed it to him, and the customs man carried the heavy flower box to the *Premier*. He carefully put it down on the deck in the ship's smoking room.

Once the ship was under way, the chief engineer was admiring the flowers. Having a lady's hat pin in his hand, he playfully stuck it into the dirt around one of the plants. The pin hit "something" hard. Scraping a half inch of soil away, the surprised sailor discovered a tin of opium. He dug around and found numerous opium tins buried inside the box. When the engineer told this to O'Brien, he knew he had to inform the customs officer. He was older, wiser, and had learned his lesson.

The customs officer was not on the *Premier* for this run. When the ship docked in Port Townsend, O'Brien pointed out the "woman with the flower box" to a young man, who promised to be discreet and tell the customs official, but what he didn't know was that the personable youth was a reporter for a Seattle newspaper. The next thing the captain knew was what he read in the headlined story in the next morning's paper. The U.S. Collector of Customs wasn't pleased, to say the least, and O'Brien took a "berating" from him over the matter. The woman was finally caught several months later.

* * *

A couple approached him one day and asked to be married onboard. They had heard that a ship captain had the legal authority to do this. This was the first time such a request had come up, and O'Brien had to think it over. Since he had a master's certificate for ocean sailing ships, the captain decided he could legally do this. The ship's agent from Port Townsend was in O'Brien's stateroom and volunteered to be the witness.

The young couple brought along their aunt and uncle, and within one minute, O'Brien had married them for life. The ceremony went so fast that the agent came over and kissed the bride in celebration before the husband did. The couple had a marriage certificate with them that O'Brien then signed. The bride gave it to her uncle to be recorded in Tacoma, but unfortunately the uncle mislaid the document.

Some months afterward, the aunt decided to sue and get a divorce from the uncle. When the matter went to trial, the niece was the main witness for her aunt; during her time on the witness stand, the opposing attorney objected, saying that in the eyes of the law the niece was a criminal. He argued that she wasn't legally married and was therefore living with a man who wasn't her husband; accordingly, her testimony was not credible and could be struck from the record. The proceeding was stopped so the niece could prove she was indeed married.

The aunt and niece came to the *Premier* and told O'Brien their tale of woe. He decided there was a way to fix the problem. O'Brien took out his official log book, went before the justice of the peace, had a certified copy made of the log, and gave it to them. The court in the divorce hearing accepted this as proof that the niece was married. O'Brien wrote later, "And they have been married now for forty years."

* * *

O'Brien took risks in his business life, as well as when he had to make life-or-death decisions as the ship's captain. A passenger friend alerted him to the profit potential of buying lots in Fairhaven, a small town on Bellingham Bay in Washington state. He picked out two lots, including one that cornered on a street, and the friend said he would hold them until John could raise the $1,600 for both. O'Brien talked to his friends and acquaintances in a very convincing manner and sold one lot for $2,000. He brought the buyer to the company's office, sold the lot to the man, and after this deal went through, the owner said he'd charge only $1,200 for both lots. O'Brien went out, sold the second lot for $2,500, and ended up clearing $3,300 without putting any money down. Multiplying these numbers by a factor of thirty will give an equivalence of these sums in today's dollars.

When onshore, Dynamite Johnny liked a "hearty bit of gambling" in high-stakes games. Flushed with success from his real estate venture, the captain came to another "heavy" poker game when the mayor of Seattle invited him to sit down with a few friends. The game had a fifty-dollar limit, and he waited at the full table for a seat opening. After twenty minutes, one player lost $500, said that was all he had, and left. O'Brien took his place.

He had $1,800 in his pocket from the real estate deal, but it wasn't long before he had lost $400 of it in the game. O'Brien then decided he would play until the game was called or he had lost every dollar he had at the table. He soon was in the middle of a large jackpot, with every man betting heavily.

When O'Brien threw three cards down and took three new ones, he decided not to look at them. The raises continued as the other players looked at every one of their cards and continued to bet large amounts. The captain also continued betting without looking at his cards, although toward the end he started making smaller bets. The other players didn't know what to do, because even O'Brien didn't know what cards he had.

When the showdown came, the captain turned over his cards and had four jacks, the high hand for the game. He had won over $3,000, which was then equal to a full year's salary. From that deal on, O'Brien felt he couldn't do anything wrong when gambling. But his luck had been spent, unfortunately, on that one giant jackpot. Over the next year, he lost $23,000, found himself in financial problems, and decided that he would have been better off to have lost the $1,800 at that one sitting. Nearly ruined financially, Dynamite Johnny decided never to go beyond a "two-bit" limit—and never did. He saved his salary with Emily's strong "encouragement" and worked himself back into financial solvency.

12

CLINGING TO A MAST

In June 1889 a savage fire almost destroyed Seattle's business district and the waterfront. The *Premier* carried emergency fire engines from Port Townsend, forty miles away, to help fight the conflagration. The residents came together to help in the rebuilding, and businesses opened up in tents in front of the burned-out hulks of their buildings. The city slowly rebuilt from the ashes.

On a more personal note, Emily had traveled to Portland to visit her parents and left behind her trunk of valued papers and personal items. John stored them in the strong room of the Arlington Dock Company, which also burned to the ground in the massive fires. The trunk was reduced to ashes along with the building and dock. Among the valuable papers lost was the will of Emily's father, which provided that ten thousand acres of land he owned would go to Emily. Her father had owned the land for forty years, dating back to a Mexican land grant, and part of the vast tract extended into the City of San Diego. The will, unfortunately, had not been recorded, and the property was later sold by her relatives in violation of the unproven will. Their dreams of wealth also vanished in the Great Seattle Fire.

Captain O'Brien enjoyed four years of prosperous runs on the *Premier*. By 1892, with direct railroad connections completed between Seattle and Vancouver, British Columbia, the heavy passenger and cargo trade enjoyed on the *Premier*'s runs declined. The voyages became unprofitable, and O'Brien wired the owners that it was impossible to make money now on the *Premier* and recommended the ship be docked. They agreed. The owners also informed O'Brien he would be on full salary until conditions improved or they secured another vessel.

When the word was out that Dynamite Johnny was available, he was quickly offered the command of the *Charles W. Wetmore*, an iron whaleback steamer based in Victoria. The ship looked like a "large floating cigar with a stub nose." It had been constructed in Duluth, Minnesota, and used on the Great Lakes to haul grain. The vessel was 265 feet long and 38 feet wide with a 24-foot depth; an inner skin was constructed 4 feet inside the keel, which was intended to make the vessel safer. The ship's elliptical form was supposedly designed for less resistance to wind and waves over the typical bow and sides. The hatches were huge iron plates that had to be bolted down, and this design was hoped to keep the holds from being inundated by large waves.

The *Wetmore* had just hauled 87,000 bushels of grain from the Great Lakes down the St. Lawrence River and across the Atlantic to Liverpool. Sailed back to the West Coast as an experiment, the mate told Captain O'Brien about its history—one seemingly filled with bad luck.

For starters, the day after the ship reached Liverpool, the mate found the captain dead in his cabin from "unknown causes." The ship ran into storms and heavy waves when returning to New York, a situation that was compounded by steering-gear breakdowns. The trip from New York went "okay" until the *Wetmore* was off the Columbia River bar. When the vessel's balanced rudder broke, the ship drifted close to the breakers; an English steamer sighted it, gave an expensive tow, and hauled the ship to Astoria. The *Wetmore* had trouble in San Francisco when docking, and the owners had just finished paying for the repairs caused by her grounding ashore when entering Victoria Harbor.

Concerned that there was a large difference between running loads of grain over the Great Lakes versus one-way voyages on the Pacific Ocean, O'Brien quickly discovered his concerns were real: The "steaming cigar" steered erratically and was a problem vessel. He found out how bad on his first voyage to Portland with a shipment of coal. When crossing the Columbia River bar after unloading his cargo, he discovered the ship's unmanageability. He wrote:

> Drawing two feet less than nothing, she would climb over a swell and fall into the trough, then strike the ocean with her flat nose, shiver, and shudder, fore and aft. One felt that the next sea she struck would finish her.

The captain managed to have "so called luck" in sailing her for five months in the coal trade from British Columbia to San Diego. Leaving that harbor on one of her last voyages, O'Brien sailed the ship north for Puget Sound. The vessel ran into a strong northwest wind and sea. The ship was pounding into the hard sea, and although the captain slowed down to avoid some of the pummeling, the engineer reported the ship was badly taking on water. The pumps were activated and needed to be kept constantly going.

O'Brien and his mate raised one of the hatches in the howling winds to check on the conditions. What they saw sent a chill down their spines: Numerous rivets had sheered off from the stress, and seawater was spurting into the hold from every side. The pumps couldn't keep up with the increased leaking of this unlucky ship. The captain ordered his carpenter to quickly make wooden plugs that other crewmembers pounded into the many holes once secured by rivets. The use of the plugs and continual pumping allowed the *Wetmore* to limp into a San Francisco dry dock, but with choked pumps and four feet of water inside its holds.

An inspection indicated over two hundred rivets had popped out, from her bow to the midsection, all due to how her snub nose plowed down into the heavy seas. Temporary repairs were made, including replacing bad rivets and using wooden braces to double all of the single-angle iron stanchions, or pole supports to the deck. Thirteen of the forward ones had been twisted and corkscrewed on arrival. The owner wired O'Brien instructions to take the steamer to Everett, Washington, where he had a shipbuilding plant on the Snohomish River. Strengthening and repairing the beaten ship then cost $30,000, which was an extremely expensive repair job.

When the vessel was ready, a dense fog hindered the trip to Tacoma, and O'Brien had "considerable difficulties" with the ship's compass. He was able to navigate to the coal bunkers, however, to begin loading its cargo. With the ship's nine hatches filled in twelve hours, the ship became self-trimming and ready for sea. O'Brien took the *Wetmore* south from Tacoma with 3,200 tons of coal on September 5, 1892.

The mate and Dynamite Johnny talked about what to do with the compass problems, but they couldn't come up with a workable solution. Given the unreliable device, O'Brien didn't feel at ease, and this trip—like the others—was not off to a good start. The ship slowly made its way down the Washington coast toward Oregon. During this time, O'Brien calculated that the compass had from a "ten to twelve degree of error," by sighting buoys after determining what the original reading had been. Before he could rework more accurate calculations, a dense fog enveloped the ship.

At night the *Wetmore* passed the Columbia River to the east, and although the sea was calm, O'Brien stayed up. The thick fog continued to blanket the vessel, and he couldn't trust the magnetic readings. He couldn't use the stars to sight by. By using dead reckoning and overadjusting for the compass errors, he navigated the ship to forty miles off Cape Blanco on the Oregon Coast, however, the most westerly part of that state and more than two-thirds down.

It was midnight. O'Brien was lying on the couch in the chartroom, thinking of his past years in the South Seas when they sailed with clear skies and no fog to worry over. He then felt a slight trembling inside the ship, and it seemed to slow a little. Realizing the cigar ship was touching bottom, O'Brien rushed to the bridge and shouted, "Hard port your helm. Let her go west southwest." The ship touched bottom ever so lightly at intervals of a few seconds, but the *Wetmore* kept swinging out to the west and away from land. This was encouraging, because before he gave the west-southwest heading, the ship was about stopped.

William Holmes, a young man from San Diego, was then on the bridge. He offered, "Captain, this is just a little sea quake. I have experienced them before in these southern waters."

"Sea quake, hell—the ship's ashore!" snapped O'Brien. He gave the mate orders for all hands to swing out the boats, just in case they were needed. At the time, the sea was a "mill pond," and in the dense fog, Dynamite Johnny could hear the moaning sound of the Coos Bay buoy that warned about a nearby sandbar. He knew at once his ship was a little north of the town and had plowed into the shallow sandy waters between Coos Bay and the mouth of the Umpqua River. The compass had either worsened or was off by more than he had calculated—and they were fortunate in that his adjustments took the ship away from the rocky shoals just off land.

The *Wetmore* then trembled deeply and came to an abrupt stop. The gentle swell of the Pacific swung the ship's head to the south, due to her being a few feet into the bar by the stern. He searched through a tide book and found that it was just time for a spring flood tide, which could lift the steamer off the sands. O'Brien could only hope the smooth weather would keep until the next high tide, and he became optimistic the ship might just get off. He ordered the hatches opened and for all hands to start pitching the coal overboard on the inshore side.

For the first few hours, everything seemed to be going to plan. The crew in the foggy darkness had moved over sixty tons of coal from the holds into the sea. As a long iron runway connected each hold, the crew muscled wheelbarrow loads back and forth from stem to stern. The captain at times fired off rockets, and the crew watched the high arcing flares vibrate in the mists as they descended into the ocean to disappear. A sailor pulled the whistle cord to pound off long blasts in the code of distress—but no one came.

The Pacific Ocean's swell unfortunately then quickly increased. O'Brien exhorted his men to keep going, but he knew a storm was crashing in. He then had to order the crew to stop work and secure all hatches. The winds whistled in an eerie sound as the rollers rocked the ship back and forth. Large waves began to crash over the railing. At four o'clock in the darkness of night, the winds and sea increased to where the crew shouted for everyone to abandon ship.

The captain told them they were close to the Coos Bay lifesaving station, and that in an hour or two, the lifeboat would be out. He pointed out that the swells now increasing and breaking on their weather side would swamp any attempts to leave. "You're safer on board this iron ship," he yelled.

The chief engineer was too worried, however, and he demanded the launching of the inshore boat, loudly arguing that it was smooth enough on that side. Pointing to the lee side, he said, "We're only one-hundred yards away from land. I can hear the breakers."

Knowing the dense black fog made any estimate like that a pure guess, O'Brien shouted back, "It's much longer than that, probably one-half to three-quarters of a mile, and you don't know how bad the breakers might be." The engineer was insistent, and sailors began to agree with him.

The captain grabbed a nearby wood post and slammed it down noisily onto the metal deck. With their attention gained, he said loudly to the engineer:

> If you want to go ashore, then take a lifebelt and go. But if you place any value on those thick hides of yours, you will remain until daylight. I warn you, or any other who tries to lower those boats without my orders, that you'll be in a warmer place than now and inside of a few seconds, for when I shoot, it will be for good and sufficient reason.

The engineer knew that Dynamite Johnny had a revolver on him and would use it. The man knew well enough to obey, for they had clashed once before. The man had refused to start the pumps after the ship had left the San Francisco dry dock. The ship was covered with cement and debris from the repairs, and O'Brien told the chief mate to wash it down while he talked with customs officials. On his return, the mate told the captain that the chief engineer wouldn't start the pumps until the ship was outside the bay. When O'Brien found the engineer, he asked coolly, "Have you any particular reason for refusing to start the pumps?"

The man shook his head. O'Brien pointed at him and yelled, "Mr. Chisholm, I will give you exactly five minutes to have water running through the deck hose, and if it is not, then you will take your little bag and what money is due you, and this ship leaves with another chief engineer." Chisholm looked at the captain with eyes full of hatred, but he left and within five minutes had the hoses working.

On the grounded *Wetmore*, the crew at daylight saw they were over half a mile from the shore, and the heavy breakers were crashing on the beach. When a lifeboat from the Coos Bay station finally came, all hands were safely taken ashore and taken care of. O'Brien wired the manager from land about the disaster, and he responded, "I'm on my way immediately."

The winds and waves blew hard from the southeast for the next twelve hours and then moderated. The ship unfortunately moved only slightly and seemed to be solidly wedged in the sand. When O'Brien heard that "a bunch of beachcombers" were going to board the ship and take possession of her as a derelict, O'Brien asked the captain of the lifesaving station to take him back. Dynamite Johnny hadn't been on the *Wetmore* for more than two hours when he heard a boat approach. Hailing the group of men, he asked what they wanted.

"Who in the hell is that?" sounded a voice back.

"This is the master of the ship. If you have any message for me, say so! If not, then paddle back to where you came from." After curses to one another, the would-be salvagers left.

O'Brien kept a lonely vigil that night on that ghost ship. The next day, he watched through his glasses as a large tug towed three boats filled with men. The manager, Captain James Griffiths, was on the tugboat and bringing "near one-hundred men" with shovels to get the coal over the side. Large wooden pumpers were also hauled onboard to pump out the engine room. Workmen were soon swarming over the ship as if it were a large anthill.

About 2:00 P.M., the captain noticed the barometer falling rapidly, and the hand indicator was actually quivering. Looking at the southwest, he saw "grayish red and green" storm clouds. The sea again began rising, and work came to a stop. A few hours were left before the sun set, and the men began securing the hatches back on the holds. Everyone left the ship, except for Captain O'Brien and the young wheelman, William "Billy" Holmes, who wanted to stay. The chief mate pleaded with the captain to leave, but O'Brien was firm when he ordered, "Get in the boat before the winds increase!"

They shook hands and the mate said, "I feel that we will not meet again." And they never did.

As soon as everyone left and was safely on the way to shore, O'Brien told Billy that a hard gale was going to be on them very soon. They had to take provisions and blankets to the forward mast. The forecastle head seemed well out of the water, and the sleeping quarters for the crew were located in the lower section of the shovel-nose bow.

The terrible gale struck with full force at night, and its seas made a clean sweep over the ship from aft to bow. After eating what they had secured from the galley, each lay down in an upper bunk, the light was turned out, and both were "soon oblivious to the breaking seas and howling gales."

After midnight, O'Brien awoke with a start. Seawater was "oozing" through his blanket, and his hand struck cold water when it dropped over the side. He shouted, "Billy, this walleyed hoodoo is sinking! You'll have to swim for the door!"

"Where in the hell am I?" anxiously replied the youth.

By this time, O'Brien had jumped out of his bunk and was up to his neck in chilling saltwater. When he yelled, "Where are you?" and didn't get an answer, John ducked into the saltwater and groped around. When he caught one of Billy's legs in the water, he jerked it toward the nearby door. The sea was over its top, but the hatch door was fortunately open. O'Brien slid through the water, underneath the door, and pulled the young man through. The corridor was also filled with the ocean, and coughing and sputtering, they had to take deep breaths, swim underwater, and make their way to the companionway that led up.

Once outside, they climbed the narrow iron ladder to the upper deck of the forecastle tower and opened the door. Breakers were everywhere. The rollers continued slamming over the deck with rooster tails of sprays and tons of greenish, chilling saltwater. When they looked out, they saw that four of the five towering masts had snapped off. The pilothouse and crew's quarters had vanished, along with the provisions that had been stored in the pilothouse.

O'Brien spotted a fire on the beach, and this heartened them. "Billy, we'll weather this out, just you see," he said. They closed the door and found two empty boxes to sit on. By this time they were very cold and sopping wet. Fortunately they had turned in with their clothes on—just in case something happened—but they didn't have shoes or hats. They spent the remainder of the night inside the forward tower, shivering and trying to stay warm.

When daylight came, the storm had somewhat subsided. They opened a compartment inside the tower and found a sailor's snacks left in a bucket. They had a box of soda crackers, three tins of condensed milk, two tins of clams, and a bottle of freshwater. They shared part of the crackers and clams for breakfast but held onto the milk and water for later.

After the meager breakfast, they walked onto the forecastle deck and found the seas still making a clean sweep over the ship. The vessel seemed to have badly sunk both fore and aft, and they thought it wouldn't be long before she sank out of sight. After one large roller crashed down the deck, throwing spray over them, the *Wetmore* shuddered and seemed to settle further into the ocean.

They decided to get themselves as high as they could on the remaining mast. Finding heaving lines running to the forecastle head, they used the ropes to climb from the shrouds to the mast. They climbed as high as they could and then lashed themselves to it; O'Brien gave Billy the "upper berth."

From their perch, they saw a number of people on the beach. An hour later, they heard the deep boom of a lifesaving mortar and watched the line sail toward the ship. Although the lifesavers were trying to reach the vessel, it was clear they couldn't succeed because the distance was too great.

The long storm was too dangerous for any boats to venture out. The squalls seemed to increase when darkness set in, and then the seas rolled in twenty-feet high with an overhanging crest that thundered down the ship, covering them with its cold spray, even though they were perched high up. The *Wetmore* shook with each hit and seemed to slip a little further off the sands into deeper water. The vibrations were so strong that had they not been securely tied, the two would have been shaken off "the way a dog attacks a bone."

To occupy their time, Billy and Dynamite Johnny told each other the stories of their lives. They sang all the songs they could remember, and their first long night in the rigging was "truly a nightmare." When daylight finally came, the two divided the last of the condensed milk, each dipping his fingers into the thick liquid. They shared the last tin of clams and the crackers. But for a small portion of water left, soon to be gone, they had no more food or drink.

They watched as three lifeboats in one day attempted to venture out, but the breakers were impossible to row over. They saw one of the boats capsize and then right itself, but the thunderous wash carried the rowboat back to shore. Time and time again, lifesavers were turned back. Their second night was as bad as the first since it was so difficult to sleep.

On the third day at low tide, O'Brien told Billy he couldn't sleep this way. He was going to climb down to the forecastle deck to have a few hours of shuteye. He told the young man to keep the end of O'Brien's rope. When he saw the breakers getting too bad, Billy was to tug on the line and get O'Brien back up.

The captain was sound asleep when the seas began to rise, and Billy pulled on the rope for ten minutes before O'Brien woke up. It was probably both the pulls and the cold sea splashing over him that did it. Although he was covered "with several seas," O'Brien was quickly back up the mast, thankful he had kept his rope tied; otherwise he would have been swept overboard. Later that afternoon the Umpqua River lifesaving station boat came within a few hundred yards of the ship, but the savage seas prohibited any further approach. In fact, O'Brien motioned them to go back.

After the third day, the two didn't feel the pangs of hunger as much, nor did they notice the lack of water. The captain wrote later he thought this was due to their being "constantly wet with the continued sprays from the sea, that our bodies just condensed enough water to keep us alive." More than likely, battling the elements and trying to stay alive on the tall mast kept their attention from these deprivations.

At low tide on the fourth day, the captain spotted part of a blanket tangled around an iron bar on the deck. Since Dynamite Johnny had to stay active no matter what, he began climbing down and told Billy to yell as loud as possible if he saw a roller. O'Brien reached the deck between breakers and started tugging at the piece of blanket.

Billy was so intent on watching the captain, however, that he failed to see a rising comber speed in. O'Brien was similarly focused on getting the blanket. When he heard the breaker's hissing and crashing, the captain didn't have a chance to get out of its way. He grabbed an iron railing and held on to it, hunched down with his head to his knees, as the green, cold, towering wave rose over him and crashed down. After the ocean surged away, Dynamite Johnny felt as if he had been flattened like a pancake, every bone in his body broken.

Realizing that most of the blanket had been ripped away, he swore at Billy, "You walleyed, transmogrified, A. P. A. of a dirty Siwash, why in the hell didn't you yell?" When he reached the mast, he saw the young man crying. Billy choked out he was sorry, but he couldn't keep his eyes off what the captain was doing.

O'Brien told the kid that it was okay. (Note: *A. P. A.* refers to the American Protective Association, an outfit Dynamite Johnny had a long-standing feud with, dating back to when they apparently framed him in Portland, Oregon; those lies, he wrote, cost him the command of the *Kate Davenport*, but he doesn't go into the details.)

The fourth day was a continuation of the cold, weary storm. From the *Seattle Press-Times*, September 22, 1892:

> Captain O'Brien's Danger: Precarious Position on Board the Wrecked Whaleback: Marshfield, Oregon, Sept. 22—A heavy southwest swell is breaking over the *Wetmore* today, and fears are entertained for the lives of Captain O'Brien and his watchman who are aboard the wreck. An effort will be made to take the men off this afternoon. A diver with a complete diving outfit arrived today, and as soon as the weather permits, will go down and inspect the hull of the vessel.

On the fifth day, the storm broke and the winds began dying down. Once more, a lifeboat took on the job of trying to rescue them. They watched again as this boat capsized in the rough water and rolled end over end. By this time, they had told all of the stories they remembered about their lives, and the two men settled in for their fifth night on the mast. They were both growing weak from the elements and lack of food and water.

The sixth morning came and brought sunshine with it. This was a good omen, although O'Brien worried about Billy, who was showing signs of going crazy. The lack of sleep, constantly being on guard, no provisions, and the cold had taken their toll. At noon, the captain watched a tug tow a lifeboat over the breakers and bar. He told Billy, "Brace up—this is our last day here!" but the youth didn't respond.

The *Wetmore* was now listing badly, and they had to get off that day. The ship had sunk at such an angle from the sandy bottom that if they had fallen, they would have dropped straight into the ocean. Hearing a boom, O'Brien watched the projectile with its line arc toward them, but this one missed the mast. The captain couldn't decide if this shot came from land or the lifeboat off the breakers. A half hour later, he heard the swish of another line past his face and grabbed it. Even when O'Brien pulled the light line to bring in the heavier rope, Billy's listless eyes showed no interest.

The captain reached over and tied the rope around Billy, then waved to the lifesavers. He cut the young man's lashing, and the seaman dropped into the churning seas. The rope with Billy attached was jerked toward land. It seemed "ages to him" before the lifeboat outside the breakers safely hauled in the nearly unconscious lad.

Lines were fired again to the mast, but they missed, one after another. The afternoon sun waned, and night would soon come. When O'Brien felt the line strike the mast above him, he made a frantic sweep with his arm, grabbed the line, but almost lost his balance to fall into the sea. He yelled out, "If you can't get me off today, do you think you could come back next week?"

O'Brien was tired and found it difficult to pull in the heavier rope. The captain finally did this with aching arms and tied it around his belly. He motioned to the lifesavers by shore and dropped into the choppy waters. Being exposed so long to the elements, O'Brien didn't feel the cold of the sea. Choking and limp, he was pulled through the breakers and finally onto the lifeboat. Given a glass of brandy to sip from, he considered himself lucky to be alive. The two were taken to a nearby hotel, and both slept for "a day and night" before waking.

Once he had spent time with a worried Emily and his family, O'Brien met a company officer. The general manager said:

> I do not blame you for the loss of the *Wetmore*; however, you were at fault for not remaining at the dock until you had your compass adjusted. I'll overlook that, as I'm sure you wanted to leave on time and not be criticized for staying in port with a full cargo load. I'd like to ask you to go back to Coos Bay and see if it's possible to save the ship.

Back on the Oregon beach, O'Brien took different bearings and decided the pounded, wrecked ship was 500 yards from shore. When he walked down the beach, O'Brien considered the skeleton wharf that would need to be constructed to get to the ship. As he made his calculations, he felt his feet sinking in the sands. He was in quicksand, and this was all he needed to know. Dynamite Johnny told the manager about the half-submerged ship and deadly quicksand, ending with the conclusion, "She's a total loss."

Billy Holmes recovered and continued his maritime career. Unfortunately, he drowned some years later on the S.S. *Valencia* with 130 others on the bleak shores of Vancouver Island. He was at the time the ship's chief mate.

* * *

Captain O'Brien quickly received word that with traffic building on the Seattle to Victoria route, his old company, the Canadian Pacific Navigation Company, wanted to give him back his old command on the *Premier*. He agreed, but by the time he arrived, the ship had already left. Captain B. Gilboy was the master, and the vessel left Port Townsend on the afternoon of October 8 that year for Seattle. Owing to Gilboy's error, a heavy steamer slashed into the *Premier* that same day and drove both ships onto a beach. The two were joined for twenty-four hours before a tug could pull them apart. Four passengers were killed and twenty injured.

After investigating the shipwreck, O'Brien decided to put in a bid to raise the *Premier*. Five bids were made, including his winning one of $2,800. Captain T. P. H. Whitelaw, the highly experienced and well-known wrecker, put in an unsuccessful bid of $20,000. Knowing one another dating back to the *Umatilla*, when

Whitelaw saw O'Brien, he commented, "John, I never thought you were crazy, but I now know you must be. Or else you must have some thousands of dollars to lose. I feel sorry for whoever goes on your bond."

Onlookers wondered how he could refloat the ship with the forty-foot hole in her side. His plan was to nail a raft of planks over the hole, put in airbags, and then use pumps, tugs, and a high tide to float her away. O'Brien couldn't wait to get into this effort, and he had only fifteen days to accomplish the salvaging, according to the bid conditions. On the first day, however, he met the salvager whose bid was next highest. The man, Commodore Irving, wanted the contract badly and hadn't expected his bid to be topped. He asked O'Brien what the captain would sublet his contract for.

Dynamite Johnny told him 50 percent of the contract price and $500 in cash. Irving said, "O'Brien, come with me to Tacoma." He did and was $500 richer. When on the small tugboat steaming to the wreck, Captain O'Brien turned to the wrecker and said he would work for free to help raise the ship. The *Premier* was successfully raised, a tugboat hauled her to a nearby port for repairs, and O'Brien was a total $1,000 richer after his expenses.

During these efforts, the heirs of the four dead passengers filed a claim of nearly $50,000 against the *Premier*. The judge would later rule that a total of $30,000 was owing to them for negligence. A U.S. Marshal traveled to Port Townsend, the port for clearing vessels with papers, to seize the vessel in satisfaction of the award. When the owners heard this, they asked O'Brien to somehow take the ship away from the jurisdiction of the United States. He made out the required voyage papers—or clearance papers when approved by the authorities—from Port Townsend to Victoria for the now-afloat vessel. O'Brien then asked the retiring captain, Mr. Gilboy, to clear his vessel for Victoria.

Whether he received the proper papers or not, Dynamite Johnny had already contracted with two tugs to tow the *Premier* over the international border. Gilboy cleared the ship as wanted, but just as he was to board a steam tender, the U.S. Marshal stopped him. The officer asked Gilboy when the *Premier* would be afloat, and the captain answered "in a very short time."

As Gilboy boarded the tender, the marshal saw the *Premier* on the horizon with the tugs pulling her away. "Why, hell, there she is! She's going to Victoria!" the marshal exclaimed. "I order you in the name of the United States to take me to board that damn ship." Gilboy stepped away from the vessel, and all lines were cast off. Now realizing O'Brien had sent Gilboy to delay him, the U.S. Marshal in the commandeered tender steamed after the ship.

The race was on. And O'Brien in command of the *Premier* was in the lead. Thick smoke poured from the smokestacks of the steam tugs as the U.S. Marshal implored the tender's crew to put all effort into catch those "law breakers."

O'Brien and his tugs reached Victoria, however, one hour before the tender did. The U.S. seizure papers were worthless in Canada.

The newspapers created a "hue and a cry" when the news was received that the *Premier* had shipped into Canada to avoid U.S. jurisdiction. The newspapers had a field day in labeling Captain John A. O'Brien as a pirate and ship stealer. The charge of ship stealing was later leveled against him, but there were no legal grounds or laws then prohibiting his actions. Years later, when O'Brien was named the U.S. inspector of hulls and boilers for the District of Puget Sound, some "A.P.A. friend of mine" wrote the department in Washington about his "stealing" a vessel from the United States, and O'Brien lost the position. The *Premier* was renamed the *Charmer*, and the ship was never brought over the international line to American waters due to the risk of its being seized.

Since the times were very bad for shipping, O'Brien took the position of mate on the *State of Washington*, which plied the Puget Sound. After two weeks on the stern-wheeler, he was asked to take command of a passenger and freight vessel named the *Utopia*. This move soon took him and this ship into the frigid waters of Alaska and the Arctic.

13

THE FIRST ALASKAN RUNS

O'Brien's home base was Seattle, Washington, and his command of the *Utopia*, a relatively small steamer of 425 tons, brought him even more challenges. This vessel first carried passengers and freight on the short haul from Olympia, the state capital of Washington on the lower Puget Sound, to Vancouver, British Columbia. Built in Seattle, the three-year-old wooden steamer was 124 feet long with a 25-foot beam. Her low draft allowed her to run into shallow inlets and land passengers and freight directly without using lighters, or the smaller boats used in transit.

Although Dynamite Johnny was untried in navigating the dangerous Alaskan waters, he soon was captaining the vessel to ports in the shallow inlets—such as Ketchikan, Sitka, Petersburg, Skagway, Cordova, Seward, Anchorage, and Dutch Harbor—with unknown names before the Alaskan Gold Rush. He completely explored the risks and beauty of the Inside Passage, the sheltered, island-packed route from Seattle along the coast to Skagway, which is located above Juneau in southeastern Alaska near British Columbia.

Navigating Alaskan waters was always fraught with danger. Understanding the safest route through the narrow passages of multitudes of islands, reefs, inlets, and waterways was intuitive and couldn't be based on the imprecise charts of the day. Shallow, razor-sharp shoals and rocky bottoms were deceptively hidden even under a bright afternoon sun and brilliant-blue waters. Blinding, shrieking

168

winds and snowstorms made winter passages particularly difficult for the captains on watch, obliterating barren landmarks, wiping away navigational checkpoints, and masking deadly icebergs. The smallest error in one's course could slash open a ship's seams before anyone could man the lifesaving boats and avoid the quick death of hypothermia. Driving rainstorms or choking fogbanks could arise any time and jeopardize what once was a safe passage.

It was these voyages into the ocean wilderness of plunging cliffs, rocky shoals, and countless icebergs, however, that brought about O'Brien's prominence as an Alaskan maritime legend. He learned the waters from Prince William Sound and Cook Inlet to the frigid Bering Sea, including the ways to flow with the currents of icebergs but avoid their deadly risks. Travelers became so confident of his encyclopedic knowledge of these treacherous waters that they wouldn't sail under any other captain. They booked reservations months in advance to sail with O'Brien.

Dynamite Johnny became enchanted with the scenic wildness of this expansive region. Broad glaciers had carved the vibrant crags and valleys, their colors ranging from suppressed grays during overcast days to brilliant browns and greens when sunny. Chalky glacier lakes with fine granite silt color the waters and beaches, from a dusty green under the sun to dark grays under the clouds. Even in the summer deep snows coat soaring peaks and blanket canyons, the rocky edges covered with thick fir, hemlock, and pine trees that plunge into the sea. The brilliance of the greens, reds, and blues of the many flowers and trees in spring, however, die into the frozen landscapes, chilling winds, and frigid snows of winter.

John Muir wrote in James Winter's narrative *New York to Alaska Voyage of Steamer "Dolphin" May to July, 1900* (captained by O'Brien):

The first stop made by the Alaska steamers after touching at Seattle, Port Townsend, Victoria, and Nanaimo, is usually at Fort Wrangel, the distance between the last two places being about 600 miles. Wrangel is a boggy place, but is favorably situated as a center for excursions. Indians may be seen on the platforms of a half dozen stores, chiefly grim women and chubby children with wild eyes. Most of them have curiosities to sell when a steamer arrives, or basketsful of berries, red, yellow, and blue. Many canoes can be seen along the shore, all fashioned alike, with long beak-like sterns and prows.

The coast climate is remarkably bland and temperate. It is rainy, however, and an Alaskan midsummer day is a day without night. In the extreme northern portion of the territory, the sun does not set for weeks, and even as far south as Sitka, the rosy colors of evening blend with those of the morning, leaving no darkness between. Nevertheless the full day opens slowly. A low arc of colored light steals around to the northeast with gradual increases of height and span, the red clouds with yellow dissolving edges to subside into hazy dimness, the islands with ruffs of mist about them cast ill-defined shadows, and the whole firmament changes to pale pearl-gray.

During the winter, snow falls on the fountains of glaciers in astonishing abundance, but lightly on the lowlands of the coast; and the temperature is seldom far below the freezing point. Back in the interior beyond the mountains, the winter months are intensely cold, but fur and feathers and fuel abound there.

From Wrangel, the steamer travels up the coast to the Taku Glacier [with numerous glaciers] and Juneau. After leaving Juneau, the steamer passes into the Lynn Canal [the route on which O'Brien wrote he met Jack London], the most sublimely beautiful and spacious of all the mountain-walled channels you have yet seen. The Auk and Eagle Glaciers are displayed on the right as you enter the canal, coming with effect from their far-reaching fountains and down through the forests. But it is on the west side of the canal, near the head that the most striking feature of the landscape is seen—Davidson Glacier.

* * *

O'Brien had been in command for only a few days when the inevitable conflict came about with one of the "hard case" crewmen that sailed during these times. The *Utopia* was soon to leave her Seattle dock. The captain came onboard at 9:00 P.M. Before going to his room, he walked around the passenger deck as part of his inspection. He spotted a "rough looking fellow" who was tapping sharply on a stateroom door and rattling the doorknob.

As Captain O'Brien walked toward the scene, the large man started to saunter away. "Are you one of the deckhands?" he called. When the answer was "yes," O'Brien ordered the man to get below where he belonged. The crewman did as he was told but took his time.

Fifteen minutes later, a well-dressed, delicate-looking lady came to O'Brien's cabin, knocked timidly on the door, and asked in a shaking voice if he was the captain. Dynamite Johnny asked her what the problem was. The passenger told him that one of his men was trying to break into her stateroom. Shaking his head, the captain assured her he'd take care of this and quickly left for the deck.

Confronting the unshaven, unkempt sailor by the same stateroom door, O'Brien told him to get off the ship. The man cursed back, and a "beautiful mix up of rough and tumble" took place for a few minutes. O'Brien's fists drove the crazed crewman up the cargo plank on "all fours." However, the man turned around, came down, and cussed out the captain with words that made his "blood boil." Spotting a nearby five-foot crowbar, O'Brien grabbed the heavy iron and drove it at the man, who now attacked with bull-like rage. The pointed end struck the enraged man in the chest; he fell with a groan on his back to the deck.

O'Brien worried that he had seriously injured the fallen crewman. He was on the moaning sailor in an instant and threw his jacket back. The captain was relieved when he saw the bar had only pierced the coat and the skin wasn't broken. O'Brien kicked the sailor lightly to let the man know he could get up. And get up he did. The beaten sailor shakily got to his legs, and with a loud, guttural yell ran down the deck, jumped off the ship, and disappeared into the night. O'Brien wrote later: "The man is still going. He never came back for the day's pay that was due him. We left at once, as I didn't feel like going to jail for my foolish impetuosity."

As if this experience wasn't enough, the mate reported later that the ship's "first-class" cook was now missing. An investigation concluded that the seaman had gone overboard by climbing through a large porthole at the ship's stern. The following midnight, the Swedish watchman woke O'Brien in his cabin. He excitedly told the captain he had seen the poor cook's ghost prowling around the ship. He had seen the apparition come onto the vessel over the stern and go into the galley. "I will show you him, captain; he is there now looking inside his sea chest."

His curiosity aroused, O'Brien followed the seaman into the galley. But the room was empty, and he could hear only the pots and pans banging against one another with the ship's motion. After giving the watchman a "calling down" for taking him on such a "fool's errand," O'Brien went back to bed. The next night, the watchman again woke him up. "Captain, come—please come!" the man insisted. "I saw him plainly come over the stern a minute ago and he is back in the galley."

"You big Swede, go back at once and grab that ghost. Bring him to my room! I'll make room for him to sleep on this sofa. After he spends the rest of the night with me in this room, he will never come on board the *Utopia* again. Go now and do as I say!" The watchman left. O'Brien wrote later, "Needless to say, I heard no more about Mr. Ghost."

This particular voyage was to the Frazer River in British Columbia, where the ship took on a full cargo of canned salmon. After passing through the Rosario Straits, a heavy southwest gale with shrieking winds, freezing cold, and midwinter snows enveloped the vessel. The conditions prevented O'Brien from taking his usual sea route to Seattle and forced him to take a detour through Deception Pass, a narrow, usually avoided channel at the head of Whidbey Island off the Washington coast. The ship veered to the southeast and approached the white-capped entrance on a gray, stormy dawn.

Sweeping his binoculars from the dark beach sands to the channel, he thought he heard a nearly imperceptible sound to windward. The captain trained his glasses to the site and picked up the outline of a small sloop with two men hanging to its broken mast. He blew several sharp blasts on the *Utopia*'s steam whistle to let them know the ship had spotted them. O'Brien ordered the vessel turned toward the derelict and a nearby seething reef in the worsening maelstrom.

The ship bounded into the rollers with roostertails of spray blasting over the bow, and as the vessel pounded through the frothing seas, the small craft ahead seemed to disappear when it slid down the trough of a large wave. The steamer was one hundred yards from the jutting rocks on which the sea was breaking high and close to the broken craft. Knowing the futility of any rescue by a lifeboat in these waters, the captain gave his crew orders to bring the ship closer to the derelict and then throw down rescue ropes.

He felt a strong tug on his sleeve. O'Brien turned to face one of the ship's owners, who happened to be onboard. The owner protested loudly against the captain's risking their ship by approaching the reef so close. Dynamite Johnny looked the man straight in the eye and said coolly, "You know me and your old ship will come to no harm. It would be hell not to at least try and rescue those men."

He ordered the men by the rail to get ready to throw the ropes down. O'Brien took over the wheel and brought the ship closer to the wreck, while the vicious currents hampered its maneuverability. One crewman on deck gave a loud gasp when he realized how close the ship was coming to the rocks. The ship was forty feet from the now submerged sloop and the seething sounds of the saw-toothed reef.

The men threw ropes toward the wrecked sloop, and two of the lines reached the craft. The numbed men couldn't hold onto the ropes, however, and the *Utopia* slowly slid past the wooden hulk and the bleak, white-capped rocks. "Hold on boys!" O'Brien yelled through the din. "I'll bring the ship alongside and take you off in short time."

The owner's face showed his nervousness at what O'Brien was doing—but he stayed silent. There was nothing else he could do. Dynamite Johnny turned the *Utopia* around, and it quickly came to a ship's length from the rocks and wave-washed sloop. He ordered two of his strongest men to stand by the railing and ready themselves to lower lines to the two seamen. The *Utopia* rocked over the small craft, while a large wave crashed over the reef. The numbed men below reached out for the thrown lines just as a large, white-washed roller inundated the battered sloop.

When the "big sea" surged away, only the barest outline of the submerged, shattered hull was visible. The two men had disappeared and were never seen again. O'Brien and his men observed a moment of silence. The *Utopia* turned back on course, and the men cautiously worked their way through the tidal currents and storms of Deception Pass. There wasn't much talking: Death is hard to accept when it's that close.

Newspaper reporters flocked to O'Brien when the news of the storm's savageness and the men's disappearance became public. Two days later, he received a letter that was apparently from the widow. It read in part, "If your report is true, then I have been left without both a husband and a son." O'Brien's description of the sloop, men, and location had proven her so unfortunate loss. He would never forget that.

* * *

His own near-death experience then awaited O'Brien, and it involved another historical figure. The *Utopia* was chartered to take a full cargo of freight and one hundred prospectors to the Susitna region in the Cook Inlet, above Anchorage. O'Brien took the Inside Passage route to Sitka, where he re-coaled and laid out the course through and around the Gulf of Alaska into the inlet. While in Sitka, he felt the first stomach pains that would prove to be another "one of my many close calls to the 'Great Beyond'."

The *Utopia* sought refuge in Seldovia Bay with two other vessels, all loaded with "impatient miners," while they waited for the ice floes to clear sufficiently so they could continue crossing northward into the Cook Inlet that led to Anchorage and Susitna. Located on the southernmost portion of the Kenai Peninsula, the tiny settlement of clapboard houses and log cabins had "many more" passengers on the ships than residents in town. Craggy, forested hills of snow and ice surrounded the beachfront and meandered upward to impressive mountains. While anchored there, the pains in O'Brien's stomach became so intense that he lost consciousness.

Not only were no doctors onboard the *Utopia* or the other ships, but apparently there weren't any in the small town either. Travelers onboard his ship hunted down a man who once had been a surgeon—but was now another fortune-hunting prospector. When the ex-doctor examined O'Brien, he found the "burst tumor"; he told others outside the ship's cabin that the captain had "about one chance in a thousand and that chance was an operation."

With O'Brien's stomach turning black, the prospector returned to the room and said he not only was unprepared to perform the operation but also didn't have any instruments for such a serious procedure. O'Brien painfully rose from his bed and whispered coarsely, "Doc, I heard you say I had a long chance to pull through. I'm a sport and God knows I don't want to die in this damn place. Go ahead. All you need is a knife and scissors."

Since the ship was rolling too hard in the waves, his men carried him off it to land. The weather was bitterly cold, and the carrying seamen slipped numerous times over the ice, dropping him hard to the ground. Half an hour later, O'Brien was in a ten- by twelve-foot crude hut, "surrounded by ice and snow, twenty miles from nowhere." The surgery table was three planks set over two packing boxes. The knife and pair of scissors lay next to him.

The now-doctor turned to the nearly unconscious O'Brien. "I wish to have an understanding," he said hesitantly.

"You mean as to your pay," O'Brien feebly replied. The prospector nodded.

When the captain asked what this would be, the man answered evenly, "I usually charged for an operation like this from twelve-hundred to fifteen-hundred dollars, but in this case I will charge you only one-thousand." In the inflated times of prospector expenses, the charges for any services quickly became unreasonable.

O'Brien told him, "Then the deal's off. I only have one-hundred-and-seventy-five dollars." The man said he'd take that and O'Brien's note for the difference.

"If I come out of this," O'Brien whispered, "then you'll have to wait some before the note is paid." This was agreeable. The man quickly wrote out the note, and O'Brien slowly scrawled out his signature.

It was now time to get down to business. The knife and scissors were "honed to razor sharpness and roughly sterilized." O'Brien never knew what the "conscripted doctor" used as an anesthetic. Although he felt no marked pain, he was conscious at times during the procedure. He saw "coagulated blood clots" removed, as was four inches of his intestine. Then he fell completely unconscious.

He awoke to "the most agonizing pain" and a mess boy hovering overhead. His words quickly put the boy in flight. The youth raced off pell-mell to find the doctor, who returned to give O'Brien an injection of morphine. The captain again lapsed into unconsciousness, and there he lay inside the cold hut of ice and snow for several days. No one held out much hope for O'Brien; even he "saw death stalking inside the cabin door."

The ship's mate visited one day and solicitously said, "Captain, the doctor doesn't think you'll live. Do you want me to write a letter to your folks?" O'Brien declined. He did tell the seaman that if he died, the mate should get four men to take his body to the "glacier you see there" and leave him on its top.

O'Brien had even more problems if he lived. During this time, the *Utopia* had discharged its cargo and passengers; however, the ship's coal supply was very low. Owing to mistakes made in Seattle and by him, the ship didn't have enough fuel for the homeward journey. The captain told the mate to take the crew at "low water" and dig the needed coal from a small formation in the bay that was accessible only at low tide. The men worked for two days, but they unearthed only ten tons of coal. They needed ten times that amount. When the crew refused to do any more of the hard work, O'Brien also had a mutiny on his hands.

The mate told O'Brien that one hundred tons of poor-quality coal could be purchased "five miles away" for $300. The problem was the ship and captain didn't have the money for such a purchase. One hour after the mate left, a tall, lanky, bearded man came to the cabin door and asked to be let in. O'Brien "whispered a welcome" after he entered.

"When will the *Utopia* sail?" the would-be traveler inquired. The man looked like a deputy sheriff, but even in his condition, O'Brien knew they didn't exist in the tiny, basically lawless settlements his ship visited.

"This is uncertain," replied the captain. He told the questioning man about the lack of coal and not having the needed $300. The stranger without further word pulled out a large roll of cash and handed it to O'Brien. The amount given was $500. The captain handed him back $200, saying, "All I need is what I've kept." The stranger gave a thin smile and nodded his head.

When the man asked what the fare was to Seattle, O'Brien told him that it was fifty dollars. He immediately counted out the money and handed it to the captain.

"What's your name?" said O'Brien. "I want to give you a receipt."

"Smith," said the man. "Just Smith, Skipper."

The man named Smith took care of O'Brien. He kept the cabin clean, tended to O'Brien's wounds, and brought food. The mate bought the coal and arranged its delivery to the ship. In addition to the quick charity of "Mr. Smith," Captain O'Brien did wonder about the two heavy-framed revolvers that Smith carried, one nestled in a holster under each armpit.

When the *Utopia* was ready to sail, the mate and Mr. Smith helped O'Brien walk down to the dock and board the lighter for the ship. Once he was hoisted aboard, Smith helped him to his room. After the ship was under way, O'Brien charted the course and then slipped into a very uneasy sleep.

After sleeping restlessly for eight hours, Dynamite Johnny awoke with a feeling that "all was not well." He called as loud as his voice allowed—but no one came. He threw a medicine bottle at the window, and the shattering of glass quickly brought the mate into his quarters. O'Brien asked what was going on. He couldn't hear the engines and wanted to know where the ship was and why the engines weren't working.

"Captain, the coal is very bad. The engineers and crew had a 'consultation' and it was decided to not sail further until we have better coal. We turned around and anchored under the lee of Cape Elizabeth."

"Why wasn't I told about this?" yelled O'Brien, who then gripped his side in great pain.

"We didn't think you were in shape to argue about our taking the ship back."

"Get me Mr. Smith," demanded the angry captain. Once he appeared, O'Brien told him about the mutiny and said matter-of-factly, "Mr. Smith, would you kindly lend me your revolvers for just a short time. You see the crew needs a little convincing."

"I am as anxious as you are captain in getting to Seattle—but I'd hate like hell to see you shoot up the crew to do so. You're still a very sick man."

"Mr. Smith, my body might be weak, but my mind is as clear as a bell, and you can be rest assured there will be no killing unless it is absolutely necessary." Smith handed over his revolvers to O'Brien. Intent on getting to Seattle, his newfound friend helped the struggling captain to his feet, up to the deck, and into a deck chair. Pointing a revolver at the mate, Dynamite Johnny quickly got the man's attention and told him to assemble the crew. "Now!" he ordered.

All hands quickly assembled in a line in front of him. With the tall Smith behind, O'Brien held the revolvers in his lap, each one resting on a blanketed upper leg and pointed at the crew.

"Some hours ago, this vessel was underway and making eight knots [about nine miles an hour] bound for Juneau, where I intended to obtain fuel and provisions. We don't have sufficient amounts on hand to make that point." Staring unemotionally

ahead, his voice was steady, his eyes fixed. "You men—without consulting me—have taken advantage of my illness to take the ship back to this anchorage. That action is mutiny."

A few men looked down at their feet or away from O'Brien. "Mutiny means death to those who refuse to obey my orders—and by the Eternal, any man among you, who refuses to carry out my orders in getting this vessel underway, I will shoot to kill as long as there is a bullet left in these revolvers."

Only the sounds of the wind and sea were heard in response. Throwing aside the blanket, O'Brien immediately rose to his feet, while two seamen began moving away. Pointing one pistol at the two and waving them back, O'Brien herded the sailors back into the line. Knowing the engineer was a prime culprit in the men's decision, Dynamite Johnny took several deliberate steps toward the sailor, who remained frozen at the spot. "Are you going to get the steam up now and ready the ship to be underway," he yelled at the engineer. O'Brien pointed one of the revolvers directly at the man's head. "If that coal is good enough to steam on for eight hours, it's good enough to get into Juneau. And I want steam up in this old tub and I want it in a hurry. If you refuse, in less than five seconds, you will be in Hell."

The sailor couldn't speak at first. "Captain," he finally stammered, "you'll have your steam inside half an hour."

"Then get a move on!" At the time O'Brien thought that he was just weak enough and foolish enough to shoot if the engineer refused, or anyone else for that matter. The captain walked unsteadily down the line of sailors. With one pistol pointed in his left hand, the other raised to the sky, O'Brien stared each man down. He knew he was being understood.

"Now get this ship going!" The men scattered. The boilers clanked in building up steam, the engines fired up, and the anchor raised noisily. Inside of one hour, the *Utopia* was on its way to Juneau, the rough and tumble "Capital of Southeastern Alaska." Wrapped in the blanket with his friend Smith alongside "attending to his few wants," the ever-watchful O'Brien stayed awake through the day and into the night. He clutched the revolvers until the ship arrived in port several days later.

When they safely arrived in Seattle, the captain believed he had escaped trouble from his threatened use of the firearms, because the men knew they were as much at fault as he was. When the *Utopia* docked, "a gaunt ghost of a sailor" met his friends, who learned he was still alive after his reported death. His wife Emily couldn't believe this skeleton of a man was the same one who had left the family a few short months before on an Alaskan voyage. O'Brien's weight had plummeted from 180 pounds to 130 pounds, and he was quickly hospitalized.

The captain spent a month recuperating in the hospital. One year later, he underwent another operation on his appendix. Although the doctor told him to be very careful with any activities, the following day O'Brien walked up the steep gangplank to his ship. When he reached the deck, he felt a "stinging, oozing sensation" at the incision. He held one hand over the place, and then realized he was holding half of his intestines in that palm. O'Brien held them in and leaned over the main rail on his back to "force them back where they belonged." Not feeling any particular pain now, he walked up to the pilothouse, got the ship under way, and, as he later wrote, "That's that."

But what about his mysterious friend, Mr. Smith, the man in his midthirties who was in such a hurry to leave for Seattle? The tall, confident man was Jefferson Randolph Smith, also known as Soapy Smith—a notorious swindler, gambler, and saloonkeeper with a very checkered past. His life now the subject of books, plays, television accounts, and movies, he had been born to a wealthy Southern family that met financial ruin at the end of the Civil War. It was in Fort Worth, Texas, that Jefferson Smith began his career as a confidence man, and he formed a small, close-knit gang of scoundrels, rogues, shills, and thieves to work for him, soon becoming a well-known crime boss. The "king of the frontier con men" spent the next twenty years as the leader of one of the most infamous gang of swindlers ever assembled.

His nickname came from his successful con game using bars of soap, which Denver newspapers headlined as "The Prize Package Soap Sell Swindle." In front of a street crowd, Smith hawked the advantages of buying his soap. He then pulled out his wallet and wrapped paper money from one to one hundred dollars around a few bars. Mixing the money-wrapped packages with numerous wrapped bars that had no cash, he sold the soap to the crowd for a dollar a cake. A planted shill in the crowd would buy a bar, tear it open, and loudly proclaim that he had won some money, waving this around for everyone to see. Box after box, soap packages sold for ten times their value. More often than not, victims bought several bars before the "sale" ended.

Smith announced later during the frenzy that the hundred dollar bill still remained in the "un-bought" pile. He then auctioned off the remaining soap bars to the highest bidders. Through sleight of hand, the cakes of soap wrapped with cash were hidden and replaced with packages that had no money, and the only money "won" went to members of "the Soap Gang." Smith quickly became known as Soapy Smith throughout the western United States, and he used this swindle for years with great success. This and other scams helped finance Soapy's criminal operations by buying off police, judges, and politicians. He built three major criminal empires: the first in Denver, Colorado (1886–1895); the second in Creede, Colorado (1892); and the third in Alaska. He was forced to leave the first two cities when an enraged public rose up and forced the politicians to finally take action.

His men sailed frequently on O'Brien's ships, although Smith kept his gamblers under control on this trip. Dynamite Johnny and Soapy Smith with his men would see each other again on these voyages into the remote towns on the Alaskan coast—the Klondike Gold Rush was now under way.

* * *

In August 1896, Skookum Jim Mason, a member of the Tagish First Nations Indian tribe, led three others down the Yukon River from the Carcross area in the northwest Canadian interior, looking for his sister Kate and her husband George Carmack. The party included Skookum Jim, his cousin (known as Dawson Charlie or sometimes Tagish Charlie), and his nephew. After meeting up with George and Kate, who were fishing for salmon at the mouth of the Klondike River, they ran into Nova Scotian Robert Henderson, who had been mining gold in the Yukon on the Indian River, just south of the Klondike. Henderson told George about where he was mining and that he did not want any "Siwashes" (meaning Indians) near him.

On August 16, the Skookum party discovered rich placer gold deposits in Rabbit Creek, which was located nearby. It still isn't clear who made the actual discovery; some accounts say it was Kate Carmack, while others credit Skookum Jim. George Carmack was officially credited with the gold discovery because the actual claim was staked in his name. The group agreed to this action because they felt that other miners wouldn't recognize a claim made there by an Indian.

The reports spread rapidly to other mining camps in the Yukon River valley. Rabbit Creek was later renamed Bonanza Creek because so many people flocked there to search for gold. Miners who had been working creeks and sandbars on the Fortymile and Stewart Rivers rapidly left to stake out the Bonanza, Eldorado, and Hunker Creeks. Robert Henderson—who was mining a couple of miles away over the hill—learned about the discovery only after all of the rich creeks had been claimed. The news reached the United States in July 1897, when the first successful prospectors arrived by steamer at two western ports and set off a stampede of would-be prospectors into the Klondike.

The scene in Seattle as O'Brien landed from another trip was one of total bedlam. The charge into the Klondike didn't start slowly and build to a climax; it started instantly when the first ship of gold-bearing prospectors docked. The first men reached San Francisco on July 15 and Seattle two days later after a month's journey on the *Excelsior* and *Portland*, respectively. With the California newspapers reporting the incredible riches brought back, the *Seattle Post-Intelligencer* chartered a tug, loaded it with reporters, and sent it off to intercept the *Portland* as she approached the sound. Loaded down with gold nuggets and ore, the prospectors were glad to trade news of the Klondike for news of the outside.

"GOLD! GOLD! GOLD! GOLD! Sixty-Eight Rich Men on the Steamer Portland; STACKS OF YELLOW METAL!" headlined the newspaper. The scene experienced in San Francisco was now repeated in Seattle. Rough, ragged, bearded men staggered down the gangplank, lugging down sacks, suitcases, and blankets swollen full of large gold nuggets, big flakes, and heaps of glittering gold dust, as the thousands of spectators yelled, "Hurrah for the Klondike!" A former coal miner had $50,000 in gold alone in his leather grip; although bound tightly with three straps, the weight was so heavy that the handle snapped off when he stepped onto the dock. Another dragged a heavy bag down the plank; he had two other sacks full of gold in his stateroom. One man had $100,000 in dust and nuggets tied up in a blanket, and he had to hire two others to help him drag it away. These men were so wealthy they could buy entire towns.

Reporters milled around each prospector, while the police struggled to hold back the crowds rushing in. Lives changed instantly as gold-crazed people tracked down the men to find out the precise location of the gold fields or to come up with a story to get part of it. Some prospectors eventually succumbed to the diseases and ill health they suffered in their successful quests. But by 9:30 A.M. on the morning of the *Portland*'s arrival on July 17, 1897, the city's streets were so jammed with people that some of the streetcars stopped running—but, then again, the streetcar operators were quitting anyway to rush to the Yukon. Store clerks quit, doctors and dentists closed practices, the *Seattle Times* lost most of its reporters, and dozens of policemen walked away, as thousands left their occupations to search for the fabled gold. Even the ferry between Vancouver and Victoria, British Columbia, had problems loading because most of the crews had already left for Alaska.

Soapy Smith quickly assessed the situation as one nearly too good to be true. He encountered an ex-policeman by the name of Willis Loomis on the Seattle streets. "I'm going to be the boss of Skagway," he casually told Loomis. "I know exactly how to do it, and if you come along, I'll make you chief of police." Smith would quickly work to build an empire headquartered in Skagway and soon became "the King of Skagway" during this incredible gold rush.

Within ten days of the ship's arrival, 1,500 passengers had left Seattle, and nine ships ready to sail were in the harbor. Their decks were so tightly packed that the legs of sitting prospectors dangled over the decks. Countless others joined the migration to the West Coast and were glad to take the ships being pressed into service. The colorful mackinaw, high boots, and thick caps became the dress at the wharfs and on streets alike. "Klondike or bust!" became the motto, as a vast migration of eager, optimistic people stampeded to get to the Yukon and its treasured gold fields, not thinking about the rugged, distant, savage wilderness or the frigid, lawless settlements that awaited.

Most prospectors landed at Skagway, Alaska, or the adjacent town of Dyea, both located at the head of the Lynn Canal. From these towns they traveled the icy, treacherous Chilkoot Trail and crossed Chilkoot Pass, or they hiked up steep White Pass into the Yukon to proceed overland to Lake Lindeman or Lake Bennett, the headwaters of the Yukon River. Thirty grueling miles from where they landed, prospectors built rafts and boats that would take them the final 500-plus miles down the Yukon to Dawson City, near the gold fields. The prospectors had to carry over the passes a year's supply of goods—about a ton, more than half of it food—just to be allowed to enter Canada.

At the top of the passes, the long line of laden-down prospectors encountered Canada's North-West Mounted Police (now the Royal Canadian Mounted Police), who enforced the regulation. This post was put in place to avert the severe food shortages that had occurred during the previous two winters in Dawson City. When the bulk of the prospectors arrived at Dawson City, however, most of the major mining claims of the region had already been filled. And they had to find a way to survive in order to be able to prospect for gold.

14

JACK LONDON AND THE GOLD RUSH

Dynamite Johnny watched the gold rush from the best seat available. On his ship's voyages from the gold-crazed docks in large cities to the rough, lawless settlements at Skagway or Nome, he brought thousands of prospectors to their jump-off places for the gold fields. Usually well provisioned with new gear, the excited men milled about on overcrowded, cold decks with their visions of wealth. On their return back, O'Brien saw the broken-down, sick, and discouraged men who had lost their dreams along with their money, their supplies, and the health they once enjoyed.

In July 1897, the *Utopia* was anchored at her Seattle dock when two men came into his stateroom and chartered the ship to take prospectors and freight from Seattle to Skagway. The earlier docking of the *Portland* in Seattle had shouted to the Pacific Northwest about the unearthed riches. Gold fever had enveloped the West Coast, and Seattle was the closest major U.S. port city leading north to Skagway, where gold-lusting men could begin their precarious journeys over the White Pass and Dyea trails.

Although the ship had accommodations for only thirty people in the staterooms and four hundred tons of freight, when the *Utopia* sailed, 134 passengers were onboard, along with extra freight. Men slept on mats and in blankets on decks, in the dining rooms, and stacked in the sleeping quarters. Four "prominent businessmen" slept on the floor in Captain O'Brien's room. Every person he met on the Seattle streets wanted to somehow get to the "golden North." When O'Brien told them about the lack of accommodations, they replied, "Captain, just give us a place to spread our blankets—that's all we want."

O'Brien complained to the owners about the overcrowded condition of his ship; but "somehow" they secured permission from the inspector of hulls and boilers for the grossly overbooked voyages. The fare was fifty dollars for each passenger and forty dollars per ton of freight; with the increased numbers of travelers and freight, the *Utopia* was now bringing in over ten times the money it had before.

Among the passengers onboard, O'Brien discovered his friend, Soapy Smith, who had saved his life, and his gang of gamblers. When the two met, they talked about the old times and the gold rush. They talked like old friends who had found the best way of earning a living in this mad scramble of crazed humanity. O'Brien then told him:

> I have an obligation to talk to you about the numbers of your gamblers that are on this ship. I'm asking you as a personal favor to keep them on check while aboard. If I find out that any of our passengers lose their little stake of money to your crowd, it will have to be returned. You know, Mr. Smith, that I have been in trouble on this ship before, but I came out on top. And thank you, sir, for your two revolvers!

Soapy Smith laughed heartily at the last sentence and said he would pass the word along. He gave his word to O'Brien that "there will be no cause for our friendship to cease." And Mr. Smith kept his word.

On the second day, however, Dynamite Johnny learned that several of his crewmen were a "half sea's out from drinking liquor." A troubling fact was that one of the chartering men was selling the whiskey to the crew. Now seeking their fortune on the way to the gold fields—but in a different way—an "unfrocked priest" and a "disbarred attorney" were the ones who had chartered the *Utopia*. When O'Brien discovered two five-gallon containers of liquor in the ex-lawyer's room, he threw them into a choppy sea.

When Dynamite Johnny walked aft to check further on his ship, he heard the click of footsteps approaching from behind. Turning around, he came face to face with the ex-attorney, who hissed, "Damn you, you threw my whiskey overboard! And, by God, you're going overboard!" The man reached to draw his revolver out, but O'Brien threw a quick uppercut. The punch landed under the man's chin, and he crumpled unconscious to the deck, the gun spinning from his hand. O'Brien brought him to with a bucket of saltwater and dragged him to his room with the help of two passengers. The captain kept the man's revolver and warned him that the next time he got into trouble, O'Brien would lock him up, charter or no charter.

The ship anchored off Skagway in late August. The first vessel carrying prospectors had arrived a mere three weeks before, and O'Brien saw lines of tents and makeshift driftwood shelters starting inland from the wide beach and flatlands, with a scattering of crude wood and log structures sweeping behind. Towering mountains surrounded the level valley, gouged out millenniums before by glaciers that had long since vanished. Since no docks had been built there yet, vessels relied on the cargo-carrying lighters to take their freight and passengers to shore.

O'Brien told the "lighterman" that he would have to look to the charterers for payment, pointing out the two men who were now on the beach. The captain showed the owner the charter agreement, which plainly stated the organizers were to pay all expenses for the loading and discharging of passengers and freight at a port.

The lighterman did get his money, but not from the charterers, as they had paid their individual ways, were the first onto shore, and had disappeared. Each passenger had to pay his own way ashore, including freight, provisions, and luggage, and the anger and indignation were high since these charges were "gold-rush high." The passengers held a miner's meeting onshore and quickly agreed that the ex-clergyman and ex-attorney would either "pay up or be strung up." Leaving their possessions with others to guard, most of the men then fanned out in their pursuit.

O'Brien later watched a group approach on a lighter with the two charterers in the middle. He gave them permission to come onboard. The men forced the organizers to the deck and surrounded them and Dynamite Johnny. A large, bearded man said, "Captain, we've brought the two sons of sea cooks here. They say they own the bedding and blanketing stores onboard, and from the sale of this stuff, they'll pay us for the lightering expenses we had to pay. With your permission we're going to have them do this for us."

Seeing that the two organizers had certainly talked quickly enough to save their skins, the captain nodded his approval. The group noisily stomped away to take a stairwell down. While the ex-barrister unloaded piles of blankets from the ship's storeroom, he had to withstand the men's insults—and he was lucky at that. Meanwhile, a small boat rowed toward the *Utopia*. Once its bow touched the ship, the man behind the oars shouted, "Hey, fellows, that Siwash who owes you money already cheated a Seattle widow with small kids from all of hers. He ought to be hung! And I hope you do that now!" A group of men on deck began talking among themselves with loud voices, grunts, and a few cries of "Hang the devil!"

Only one U.S. Marshal represented the law in Skagway, and the tiny place was lucky to have him. He was helpless with this type of group and had already decided to stay on land since O'Brien was on the ship. With hundreds of tough, grizzled men in tents getting ready to trek over the White Pass Trail, there wasn't much law that he could enforce—and one more man being strung up didn't make a difference.

Grabbing a bunch of the blankets now on deck, one clear-thinking prospector yelled, "That can wait! Let's take those blankets to shore and sell them. We need the money!" The mob chose getting their money back over stringing up a lawyer— for the time being. Two prospectors stayed behind on the ship with the ex-barrister until everything was sold. The man was very lucky. Word was received the next day that the blankets had been sold and the money returned. He was then released, left his partner behind, and disappeared from Skagway. O'Brien learned later that the instigating rower was an ex-convict who had recently been released from "doing hard time."

Leaving Soapy Smith and his first contingent of men on Skagway, the captain steamed away from that lawless place for another. He took thirty miners and their supplies on the *Utopia* to nearby Dyea, a landing place farther north up the Lynn Canal that was also used by prospectors to march inland into the Yukon. According to his written memoirs, it was on the trip to Skagway and Dyea that O'Brien met Jack London and entertained him with the stories of Wolf O'Malley.

When the *Utopia* anchored off the growing settlement, he allowed the miners to use his two longboats to ferry their supplies and men to shore. Dynamite Johnny was doing everything possible to keep the prospectors from ganging up again on the one charterer who was still onboard. When these boats couldn't offload all of the provisions, the miners had to hire a fishing sloop. When they needed to pay the sloop owner for this use, the men were again very upset.

When the sloop was ready to leave the *Utopia* on its last trip into Dyea, the prospectors stared at the ex-clergyman on deck, who was being guarded by a customs officer and O'Brien. Hearing the captain tell the men he wouldn't allow any "stringing up" onboard his ship ever again, not as long as he was the officer in charge, the charterer ran for this protection. As the sloop pulled away, however, the upset men cursed the ex-clergyman, reached for their revolvers, and started firing at the ex-priest. As bullets whizzed close to their heads, the three men fell flat onto the deck. When the customhouse officer turned over the ex-priest, he found the man had turned to a "deadly pale" color. A bullet had ripped through his clothing under his left shoulder; the man was bleeding from the wound but seemed to be "otherwise okay."

When the longboats were returned the following day, O'Brien hauled up the anchor and steamed back to Seattle. Already onboard were twenty-five "disillusioned and disgusted" miners who had found the hardships to Chilkoot Pass from Dyea to be more than they could stand. Dynamite Johnny never heard what became of either charterer, although the defrocked priest recovered from his wounds. With these rough, lawless men, those two were off to a very bad start, especially since Soapy Smith's crowd of "gunmen gamblers" wouldn't hold anyone off from hanging them later.

When the captain arrived in Seattle, he was offered the command of a "well equipped, little steamer," the *Rosalie*, to haul more freight and passengers. Built in 1893, the four-year-old ship was 136 feet long with a wooden upper deck. He knew the owners dating back to his Canadian Pacific Navigation Company days, including the company president, Mr. Charles Peabody. These owners were "light on capital," and Peabody even told the captain:

> Captain John, we still owe four-thousand dollars on the *Rosalie*, and although we know you'll make good, we cannot pay you the salary you'd like. We can credit you each month from net earnings, and when this amounts to fifteen-hundred dollars, we'll give you that sum, or in stock, with the understanding that you'll keep our vessel out of trouble.

O'Brien's gambling nature came out again, and he quickly accepted.

* * *

Born in San Francisco in 1876, Jack London was basically a self-taught man with limited formal education. While still a teenager, he was forced to earn money to help support the household. He worked at a series of unskilled jobs but constantly sought a way out of the dead-end life of being a "work beast." He sailed the waters of San Francisco Bay, first as an oyster pirate, then some say as a member of the fish patrol, apprehending his former partners in larceny. In 1893, at the age of seventeen, he signed on as a seaman with the seal-hunting vessel *Sophie Sutherland*. The experiences of these seven months at sea not only taught him much about life but also provided him with raw material for his writings.

Being young, healthy, and in search of wealth and adventure, he made up his mind to head to the gold strikes in the Klondike. With financial backing by his sister and brother-in-law, he looked in 1897 for a steamer bound for the Alaskan Inside Passage and ultimately the gold fields.

Jack London boarded the *Umatilla*—the vessel on which O'Brien had received his nickname—in San Francisco. On the morning of July 25, 1897, the *Umatilla* housed hundreds of passengers, sixty-one of whom were bound to Juneau in the Alaska Panhandle. The rest would leave the ship at Victoria, Port Townsend, or Seattle, hoping to find passage farther north from one of those busy Puget Sound ports. The sixty-one fortunate enough to continue on would transship to the *City of Topeka* at Port Townsend, Washington, and continue on their way to Juneau. Among this group were London and his brother-in-law, J. H. Shepard.

Before the transfer at Port Townsend, London and Shepard formed a group to prospect together in the Klondike with three others by the names of Thompson, Sloper, and Goodman. This is significant, as Thompson kept a diary that is the prime source of information on what London did. They made the eight-day trip in the *City of Topeka* with a stopover at Victoria, up the passageways, and finally to Juneau. Once there, Thompson's diary does not specifically mention how London and the others made their way from Juneau through the Lynn Canal passage to Dyea.

With huge glaciers and mountain ranges stretching nearly one hundred miles, the Lynn Canal is the longest glacial fjord in North America. Although Thompson's notes seem to indicate they took "Indians and canoes," which would be a long, arduous trip, scholars such as Franklin Walker in *Jack London and the Klondike* states no one knows for sure. Captain O'Brien's handwritten memoirs do go into the specifics of his conversations and relationship with Jack London, however, and these writings are known for their accuracy and detail.

O'Brien describes how London listened to him tell the sea stories about O'Malley, the hard-case mate of the *Edwin James*, and made "copious notes" with his stub pencil, although it is not known for sure the extent or if this is who the character Wolf Larsen in *The Sea-Wolf* is based on. According to London, most of the events in that book were drawn from his own experiences aboard the *Sophie Sutherland*, but scholars still debate whether his inspiration was more from the "sea yarns" related by others or newspaper accounts about Captain Alexander McLean, which O'Brien also brings up. In any event, London's experiences in the Klondike brought about his novels *The Call of the Wild* and *White Fang* and his memorable short story "To Build a Fire," among other stories and books.

O'Brien penned:

> The winter months without any aids to navigation were very hard on shipmasters; many a voyage I made from Seattle to Alaska without a chance to take my clothes off until arriving at our final landing at Skagway or back in Seattle.
>
> It was on one of these trips that I met Jack London on his way to Dawson and seeking his fortune. I liked the man, and after our introduction, I invited him to my room. After a while, I began reminiscing about my Hawaiian and South Sea Islands experiences. He was intensely interested, especially about that wonderful demon of a mate I had on the barque *Edward James*. I told him about how he [O'Malley] chased a man up to the foremast of the yard and let him drop one-hundred-and-forty feet; caused men to jump overboard; his sealing experiences in the Bering Sea; his killing his Russian guards, and when they imprisoned him on Copper Island off the coast of Siberia, his escape; his final voyage with me to Tahiti in the South Seas; and my leaving him on the Island of Bora Bora with only a bandana, handkerchief, and case of gin.
>
> Jack London took all kinds of notes during my telling of the story, and said, 'If I make a stake in the mines, I am going to build or buy a small vessel and sail her all through those waters (which he did in the sloop *Snark* with his wife and a Japanese boy—the latter I met in Honolulu some nine years ago. He is a dentist there and told me all about the voyage.)'

According to a respected maritime treatise of the times, *The H. W. McCurdy Marine History of the Pacific Northwest*, the "legendary" career of Captain Alexander McLean is "generally considered" to have been the inspiration for Jack London's *The Sea-Wolf*. Among these exploits was McLean's ramming his small sealing schooner, the *Mary Ellen*, into the side of an armed Russian sea cruiser and the subsequent kidnapping of ten of her crew; firing salvos of potatoes from a "saluting" cannon onto a rival sealing schooner; and talking the U.S. State Department into intervening on his behalf at an international tribunal at The Hague when the Russians confiscated his schooner, *J. Hamilton Lewis*, while he was in the act of robbing the Siberian seal rookeries.

As a result of the State Department's efforts, the Russian government awarded him $50,000 damages. Leaving the sealing trade, Captain McLean tried his luck with a mining expedition in the South Pacific and as a steamboat skipper during the Klondike Gold Rush. He then returned to the seal hunt, which was illegal for Americans. McLean ended his days as a tugboat skipper in Vancouver, dying by drowning after an evening of drinking in 1914. An investigating coroner's jury held that he had accidentally walked off the end of a wharf between two moored vessels and drowned.

Captain O'Brien continued in his memoirs:

There is no doubt that Alexander Mclean was also a participant in the story, but as the newspaper *Vancouver Province* of some twenty years ago said in an article on *The Sea Wolf*, they could not see how Jack London could portray the character of Alexander McLean as he did in his story, as both Alexander and his brother Dan's everyday life was beyond reproach; that of course most of the sealers would raid seal rookeries, when no Revenue cutters were in sight—and other unlawful acts while on a seal hunting cruise—but as to his brutal treatment of his crew: NEVER.

I knew the McLean Brothers well in Victoria, B.C., met them socially and otherwise many times, during the years from 1885 to 1887. Their schooners and the barque *Alden Besse*, which I had command of, were moored together off the Hudson Bay Dock in Victoria harbor. For weeks at a time, in the fall, while we were awaiting our Chinese laborers to take to Hong Kong—in all my associations with the McLeans—I found them square-upright men.

On the other hand, to verify my statement as to who was the "Sea Wolf" that Jack London wrote of—outside of the notes I gave him—I recall an evening in my cabin on the S. S. *Victoria*, while bound for Nome, Alaska. I was entertaining some passengers, telling them of this hard case mate of mine, and when I finished, one of my guests stood up, came towards me, and said, "Captain O'Brien, I own the adjoining ranch to Jack London in California, and one night, I was sitting on Jack's porch, listening to how he wrote 'The Sea Wolf,' and he told me, word for word, just as you have related it."

And again in 1912—when he came around the Horn to Seattle aboard the four-masted barque *Dirigo*, he called on me, but unfortunately I was away. My oldest son, Ned, entertained Jack London, and during the conversation, Jack mentioned how sorry he was not to have seen me, as he wished to renew our acquaintance of Alaska days.

* * *

Before the gold rush, Dyea was a trading post made up of one log building that was used for trading, the post office, and a residence. By the time Jack London was there in August, hundreds of would-be prospectors were living in a boisterous tent city on the beach. Leaving the raw, tiny settlement, Jack and his partners decided to hike the trail from Dyea Beach to Lake Linderman, a distance of twenty-eight miles that would take them over a very difficult pass. They ported their heavy provisions and supplies by themselves and hired an Indian pack train to work up the dreaded Chilkoot Pass, which was also known as the Golden Staircase.

The trail over this pass was steep and hazardous, rising a thousand feet in the last half mile; packed with deep snow and drifts during winter, the slopes averaged a terrifying 50 degrees. Since it was too steep for pack animals, prospectors had to pack their equipment and supplies over 1,500 steps carved into the ice just to travel up the pass. A continuous line of would-be prospectors with heavy loads snaked up the dizzying incline; an estimated 100,000 people were in this gold rush, and using different routes, about 30,000 made it to Dawson City by the end of 1898.

After the arduous trek over the pass, the trail makes its way to Lake Linderman. In his book *John Barleycorn*, London wrote of his "splendid physical condition" and that once down the pass, he could pack 150 pounds of supplies a distance of three miles, four times a day—or daily he trekked twenty-four miles, of which twelve were with the 150-pound burden. He described Lake Linderman in his book *Smoke Bellew*: "Lake Linderman was no more than a narrow mountain gorge filled with water. Sweeping down from the mountains through this funnel, the wind was irregular, blowing great guns at times and at other times dwindling to a strong breeze."

This lake was the prime location where boats could be built and men could navigate through the connecting lakes to the Yukon River and make the long journey to Dawson City. London's group lived in their tents and built a roughly made boat with four oars, a mast, and a square sail; it was named the *Yukon Belle*. They sailed in September from Lake Linderman toward Dawson City, as did many other gold-struck men, arriving in great numbers to the surprise of the good people of Dawson City. This route took weeks of hard paddling over a dangerous water route that turned out to be a nearly six-hundred-mile trip to Dawson City and the Klondike. The rapids were particularly risky, including the very dangerous White Horse Rapids on the first part of their voyage.

The jutting rocks and reefs were formidable due to the low water then present in September. Many miners decided to port their outfits and boats around the rough water over land. London wrote about this experience in running the rapids in *Smoke Bellew*:

> When we struck the "Mane", the *Yukon Belle* forgot her heavy load, taking a series of leaps almost clear of the water, alternating with as many burials in the troughs. To this day, I cannot see how it happened, but I lost control. A cross current caught our stern and began to swing broadside. Then we jumped into the whirlpool, though I did not guess it at the time. Sloper snapped a second paddle and received another ducking.

With more close calls on the seething river, its white, rolling currents crashing around huge rocks, London's group finally made the trip through this and other obstacles to close in on Dawson City.

The group decided to stop at the mouth of the Stewart River, which was eighty miles from Dawson, and winter there. The date was October 9, only a few days before the date usually associated with the river freezing over. Staying there wouldn't be as crowded as at Dawson, and the men were not as likely to run into the food shortages and lawlessness occurring there. They had made the hard trip from Dyea in two months and the river trip from Lake Lindeman in less than three weeks.

London's group then unpleasantly discovered—as did many of the prospectors who were arriving in the area—that the claims with the best prospects of finding gold had all been taken by this time. However, he and his partners did file a claim on the Stewart River and rented a small, drafty cabin. It was late fall by now, and the chilling winter was closing in. Needing to file their claim in Dawson, a curious London decided to take the risk and traveled with others down the Yukon River to Dawson in mid-October. He found the city of run-down cabins, saloons, and muddy streets tense with officials worrying about the lawlessness, lack of food, and desperation. London remained there for more than six weeks before traveling back in early December.

Their cabin was located on one of the numerous islands on the west bank of the Yukon, just below the mouth of the Stewart River. During the winter, it was an area of heavy ice jams, whipping winds, heavy snows, and abject desolation. The crude, roughly hewn structure had a sizzling hot stove in the middle, but ice circles would be etched on the inside windows. Their food was bread, beans, and bacon, with the bacon grease used to fuel the smoking, smelly slush lamps. Bathing was nonexistent, full beards and mustaches the norm, and clothing took on the pungent odors of the men, their food, and the ever-present smoke.

To while away the hours, the men would drink, play cribbage and whist, read, talk, argue, and dream about women. However, cooped up in small quarters during the winter proved to be too much, and Jack moved to a nearby cabin where he made new friends. Since the main trail from the outside world into the Klondike passed near the cabin where he lived, London was able to meet a variety of different adventurers. From ex-doctors and ferro dealers to Canadian Mounties and sled-dog runners, the men told him the stories of their lives, their dreams, and their failures—and London gladly noted these to write into the books and articles that later brought him fame.

There were considerable difficulties, of course, over the long winter: the feelings of isolation, interminable cold and difficulties in staying warm, lack of female companionship, fearsome storms, and illness. The five months of an enforced bad diet and lack of exercise brought London the frightful disease of scurvy, primarily owing to his constant diet of canned food without fresh fruits or vegetables. A lack of vitamin C causes muscle aches and weakness, a puffy face, discolored skin or purplish rashes, among other symptoms, and can lead eventually to death. A particularly gruesome aspect of scurvy is that one's gums swell and bleed, and then the teeth loosen to eventually drop out. London's scurvy became a large problem around the time of the spring thaw.

When he heard the thawing cracks of the ice over the closed-in river, Jack knew he would head home. Over the weeks, the sun rose earlier and stayed longer; the snow had left the valleys and was deep only on the ice-scarred ridges. The willows and aspens would soon bud and flower with fresh, young green leaves.

London remembered the long, hard pull over the Chilkoot, the thunderous rapids crossed, the cold cabins with hot stoves, and the men's gold claim without gold. He decided not to return the way he had come, but to travel down the Yukon River, across the length of Alaska to the Bering Sea and St. Michael, the saltwater port near the mouth of the Yukon, and then begin the long voyage south to San Francisco.

The men on the islands had waited impatiently for the ice to break up. When they heard the rumbling upstream and finally saw the crashing, grinding ice floes, they knew they could soon start for home. Since the original men in his group had already taken different paths, London and a friend, Doc Harvey, tore down the cabin and made a crude raft that they floated to Dawson City. Although steamers plied the river from Dawson City to St. Michael, London took a small boat, "home-made, weak-kneed, and leaky," that had a sail. He left Dawson and the Klondike on June 8, 1898.

With two other newfound friends, London sailed down the Yukon River in the rough-hewn open boat, which became their home for the next three weeks. The three of them had decided to make this a pleasure trip, especially after the traveling before when carrying heavy loads on their backs or dragging sleds for days. As London wrote in his diary, "We now hunted, played cards, smoked, ate, and slept, sure of our six miles an hour, 144 [miles] a day." The unnamed boat—apparently because of its roughness and the short trip—crossed the Arctic Circle and took its occupants past lonely trading posts, deserted fishing villages, native towns, and seedy settlements in a beautiful setting.

After they finally reached the Bering Sea, it took them five days to row and sail up the coast through stormy weather to reach the port of St. Michael. London penned in his journal the following:

> Our last taste of the Bering Sea was a fitting close to the trip. Midnight found us wallowing in the sea, a rocky coast to the leeward and a dirty sky to the windward, with splutters of rain and wind squalls which soon developed into a gale. . . . We shortened to storm canvas and ran before it, reaching the harbor of St. Michael just twenty-one days from the time we cast off the lines at Dawson.

St. Michael was a tiny, rustic port with gray mudflats, crude buildings, desperate men, and no docks. The date was June 28, and London soon found a job "passing coal on a steamer heading south to warmer waters." The last entry in his journal read: "Leave St. Michaels—unregrettable moment."

Somewhere between St. Michael and Victoria on this steamer, he burned himself so badly that he had to give up the job. It is possible the scurvy had caused him physical problems or mental lapses. An explanation can also be found in a passage in London's *John Barleycorn*, as noted in Franklin Walker's *Jack London and the Klondike*:

> I remember passing coal on an ocean steamer through eight days of hell during which time we coal-passers were kept to the job by being fed whiskey. We toiled half drunk all the time. And with the whiskey we could not have passed the coal.

Being drunk could also have done it.

He traveled steerage from Victoria to San Francisco and arrived home in early August of 1898. He found out then that his stepfather had died, and his remaining family was now dependent on his support. The United States was in an economic depression, he was an unskilled worker, and he was recovering from scurvy. He was unsuccessful prospecting in the Sierras, and London took odd jobs when he could find them, including "lawn work."

He wrote new stories based on his experiences in the Yukon; he revised stories he had written before he left—but they were all rejected. He had pawned almost everything he owned and was in desperate financial straits. Then in May 1899 London received forty dollars from a magazine when one of his short stories was published, one that had been rejected by others.

London continued to follow his calling, hoping to succeed, and he went on to become one of America's greatest writers. In January 1903 he submitted the completed manuscript of *The Call of the Wild* to the *Saturday Evening Post*. He received a check for $750, a very good sum and more than a year's salary. Less than one month later, Macmillan Publishers bought the book rights for $2,000. The book became an American classic.

The Sea-Wolf was published one year later and became an instant best-seller. London wrote many articles and stories, yet his greatest works were always about the far north—such as *White Fang* and *The Call of the Wild*—and the sea. As seen in these books, a constant theme he explored was man's struggle against nature's indifference and cruel power. London later wrote about his year in Alaska: "It was in the Klondike that I found myself. There, nobody talks. Everybody thinks. You get your perspective. I got mine."

Jack London died in 1916 at the very young age of forty. During his lifetime he wrote twenty-two books, forty-nine short stories, and six short-story collections, not to mention different memoirs, essays, and nonfiction. His literary executor quoted a "Jack London Credo" in an introduction to a 1956 collection of London's stories:

> I would rather be ashes than dust!
> I would rather that my spark should burn out in a brilliant blaze than it should be stifled by dry-rot.
> I would rather be a superb meteor, every atom of me in magnificent glow, than a sleepy and permanent planet.
> The function of man is to live, not to exist.
> I shall not waste my days trying to prolong them.
> I shall use my time.

15

ARCTIC DANGER— AND LOSS

On one fall trip, O'Brien learned that a large number of miners were in Skagway anxiously awaiting their return to Seattle so they could rejoin their families across the country. When the captain told this to Mr. Peabody, the president of the company owning the *Rosalie*, he responded:

I'm afraid you'll come home with a light passenger load this time. The *City of Seattle* sails in thirty-six hours, and she has the finest of accommodations at fifteen knots. As you know, the *Rosalie* isn't as plush and steams at ten knots. With the *Seattle* leaving before you, unfortunately I don't think this voyage will be a good one for us. It'll get all the people waiting to get back here.

O'Brien smiled back, saying, "Mr. Peabody, we may pleasantly surprise you upon our return."

The captain loved any challenge. When the *Rosalie* left its Seattle dock, Dynamite Johnny told his chief engineer about the *City of Seattle*'s speed and asked him to work their little steamer as fast as she would safely go. Having no passengers at Ketchikan, the ship steamed past the port in the middle of the night. When approaching Juneau, he told the half-dozen passengers what was happening and used the ship's lifeboat to ferry them to port, again saving time by not docking and then steaming back to the traveling lanes. Four hours after the *Rosalie*'s passengers arrived, the *City of Seattle* docked; when its master, Captain Connell, heard that the *Rosalie* hadn't shown up yet, he told his ongoing fares to go ashore, enjoy themselves, and return before 3:00 A.M. when the ship would leave for Skagway. He assumed O'Brien's slower boat was still on its way.

At midnight, the *Rosalie*'s sailors—who had rowed the lifeboat to Juneau—had spent the expense money O'Brien had given, "probably in the gambling saloons." They wandered down to the dock and the *City of Seattle*. When an officer recognized O'Brien's seamen, he asked where their ship was. The answer of "close to Skagway by now" drove an upset Captain Connell into action. He blew the ship's whistle with three long blasts, signaling an emergency to the crew, and hurried three officers into the town to bring his passengers back.

Already pulling a fast one on the *Seattle*, O'Brien brought his ship into Skagway at daybreak. He didn't blow the whistle for one hour, as he didn't want to alert the *Seattle*'s shipping agent about the *Rosalie*'s whereabouts. He needed the time to hire all of the freight men he could—at double the usual rate of seventy-five cents an hour—to unload the goods and freight in "fast time." His officers then combed the town to find all of the customers they could. The purser and O'Brien raced to the lodging houses, hotels, and gambling saloons for anyone who wanted passage now to Seattle on the *Rosalie*. They told people his ship was sailing in two hours—which would be a very fast turnaround.

Some asked O'Brien why they should sail on his ship when the *Seattle* would be arriving there "a day or two" ahead. The captain replied if that vessel came into Skagway before they left, then every person would get their money back. Due to this commitment, he had a full list of passengers on the *Rosalie*, including people he had to pick up in Dyea. Just before leaving, however, his ship's agent became furious with O'Brien for making these deals without consulting anyone. Had he done so, of course, no company officer would have supported the higher unloading expenses or "money-back" guarantee. The agent worried that the *Seattle* would make the port before the *Rosalie* could leave. Dynamite Johnny countered he would pay from his own pocket the extra expense incurred to get the freight off if he didn't arrive in Seattle with a full list. On these terms, the *Rosalie* sailed from Skagway, and the captain had two conditions to meet: beating the *Seattle* out of Skagway (which he did) and bringing a full list back to Seattle.

The next stop was Dyea, where O'Brien was to pick up eighteen more passengers from a launch. There still was no sign of the *City of Seattle*. Two hours after picking up the Dyea fares—and steaming at full-speed ahead on his return—the two ships passed. O'Brien gave a "salute" of long whistle blasts, which was answered by "short, snappy little puffs of steam," showing that his old friend, Captain Connell, was not in the best of moods since he still had to make Skagway.

Dynamite Johnny stopped at Juneau, picked up his sailors, and steamed to Seattle. Although the *Rosalie* arrived there two hours after the faster *City of Seattle* did, O'Brien came with a full list—meeting the second condition—and the passengers were happy with the *Rosalie*'s arrival time. Mr. Peabody was pleased with the full load and top revenues, so he didn't ask O'Brien to pay the extra labor charges. The captain said their chief engineer was the one most responsible for the success: He had increased the ship's speed sufficiently to make the race possible, and O'Brien had been counting on that. This matter could have been very costly to the captain if he didn't get a full load or cut corners as well as he did.

* * *

Gold fever seized people then as strongly as a drug addiction. One prospector-passenger from St. Louis on the *Rosalie* said he and his wife had mortgaged their home, leaving little for the family, gambling he could find enough gold for them to be rich. The next day, the mate came to O'Brien's cabin and said one of the passengers had dropped dead. The captain cleared the crowd away on the deck and looked down: It was the man who had mortgaged his home, but now he had "such a sad" look on his face.

When O'Brien searched the body, he discovered the dead man's address in St. Louis and a money belt with $1,800. The captain counted out the money in front of the people. He told the milling prospectors that once they docked in Juneau, he would ship the body, money, and personal effects to the wife at that address. As soon as he said this, two men stepped forward and said the money was theirs: They had given it to the man for safekeeping.

The men told O'Brien they had been friends with the deceased since they were "boys," but now with their friend dead, their heading to the gold fields had come to an abrupt end. They would leave the ship at Skagway, and after selling their gear, would join the ship at Juneau and accompany the remains back home. The captain said he believed them, but since they didn't have any written proof that this was their money, he felt it was his duty to pay for the embalmment and send the balance by Wells Fargo Express to the wife. When the two bearded prospectors agreed, he believed they were honest but still did what he had said.

The widow later sent O'Brien a letter thanking him for forwarding the money. This had belonged to the two young men, as they had stated, and she had given it back to them. The woman finished the letter by writing that she was now left alone with two children and a mortgage on their "little home but would manage." She also was one of those honest persons that the captain remembered for his life.

O'Brien wrote in his memoirs:

> In the four years of the Yukon Gold Rush, I saw and came in contact with many similar cases. By the hundreds, men would land at Skagway with high hopes, but after a week of struggling with heavy packs on their backs, trying to get over the White Pass and Dyea Trail, and then seeing the desolation of maimed men and dead

horses strewn over the steep trail, they'd sell their outfit for a fraction of what it cost them and return to Skagway for the next steamer to Seattle.

Having carried one hundred pounds of provisions into the Yukon for two hundred miles over a "blazed trail" twenty-five years before, Captain O'Brien knew precisely what these men found instead of their dreams of wealth. He shipped the goldseekers, complete with outfits, sleds, and dogs in crates, and then brought back the broken bodies of the men, with muddy, torn clothing and no animals.

After eighteen months, the traffic to Skagway and Alaska was so heavy that the owners of the *Rosalie* bought a controlling interest in the *Farallon*, another passenger and freight vessel, as well as buying outright the *Dirigo*. These three ships would become the foundation of the much larger and famous Alaska Steamship Company.

* * *

The passage through the Alaskan waters, with its icebergs, hidden shoals, surprisingly thick fogs, and unexpected terrible storms, was always fraught with danger. Serving Alaska was a difficult task—it's nearly 600,000 square miles of the earth's surface, but its total population is still limited. The people were scattered in numerous tiny towns, so the steamships had to call on ninety-two different ports. The closest, Ketchikan, is 750 miles north of Seattle, while the farthest is Kotzebue, which is 2,850 miles from Puget Sound and above the Arctic Circle. To get there from the United States, ships traveled the Inside Passage, the thousand-mile corridor that stretches from Seattle to Skagway and is nearly a continuation of the great inland sea of the Puget Sound of the Pacific Northwest. Myriads of glaciers, countless narrow waterways, hundreds of islands, and numerous straits separate these ports in what is the most rugged of country, coast, and ocean. Hidden spirals of rocks, floating icebergs, strong tides, Arctic blizzards, fog, sleet, and snow seemed to appear at will in the path of any ship.

O'Brien's *Rosalie* had left Juneau for Seattle and was thirty-five miles away when he sighted through the mists a vessel piled up on a small island named Midway. He recognized the beached ship as being the line's *Dirigo*. Coming alongside at noon, the captain found one of the owners in a "state of collapse." The man later told O'Brien that he had relieved the pilot some twelve hours before at midnight. Minutes later, the owner saw the rocky inlet dead ahead and too close to steer away from. Although there were no fatalities and the ship would be later recovered, O'Brien took the man to Fort Wrangel for medical help. They had bought the steamer just months before.

Dynamite Johnny had several close calls with the *Rosalie*, and these voyages were especially dangerous on the small ship during the winter months. On one "blizzardly day" while crossing northward over Dixon's Entrance, he was approaching the pilothouse and keeping a "strong" look at the sea. Through the snow, he suddenly saw breakers and the "black heads" of the nearly covered rocks on both sides of the ship. O'Brien literally flew up the ladder into the pilothouse, pushed the pilot aside, and ordered the ship stopped, then full-speed astern. The two men watched the land mass looming ahead. The *Rosalie* handled "beautifully" and slid to a slow stop as the land seemed to push closer. At the last moment, the ship's propellers bit into the ocean and began to pick up speed in reverse. The *Rosalie* would live for another day as it just missed those rocks.

He had other close times, including one when another blinding snowstorm with biting winds engulfed the ship when it was seven hours out of Skagway in the Lynn Canal and bound for Seattle. The ship's searchlight pivoted to catch navigation marks, but the conditions became so bad that the snow blocked out most of the light. From his telescope on that night, O'Brien suddenly picked up the chilling sight of breakers not more than fifty feet from one side. He stiffened, knowing there wasn't anything he could do except continue on course and pray. "Had we been ten feet closer, it would have been 'taps' for all of us."

Years later, however, the Canadian Pacific liner *Princess Sophia* came by the same reef (Vanderbilt Reef) on a dark, snowy night and wasn't so lucky. When the steamer stranded on the reef on the morning of October 24, 1918, it became one of the worst disasters ever on the West Coast. Due to the blizzard conditions, the 356 passengers and crew onboard were trapped and couldn't be rescued. After the *Princess Sophia* remained stuck on the reef for most of the following day, the weather and seas became worse. The high winds and tide then combined to lift the vessel's stern off the reef and tear away part of the hull. The damaged steamer then pivoted so that the bow headed differently as water flooded inside. It then slipped backwards under the water.

When rescuers returned the next day, all that was visible was the mast sticking out. Everyone aboard had died within minutes, with many suffocating after being covered by the bunker oil that coated the water. The only survivor was a dog, believed to have belonged to a wealthy couple that had been aboard. The death toll made this the worst maritime disaster in Pacific Northwest history.

On another voyage, the *Rosalie* passed close to a small island that was located thirty miles from Skagway. The crew spotted the mast of a sunken steamer weaving fifteen feet above the ocean froth. The *Rosalie* stopped, but no one could be seen alive, and only debris was washing against the island's gray shoreline. They later learned that the vessel that had gone down with "numbers of miners" was the *Hassler*. Every person onboard perished when the 151-foot ship slammed into an uncharted rock in February 1898. No one knows how many died that freezing night, and some estimate that more than one hundred people perished.

Some months later, the Canadian Pacific Navigation Company's steamer the *Islander* left the Skagway dock bound for Vancouver and Victoria. This ship was the same one that only a few years before had steamed to Vancouver to take passengers off O'Brien's *Premier* during the smallpox scare. Dynamite Johnny had talked with her master, Captain Foote, a few minutes before she sailed. The ship some hours later struck an iceberg and went down with a heavy loss of life and up to $3 million of gold nuggets, bars, and dust. The August 20, 1901, edition of the *New York Times* ran the following headline about the *Islander*: "SUNK BY ICEBERG; SCORES DROWNED; Sixty-eight Lose Lives in Sinking of Steamer Islander. CALAMITY ON THE PACIFIC; Vessel Had Sailed from Skagway with 198 Passengers, Many Laden with Klondike Gold – Wild Scenes Followed Collision – Blame for the Captain."

Two hours later, O'Brien's ship passed the point where the ship sank. The *Rosalie*'s searchlight swept around the area to avoid hitting the same icebergs that had caused the *Islander*'s loss. The crew didn't find any signs of the steamer, as the ship sank in water that was 260 feet deep. According to O'Brien, one Captain Quinn located the wreck in the deep much later with an electric light attached to his diving bell. The undersea explorer saw a man's skeleton in the forecastle, but he didn't find any of the gold.

"The Alaskan waters certainly took their toll in wrecks and lives," O'Brien wrote. Downright error and stupidity also contributed. The captain had taken his vessel through twenty miles of a rock-infested channel, called the Wrangel Narrows. He told the pilot, supposedly "one of the best," to call him if the ship ran into a snowstorm. O'Brien headed to his cabin for some sleep and settled down in his clothes on the sofa.

He had been asleep for two hours when heavy knocks sounded on the door. Awakening, he let the person in. A wealthy Seattle railroad man, by the name of H. C. Henry, told him, "Captain, you need to come on deck. Your pilot is drunk. I saw him and a passenger drinking from a whiskey bottle, and it is badly snowing outside."

O'Brien was out and into the pilothouse as quickly as if someone had yelled, "Fire!" Looking through the snowy window to see what was out there, O'Brien yelled, "Why didn't you call me, pilot?"

The man shrugged his shoulders and replied nonchalantly, "This is only a passing snow squall." Once the pilot spoke, the captain knew he was drunk.

"Have you passed Cape Fanshaw?"

"Yes, a few minutes ago." O'Brien wasn't going to accept anything this man said as being accurate or truthful. A bad reef with rocky spires was near Cape Fanshaw, which is a landmass that juts out into Frederick Sound below Juneau. The captain looked quickly at the compass binnacle and saw the ship was forty-five degrees off her course—and had to be heading into that reef.

Dynamite Johnny yelled to the wheelman, "Hard helm over now!" The sailor threw the wheel around, and the ship quickly began swinging away. Not in a good mood with the pilot, O'Brien told him he was drunk and to go to his quarters. When the pilot refused, Dynamite Johnny threw a hard right to the drunk's jaw and knocked him out of the pilothouse. A few minutes later, the pilot struggled to get up from the snow-covered deck.

When the *Rosalie* cleared Cape Fanshaw, O'Brien realized the old course would have taken the ship onto the reef. Once he picked up the outlines of the cape, the captain swung the ship around to anchor in the lee of that land mass; any further travel was impossible as the snowstorm had reached blinding proportions with howling winds and even worse waves. In the morning, the ship sailed to Juneau but wasn't able to reach the port until night. The blizzard continued with such ferocity that the ship's sailors could not rope the ship to the dock. To allow the passengers and freight to leave over the bow, O'Brien had to nose the *Rosalie* head-on against the dock, all while the propellers were slowly moving ahead. Once the unloading was completed, he backed the ship away and continued to Skagway.

There is no question Captain O'Brien was one of the best ship masters to ever sail the seas, especially in the waters of Alaska and the Arctic. He enjoyed near-total—if not complete–recall of what he had previously seen, heard, or experienced in sailing his routes, and he was intuitive. It is also clear that O'Brien had good fortune on his side. There were times when only divine intervention, as he called it, had saved him and his passengers.

* * *

O'Brien came to know numerous well-to-do and famous men when they steamed back and forth over the arctic waters on the *Rosalie* and other ships under O'Brien's command. The two that became his closest friends were railroad contractor Michael J. Heney and author Rex Beach. Michael Heney was a railroad builder of international renown, best known for building the first two railroads in Alaska, the White Pass and Yukon Route Railroad and then the Copper River and Northwestern Railway. When the Klondike Gold Rush came, Heney was ready. He visited the Skagway area to survey the potential routes into the interior, which resulted in the White Pass and Yukon Route. His life inspired several books and at least one movie, and a glacier, mountain, and range of mountains in Alaska bear his name.

Dating back to his days on the *Premier*, O'Brien knew Heney. When O'Brien was leaving Bellingham for Puget Sound ports on a hot day with four hundred passengers, the agent introduced the captain to Heney. He told O'Brien the man had arrived too late to get a berth onboard and that Heney had just finished a contract with the Canadian Pacific Railway. He hoped the captain could find a berth for Heney, as the passenger was tired and wanted to lie down somewhere.

Despite Heney's being up all night on business, O'Brien saw a tanned, handsome young man with "smiling black eyes." Dynamite Johnny told him the *Premier* would sail in twenty minutes, and he would find a berth for Heney on the ship.

Leading the man to his quarters, O'Brien said, "On a day like today, a nice cool drink would be in order. And then we'll see about the berth."

After the "refreshments" were served, O'Brien drew the Japanese partitions aside and showed the bunk. "My bedroom is yours," he said, "until we arrive in Seattle."

Heney protested and said, "I can use your sofa, if that's okay with you."

O'Brien smiled and replied, "I'll be up most of the time on the bridge, so that's decided." The thankful Heney spent the time sleeping on the captain's bed, and the two became good friends.

Spending several years on survey and work crews learning about construction as the Canadian Pacific Railway worked its way through the British Columbia mountains, Heney picked up extensive railway building and engineering skills. By the time he was twenty-one, he had earned the title of "railroad contractor." Moving to northwestern Washington in 1887, at age twenty-three, Heney handled railroad construction projects and made Seattle his permanent home. During the last twenty-three years of his life, he devoted much of his time to work in Alaska.

Construction on the White Pass and Yukon Route geared up in Skagway in June 1898. By early August, Heney had two thousand men working on the rail trail. During the two years it took to build the railroad, Heney often worked eighteen-hour days, traveling the right-of-way by horseback to oversee the construction. With his confidence and energy, he inspired and demanded a level of performance beyond what was expected of such unskilled crews. If he heard of a slowdown or difficult job, "Big Mike" would take charge, help do it himself, and exhort his men to complete the task—which they did.

After the 110-mile White Pass and Yukon Route was officially completed on July 29, 1900, Heney's men surprised him with a farewell dinner to honor his kindness and courage. A total of thirty-five thousand men had worked at different times to build that railroad. He would then turn to constructing the Copper River and Northwestern Railway projects.

Author Rex Beach also met O'Brien during this time period. After working as a lawyer and spending five unsuccessful years prospecting in Alaska during the gold rush days, Beach turned his hand to writing. Much of his work featured his real experience with gold mining, claim jumpers, and dishonest officials. In 1906, his first book, *The Spoilers*, became one of the best-selling novels of the year; it was based on a true story of corrupt government bureaucrats stealing gold mines from prospectors, which he witnessed while he was prospecting in Nome, Alaska. He became a successful screenwriter and film producer and authored more than thirty novels, many of which were adapted to the screen. O'Brien and Rex Beach were friends from their first meeting.

* * *

The now well-known Alaska Steamship Company needed all the ships it could find to carry the hordes of optimistic gold rush prospectors to the gold country and then bring them out. When the company decided to purchase a vessel docked in New York and use it on the Alaskan runs, it sent Captain O'Brien by train to New York City. In April 1900, he took command of the steamer *Dolphin* to sail it around the Horn to the West Coast. The chief engineer, James M. Winter, wrote a book about the voyage titled *New York to Alaska Voyage of Steamer "Dolphin" May to July, 1900*. The original handwritten log of the voyage had been presented in later years to President Franklin D. Roosevelt for his museum and library at Hyde Park, New York. The demand for the log in book form finally became so great that it was then published.

After successfully bringing in the *Dolphin*, O'Brien in August 1901 next accepted command of the steamer *Manauense*. The charterers had commissioned this vessel to carry a full load of provisions and mining equipment to St. Michael, far north in the Bering Sea, where Jack London had ported from on his return to California. After a trip that included a broken main shaft, O'Brien brought this ship safely back to Seattle. With no further charters secured for the *Manauense*, he accepted the command of the *Eureka*, a very large "Great Lakes" steamer of over three thousand tons.

The captain's first voyage with the *Eureka* was uneventful when it hauled loads of grain from Portland to San Francisco. He made several coastal voyages like this, after which the ship was chartered to take a load of lumber and railroad ties for the Kansas City, Mexico, and Orient Railroad to the seaport of Topolobampo, Mexico. Topolobampo is a port on the Gulf of California in northwestern Sinaloa, which is the Mexican state bordered to the north by Sonora and to the west, across the Gulf of California, by Baja California Sur.

O'Brien had left explicit orders for the second mate to call him when he spotted land. Coming onto the bridge around midnight, the captain couldn't believe that he saw "what looked like trees on low land." He immediately ordered the wheelman to swing to starboard, but the large, heavily loaded ship didn't turn. It stopped—the *Eureka* was now aground. "Didn't you see that land?" he questioned the sailor harshly, who quietly replied, "I just saw it, captain."

Dynamite Johnny ordered the chief mate to haul the port and starboard anchors aft, as far as the cargo booms could carry them. The men took a hawser from the ship's stern and made it fast to the anchor flukes. With the hawser pulled taut with the boom, both anchors were lowered to the ocean bottom. With the sea "comparatively calm," the men waited for high tide. A few hours later, the tide began sweeping in and the ocean became higher. At that time, O'Brien ordered the engines powered full astern and the windlass used to pull the hawser attached to the anchors. The combination of tide and pull toward the anchors brought the ship into a slow, soft slide back into the sea. After two minutes, the *Eureka* was off the bottom.

O'Brien was happy that "not a stick" of his load was lost. When the vessel docked at Guaymas, the Mexican port of entry, O'Brien ordered a diver to check the ship's bottom. The paint wasn't even scratched from the soft sands. He had been lucky and told everyone so. When it turned out that the second mate needed glasses but didn't tell anyone, the captain kept him on, but he told the seaman to forget about doing any pilot or wheel duties.

With more provisions onboard and customs cleared, the ship arrived off To-polobampo, but the captain discovered that there weren't any buoys or beacons to navigate by. The channel twisted its way for "eight or ten" miles, and numerous sandbars barred the way. With good use of the given sailing directions and a leaded line to plumb the depths, the ship made the port on a "glorious evening." He found the native Mexicans to be a "happy, go-lucky lot," and fifty came onboard in colorfully dressed groups to sing around the decks and play their guitars. Before leaving, O'Brien had the steward give them "refreshments," and the stopover turned out to be a very pleasant one.

Hearing the news of the great ship's arrival, thirty Mormons traveled there from an American colony of five hundred missionaries who had settled in a valley forty miles away. They said they were "contented and happy" with their decision, but they came to trade for whatever was useful. When they left, the ship was well provisioned with fresh fruits, vegetables, and poultry, and the Mormons now owned ropes, tools, and paint.

* * *

When the *Eureka* returned in 1902 to Seattle, the ship was chartered to Nome, Alaska. Four years before, three lucky prospectors had discovered gold in the beach sands and river tributaries close to Nome. Others shortly discovered flakes and nuggets for forty miles along the shoreline in either direction from the isolated and tiny settlement. News reached the gold fields of the Klondike that winter, but the coast was icebound that season. The area is frigid during autumn and winter, as Nome is 102 miles south of the Arctic Circle and 161 miles east of Siberia.

When the news finally reached the outside world, then the real stampede began. Thousands of men poured into Nome during the spring of 1900, as soon as steamships from the ports of Seattle and San Francisco could reach the north through the ice. During that summer alone, more than $2 million worth of gold was taken from the beaches of the now booming city. In that year a tent city mushroomed on the beaches and treeless coast to the water's edge and reached thirty miles from Cape Nome to Cape Rodney, a point of land on the Bering Sea, located northwest of Nome. Buildings of finished board lumber had been constructed as early as 1899, however, as soon as ships could reach Nome with supplies.

An estimated forty thousand people rushed there in 1900, including latecomers to the Klondike Gold Rush that had started three years before. Many of these fortune seekers left when they found the best claims were already taken or the conditions were too lawless and tough for the stay. Once the largest city in Alaska, estimates of Nome's population at one time reached as high as twenty thousand, but the highest recorded population in 1900 was 12,488. The U.S. Census of 1900 listed one-third of all whites recorded in Alaska as living in Nome. The gold camp's heydey was the first decade of this century.

Charles Madsen in *Arctic Trader* (written by John Scott Douglas) later told his experiences of coming to Nome and the Arctic in 1902 with gold fever, only to set up a trading and then guiding business instead:

The ship's anchor splashed overboard more than a mile off the beach at Nome. As our vessel rolled in the heavy swells, I stepped out into the icy breeze to mingle with others crowding the lee rail. A lighter rose and fell as it was drawn toward our vessel by a bobbing launch. Beyond these boats, across a gray expanse of tumbling seas, the beach was dotted with tons of machinery left to rust after miners had abandoned their claims. Most prospectors, I had heard, were now working in the island creeks, but there were still quite a few busily toiling in the sand. Above the beach, outlined against the loom of low, distant hills, was a town of respectable size, composed of white commercial buildings, unpainted shacks, and numerous tents.

The crew lowered a ladder as the launch towed the lighter barge alongside. It was flat-bottomed, and to prevent passengers from falling overboard, had railings along the sides and rowboats at either end. Although the ship was rolling wildly, the barge was finally loaded with people and cargo, and the launch towed it through the heavy swells. Beyond the breaker line, the after-end was brought about toward the beach. Two crewmen slid the rowboat overboard, and one took his place at the oars.

He was joined by a gold prospector, his wife, their children and several bearded men. I helped lower the other boat and was told to climb aboard. I steadied two nervous young women who followed me, and when the boat was full, the man at the oars pulled away. The women gasped as we shipped water in the crashing breakers. The boats soon grounded, however, and the young ladies in ours were lifted from it and carried up the beach by two men I took to be their husbands.

Miners left their operations to greet us. In answer to a question, one showed me a rocker into which he had been shoveling beach sand and gravel. It was a box resembling a cradle, with a dozen riffles or cross-bars secured to a canvas-covered, sloping bottom. My heart quickened at the sight of glittering particles of gold caught in the riffles. To a young seaman like myself, who had worked for small wages, it looked like a fortune.

Several boatloads of passengers were brought ashore before my baggage reached the beach. Carrying it to an unoccupied place high on the strand, I set up my tent on the bank of a river. It made a northward loop, creating a slough separating beach and town, before flowing into the sea. Across this lagoon, an enterprising settler had constructed a toll bridge. Women and children could cross free, but I had to pay a small charge to get my first glimpse of Nome.

The streets were deep in mud, although flanked by board sidewalks. The mud served as snow for the dog-teams and sleds that prospectors had brought into town. Walking along the sidewalk, I brushed shoulders with bearded miners, a few accompanied by wives and children; with an occasional dancehall girl, dressed in the height of fashion; and with visiting Eskimos, round-faced and curious-eyed, clad in fur parkas, skin trousers and boots. From gambling dens, bars, and dance halls came the sound of raucous voices and shrill laughter, the mechanical tinny beat of pianos, the wail of fiddles. Stores that outfitted miners, like the streets, were crowded, particularly the large establishment run by the United States Mercantile Company. I stopped to watch several new arrivals emerging from the store with new mining tools and other gear.

Finally I entered several dance halls. But the girls, made up with rouge and mascara, flaunting their charms with low-cut dresses and high skirts, made me feel shy and uneasy. Their strident, honeyed, or wheedling voices, when they invited me to dance, left me completely cold. Perhaps their contrast with the fresh, youthful charm of the girls I'd known in my Danish homeland was too great.

* * *

On this voyage of the *Eureka*, Dynamite Johnny's two sons, Ned and Frank, joined him. He was pleased not only that his sons enjoyed the ocean as he did but also that they were able to be with him on a long voyage. Ned was the oldest and at age twenty-two was the second mate; he had been to sea for a number of years and was a "powerfully built" young man. His seventeen-year-old, six-foot brother Frank was onboard as a guest. Frank was considered a champion runner, able to run the hundred-yard dash in less than ten seconds, but he "overdid" himself in training and collapsed. The doctor recommended that the ill youth take a trip to sea because the saltwater air would do him well. Frank was to stay on deck and avoid any strain.

When discharging the ship's cargo off Nome, the mate called Frank to the main hatch and said, "You're tall. Could you lift up this cargo block and hold it while I shackle it to the boom link?" The young man was like his father and didn't know the word *no*. Without a moment's hesitation, he lifted the forty-pound iron block over his head at arm's length. The strain was too much.

A stream of blood gushed from his mouth. Frank ran to the galley and grabbed a handful of salt, then tried to swallow it—an old remedy but tough—to stop the bleeding. It wasn't successful. When the captain heard that his son was ill, he grabbed a bottle of Friar's Balsam from the medicine chest. (Friar's Balsam is resin from the benzoin tree, and the liquid benzoin is used as an inhalant and a medication, among other uses.) After pouring some of the contents down Frank's throat, the internal hemorrhaging partially stopped.

He sent for a doctor, who then examined his son onboard the ship. Slipping in and out of consciousness, Frank was in serious condition and quickly taken to a land hospital. Seven days later, the doctor told Captain John that his son would die unless sent back on the next ship to Seattle. Although the steamer *Roanoke* was sailing the next day, it was completely booked. With his contacts and the emergency, O'Brien was able to secure two berths in a small room, one for Frank and the other for Ned to look after his sick brother.

An attractive woman of thirty watched as the "deathly still" Frank was brought onboard the steamer and taken to his room. She walked up to Captain John and asked if that was the room he was going to stay in. O'Brien nodded and told her it was the only one available. The woman said, "I have a large comfortable room all by myself, and your son with his brother is going to occupy it. I'll take theirs."

The captain first politely refused, but the woman insisted. He offered to pay her the difference in the room prices. She answered, "I once had a brother who looked very much like your son. In his memory, I want to help and take care of him during the voyage." She told the purser to take her belongings from her room and exchange them for what was in the smaller one. The woman watched over Frank as a sister or mother would. O'Brien later wrote: "She, God bless her, was known in the North as a 'woman of the night.' From that day forward, I have always shown those unfortunate women the utmost consideration and courtesy if they were passengers on my ships."

Frank arrived safely in Seattle, thanks to the woman's care, but the captain never saw her again. His son never fully recovered and for years tried to regain his health.

* * *

The next trip to Nome was also "full of tragedy and thrills," and Captain O'Brien was in port on the *Eureka* with Ned. Buffeted by gale winds on this October 1903 journey, the same conditions were present in Nome while he oversaw the cargo being unloaded. The job was nearly complete when one sailor pointed out a ship's lifeboat that was slowly approaching. Although its brig sail was set, the seamen were rowing and were obviously very tired. After the boat tied up to the much larger steamer, the officer in charge came onboard.

Dynamite Johnny recognized the man as Captain Harriman, who formerly commanded a sailing ship. Harriman handed him a letter from Captain Ames, who was the master of a company sister ship, the *Meteor*. The note read that Ames sent the lifeboat and Harriman to find help since the *Meteor* was in serious trouble. Loaded with 3,500 tons of cargo, the ship had lost her rudder and propeller. Now anchored in sixteen fathoms (ninety-six feet) of water, the *Meteor* was located some miles off Yukon Flats, seventy-five miles south of Nome. The longitude and latitude were set down. Captain Ames wanted O'Brien to come out and bring the *Meteor* back.

The unloading was completed late that night, and the *Eureka* sailed toward the Yukon Flats at 4:00 A.M. O'Brien wanted to get there before anyone else could, because any ship that saved the *Meteor* would claim—and receive—a handsome salvage award. Before coming to the *Eureka*, however, Harriman had told others in port about the *Meteor*'s condition and need for towing. Dynamite Johnny wanted to save those fees for the company and took Harriman with him before he alerted even more captains.

The winds were chilling, the seas frothy, and the travel rocky, but O'Brien steamed to the location. At noon his ship was precisely at the given coordinates—but the *Meteor* was nowhere to be seen. The crew of the *Eureka* searched the area, but the *Meteor* had disappeared. Captain John quickly decided it was more likely the currents had swept the ship away than the waves had overcome and sank the vessel.

He called Harriman into his cabin and asked him what the weather conditions were like when the ship anchored. The information wasn't helpful. On a hunch, O'Brien told his mate to drop the starboard anchor overboard and play out thirty fathoms, or double what would have hit bottom. A moderate wind on another gray day was blowing from the east with light snow flurries.

They noticed the ship's head was pointing to west southwest and not into the wind, which indicated that a very strong current was sweeping to the east toward Yukon Flats, twenty miles distant. With the wind and current joining in the same direction, O'Brien concluded that the *Meteor*'s anchors weren't enough to stop the ship from drifting away.

He sent a sailor aloft to keep watch, promising him ten dollars if he discovered the *Meteor*, and the *Eureka* steamed in the direction of the currents and land. As time passed, O'Brien couldn't believe the missing ship was this far away with two anchors down. Something was wrong, or the anchors had ripped away.

Over an hour had passed and the ship was still steaming ahead at full speed. Although the visibility was poor, the lookout suddenly shouted out that the ship was ahead. The captain stopped the engine and took a sounding: The depth was seven fathoms, or forty-two feet, much lower than anyone thought and as he had unfortunately anticipated. The *Eureka* started moving forward again and was soon within hailing distance of the *Meteor*. O'Brien yelled through his megaphone, "How much water are you in?" When the answer came back, "Sixteen fathoms," he shouted, "No, you are in five fathoms—and your anchors must be gone. It won't be long before you are ashore on Yukon Flats."

Knowing that both ships were in shallow shoal waters, the crews worked quickly. Seamen rowed a ten-inch hawser to the crippled ship, attached it, and began the tow. This was a tough tow, since the *Meteor* was without a rudder, was deeply laden, and had no anchors. The ship slowly swung back and forth in the ocean troughs while the slower moving tow ship had to compensate for the out-of-control paths—and this zigzagging continued for hours. When the *Meteor* rode off in a different direction, the men on the *Eureka* were forced to use their windlass to slowly tighten the wayward steamer back on course.

This continued for twenty-four hours until the crews sighted the steamer *Nome City*. O'Brien signaled the ship that he would like them to join in the towing. With two ships sharing the task, controlling the helpless vessel would be easier. Ever mindful of receiving a share of the salvage award, the *Nome City*'s captain quickly agreed. The combination proved successful, since both boats could tow in different angles and keep the *Meteor* relatively under control. The passengers onboard the *Nome City* rebelled after two hours, however, arguing they had paid for a passage, not a slow ride on a tugboat. The captain soon signaled he would have to let go. After O'Brien acknowledged the communication, the *Nome City* cast off the hawser. The vessel approached the *Eureka*, and the *Nome City*'s captain told O'Brien why he was leaving. The ship then steamed away with three long blasts of her whistle and disappeared into the snowstorm, leaving the lonely vessels in freezing cold, swirling snow and the moderate gale winds now blowing.

With darkness falling, lack of visibility joined these miserable conditions. During the night, a few crewmembers made matters even worse. Tired of the constant slowing, stopping, and pulling, these sailors slipped the hawser from the towing bits. The rope pulled away into the ocean. When this was discovered, a longboat had to be lowered and rowed back to the nearly indistinguishable lights of the *Meteor*.

With snow falling and high waves rolling, the cold crew and O'Brien tried to find the hawser. As it was still attached to the *Meteor*, the men didn't find the rope until they were nearly to the bobbing ship. Once the rope was reattached to the *Eureka*, O'Brien warned his crew about the consequences of anyone again "messing" with the tow. The seamen had the choice of sharing in a salvage award or being "put in irons on bread and water until we make port." Their decision was quickly made.

The crew worked hard, and no more problems occurred. The hard slog through the snows and cold lasted for seven days. Although trying to make Dutch Harbor in the Aleutians, O'Brien finally decided the conditions were so bad—with bitter cold and "scum" ice now forming on the ocean—that he would find a close bay on the south side of St. Paul Island, the largest of the Pribilof Islands. The ships were far in the Bering Sea, about two hundred miles north of Unalaska (the tip of the Aleutian Islands), and the Siberian coast was roughly five hundred miles away. He intended to offload part of the crippled ship's cargo to the *Eureka* and bring the *Meteor* into a better balance for the tow.

The problem was the captains misunderstood what the other was going to do. O'Brien thought he had communicated his intentions to Ames and signaled for the ship to let go of the hawser. In the safety of the bay, O'Brien would offload with both ships lashed to one another—but first he had to see how safe it was. He didn't communicate this very well. Thinking the *Eureka* was going to abandon them, Captain Ames refused to toss the thick rope back. O'Brien then untied the hawser and sailed away.

The horrified men on the *Meteor* couldn't believe what was happening. They were being abandoned in the ocean by the one hope they had. Captain Ames exploded and called O'Brien every cuss name in the book, including the famous "damn walleyed A.P.A."

For several hours, the crew of the *Eureka* searched for the west side of St. Paul's Island, but the heavy snowfall was so bad, nobody could find it. During this time, the *Meteor*'s crewmen were nervous at best. Steaming back to the *Meteor*, O'Brien explained more fully what he had tried to do—and then reattached the tow.

With the tortuous dragging again underway, two more days slipped by. The ships found the sun partly shining, and by the morning of November 10 they were three hundred miles southwest of Dutch Harbor. The mate then noticed that the *Meteor* seemed to be down by its bow. O'Brien signaled Captain Ames to let go of the bow hawser and they would attach it to the stern to alleviate the bad trim. He agreed.

After the line was hauled in, Captain John took the longboat over to the *Meteor* to be sure everything was understood, putting his son, Ned, in charge as second mate of the boat. At the time a very heavy sea swell was running with strong rollers. The thermometer was barely above zero. Although the wind had died down, the weather conditions were so cold that a "thin shimmer of ice" now covered the ocean when the longboat tied up.

Ames told him the ship was lower by its bow because he had ordered his men that night to throw overboard a large quantity of dynamite being hauled. He didn't want the risk of an explosion. O'Brien asked if there was any way to jury-rig a rudder to keep the ship from "yawing all over the ocean." With the tow being from the stern, Captain Ames didn't have any ideas.

Captain O'Brien, Ned, and his sailors rowed the longboat back. When the sailors hooked the boat onto the davit tackles, the ship was heading into the sea "in fine shape." The boat was hauled up, and the men started climbing up and over the side. With nearly all of the men onboard, the *Eureka* slid deeply into the trough of a heavy swell, and the longboat was four feet out of the water. The boat swung fifteen feet away from the mother vessel and returned with a crash against the ship's side, completely flattening the boat's side and splitting her open.

The boat's crew with Captain O'Brien had climbed out before then, but Ned was last and clinging to the smashed side. The *Eureka* rolled far down into another trough, and the broken boat swept out again in a sharp angle. With Ned still trying to climb out, the boat froze for an instant at its apogee, then swung fiercely back with him on the longboat's outside. Ned was caught in the middle when the heavy boat smashed into the *Eureka*'s iron sides.

Watching the heartrending crushing of his son, O'Brien was speechless. His son gave a weak wave and then dropped silently into the foaming sea. Standing on the deck, O'Brien wondered later why he didn't jump immediately after Ned instead of standing frozen and staring at the sea. Bobbing by the ship, his son spoke the barely audible words, "Good-bye, father. Tell mother I was thinking of her," and this jolted O'Brien into action.

He shouted back, "Good-bye nothing! Keep that black head of yours above water! We will have you in the boat in less than no time!" His first inclination was to leap into the cold waters, but the freezing conditions would be deadly for anyone who tried.

Seeing his son was drifting toward the stern, he ordered that the engines be stopped. Unfortunately, the command to lower another boat took five minutes because the longboat's ropes were fouled on the deck. Once his son passed by the stern, O'Brien ordered the ship's engines back on, which brought the *Eureka* into the waves to launch its remaining longboat.

Dynamite Johnny jumped into the second boat with three sailors, and it was dropped into the ocean. The rolling seas by now had already carried Ned over 150 yards away. When a high roller picked him up, his head raised high into the air, but then he was swallowed up when it crashed down. The men leaned hard into the oars, and in five minutes the rocking boat was within twenty yards of Ned. Before they could reach him, O'Brien's son disappeared under the sea. The shock and hypothermia had overcome him.

The sailors rowed to where they thought Ned had vanished. Raising an oar high into the air, O'Brien drove it down through a thin layer of ice, hoping his son would take it. He didn't. He tried again and this time let go. Several seconds later, the tip surfaced fifteen feet from where he had rammed it down. The oar must have partially struck his son, he thought, and the captain instantly went into action.

O'Brien impulsively dove into the shockingly cold murkiness and swam toward the oar. With his body shaking involuntarily, he felt his arms crunch through thin ice and his body being carried upward by another surging swell. When he was almost to the oar, a hand came up and closed around it. The captain grabbed his son's wrist and began to tow him to the longboat. O'Brien learned later that the oar's glancing blow on Ned's head had awakened him from his stupor, and he had reached for it.

One sailor lowered his oar over the boat's bow to the captain, who grabbed it with his free hand. The men slowly pulled him up while he held to his son's wrist. The sailors then helped him pull Ned from the ocean.

A doctor was onboard who was working his way home after a bad gold-seeking experience. Watching what had happened from the deck, he was with Ned in seconds after the man was brought over the railing. This doctor didn't hold much hope for him at the time, noting the time spent in the freezing ocean. An hour passed before Ned started breathing normally.

Although no bones were broken, Ned had serious internal injuries and masses of deep bruises that coated his back and arms. The physician was hopeful O'Brien's son could recover somewhat, however, due to his splendid physical condition, and tended to him for the remainder of the voyage. In the middle of November, the *Eureka* reached Cape Cheerful, a "bold rocky cliff" some eight miles from Dutch Harbor. The sun was shining for the second time since the ship left Nome. When the *Eureka* entered the spacious harbor, the ship dropped its tow and maneuvered around the *Meteor*. The two ships were lashed together, and the *Eureka*'s crew then dropped its anchor for both vessels.

After a spare propeller and handcrafted rudder were installed, the *Meteor* was thought to be sufficiently seaworthy, although not able to steam on its own for the entire trip back to Seattle. The *Eureka* then started another long tow. The bad luck continued when the hawser parted a short distance from Dutch Harbor. The heavy seas and previous hard use had weakened the line, and it gave way after a series of heavy waves smashed into the vessels.

When Captain O'Brien couldn't turn his ship around in the narrow channel, he had no alternative but to continue on alone. Another ship that was escorting the two vessels, the *Manning*, attached another hawser to the *Meteor* and brought her back to Dutch Harbor. A steam tug then continued the efforts to bring the *Meteor* south for permanent repairs.

The *Eureka*'s journey was again troublesome, as the ship ran into more winter storms. The waves caused such severe rocking and pitching that the boilers ripped from their mounts, slammed against one another, and caused considerable damage inside. Its course through the Juan de Fuca Strait came headlong against another severe gale. These great waves engulfed the vessel, and one huge, rising monster nearly rolled it completely over. The *Eureka* and O'Brien fought through this for thirty-six hours, and at one time the vessel was within one mile of the deadly rocks on the Washington coast. When the storm conditions mercifully weakened, O'Brien was finally able to make Seattle's safe harbor.

His son was hospitalized, and two operations were necessary on his stomach to repair the internal injuries. Ned returned home an invalid, joining his brother who was in the same condition. Both men would fight to recover together, however, and although limited in what they could do, enjoyed basically normal lives. The O'Briens also had a daughter, who was then attending a boarding school, and a young son, John, then living at home and born in Vancouver, when the captain was working for the Canadian Pacific Navigation Company.

The lawsuits over the salvage of the *Meteor* quickly ensued, and the court awarded a grand total of $57,000, which was a large sum for ship salvage. Given the terrible weather conditions, what had to be done, the risks, and the injuries to O'Brien's son, this total amount seemed reasonable then—and worth over a million dollars today. The owners of the *Eureka* received the great bulk of the award, or $50,000. O'Brien received $2,500; the chief engineer got $1,000; Ned received $500; and the individual crew members were awarded $100 each. Other vessels such as the *Nome City* and the tugboat sought compensation, but the judge didn't award them anything. Even though the court awarded "extra" compensation for the men, the amounts seem low, given they were the ones responsible for the successful salvage. The owners, however, were the legally responsible parties and the seamen were their employees. Although the same results would generally be decided today, company policies now, worker's compensation, and a more favorable legal climate would certainly increase what the men would receive.

After the hard luck on this ship, Dynamite Johnny was ready for a different vessel. When the *Eureka* didn't secure any charters during the winter months, he had the excuse to take another command, but O'Brien would still be voyaging into the dangerous waters of Alaska and the Arctic.

16

THE RAILROAD MAGNATE AND NEAR-DEATH EXPERIENCES

Ships changed on O'Brien, but life onboard didn't. He accepted the command of the steamer *Olympia*, an English-built vessel placed under the American flag during the 1898 Spanish-American War. This vessel had limited first-class accommodations, but with the prime destination being Nome—despite the gold rush having started a few years before—her b'tween deck was crammed with gold-hungry passengers and her holds filled with their provisions and supplies.

Two days after leaving Seattle on its maiden trip, a delegation of prospectors knocked on the captain's door after breakfast. They told him the accommodations and food were "okay," but their waiters and steward were grifters: They charged for a second cup of coffee, equivalent today to the cost of the entire meal. O'Brien immediately called for an "inspection" of the entire steward's crew, including the waiters, that morning at the main hatch.

The chief steward, a large, beefy Englishman who was an ex–prize fighter, stood silently by while the captain took over. Dynamite Johnny warned the group that anyone found "grifting"—or fraudulently taking someone else's money—would wear a sign on his back with the word *grifter*. The captain would disrate the man and replace him immediately with one of the defrauded passengers. The captain told the men they were being paid a monthly salary, and any passenger was welcome to tip them for good service, but that was the extent of it.

212

O'Brien turned to the passengers who had complained and said, "Now point out who stole from you on the coffee." When the men hesitated, he said pointedly, "You need not fear any retaliation by the waiters. I will take care of that on my end." When still no one came forward, O'Brien sent the steward's department on their way.

The heavily built chief steward caught O'Brien alone. "You have no right to call my men down the way you just did."

The captain turned around and yelled into his face, "What! I have no right to call down your thieving gang! I am the King of this ship. If you or anyone else acts differently, you will be disrated. If you open your trap in criticism of my actions, you will be disrated at once. And don't test me on what else I'll do!"

Although the chief steward didn't say anything in response, Captain John saw a "snake-like-look creep onto his face" before he quickly turned away. O'Brien didn't have any further problems with the waiters.

Once the ship reached Nome, the passengers began disembarking. The steward then arranged for a "large group" of longshoremen to pay for eating their breakfast onboard instead of leaving to eat on land and then returning to unload freight. When these men began eating in the crew's mess, one sailor complained loudly to the steward about this intrusion. The man was a burly, strong-looking chap named Barney, and the two were soon shaking their fists in each other's face. Both stormed to the stern, and the fight was on. Dynamite Johnny said later this was one of the most brutal ones he had ever seen.

Every crewman came running to watch the fight as the two men furiously exchanged blows. Passengers still onboard and longshoremen ringed the fighting men and began waging bets. With the two combatants bloody and bruised, the sailor finally landed a strong blow to the steward's jaw, and he sagged to the deck, followed by Barney who slumped to his knees. The vicious fight was over, and the deck was covered with blood.

Both men were injured, with large swatches of bruises, abrasions, and cuts over their bodies. The steward had suffered a broken nose and several broken ribs, while Barney ended up with a fractured jaw and both eyes swollen shut. The *Olympia* soon left on its return trip, but the steward still remained in his berth. Seeing both men in bandages, O'Brien ordered Barney to be the steward's nurse until the ship docked, deciding there was no reason to be shorthanded, especially when their fighting brought about their injuries. During this time, they became friends, which wasn't that uncommon for brawling seamen and part of the respect given for a "fair" fight when only fists were used.

During these times such physical conflicts were an unfortunate part of any ship's voyage. And over time, O'Brien consciously tried to avoid fistfights with crewmembers. He saw the increasing power of the laws and courts. (In 1915, the federal Seamen's Act was passed, which reduced penalties for disobedience and regulated the hours worked, wages paid, and specific levels of safety, among other changes.) For years he looked for a way to compliment any sailor he had previously disciplined, otherwise known as "decking" someone who had been disorderly or wouldn't follow orders. That seaman normally would try his best afterwards to do his job. O'Brien demanded and commanded respect, but despite this, challenging situations continued to arise.

On this voyage, angry passengers stomped up later to O'Brien at midnight when he was on the bridge. They complained bitterly about the noise from a gambling "den" that kept them awake. The captain grunted he would do something about this, angered that any involved crewmen knew he couldn't leave the bridge on a foggy night such as this one—or so they had thought. He stopped the ship's engines and let the ship "run her way out." When the vessel stopped, he told the bridge officer that if he heard or saw anything out of the ordinary, to sound four short whistle blasts and O'Brien would immediately return.

When he stared down the dark main hatch, O'Brien could make out a long table with flickering oil lanterns strung overhead. Seamen, passengers, and even waiters were gambling in "full swing" and in a raucous setting. His blood was boiling over the crew's violation of his no-gambling order.

Captain O'Brien jumped down the gangway and shoved his way through the crowds to the table. Yelling "you, damn walleyed, transmogrified A.P.A. sons of Siwashes, haven't I told you not to gamble!" he punched at every crewmember involved, especially the white-jacketed stewards. Grabbing the table with its money, dice, and cards, he threw it over as people shrieked and ran for the gangway. O'Brien smashed the oil lamps, one of which burst into flames. Before the fire could spread, however, he smothered it with a blanket.

"That was the last of the gambling," he said, "and the passengers received their paid for sleep." Returning to the bridge, the captain started the engines again and continued on. The fog lifted a few hours later, and the ship soon docked at its next Alaskan port.

On the next trip, the ship was to haul a large cargo of lumber to Alaska for bridge building. With the loading nearly completed, Captain O'Brien lit a cigar. He was passing the number-two hold on his way to his cabin when a crewman shouted, "Look out!" He couldn't react fast enough. A stack of lumber crashed into him and knocked him from the deck into the hold. He fell thirty feet, head first. Throwing his arm out in protection, O'Brien slammed into the b'tween deck hatch combing, breaking his arm above the elbow but changing his fall. He slammed onto the hold's deck on his side.

A sailor slid down the ladder to O'Brien's side. Blood was flowing from his mouth, a bad sign that indicated internal injuries, and his first words were to ask for a priest. When a doctor climbed down into the hold, Dynamite Johnny refused to be moved or to receive a morphine injection until his called-for priest came. Although he could scarcely move his lips, O'Brien confessed his sins, but as one person later observed, "He wouldn't have had the time to talk about all of them."

Crewmen hoisted the captain through the hold while strapped to a cot, and an ambulance hurried him away to a local hospital. O'Brien had received serious injuries in the fall: All of his ribs on the left side—the side he fell on—were broken. A broken rib had punctured one lung, he was bleeding internally, and his collarbone was broken. The left side of his head was "smashed and swollen" with a "slight" fracture. O'Brien would be in hospitals for more than a month. Many thought he was lucky to be alive, but O'Brien amazingly fully recovered, although his nine lives had nearly ended with this one.

When he was conscious, Dynamite Johnny asked to be transferred to the marine hospital in the city to complete his recuperation there. When discharged, he signed both hospital and doctor bills, asking that they be sent to the owners of the SS *Olympia*. Twenty-four hours later, he was assigned to command the steamship *Edith*.

When the stevedores were loading his new ship with railroad construction materials bound for Valdez, Alaska, O'Brien paid a visit to the Sisters of Charity Hospital, which was the previous hospital he had stayed in. He wanted to thank them for their many kindnesses, especially when he lapsed into unconsciousness for several days from "complications" and a fever. When he asked if they had received their payment, he was shocked to learn that the bill had been returned. The *Olympia*'s owners had told them to look to him for payment.

O'Brien was "dumbfounded" that he had nearly lost his life while working for the owners, but they would be the "one in a hundred" that wouldn't pay for the medical bills. He paid the hospitals and doctors what he could and monthly thereafter until everyone was paid in full. As the owners had continued his salary while he was recovering, however, O'Brien decided to stay with them. This result, of course, would be completely different today. Before the era of worker's compensation laws—and today's ever-present personal injury attorneys—companies had very limited legal obligations to pay for the medical bills of employees who were injured on the job.

* * *

Dynamite Johnny completed his last trip on the *Edith* with construction materials bound for Valdez, Alaska. After that one run, the Alaska Steamship Company in 1905 transferred the fifty-four-year-old O'Brien to run a brand new 4,000-ton freighter, the *Seward*. This ship was headed on its maiden voyage for Katalla, an "exposed, open" port in the Gulf of Alaska. It was loaded down with railroad construction materials to make Katalla the shipping point for the Kennecott Copper River deposits.

O'Brien's great friend, M. J. Heney, had already built the long, tortuous White Pass and Yukon Route through Canada for the Alaskan Gold Rush. Known as Big Mike or the Irish Prince of Alaska, he next turned his attention to the substantial copper and coal deposits discovered by the Copper River in Alaska. He surveyed a route, bought land, established a tent camp named Cordova, and started construction of his railway. Work on the railroad began from Cordova in April 1906, and the town grew rapidly. Rivals began constructing a competing line, with the major difference being that one ended at Heney's Cordova and the other at Katalla, which was located fifty miles southeast of Cordova by land. The dramatic conflicts between the different construction crews included trading gunfire, dynamited passes, and destruction of equipment.

The Guggenheims and J. P. Morgan owned the ore deposits, and a Morgan-Guggenheim–backed venture had made a substantial investment in Katalla to be the shipping and railroad head for the mined copper. They were attempting to build a breakwater then for ships to connect with their ore-filled railroad cars. The port facilities were in the first construction stages, and the railroad line started from the Kennecott copper mines and great deposits—located a distance away—to end at the Katalla terminus. Heney had made a huge gamble in deciding to end his railroad at Cordova. For Dynamite Johnny, however, Katalla Bay was not a safe harbor. Severe gales raged through that wrecked the small cargo lighters offloading cargo, so he told Heney that Cordova was by far the better port.

In Seattle, the dockworkers loaded the huge *Seward* to where it squatted two feet below her Plimsoll line. O'Brien then refused to permit another hundred tons of steel railroad rails to be loaded onboard. Although a heated argument ensued with the shipping agent, he doggedly held to his position. He pointed out the ship was already two feet under her legal loading limit and concluded, "If you put another hundred tons on the deck and this ship hits gale winds, she'll never get to port."

The ship arrived off Cape St. Elias, twenty-five miles from his destination, in a "smothering snowstorm and a hard easterly blow." The lookout couldn't see the cape, and the conditions were dangerous. As daylight broke, O'Brien watched as a "mountainous sea" surged toward the ship and smashed into it, its swirling, green water flowing over the decks from bow to stern. The *Seward* was heavily laden, with a locomotive and tender lashed to its deck and hundreds of tons of railroad iron inside its holds. When the great sea struck, the ship trembled throughout, and the *Seward* slowly began to sink into the frothing green seas. At the time, the vessel was proceeding at a slow rate of speed, and O'Brien watched through the swirling snowfall in part amazement as the forecastle completely disappeared under the sea.

Realizing that his ship was going under, he instantly changed his attitude and decided to speed the ship up. Grabbing the bridge "speaking tube," O'Brien yelled for the engineers to give it "all she had" and go even faster than full-speed ahead.

He put the helm hard to starboard so the ship slowly swung into a huge trough in the sea. With the *Seward* inside that swell, the captain steadied the course to keep her inside the trough and away from the high rollers that nearly engulfed the ship. He anxiously judged that his vessel wouldn't sheer its sides on the outside reefs. When this conclusion proved accurate, he continued on that course.

The ship staggered through the high seas, as O'Brien hoped to bring her to the lee side of St. Elias before "she went to the bottom." After five minutes of plowing under the frothing ocean, the captain noticed that the *Seward* begin to roll up very slowly. It wasn't long before he saw part of the submerged forecastle, and this meant the ship had broken out "somewhat" from what he hoped were freak waves. Slowly the deck appeared, and O'Brien felt this crisis was passing.

Fortunately, every door around the decks and houses had been secured before the seas overwhelmed her. O'Brien was also thankful he had taken a hard stand against loading the additional tonnage of heavy rails. Even then, he had to keep the engines churning at full-speed ahead, with the occasional abrupt turn into a rogue wave's huge trough to deny Davy Jones his due that day.

Vibrations continuing to race throughout the structure, the overloaded ship submarined through heavy waves and gale winds toward its destination. That afternoon the snow let up, and the ship entered Katalla Bay before dark. The *Seward* anchored in the cove, close to where the Morgan and Guggenheim investors were building their breakwater. Although workers were already constructing the railroad from Katalla, the captain still felt this didn't make any sense if the harbor wasn't safe. He would soon find that out again.

The next day the crew was able to offload three hundred tons of rails to lighters that chugged them ashore; however, the seas were still too rough to take off the locomotive and tender. When a bad easterly gale stormed in the next day, the winds and waves forced O'Brien to drop a second anchor overboard with ninety fathoms (540 feet) of chain on each one. The winds blew so fiercely that the ship had to steam from slow- to half-speed ahead just to keep from being dragged—even with its heavy anchors down—onto land. One gust blew the two-hundred-pound mate off the forecastle down to the main deck. The man fortunately wasn't seriously injured, but he was severely bruised. Offloading any cargo was impossible under these conditions.

The blinding snowstorm and frightening winds continued for days. On the eleventh day, Dynamite Johnny noticed his ship was "some distance" from where it had originally anchored. He ordered the crew to use the windlass and heave in the slack of the port anchor chain. After fifteen fathoms (ninety feet) was brought in, the crew discovered with some apprehension that the chain had snapped from the currents and stress. With the engines going slow, the ship headed into the wind. When O'Brien ordered the starboard chain "hoved in," the men found this anchor had also parted after thirty fathoms (180 feet) was taken in.

With both anchors gone and only three hundred tons of cargo offloaded, the *Seward* was in a dangerous situation inside Katalla Bay. Not knowing how long the horrid conditions would continue, O'Brien decided to steam to Cordova, where its dock was small but the bay was better protected. He could offload the remaining 3,700 tons of cargo there.

O'Brien signaled the authorities in Katalla of his plans to leave for the Prince William Sound and Cordova. In case this communication had been missed, he wrote down their plans and destination, put the notes into bottles, and threw them overboard. The currents and winds quickly began sweeping the containers to the beach, where the railroad men could pick them up.

The conditions were still bad, but the ship made it to Cordova. Once the *Seward* docked, the first person onboard was M. J. Heney, who had invested great amounts of money on his gamble to build the railroad from there. Believing also that Katalla's harbor was unsafe, Heney had already built a few miles of the railway, despite the opposition of the Morgan-Guggenheim interests.

The ship unloaded all of its cargo at the dock in short time, as opposed to the dangerous eleven days spent in Katalla. The *Seward*'s horrendous time at that port and its successful travel to Cordova gave strong support to Heney's decision to build where he did. The steamship manager had asked O'Brien to check out the proposed final plans for building the Katalla jetty. The captain later told them the conditions he had seen would prohibit any dock unloading, concluding, "Neither ships nor that jetty could possibly survive the force of wind and sea, especially what we experienced for the days we were at anchor."

O'Brien had kept a log for each day from leaving Seattle to docking in Cordova and handed this to his manager. The man passed the report to New York, according to O'Brien, and with his strong recommendation about O'Brien's experience, it was presented to the board of directors, including J. P. Morgan himself. The crusty multimillionaire was reported to have commented:

> Gentlemen, I don't know this Captain O'Brien personally, but I do know that we have spent more than two-million dollars in the Katalla railroad scheme. We have little or nothing to show for our money. Scow load after scow load has been reported lost because of bad weather conditions. Vessels have lost their anchors and never recovered them. I, for one, absolutely refuse to put another dollar into the Katalla breakwater and railroad.

O'Brien's forced decision saved his ship and valuable equipment that his friend, Michael Heney, needed to build the very difficult Copper River and Northwestern Railway. His experiences at both ports, along with other factors that included the destruction in the fall of 1907 of the unfinished jetty by violent storms, brought about the moving of the railroad's terminus to Cordova.

When other routes proved impassable or as ill conceived as at Katalla, the Morgan-Guggenheim venture bought out Heney's interest in his route but appointed him to be its contractor. As the construction supervisor, he is given credit for having built this demanding line. The Copper River and Northwestern Railway was one of the most difficult construction projects undertaken. Under primitive conditions and far from supplies, the railroad line crossed difficult terrain including mountainous passes and two glaciers. The multispan Miles Glacier Bridge, also known as the Million Dollar Bridge, was built fifty miles from Cordova and between those glaciers. This bridge was completed just hours before the spring ice floes would have destroyed it.

In August 1909 and at the pinnacle of his career, Big Mike sailed from Cordova to Seattle on business. On his return trip to Alaska, disaster struck while he was aboard the steamship *Ohio*. Shortly after midnight on August 27, the ship struck an uncharted rock near Swanson Bay, Canada, and began to heavily take on water. Heney led the operations in abandoning the ship and saving the passengers. To allow one more passenger to be in his lifeboat, Michael Heney jumped into the chilled water and held on to the lifeboat's stern while it was rowed ashore.

After his long immersion in the frigid waters, Heney unfortunately never fully regained his health, and as a result developed pulmonary tuberculosis. Although he returned to Cordova to supervise the railroad's construction from September through November 1909, he became seriously ill while on a business trip that winter. Unable to return to work, he died on October 11, 1910, and was buried in Seattle. Heney's greatest achievement, the construction of the Copper River and Northwestern Railway, was completed five months after his death. Between 1911 and 1938, more than half a billion dollars worth of copper flowed from the Kennecott mines.

Never married, Heney left an estate of more than $1 million to friends, relatives, and charities. In August 1910, just before his untimely death, M. J. made his will and included Dynamite Johnny in it. He first left O'Brien $25,000, which was an enormous sum of money in those days. He changed his mind, however, only a few hours later. Heney returned to his attorney's office and told the lawyer that he wanted the will changed.

M. J. said the captain was getting along in his years and that if he received the lump sum of $25,000, "He'd spend it in a year or two at the most. I know him. I wish to give him $150 a month, or $1800 per year, until he dies." The wisdom of his friend was borne out. Once the monthly payments were made, O'Brien received over $37,500 before he died. When in Seattle, the captain headed to his friend's grave every Sunday and "had a talk with him as I did before—R.I.P."

Rex Beach portrayed M. J. Heney's character in his story *Iron Trail* as the railroader, Murray O'Neil. The honest engineer (O'Neil) fought with a corrupt promoter (Curtis Gordon) for the right to run a railroad through Alaska's gold country. Although Gordon used crooked means to edge ahead, O'Neil finally managed to emerge victorious. According to O'Brien, the book was based on fact, and even he had a "minor role": Captain Johnny Brennan, the master of the steamer *Nebraska*, that struck a hidden rock in Alaskan waters and sank. Although loaded with cargo for O'Neil—who always sailed with Captain Johnny—all hands were saved, including O'Neil, who managed to swim to shore. The book was published in 1912 and was based, according to the captain, on the experiences that O'Brien and Heney shared with Rex Beach after they met on the *Rosalie*.

* * *

O'Brien commanded other ships for the Alaska Steamship Company, including the *Oregon, Yucatan, Alameda*, and *Northwestern*. While captaining the *Yucatan*, the ship stopped at Katalla on its way to Valdez. The U.S. Marshal at Katalla, Jim Lathrop, boarded and told O'Brien that he wished to buy passage for himself and a "passenger" to Valdez. Lathrop said the prisoner was a "murderous devil" and had shot two loads of buckshot into a railroad foreman. The marshal wanted to know if the captain had a room where his prisoner would be "safe" until their arrival in Valdez. O'Brien showed Lathrop the available rooms, and the marshal took one.

Dynamite Johnny and Lathrop went ashore in a lighter and walked to the jail where the prisoner was kept. When the door was opened, O'Brien saw a "dark, vicious-looking man" of about forty. Staring at the captain, the prisoner, whose name was Carbone, had the look of a "caged wild animal." He couldn't attack anyone, however, because he was bound with leg and wrist irons. The man raved in Italian at the marshal, who spoke politely back. O'Brien told Lathrop he indeed had a "bad hombre," noting the "smoky" eyes, and that this one needed to be closely watched. They agreed Carbone was of the "killing kind."

The marshal brought the prisoner onboard that evening and put him in the quarters "prepared" for him. O'Brien assigned one seaman to keep watch on the room and Carbone. All seemed to go well during the night, and the ship was steaming up Prince William Sound at eleven in the morning. The sun shimmered over the snow-capped mountains, and the passengers were enjoying a beautiful day on the promenade deck. The ship was to arrive in Valdez in a matter of hours.

Captain O'Brien learned later that Carbone had complained to a summoned doctor that his wrist irons were hurting him. He asked the doctor to loosen them, which the physician did. Another Italian-looking man—and thought to be a member of the Mafia—was seen dropping something into the ventilator that led into the prisoner's room. When questioned, the passenger said he had sent down some tobacco, but a later examination of the room didn't find that substance.

Soon afterwards, Carbone began calling for the "keeper." When the sailor opened the door, the prisoner had the handcuffs off one hand and a six-inch knife held high in the other. When he slashed at the seaman, the knife ripped through the man's clothing, and he fell to the ground as if hit by an axe. The second mate rushed the Italian, but he stopped when the knife sliced down and nearly severed his thumb from one hand.

The prisoner stumbled from the room. Now on the loose, he clanged up the steps with his leg irons still on. Carbone shuffled to the saloon deck, yelling, "I'll kill every one of you." Having heard the commotion from his room located only fifty feet away, O'Brien was quickly—perhaps too quickly—on the scene. Carbone's path led directly to a female passenger, who was frozen with fright, as O'Brien ran toward both of them. When the crazed man stopped in front of the woman, the captain reached for her and heaved her out of the way.

The knife flashed in the sunlight as the captain yelled for the man to drop the knife. "Drop it, damn you! Drop it!" he shouted.

The prisoner yelled, "I'll kill you!" The two lunged at each other, the prisoner's knife slashing at Dynamite Johnny. The captain caught the knife hand by the wrist and drove a hard blow to Carbone's face. As the man stumbled, he grabbed the knife with his free hand and with curses drove it again at O'Brien. Captain John was not quick enough this time: He felt the knife's "red hot searing" as it plunged into him.

He grabbed the arm with the knife, and using his leg, tripped the enraged man. Both fell over the side of an open stateroom door, with O'Brien landing on top. When they fell, the captain lost his grip on the knife arm and felt the weapon's point in his back. With the killer trying to knife him again, O'Brien punched Carbone hard in the face and then grabbed him around the throat. O'Brien held to him tightly, trying to keep the man from slicing into his back—but then he felt the blade again.

Two ship officers finally ran over to the fighting men, and one kicked hard on Carbone's arm to knock the knife away. They then dragged the deranged man from underneath O'Brien. As they forced him back to the room, Carbone's screams continually cut through the ship and the low conversations of the frightened passengers.

Dynamite Johnny tried to get up, but the intense pain in his stomach doubled him over. He fell back into a pool of his own blood. The doctor and mate picked the captain up under each arm and dragged him toward his own room. With his blood dripping onto the deck, the floor became covered with the splatters. O'Brien didn't feel particularly weak, but he strangely seemed numb over his entire body. The doctor's wife, who was a trained nurse, was along on the voyage. She and her husband stripped away O'Brien's blood-soaked clothes and put him into his berth.

When the doctor probed the deep wound, his instrument disappeared completely inside it. Withdrawing the tool, he shook his head at the depth. Seeing this, O'Brien asked, "Did it go all the way in? If it did, then give me a stiff drink of whiskey, and I'll sing 'Sweet Rosie O'Grady' before I pass out." The doctor replied he could have the drink, but they needed to rush him to a Valdez hospital once the ship docked. Until he could sew O'Brien up, they kept direct pressure on the wounds, including those on his back, to try to control the bleeding. Already weak from the loss of blood, his chances of living were slim and ebbing away each hour.

The prisoner was again locked up, was placed in irons, and had both the U.S. Marshal and a sailor guarding him. But for the blood being washed off the decks and a critically injured O'Brien on his bunk, life on the ship seemed to go on as if nothing had happened. Once the *Yucatan* arrived in Valdez, seamen quickly carried the captain away to the hospital. Three doctors took turns sewing up the wounds, including the stitching and "plastering" of his cut-up intestines.

When he awoke from the anesthetic, a doctor warned him that he couldn't move for ten days: He would rupture his sutures and bleed to death. O'Brien knew he was close to death's door, but he was calm about his fate. For two days and nights, he lapsed in and out of consciousness, and the pain was intense when he was awake.

After forty hours passed, he heard the *Yucatan*'s steam whistle blow. O'Brien knew she had returned from Seward and would leave in an hour or two for home. Regardless of the risk, the captain decided he would go home on his ship, "doctor or no doctor's orders." He would rather die there than in some land hospital with its "nauseous smells." He could smell the bad odors of the last patients who had been in his bed—and knew some had died.

Dynamite Johnny waited until he felt the *Yucatan* was "fast along dockside" and the nurse was away from the room. When he slowly moved his feet over the bed's side, the pain in his stomach intensified. Holding his hand over his stomach, O'Brien slowly made his way to the closet. It took long minutes for him to bring the clothes to his bed and listlessly put them on. The hardest task was trying to work his trousers on. He couldn't bend down due to the pressure put on his intestines and the intense pain. He had to work one pant leg up a bended leg, pull it up, and then swing his other leg through. The simple act of dressing was torturous.

He slowly crept barefoot through the quiet hospital, out its front door, and into the warming sunshine. When he felt "woozy" outside the hospital, he leaned against a tree. Looking up, he saw a small wagon with beer barrels creaking over the dirt road toward him. O'Brien slowly raised his hand and quietly hailed the driver. He asked if the man could take him to the *Yucatan*. "I can't pay you now," he said, "but if you get me to the ship, I can make arrangements." The man told him to get in.

O'Brien backed into the wagon. Seeing the obvious pain the captain was in, the driver chucked his horse and cart slowly along, while Dynamite Johnny held one hand against his stomach wound. His bare feet were over the wagon's end and just cleared the ground. When the cart stopped at the ship's dock, the passengers and their friends were milling about the gangplank. "Good-bye" and "See you, again" filled the air. Some of these smiling, active people noticed a pale, elderly man with no shoes, one hand clutching his stomach, as another man guided him down from a wagon with empty beer barrels.

They must have thought the frail, sick-looking man, who shuffled up the gangway, was crazy. And he guessed they were nearly right. He asked one of his sailors to pay the driver, who stood patiently waiting below. O'Brien shuffled to his room, opened the door, locked the spring lock behind, and lay down slowly onto his berth. He had a hard time keeping from fainting, but Dynamite Johnny managed to "keep his head."

The doctor and nurse continually knocked on his door, but O'Brien couldn't get up to let them in. Eventually they sprung the lock and barged into the room. When that happened, the captain slowly swung one of his legs out of the berth. He told them evenly, "I'll kick you in the stomach if you try—in any way—to take me from this berth. I will not go back to that terrible hospital. Never!"

"Captain," said the doctor in a soothing voice, "If you go back, you will come out all right. You are flying in the face of Providence. You'll surely die on this ship."

"If I die, sir, then it will be in a clean bed. Now I want you to leave. I'm going home on this ship and that is final. I am still the captain." The doctor and nurse stayed and tended to O'Brien until the ship arrived in Katalla, 120 miles from Valdez. When the vessel docked there, they left him and disembarked.

After the ship steamed away from Katalla, the captain felt that he couldn't bear the pain—but he did. The thought of seeing his dear wife "braced" him up, as well as that his grown children and daughter-in-law would be with him. With them, he knew that "every care would be attended to."

Time passed. When the *Yucatan* was approaching its Seattle dock, Captain John saw the manager, Mr. Trowbridge, pacing up and down the wharf. He learned later that Trowbridge was upset from a received wire that reported O'Brien would likely be dead upon the vessel's arrival. When the manager didn't see the flag at half-mast, however, he knew that his captain was still alive.

When Trowbridge and Em' entered his stateroom, the captain was already dressed in his uniform. They both were surprised when they saw him, and O'Brien looked as if he was a "long way" from being a dead man. They took him at once off the boat and by an ambulance to a Seattle hospital. After two more weeks of recuperation, he finally felt well enough to come home for a few days.

A process server then handed him a subpoena to appear in the Valdez court on the charges brought against Carbone for the stabbing of "one Captain O'Brien." Dynamite Johnny went to the Alaska Steamship Company's office to obtain a pass on the next ship going there. The ticket agent told him the officer who issued the steamer passes was out of town. The agent concluded, "It would be just fine for you to pay your fare to Valdez and I'll give you a receipt. When you return here, you can be reimbursed."

O'Brien paid the fifty dollars for his passage. The U.S. government also paid witnesses at a rate of five cents a mile, which would offset this. He appeared in court the next day. At the hearing, the defense was that the prisoner was insane, and doctors testified to this. In fact, O'Brien also testified that Carbone had to be insane.

He told the jury what he later learned when Carbone was in the Valdez jail. The prisoner had somehow gotten his hands on a large nail, perhaps from the same accomplice who tossed the knife down the ventilator shaft. Carbone sharpened the nail against the stone flags of his cell. One morning, he began screeching loudly. Hearing the curses and yells, the jailer opened the prisoner's door and without thinking ran in. "Quick as a cat," Carbone was on top of the jailer and stabbed him several times in the face with the honed nail. That was enough for O'Brien to conclude that this prisoner was not only a homicidal maniac but also crazy. O'Brien testified to what he honestly believed, even though this meant the man who had nearly killed him might not go to jail. Despite Dynamite Johnny's testimony, the trial ended with Carbone receiving a sentence of ten years at Washington's Walla Walla state prison for the shooting, with additional time for the stabbings of O'Brien and the jailer.

The agent in Valdez couldn't give him a pass to Seattle, however, so the captain once again had to pay for his passage. Carbone with two guards was ironically on the same steamer. Showing O'Brien's typical lack of fear, he asked to be let into the prisoner's room. Once there, he said, "Antonio, why did you stab me?"

Carbone stared at him—but this time without the "snake-like eyes"—and said in broken English, "I no stab you. You, good man." He told O'Brien about his wife and "little bambinos" in Sicily and then emphasized, "I no remember me stab you." Feeling he was a lucky man, Captain John walked back to his room. He learned later that Carbone was imprisoned in different places. When finally taken to a prison for the criminally insane, Antonio Carbone died mysteriously during the transfer.

Once O'Brien arrived in Seattle, he headed directly to the company office to be reimbursed for the two tickets. The officer then told him that the business wouldn't do this. Since the government fees for being a witness were about the same amount as the fares, there was no need to reimburse him. The only problem was that although this "just about" covered his expenses on the trip, he hadn't been on the company's payroll from the day he arrived in Seattle after leaving the Valdez hospital. He was again in a financial hole to work out of with Em's guidance.

* * *

Captain O'Brien had more "thrilling experiences" on the next ships commanded after the *Yucatan*. These were on the *Northwestern* and the *Alameda*, again owned by the Alaska Steamship Company. The captain found himself and the *Northwestern* in another bad snowstorm on the way to Prince William Sound. The gale conditions were so bad with strong winds and thick snow that the men couldn't catch the echo—showing the presence of deadly land or rocks—from their "weird sounding steam whistle." With 275 passengers onboard, many people were praying and trusting their safety to the captain.

O'Brien was amidships when he heard a distinct voice through the screeching winds say two words in his ears, "Heave to." He looked sharply around but couldn't see anyone. Turning to the officer on the far "weather side," he asked if the man had said anything, but the officer shook his head.

Seconds later, Dynamite Johnny heard the same words of "Heave to," and again no one was close enough to say that. He heard the words again in his ears, this time from behind his back. When he whirled around, he saw only the back of the pilothouse, and strong chills ran up and down his spine.

The captain said, "Whoever you are, I'll heave to." He gave the orders to slow the engines down. When the ship's way had "slackened," he put the helm down and brought the ship's head to the south so that the vessel was now pointing directly to the open sea.

Suddenly the lookout shouted, "I think I see a light ahead, sir!" The tiny speck of light swung back and forth and was three hundred yards away. The illumination seemed to flicker and then completely disappear. Ordering his mate to "turn the juice" on their searchlight, the powerful beam swept around until it picked up the silhouette of a small, beaten sloop. Its sails were ripped away, and the boat was wallowing in the frothing ocean. O'Brien whistled through the tube and ordered the engineers below to get the steam up to approach the sloop.

When the ship came within fifty yards of the floundering sailboat, O'Brien saw the lamp attached to the mast. As the ship swung with the deep rollers, its light bounced around as well. When a large wave dragged the wreck into its trough, everything disappeared into the blackness. A barely audible voice pleaded, "For God's sake, please take us off. We were blown off course, have little canned food left, and six men and a woman are onboard."

Although moved by the sight and the piteous voice, Dynamite Johnny shouted through his megaphone for them to hold on until daylight. "It is almost impossible to take you off in this heavy sea. We can't launch our boats. To come alongside, means our ship will smash you."

The voice pleaded, "We can't last another hour. Please help us."

O'Brien said he would. While the ship's searchlight "played" on the scene, he told the mate to keep all of the cluster lights ready and to throw the Jacob's ladder over the side on his command. He yelled at two men to ready heaving lines and quickly pull everyone in on his command. When the vessel was abreast of the beaten sailboat, sailors threw the ropes toward the people as the searchlights illuminated the sea and wreck "as bright as day." The seamen began dragging some of the people up the wet sides of the much larger ship.

When a long roll of the steamer brought the sloop close to the railing, the rest grabbed for the side ladders, and the first ones were quickly hauled up on deck. One of those who jumped, however, missed the ladder and fell back into the choppy waters by the sailboat. He bobbed up and down for an instant, only to be crushed when the sloop and the steel ship crashed against one another in a spray of sea. He then disappeared forever beneath the ocean and its shadowy, dark waves.

The crash caused the sloop to fill with ocean, careen within the large waves as if a toy boat, and then sink as fast as the unlucky man did. All the people—but for the unfortunate one caught between the ships—were now onboard save two. A man and his wife were still clinging to the ladder, halfway between the railing and the crashing ocean. When the *Northwestern* rolled up, the sailors hauled up the ladder with the motion. They were able to bring them up while the terrified woman still clung to her spouse.

Crewmen accompanied the soaking wet, shivering people to the saloon where they received dry clothing and food. While they basked in the warmth and safety of the ship, the husband told O'Brien that the man who died was his wife's insane brother. When everyone had given up hope, however, he had told them that a large ship with lots of lights would be coming to them. O'Brien didn't tell him about the voices he had heard at about the same time.

The *Alameda* brought about an episode the captain would have rather forgotten. Although he wasn't at fault, the event made Seattle newspaper headlines. The regular master of the *Alameda* was ashore in 1912, when O'Brien was acting temporarily as the port pilot and in charge of bringing vessels to the dock. The ship had taken on its fuel of bunker oil at the Standard Oil dock on the East Waterway, leaving at 9:45 P.M. and arriving a half hour later off its pier in Seattle. O'Brien planned to berth her at the south slip and already had her moving under a "dead slow" bell toward that side. The dock manager then shouted instructions for him to tie up instead on the north side.

The *Alameda* was two hundred yards from the pier. When he put the helm hard to starboard, the vessel didn't respond. O'Brien then rang for slow ahead, and as she began to swing, he ordered half-speed astern and then full-speed astern. The third engineer was taking the signals from the bridge and relaying them verbally to the second at the throttle.

The throttle engineer somehow misunderstood the directions, and he set the engine at full-speed ahead rather than full-astern. When Dynamite Johnny felt the powerful surge of the engines, he shouted to the chief officer on the forecastle to get the anchors over and fast. With the steam whistle sounding its shrill alarm, the large *Alameda* tore through Colman Dock 150 feet from the outer end, emerged on the north side, and smashed directly into the stern-wheeler *Telegraph*, driving the wooden ship hard against a neighboring wharf.

The *Telegraph* sank in less than fifteen minutes. In the stern-wheeler's engine room, one fireman was working on a condenser when the *Alameda*'s bow crashed through and grazed the spot where he was working. Shocked at the sight of the huge metal bow filling the high ceiling space, the engineer still managed to start the pumps as the huge floods of water began spurting inside. With the sea quickly rising to his waist, the man was forced to race up the stairwell and to the stern. There he jumped into the ocean. The *Telegraph* was soon resting on the bottom in forty feet of water.

Three women were injured on the docks, and lifeboats promptly lowered by O'Brien from the *Alameda* plucked several people from the sea. Fortunately no lives were lost. The damage to the *Alameda* was so slight that she sailed the next evening for Prince William Sound, only twelve hours behind schedule. The "remarkable blunder in the engine room," however, had sent the heavy iron ship crashing through the dock, demolishing a tall clock tower, smashing the outer end of the dock to pieces, and almost cutting the *Telegraph* in two. The Colman Dock clock tower had been a landmark on the Seattle waterfront; cut down by the ship's path, it rolled from the *Alameda*'s deck and was found floating the next day in the harbor. A tug towed it to the beach, the large hands still pointing to 10:23, the time of the accident.

The H. W. McCurdy Marine History of the Pacific Northwest states:

> Maritime men were unanimous in their praise for the prompt action of Captain O'Brien, particularly for his quick lowering of the anchors. The starboard anchor had caught and stopped the destructive course of the steamer after one-hundred and twenty-five fathoms of chain were out, undoubtedly preventing her from continuing her rampage through the Grand Truck Dock.
>
> Captain Howard Bullene, master of the steamer *Santa Ana* commented: "If the navigator of the wrecked *Titanic* had exhibited one-half the presence of the mind of Captain O'Brien, the most frightful disaster in maritime history would have been averted. With the same promptness, the *Titanic* could have been turned bow-on to the iceberg, when it was reported a quarter of a mile ahead, and her bulkheads would have saved her, as was done with the *Yucatan* when she struck a berg in Icy Straits."

The owner of the *Telegraph*, the Puget Sound Navigation Company, turned the claim over to its insurers. They demanded damages of $55,000. After the contested hearing, the U.S. commissioner awarded damages of $45,000. The U.S. Court of Appeals in San Francisco reduced this award to $25,000, on the basis that the market for stern-wheelers had suffered an economic downturn since the *Telegraph* was built and that the basis for calculating the damages was wrong. Salvagers had subsequently raised the ship and she was back in service by that time.

In 1909, Captain "Dynamite Johnny" O'Brien became the master of the *Victoria*, and under his command this ship became one of the most famous of the Alaskan vessels. His voyages became legendary during these risky but adventurous times when ships ruled the Pacific Northwest and Alaska.

17

THE *VICTORIA*

The *Victoria* was a long 360 feet, her beam 40 feet, and she displaced 3,500 tons. O'Brien's *Victoria* was the ship sent in when storms were fierce or a destination needed to be reached. Frequently swept by fierce gale winds and blinding snowstorms, the Bering Sea experienced ferocious waves in its shallow waters. The vessel proved her worth under these conditions, as her massive hull of wrought iron and powerful engines made her well suited for those waters and as a trailblazer. This ship pushed her way through ice floes that lesser ships couldn't try. The *Victoria* was usually the first to plow through the ice on the Nome run, and usually she was the last ship out in the late autumn. These departures were done hastily, because when ships weren't out by the first of November, insurance premiums typically skyrocketed after that date for vessels in the Bering Sea.

Nearly twenty years before, Captain O'Brien watched from the quarterdeck of the *Premier* while the ship lay alongside its CPR (Canadian Pacific Railway) dock in Vancouver. A "long, graceful looking" steamer headed to a nearby berth. "Little did he know" that years later he would be in command of this vessel in the Alaskan trade.

Commissioned in 1870, the *Victoria* began her career as the Cunard Line's *Parthia*. Designed for the low-cost immigrant trade between Ireland and the United States, the ship was built for economy and strength, not for speed or luxury. During her fifteen years of service as a Cunard liner on the North Atlantic,

229

the ship was used as much as a windjammer as a steamship. Although fitted with an 1,800-horsepower compound engine, she was fully rigged as a three-masted bark. When the winds blew favorably, the engine was disconnected from its shaft, the screw was feathered, and the boat sailed across the Atlantic on wind power to save hundreds of tons of expensive coal.

During her Cunard service, her duties ranged from carrying commercial passengers across the seas to being chartered as a British troopship during the 1881 Egyptian campaign. When sold to another company, the *Parthia* in 1885 was reengineered and fitted with a triple-expansion steam engine (where the steam passes through three chambers and generates more power), which was used on this ship into the 1950s. After being placed on voyages to South America, Australia, and the Hebrides, the ship steamed two years later to the Pacific to operate between Vancouver and the Orient for the Canadian Pacific Railway Company. Five years later, the ship returned to Great Britain for an overhaul and was renamed the *Victoria*, returning to the Pacific in 1892.

The *Victoria* operated from Tacoma to the Orient for twelve years, including being used as a U.S. Army troopship during the Spanish-American War, when she was sold to the Northwestern Improvement Company and again extensively rebuilt. More deckhouses were added in preparation for the service between Seattle and Nome in the summer of 1904. When this company merged four years later with the Alaska Steamship Company, the *Victoria* became part of its fleet.

Placed on the Nome service during its gold rush days, the *Victoria* took miners there and gold back. *Marine Digest* (1953) concluded:

> As a unit of the Nome gold fleet, this ship was considered the most popular of all—and probably thanks to its captain, Captain Dynamite Johnny. It was common for the *Victoria* to bring as much as two-million-dollars worth of gold per trip from the Seward Peninsula gold fields. Bricks of gold were shipped in canvas bags and averaged twenty-thousand dollars in value. As the ship on many voyages didn't have a safe room in which to stow the gold, it was placed on the floor of the purser's office.
>
> Many passengers swore by this strong-hulled ship. However, numbers of them credited Captain Johnny Dynamite O'Brien as the reason for this ship not impaling itself on the hidden rocks or ripped open on the deadly ice floes.

The ship was originally a coal burner but in 1910 was converted to run on oil. When steaming on coal, her bunkers and one hold would be filled with coal; during the return trip from Nome, it was necessary to hoist the coal in rolling seas to fill the bunkers. This difficult task was eliminated by the use of oil. The *Victoria* originally could haul 800 passengers, along with a crew of 140, but this number could be increased depending on the voyage. When "rolling chocks" were added, hauled loads were steadied when in bad seas. These pieces of wood or other material were placed beside cargo to keep them from rolling about or moving sideways inside a ship's hold.

During her runs, the ship had her share of "scrapes." Prior to the Alaska Steamship Company's ownership, the vessel had incidents ranging from colliding with the White Star liner *Adriatic* to running aground outside New York, but the strong ship sustained only minor damage. In 1907, the *Victoria* struck an iceberg near Nome, filling a lower hold with the sea, which rose to within a few inches of the main deck. The forward and after bulkheads held, the cargo was offloaded, and after temporary repairs were made, the ship returned to Seattle. She was completely repaired at the Puget Sound Navy Yard at Bremerton, Washington.

After the incident, the *Victoria* was in a race one year later with her rival in the trade, the steamship *Ohio*, from Nome to Seattle. Excitement ran high on both ships while the passengers watched and bet on the outcome. The *Victoria* beat the *Ohio* by nine hours and steamed into Seattle with a broom lashed to her mainmast. Another accident occurred in 1910 when the *Victoria*, now owned by the Alaska Steamship Company, grounded onto the beach on the south end of Hinchinbrook Island, Alaska, in the Inside Passage. She was refloated, however, and easily repaired.

* * *

Dynamite Johnny's first trip on the *Victoria* in 1909 took six hundred passengers, and the ship pushed through two hundred miles of ice, being the first vessel to arrive in Nome that late spring. With these large numbers of voyagers, the professional gamblers flocked to buy round-trip tickets on the trips to fleece those with the gambling spirit. Although O'Brien had posted notices on his vessel reading "No gambling allowed," he knew this by itself wouldn't solve the problem.

On his first day out on any voyage, the captain assembled the passengers on deck and told them about the "sure thing" of the gamblers lying in wait. He told the people that they had no other purpose except to rob them—especially those who were leaving Nome in the fall with their season's hard-earned savings. He talked about the numerous people who came aboard his ship "happy" with gold and money for their families, only to disembark in Seattle with suicidal thoughts and nothing left in their pockets.

He would conclude:

> You can play all the cards you want for pleasure—even for cigars—but if I ever see money on the tables, I will take it. The Red Cross will receive your donations upon our arrival in Seattle. If you think you can get it back, then you'll have to sue for it. Gambling is illegal on this ship.

No matter what voyage or time, O'Brien seemed to be always breaking up a game. The gamblers tried to stay one step ahead on this large vessel by positioning paid informers at different locations; when they saw the captain coming, they sounded out the alarm. By the time O'Brien reached the complained-about room, no money would be in sight and only a "friendly game of cards" was in progress. When this happened, O'Brien disguised himself by wearing an overcoat with high collars and walking inside a group of passengers. He would pass the sentries to watch the tables.

O'Brien then waited until he heard the words "Hit me," whereupon he would roar, "Yes, I'll hit you and hard!" and jump to the table. Screaming like a crazed man, O'Brien would grab all the money in sight. Remembering his admonitions, the passengers would run to get away. The gamblers angrily yelled back, however, that O'Brien would have a knife stuck in his back, or some other threat, but nothing of the kind ever happened. They knew the penalty and that O'Brien was the king of this ship. He also created such an angry, out-of-control scene, as he wrote later, that no one really wanted to challenge him. O'Brien understood mob psychology—he had to.

His main concern was to control his crew, whom the gamblers also liked to target. One time, the mate ran to him and said, "We can't keep steam up, as most of the men on watch are gambling with the passengers." O'Brien was surprised this time, because he had just made the rounds of the ship and had seen nothing suspicious going on. The mate told him the gamblers had found a place on the large ship that even O'Brien hadn't thought of. This was down in the last hold by the bow.

As he had done in the past, Dynamite Johnny crept to the place, this time to the forward b'tween deck hatch. Peering quietly through a crack in the hatch, he noticed a light coming from below. Lifting one of the hatches, the captain climbed down the Jacob's ladder, where he found forty men gambling at a long table with strings of lights overhead. He grabbed a whiplike stick and "came on the run," yelling again like a madman and noisily whipping the switch back and forth. Frightened by the sudden appearance of the screaming white-coated banshee, men began running pell-mell for the ladder. O'Brien threw the long table over, and the money scattered over the floor. He then ran after everyone while jabbing at them with the stick. He started laughing to himself at the spectacle of the people falling over themselves to get away.

Men were scrambling over the shoulders of others, including the white-jacketed waiters who were still in uniform, all trying to put some distance between themselves and O'Brien. Looking around, the captain saw one man running after him with his hand held high. Knowing that this had taken a serious turn, the captain decked him and located a knife nearby. When four passengers came to him and apologized, they then promised not to gamble and to do their best to stop others. Captain John accompanied them back into the hold and gathered up the money; he then gave it back, sternly lecturing them that if he had any further problems, he would hold them personally accountable. O'Brien had made a commonsense exception to his rule, which also helped end any further gambling on this particular trip.

No matter the day, a captain always had some problem to solve with his personnel. On a morning when no eggs were being served, the quartermaster decided he was special, stormed down to the galley, drove out the cooks, and fried himself four eggs for his breakfast. The steward told the captain what had happened and that several seamen were now wondering why they also couldn't have eggs. What had been a small problem had grown bigger. O'Brien found the quartermaster and called him down for his actions. When the quartermaster gave a "sharp reply" back, O'Brien grabbed him by the seat of the pants and shoulders, ran him through the passengers, and tossed him onto the forecastle deck. After disrating the quartermaster in his rank and position, he told the man to live in the fo'c'sle now with the other seamen. The captain then went back to his breakfast.

Ten seamen who worked under the deposed quartermaster, and who probably were also receiving special favors, then refused to work further unless he was reinstated. O'Brien stormed down to those men and yelled, "If you're not working in sixty seconds, each and every one of you will be fined two days' pay. And you'll be in irons. By the gods, I'll be the man who puts them on."

Taking his watch out, Dynamite Johnny counted to sixty seconds and then walked to the nearest man. O'Brien demanded to know if he was going to "turn to," but the sailor murmured something he couldn't understand. The captain yelled louder, "What did you say?"

"Yes sir, I'll turn to," the young-looking man shouted at the top of his voice. "And off he flew," said the captain later.

Nine seamen remained. O'Brien asked another one the same question, and the man replied quietly, "Yes, sir."

"Yes, what!" Dynamite Johnny stormed.

"Yes, sir!" the man yelled back. When this sailor walked quickly to start his work, the others followed.

Suspecting the disrated ex-quartermaster was behind the coup, the captain found the man. "Down on your knees!" he yelled. "Take that bucket and start swabbing the entire deck. You'll do this all the working hours from here to Seattle!" Although O'Brien's blood was still boiling, after he watched the man dutifully follow those orders for the day, his "heart relented" and he reinstated the quartermaster.

No matter what, a captain needed to be ever watchful. The seas always presented danger. On one occasion, a "large beam sea" was running, and the ship was severely rolling from thirty to forty degrees. A small boy was walking on deck in his oilskins. O'Brien was on the bridge when the ship heeled into a deeper roll than usual. He watched, mouth open, as the boy lost his footing, slid violently from the weather side to the lee side, and broke through the iron-pipe gangway rail to sail into the choppy sea.

The men threw "lifer rings" down, and the lifeboat was lowered. While seamen kept their view on the boy, men rowed the boat toward the bobbing youth.

As O'Brien and his crew approached the struggling youth, a large roller came through and surged the boat up. Still keeping the boy in sight, the men saw his oilskin blow over his head. While he fearfully flailed with his arms to try to clear the raingear away, he simply sank away in plain sight of everyone.

Despite the frothy ocean and whitecaps, the seamen held to their position by backing and going ahead. They searched for a half hour but didn't find any sign of the youth. The boy was never seen again.

O'Brien cabled the report of the loss at the next port, and the company's manager broke the sad news to the mother. The captain couldn't forget the pain and anguish that the "middle-aged woman" showed when he had to explain onboard how her son lost his life.

When passengers come aboard any ship, they also bring along their problems. The son of a well-known judge was on one voyage and became insane. He grabbed a carving knife and chased the crew from their quarters. When O'Brien heard about this, he found the youth on the main forward deck, screeching, "I'll kill any man who comes near me." The captain walked to him and said in an "easy voice" when twenty feet away, "What's the matter, son? Has someone on this ship been bothering you? If they have, I'll stop them." The judge's son didn't answer.

With the young man staring at him, O'Brien slowly walked closer. He stopped four feet away, but still out of knife range, as the captain had already had one weapon stuck six inches inside him and had "supposedly" learned his lesson. For some reason, however, the captain felt secure that this one wouldn't try to stab him.

Dynamite Johnny said quietly, "You know that I'm your friend. I am here to take care of you." He said casually, "What a curious knife you have. Where did you get it?" O'Brien kept talking in an easy voice.

Lowering the knife, the lad told the captain that he had grabbed it from the galley—or "kitchen as shore folks call it." O'Brien said he would like to see the knife maker's name and that he was interested in this. Slowing reaching for it, O'Brien held his hand open. The boy quietly handed the weapon over.

The two were silent. "Sonny boy," he said. "Come with me to my room." They chatted for a few minutes there, and then O'Brien excused himself so he could write a hurried note to the mate to at once make ready one of the spare staterooms. The room would have portholes but be stripped of anything that could possibly be used as a weapon. The physician onboard was to be alerted. When the room was ready, the mate was to let him know by another note.

The folded message came. O'Brien told the boy that no one would be able to harm him and he had a new, safe room. The captain took the youth there, talked with him until the boy lay down, and then admitted the doctor. While the doctor attended to the lad, O'Brien left for the bridge. The father met the ship upon its arrival and took his son away. He told the captain later that the young man had to be committed to a sanitarium.

Other passengers created happier times. The classic case was about one Mr. Eisenlohr, a multimillionaire tobacco importer and manufacturer from Philadelphia. He was traveling on the *Victoria* to Nome on business the first time they met, and Dynamite Johnny remembered him as being one of the most congenial men he had ever come across.

Eisenlohr was a bachelor and had a "hobby" of helping people, especially young men who were trying to enter a profession through hard work. When he came upon such a lad, he would contact a friend—the president of a college in Philadelphia—and have him write the man to make an appointment to talk about college. The president would tell the young person he had an "unknown friend" who would pay his tuition and expenses for a college degree. By this time, Eisenlohr had arranged for thirty-four young men to study at that university.

O'Brien and Eisenlohr enjoyed conversations and cigars in the captain's room when he was off duty. They talked about their experiences of love and life. When the ship was approaching Seattle, Eisenlohr handed a $1,000 check to O'Brien, telling him to buy himself "a few drinks" as a toast to their friendship. Trying to be as tactful as he could, O'Brien declined the offer, but he could tell his new friend's feelings were "somewhat hurt."

Three days after the ship's return, Eisenlohr sent a note to Dynamite Johnny from Spokane. The $1,000 check was enclosed. The letter read:

> My dear Captain. If you dare send this little remembrance back to me, I will at once send it to the American Protective Association [the basically anti-Catholic, anti-union outfit O'Brien had the longstanding feud with] in Seattle to be used in a frame-up, such as was done to you in Portland, Oregon, in 1881, when their lies lost you the command of the ship *Kate Davenport*. I know how much you love the A.P.A., and consequently, I know you will keep this memento in memory of our trip on the *Victoria*. And when you take your next vacation, don't forget old man Eisenlohr.

The following day, the captain visited the Seattle hospital to visit his two sons, both of whom were trying to recuperate from complications that arose from their tragic accidents. Born on the bark *Alden Besse* those years ago during a Pacific gale, Frank was now thirty years old. He had internally hemorrhaged while lifting a heavy weight on a ship off Nome. Smashed savagely between a rolling ship and its lifeboat in the Bering Sea, older brother Ned was also fighting to heal from his injuries.

He had helped both his sons in their battles to live a normal life. The doctors had just told the captain, however, that Frank didn't have many more days to live. For ten years, O'Brien had arranged for Frank to spend periods of time in the warmer climates of Southern California and Arizona to regain his health. This had seemed to work well, as his son had passed a physical examination at Camp Lewis to join the army. A few months later, Frank became sick with ptomaine (food) poisoning, was sent immediately home, and was now deathly ill. He had been married for only five months.

The day the captain saw Frank in the hospital, his son said, "I feel very sad you've spent so much money on me. I thought that before long I could repay you part of that, but here I am sick again. And it looks like my end is near."

Tears welled up in their eyes. The captain told his son that he was in good financial shape and showed him the $1,000 check from Eisenlohr. Frank died soon thereafter. O'Brien wrote his friend afterwards and told him how his gracious check had given his son peace in those last days. Simply showing his son that he was "in the $1,000 class" had brought happiness to Frank. Captain O'Brien was understandably appreciative of "old man Eisenlohr." The two men kept up with each other when both were in Seattle and could sit down over dinner. O'Brien once told Eisenlohr that he was going to be in the U.S. Shipping Board's service, as he had been assigned to a ship running between the Pacific and Atlantic during World War I.

The tobacco importer replied, "Captain, if by any means you are in Rotterdam in Holland, you'll find that I have a full cargo of Sumatra leaf tobacco, but due to the war, I haven't been able to ship it to the United States. If you can arrange for my agent to ship the cargo on your vessel, you will receive a bonus from me of twenty-five thousand dollars. Of course, I would pay all freight and charges."

This was a very large sum of money and in the hundreds of thousands of dollars today. O'Brien answered that if he was ever there, he would see what he could do legally, including "trying to ram every enemy submarine that showed its nose above water." Eisenlohr increased the amount earned to $30,000 if the captain was successful. O'Brien told him that he doubted he would be able to help the man, and as it turned out, he was never there.

* * *

Temporarily leaving his command of the *Victoria* during World War I, O'Brien was placed in charge of running the *Westerly*, a ship that hauled heavy cargoes of steel and war supplies. Motivated by patriotism of the "purest kind," as *Marine Digest* commented, Captain O'Brien was sixty-six years old, "almost of white hair," when he volunteered for service during the war. When O'Brien steamed out of Seattle harbor on the *Westerly* for the Atlantic, he was an officer in the United States Naval Reserve.

Headed for the East Coast, he contacted Eisenlohr about his coming. When the captain stepped off the train in Philadelphia, Eisenlohr met him at the train station with his girlfriend and sister and then showed him the "long, extravagant limousine at their disposal." O'Brien spent eight luxurious days at his friend's huge, exquisite country estate near Washington, DC, which included Eisenlohr giving a banquet in his honor with fifty invited guests. A chartered railway car brought O'Brien and eighteen of the partygoers in style to the grand estate. After the grand times, the captain took a train back to pick up his vessel.

O'Brien commanded the *Westerly* back to Seattle, but when the ship was sailing through the Caribbean at dusk, the man on watch yelled, "Submarine off starboard quarter! Submarine!" The captain swung his glasses around and picked up the wake of a periscope one-half mile away. He told the engineer through the speaking tube to go full-speed ahead, while he ordered the pilot to swing the ship to port and away from the submarine. The ship was fortunate when night and a storm quickly thundered in. The *Westerly* had escaped.

Dynamite Johnny next commanded a new coal-burning freighter, the *Ossineca*, on her maiden run. Since the vessel hadn't been "shaken out" well, it developed engine trouble before she was even out of Puget Sound. The chief engineer argued with O'Brien as to whether the ship should turn back, but he decided to continue on to San Francisco. This was a war, after all, Dynamite Johnny decided, and the ship made its destination.

After repairs were made, however, the crewmen came back onboard the ship, but they were drunk. O'Brien fired the chief mate when he wouldn't control the men. The captain had problems from the firemen, who repaired a hoist carelessly and almost killed a crewman; and in the Panama Canal during the ship's crossing to the Atlantic, sailors and engine-room personnel refused to further work. For that, he had to call in the marines with rifles and bayonets. O'Brien had trouble with the engine breaking down, and by the time the ship was in the Atlantic Ocean, he was disgusted with the entire voyage of "conscripted" men. When orders came to leave the ship in Norfolk, O'Brien was nearly ecstatic when taking the train back to Seattle and returning to his old friend, the *Victoria*. Leaving the day after his return, he captained the ship on June 2, 1918, on a voyage to Nome. Although needing to break 250 miles of ice in the Bering Sea before reaching his destination, Dynamite Johnny couldn't have been happier.

Navigating in dense fog through narrow channels with rocks and reefs, treacherous tides, and cruel snowstorms continued to test the mettle of O'Brien. On one voyage, the captain ordered the *Victoria*'s engine room to go slow through the Seymour Narrows, a passage between Vancouver Island and the mainland. With a full passenger load bound for Alaska, he reviewed the tide tables and decided the best passage through the channel would be at high tide. This is a dangerous stretch of water with a treacherous rock (Ripple Rock) in its middle "having thirty-two feet on it at high tide"—the ship was drawing twenty-five. O'Brien thought the rock was some 175 feet from land on the side where the ships usually ran, and the captain had seen the tide run at its full strength at fifteen miles per hour under certain, rare conditions.

He had the ship steaming slow around midnight to catch the narrows at slack tide before the high waters raced in; he would then bring the ship at high tide around the rock. Unfortunately a thick fog quickly set in. He continued on while sounding the steam whistle every minute and then waiting to listen for an answering echo that would indicate land or rocks ahead. When the ship was three-quarters of a mile from the entrance, he figured the vessel would have the slack water and not need to contend with the fast-moving tide currents, ones that could sweep the ship against the rock. O'Brien was wrong.

He swung the ship into her course. When O'Brien saw the red warning light close to the water's edge on an island point (Maud Island), he ordered the ship full-speed ahead to clear it. A strong tidal current suddenly caught the ship and swung it toward the rocks. Since most of the passengers and crew were asleep, only those on the bridge felt the anxiety of what could happen next.

O'Brien had a "vision" that if he started backing the ship away, before the propellers could secure a strong grip the ship would crash on the rocky face of the island with such force that it would sink headfirst. This vision showed him that the unexpected tide striking her bow could also sweep her stern when the ship's full length reached the point.

He kept the helm hard to starboard, and the *Victoria* began swinging to port, listing with the full force of the tide against her rudder. The ship swung to the north, "like a sternwheel steamer," and the ship was so close to the perpendicular cliffs of the island that the wind's wash from its proximity blew his cap off. For Captain O'Brien, this was one of the few times that the "fear of death was in his nostrils."

He ordered the engines stopped to let the *Victoria* slide on her course until she was by Maud Island. While holding his breath, he then ordered the ship turned on a northwest course as the vessel made the short run to try to pass Ripple Rock. They made it—barely—and he felt the Victoria scrape over the rocks. O'Brien threw up later over the railing, knowing how close they had come to total disaster. If he had backed the engines at first, without heeding the vision that somehow came to him, the ship would have swung out of control into the island's sheer cliffs.

Another time, the ship had left Seward and was within a few miles of the Prince of Wales Passage. When the ship was initially headed toward a valley between high hills that he didn't recognize, O'Brien asked the second pilot, "Shouldn't you go starboard?"

"Why, Captain, that's our passage dead ahead. I know it well," the pilot replied. "I was in charge of the mail boat for over a year in these waters." O'Brien still thought something was wrong. He ordered the helmsmen to make a hard starboard turn, and the ship then swung sixty degrees until it cleared the point. When the pilot angrily left the bridge, the captain told him, "If I'm not right, then you can order the most expensive suit of clothes in Seattle and charge it to me."

Minutes later, the ship came to what was called Lone Tree Point and its warning light. It was now clear the hard swing off course had brought the *Victoria* to the correct one. Seeing his mistake, the pilot knew his directions would have grounded the ship. Returning to the bridge, he turned his back to O'Brien and said loudly, "Captain, would you give me a swift kick? I would have sworn that I was right and you were wrong. The suit is yours."

"I don't want a suit," snapped Dynamite Johnny. "All I want is to get this ship safely back to Seattle. And to be told whenever you're in doubt."

Trouble could surface even when a ship was anchored. While lying at anchor in St. Michael harbor in the late fall, bad winds and waves kept 275 passengers from leaving the ship and the same number from embarking. O'Brien had given the ship ninety fathoms (540 feet) of chain to let her ride out the storm, and the bottom where the *Victoria* anchored was "fairly good holding ground." Believing the ship was safe as long as the current winds prevailed, he left orders to call him if they increased. He went down to his quarters to sleep.

The winds increased after midnight, but O'Brien wasn't summoned. When he came on deck that morning, he noticed that the ship had changed its position from its anchorage. Walking around the vessel, he asked the watch if he had sounded the depths to find how much water was underneath her. The mate replied that the ship, both fore and aft, was two feet clear of the bottom. With the winds dying down, O'Brien relied on this opinion and went ashore to see about getting those passengers onboard.

While talking on the dock with the agent, Dynamite Johnny began to worry that his sailor was wrong about the soundings. From shore, it seemed the ship was stuck in the mud. Quickly heading back, he discovered that the vessel was "fully four feet in the soft mud." What he told that mate then would have kept him "sewing buttons on his clothing for a month." Not to mention he felt responsible for the mistake.

O'Brien now had a large list of passengers onboard and on the dock, and the *Victoria* was stuck on the bottom in mud. If a "freeze-up" night then occurred, these problems would be severely magnified. With the ship frozen in, caring for that many passengers until the ship was free would be "big trouble." The only alternative was to free the ship—and fast.

There were no powerful tugs around, and he didn't feel that the ship's engines alone could free it. When back on shore, O'Brien told the agent what had happened. If they couldn't get the huge *Victoria* under way, they worried how they could ever feed 550 passengers through the winter in that tiny village. The captain asked for a ten-inch hawser for starters, and when the agent had one in his warehouse, O'Brien bought it on the spot. Like many of these ship agents, the man was an independent contractor and not employed by the Alaska Steamship Company. The ships didn't come along that often to these port villages for one line to keep a full-time employee.

The agent agreed to let the captain "borrow" one of his small tugs to run an anchor with the ten-inch hawser at a right angle to the ship's bow. At the "right time" the agent arranged for the tug to push to sea and a stern-wheeler to pull in the same direction. Everyone then waited for high tide.

When the seas ran high, O'Brien ordered his men to put "almost a breaking strain" on the windlass as the equipment mechanically pulled on the anchor. When the pull brought the ship's bow into a line out to the ocean, he told the ship's engineer to "push like hell" and get all the power he could muster. The tug's steam engine strained to push, the stern-wheeler tugged on another hawser, and the "old" *Victoria* started to shove mud on the side with the two-foot higher sea level. She slowly came to the needed angle out, and O'Brien ordered the engines full-speed ahead. With the propeller screaming and engines smoking, the ship lurched and "off she came." This was a great relief to everyone, since no one wanted to spend a winter in the arctic of St. Michael, not to mention that Seattle was the alternative.

* * *

The last trip Dynamite Johnny O'Brien made on the *Victoria* was in November 1919 on the return from Nome. The ship had slipped through the ice choking the Bering Sea and made it to the small gold rush town of shanties, tents, and wooden buildings. The crew plucked more than seven hundred people from the beach who would have otherwise been forced to spend a long, deadly winter in that arctic city. The *Victoria* cleared for Seattle with nine hundred passengers and crewmen.

Two days out of Nome, the dreaded influenza broke out onboard. The virulent influenza pandemic was under way and would kill over fifty million people worldwide in two years. The captain had orders to call at Cordova on the way south, but when he discovered that some of his passengers were sick, he radioed the conditions to the home office. He emphasized that they had just buried a passenger—although this man had not died of the flu—and he intended to steam straight to Seattle. The office sent back its reply a few hours later in full agreement.

In a short day, over a hundred people were deathly ill with the frightening disease. Since the doctor couldn't tend to all of them by himself, O'Brien rolled up his sleeves to help. He called for and accepted any volunteers that came forward, but only a few crewmembers volunteered. The captain had decided against ordering his seamen to work with the sick. He needed them to get the ship to Seattle.

The trip south lasted six days, and O'Brien was up, day and night, for each one. He catnapped for an hour or two, but the demands for help were too much, and he didn't have the chance to change or get out of his uniform. Every fifteen minutes to a half hour, someone would tell him that another passenger had come down ill. He would race from the bridge, or from a stateroom, into the dense fog constantly surrounding the ship—not even the sun would shine.

His third son, John, was then twenty-six and sailing as a passenger on this dark voyage. He was stricken by the disease, and his father put him in the captain's berth for the trip south. O'Brien felt that his son had contracted the disease while working in a gold-mining camp at Nome. It is also likely that John came down with influenza from an infected passenger or crewmember. The captain undoubtedly wanted to spend that time with his son, but he had to watch over everyone onboard—and not just with John. At this time, O'Brien had three grown children still alive after Frank's death: his daughter, Kathleen (age thirty); John, who was now severely ill; and Ned (age thirty-seven).

Remembering his sail-ship training, O'Brien used what was onboard to care for the sick: hot water, Epsom salts, quinine, lemons, and whiskey. For those days and nights, he, one doctor, and his volunteers tended to the sick. The first step was to try to break the fever with a tumbler of hot water and two "heaping" tablespoons of Epsom salts. Two hours later, someone would give the sick person a whole lemon squeezed into a large glass of hot water, "topped off with a second mate's drink of whiskey, which meant a large drink." Even if the patient resisted, they forced the liquid down, and typically after the person took the first gulp, there was "no more hesitation in finishing the glass." One hour later, ten grains of quinine were given. The attendant after that tried to keep the sick person "well covered" with blankets.

Two people died from the flu on the fifth day, and then a third on the sixth. O'Brien wired ahead that he was docking with 160 seriously ill people and a number of ambulances needed to be ready. The captain expected to receive orders to head directly into quarantine, but when he didn't receive them, he kept the *Victoria* steaming full-speed ahead to its dock. Only three people had died, and O'Brien felt that he could have saved them if only he had onboard more whiskey and lemons. Thankfully his son, John, was alive and would eventually recover.

When the *Victoria* eventually slowed to a stop by its wharf, hundreds of waiting family members in white face masks lined the dock. Every available ambulance in the region had been sent there and were lined in multiple rows. Doctors and nurses streamed onboard to tend to the sick, nearly all of them in their staterooms or lined up in wrapped blankets on deckchairs and common areas. A police line quickly formed to keep back the milling, worried crowds that pressed ahead to see their loved ones, but they would have to wait until the sick, one by one, were brought out on stretchers. Returning on the ship for the winter, a company of soldiers from St. Michael lined up on the wharf. Due to their illness, several fell from formation and tumbled to the ground. Sirens wailed as the sick were rushed to hospitals all over the city. And more would die.

O'Brien knew he had done his best, and the doctors consoled him that he had saved lives. He started thinking, however, that he had been steaming to Alaska for twenty-three years, "all of this just for a living." After what he had gone through, he wanted to see blue skies and be away from blizzards and snowstorms. O'Brien wanted to be away from death.

For the entire voyage, he had only one glimpse of the sun and no stars to navigate under. The "miserable fog" had enveloped his ship when he first left Seattle. He remembered drifting through passes and knowing that his ship was somewhere in the Bering Sea only by the deep soundings. O'Brien had ordered a crewman to "use the lead" every hour for 650 miles, and the first distinct thing he saw when approaching Nome was the lighters at their moorings. And when he returned to Seattle, O'Brien could see only the countless ambulances waiting to take away his passengers. Even his son was ill. For all that he had done for his company, he was being paid $300 per month. Although this was a very good salary, it wasn't the riches that he had sought for all those years.

O'Brien was exhausted, he was depressed, and he looked like an old man. His hair was white; his face was wrinkled. The previously young-looking sixty-eight-year-old man had aged. The captain walked up to the assistant superintendent, Mr. Harris, and quietly said, "I'm through."

Harris asked, "You mean for the night?"

"No. I'm finished with the Alaska run. I'll have my things ashore in minutes." O'Brien walked back to the *Victoria* and said good-bye to "one of the best old ships" he had ever sailed on, "a nice enough name, but it always stuck in my throat when I had to mention it later."

His ships had carried tens of thousands of passengers and millions of dollars of gold. The company officers handed him a letter reading that "they regretted Captain O'Brien's leaving—and if he ever wished to have a command, they would be glad to give him one."

* * *

After Dynamite Johnny's long career as the *Victoria*'s captain, the ship continued to sail until 1937 into Alaskan waters as a passenger and freight liner. When war loomed, she was converted into a freighter. During the winter of 1940–1941, the passenger accommodations and most of the superstructure were removed and converted into cargo space. In June 1941, the vessel began operating in this new capacity. Painted in Navy gray and camouflage colors with guns mounted fore and aft, the *Victoria* ran supplies to isolated military settlements.

The ship continued those northern freight runs after the war until her last voyage in 1952. Found to still be in "beautiful" shape, the handwrought Swedish iron was as strong then as it was in 1870. The engines built in 1885 were still smooth and powerful, and she could steam at thirteen knots, or about fifteen miles per hour. The ship's demise was brought about by the advent of containerization: The *Victoria*'s holds were too small for the large containers of freight. For a number of years, the *Victoria* had held the title of being the oldest active vessel in the American Merchant Marine.

The strong, gallant vessel was stripped of her engines and upper works and then towed ignominiously as a lowly barge along the coast from Alaska to Mexico. She made her last trip in 1956, when towed as the barge *Straits Maru* to Japan for scrap. The career of a ship that spanned nearly nine decades had come to an end.

18

THE SOUTH SEAS AND HOLLYWOOD

After leaving his command on the *Victoria*, one month ashore was all the captain could stand. He met an old friend, Mr. Schubach, who had built a brand new twin-screw wood ship in twenty-three days. Named the *Aberdeen*, it was the "best finished ship" he had ever built. Schubach told O'Brien that the *Aberdeen*, one of the last wooden ships constructed, had been caulked so much that not an ounce more of oakum could be jammed into her seams.

O'Brien accepted the command and sailed for Honolulu in December 1919. The ship sailed well and without the problems of a newly built vessel, whereupon systems from mechanical to propulsion needed "fine tuning." Arriving in Hawaii, he had the ship caulked more on the decks and sides as a precaution. He took on a full cargo of sugar from their agents, Castle and Cook, and the *Aberdeen* soon sailed back for San Francisco. This was an "all-round successful" voyage and a warm contrast from the stormy, icebound, and at times anxiety-ridden trips on the *Victoria*.

The crew unloaded the bags of Hawaiian sugar and then quickly hauled onboard a full cargo of grease and wool bound for Boston and New York. Although the ship's holds were cleaned up in San Francisco for this new load, O'Brien ordered that a thermometer be placed inside each bunker. The sailors reported every hour on the temperature to ensure that the previous tropical run hadn't brought about an internal combustion problem with the new wool cargo. Arriving in Boston in twenty-five days by way of the Panama Canal, the ship again had a trouble-free journey. "Not an ounce of cargo became water damaged," he wrote.

The captain and his crew were so proud of this ship that they erected a large blackboard sign, "sixteen feet square," that read, "This wonder ship was built complete and ready for sea in 23-1/4 days—and made the passage from San Francisco to Boston in 25 days." Learning what they had done, Mr. Schubach wired O'Brien to bring the ship back as soon as possible to New York. With most of the previously built wooden vessels now having trouble, he wanted the U.S. Shipping Board officials to see one that sailed so well.

When the *Aberdeen* steamed so successfully past the smiling officials, Schubach invited the captain to dinner at the plush Waldorf Astoria Hotel in New York, complete with a very expensive bottle of champagne. After filling their glasses and giving a toast, he passed an envelope to O'Brien. Inside it was a check for $500, or two months' pay, which was a substantial bonus. Congratulating Captain O'Brien on the advertising coup, the owner sat back with a wide smile on his face.

Dynamite Johnny thanked him, adding, "It would be just wonderful if I could see this in real money."

"You darned old pirate," the owner said loudly, "don't you think my check is good? Come with me to the hotel cashier and I'll show you." He cashed the check and O'Brien counted the money.

"Now, my friend," O'Brien smiled back. "We can have a very expensive bottle of wine on me, your old pirate skipper." They drank well into the night, and Schubach wanted him to captain the *Aberdeen* on more East Coast runs. The following morning, however, O'Brien was on a train headed back to San Francisco, preferring the West Coast and being with his family.

He met another old friend and soon was sailing the *Glorietta* for the Matson Steamship Line on the runs between San Francisco, Honolulu, and Seattle/Port Townsend. On the first run, a crewman died of natural causes. O'Brien radioed the company in San Francisco that he intended to bury the body at sea, unless he heard otherwise within twenty-four hours. The time elapsed and he proceeded with the burial ceremonies. Just as his sailors were ready to consign the remains to the sea, the wireless operator ran to O'Brien while waving a paper in the air. The captain read that the relatives wanted the body brought back home. Had the message been received a minute later, the ceremonies would have been completed. A lawsuit in that case would have been brought today.

On the first trip from Hawaii, the *Glorietta* was lying alongside the Matson dock in San Francisco. His oldest son, Ned, who had "gone through death's door in the Bering Sea," was standing by the gangway amidship. His attention was drawn to a crewmember who was obviously drunk. Walking crookedly, the man staggered toward the ship's bow, stumbled on the deck, and pitched overboard.

Ned shouted to two crewmen standing by, "Man overboard!" and ran to where the man had gone over. The others joined him at the railing, but they couldn't spot the seaman.

Without hesitation, Ned dove into the ocean. He searched for the disappeared sailor but had no luck. After fifteen minutes, his hand finally touched the body. Tiring but still focused on his task, he pulled the man to the surface. Near exhausted from his efforts, Ned reached the dock piling with the body. Others climbed down and eventually hauled both men onto the wharf. An ambulance with sirens wailing quickly stopped at the scene, but the attendants declared the seaman was dead. O'Brien wrote tragically later, "Never having fully recovered from his near drowning in the Bering Sea, my son made the trip to warm Honolulu for his health. From this rescue effort he received a setback [tuberculosis] from which he eventually died."

* * *

When the Matson Line sold the *Glorietta* to "New Orleans investors" to run on its route to Cuba, the officers gave him the command of the SS *Dellwood*. The U.S. government through its U.S. Shipping Board owned this ship, but Matson had the management contract to run it. On his third voyage with the *Dellwood*, a union dispute erupted that put O'Brien again into the forefront. The ship was two sailors short for its crew, all of them so far being union members, and the union representative swore that the two needed men had to be unionized. The Matson superintendent wanted to employ less costly nonunion personnel. The company official later brought two nonunion U.S. Shipping Board seamen in a longboat to the *Dellwood*, and since O'Brien knew what was going on, he gave the orders for the engineer to build up steam and quickly sail away. He had already cleared customs for the voyage to Honolulu via Seattle.

Climbing up a side ladder, the captain gave the orders to the chief mate to man the windlass and haul up the anchor. When the union representative heard this, he told the mate, "You don't need to get the anchor up. We are all going ashore, and my orders are to not sail with anyone but union men."

O'Brien snapped back, "This is a U.S. Government ship, and as its master, I am their agent. You and everyone on this deck are going to sea now." The union man insisted that everyone go to shore, but O'Brien was firm that the ship was sailing and they would finish up their argument outside the three-mile limit. He ordered the mate to get the anchor up "without delay" and let the chain run into the locker without stowing it.

After turning the engine room telegraph to "full speed ahead," Dynamite Johnny looked over from the bridge and saw two launches speeding toward the vessel. He assumed the union men had hailed the boats to take them and his crew off the ship. Telling the mate to take the wheel and keep clear of ships, he quickly walked to his cabin, took out his revolver, and ran onto the bridge. When the nearest launch approached the *Dellwood* to tie up, he fired one shot over the launch's bow and shouted, "The next shot is aimed lower if you try to board us." The boat steered away, followed by the other.

The union men ran to the quarterdeck and shouted, "You are shanghaiing us out of San Francisco in broad daylight. You can't do that!" Dynamite Johnny calmly kept the revolver by his side but swung it so the men were sure to see it again. With the ship under way, he firmly told them, "If you are going to turn to, just say so; otherwise, get the hell off the quarterdeck! When I get this ship outside the three-mile limit, you'll hear from me."

As the vessel steamed down San Francisco Bay and crossed the Oakland ferryboat lanes at full speed, O'Brien was thankful that no boats were passing that way. When the ship passed Fort Point and into the open ocean, the delegate with two sailors approached the foot of the bridge, saluted him, and said, "Captain, you win, but only as far as Seattle will we go." They then left to go about their tasks.

What they didn't know was O'Brien had already discussed his plans with the company superintendant, who agreed with him on sailing directly to Honolulu. The sailor's union would tie up the ship in Seattle, and they had no freight yet onboard bound for Puget Sound, which could be picked up in Hawaii.

As soon as the union delegate told him about staying on for Seattle, the captain had the mate get them working, which included restowing the anchor chains into their lockers. He actually ordered the delegate and his "crowd" to relieve the mate on the forecastle head and the second mate in the pilothouse. If O'Brien intended to go to Seattle, the ship would have passed through the "south channel," but the vessel didn't with its different destination. When the vessel passed the San Francisco lightship, he gave the order to the "old Irish seaman" at the wheel to steer southwest by south. Staring over at O'Brien, the wheelman said, "Excuse me, sir, but did you say southwest by south?" He knew where that command would take the ship.

Captain O'Brien repeated the course to the union man, adding, "You thrugmullion—are you deaf! Or don't you understand the American language." He heard the man mutter "shanghaied" for the second time in his forty years at sea. O'Brien barked, "Shut up! Steer the course I gave you and now!"

Only a few minutes passed before the entire deck crew was back on the quarterdeck, and the delegate spoke loudly to the captain, "Are we going to Seattle, captain, where we signed on under the ship's articles?" The captain yelled back:

> The articles read for us to go to Honolulu via Seattle—and for good and sufficient reasons, I choose to sail to Honolulu first. Now listen to me. This is the last time I want to see you on this quarterdeck protesting this ship's movements. I have my orders, which I intend to carry out—and you will obey my orders. If you refuse to work, then you know the consequences.

I alone can take the ship there, and when she arrives, you are free to quit and do what you damn well please. Now get a move on—and get to work!

They resumed their tasks.

When the sailor's union learned how it had been fooled, the leaders decided to take their union sailors off the Matson ships in port. This move put considerable pressure on the company. When O'Brien returned to San Francisco with a full cargo, he didn't receive a reprimand. After all, he had only been carrying out the orders of the superintendent. This official had left Matson before the ship returned, however, and O'Brien surmised that the union's criticisms had caused the line to cave in and give the superintendent his "walking papers."

As a captain was part of management, O'Brien was mandated to follow company orders. He also had an aversion for any tactics, union or otherwise, that interfered with his operation of a ship. Short months later, he found himself in the middle of another longshoremen's strike. The union had called a widespread strike, and the owners hired blacks "by the hundreds" to load and unload their ships. The police guarded the docks, and a spare ship, the *Annie Johnson*, was berthed nearby and used to house and feed the Negro strikebreakers.

With the *Dellwood* anchored with no one available to offload its cargo, O'Brien offered to run one of the black gangs. He had been at work with his crew for not more than thirty minutes when trouble arose. A "great big Negro crewman" was using the "most profane and obscene language" while handling the dock cargo. The much shorter, older, and wizened captain "roared a volume of beautiful 'damns' at him, and told him to shut up his big mouth." O'Brien then shouted, "Cut out your bad language or I will knock seven black devils out of you."

While the captain waited expectantly for the next—and perhaps last—fight of his career, the man began to laugh heartily. "Now, boys, isn't that the limit? Did you hear that man swear and he says he doesn't want to hear mine." The big workers laughed heartily, "My God, he's a peach!" O'Brien started laughing as well, and the cargo hooks flew into the goods swiftly and furiously.

When the work was completed, those who left by car had their revolvers stuck out the windows, ready to return fire if they were fired upon. The new crews loaded and unloaded the ships quickly and efficiently. And the strike was eventually settled.

* * *

Captain Saunders, the operating manager for the Matson Line, was a longtime friend of Dynamite Johnny. When the *Dellwood* was "laid off," he remembered how O'Brien had worked to unload the ships. Saunders asked O'Brien if he would take charge of the U.S. Shipping Board's fleet that was now anchored close to San Francisco. The American shipbuilding facilities had constructed hundreds of vessels for World War I, and these surplus vessels were not needed after the war's end. His fleet would be three "unwanted, war-built freighters" that were anchored on the mudflats of Benicia on the Sacramento River.

Dynamite Johnny accepted. He was now seventy years old, and this 1921 job carried a "good" salary. Nearly fifteen years would elapse before President Roosevelt would sign the new Social Security Act, and the retirement world of 401(k) plans, adequate pensions, and IRAs was decades away. The three ships he started with were in bad condition and very rusty, as the past commanders had not sealed their ships from iron rust when in use. O'Brien oversaw the work crews that refurbished these vessels, and eighteen months later, as more ships were brought in, he was in charge of thirty-four ships with a value of sixty-six million dollars.

His work crews now numbered 143 men, and he had a "fine" corps of officers and men to carry out the work. After his first year in charge of the Benicia fleet, government officials in Washington commended him for his work, stating that the "Benicia fleet of ships were kept in better condition and cost than any of the numerous fleets owned by the U.S. Shipping Board."

As with any maritime work, O'Brien had his challenges, which included another fight at an age when most men were sitting in a rocking chair, or these days, staring at the television. He had discharged a "cowboy sailor" for carrying around a revolver and bowie knife, not to mention the man's bad attitude and work habits. The captain then learned the ex-worker hadn't left and was prowling through the cabins of a ship that had just arrived. The troublemaker was heard swearing and then disappeared into a cabin. In the captain's younger days, he would have given the sailor a "thrashing," but now he thought he would just oversee getting the man away from his operations. For the first time, he also thought there was the chance he would be "licked" instead. Dynamite Johnny was never indecisive, even now, and he immediately walked to the cabin to see how long it would be until "the man was ashore."

He found the "thing" lying in a lower berth, soundly sleeping and wearing only a short undershirt. Without a moment's further thought, O'Brien gave in to his instincts. He walked over, grabbed the man by his neck and stomach, and heaved him over to the doorway. The sailor fell but was up in an instant. When the captain rushed closer, the cowboy made a swiping blow that just missed. O'Brien caught him "with a beauty under the ear" and knocked him to the ground. The man crawled on his hands and knees from the deck and down the gangway. Looking up, he yelled at Dynamite Johnny to throw his clothes down. He did. Two of his men then rowed the fired sailor to shore; the twice-fired man never returned.

Times had changed now, and laws were in place protecting seamen from any type of abuse, whether they refused to follow orders or not. O'Brien now worried that the assaulted sailor would complain to the manager of the U.S. Shipping

Board and he would be fired. Deciding to get there before the sailor did, the captain quickly washed, shaved, put on his best uniform, and jumped into a launch headed to port. He quickly caught a train and ferry and was in the office a few minutes before the manager arrived in the morning.

He told the officer about the cowboy sailor and didn't leave out any details. O'Brien said he "licked him good" but would bear the consequences. "If you want my resignation," he concluded, "I will accept the consequences." When the manager didn't answer, Johnny left and returned to his fleet at Benicia. While waiting for his relief to succeed him, he continued overseeing the work—but no one came.

A month later, his old friend Captain Townsend—dating back to Hong Kong and other faraway ports—sailed his ship to Benicia to join the mothballed fleet. When his crew tied up the vessel, Townsend gave O'Brien a bottle of Johnny Walker Scotch. Putting the bottle in his bag, O'Brien forgot about the fine whiskey inside. The captain walked to the Oakland ferry depot, ordered his dinner onboard the ferry, and then remembered leaving his bag at the train station next to the ferry depot when he saw Captain Townsend off. Running back, Dynamite Johnny discovered that the bag and bottle were gone.

He was "very much chagrined" that he had lost the bottle because these were Prohibition days, and "the real thing" was now hard to get. Hailing a railroad conductor, he asked the man if, by any chance, he had seen a small bag. When questioned if there was booze in it, O'Brien without hesitation said "yes," and the conductor directed him to the stationmaster's office to see the Prohibition Officer. O'Brien walked there and looked through the window: His bag was on the counter, and a train conductor, someone who was presumably the Prohibition Officer, and another person were standing close by. The three men were looking at the bottle inside the bag and laughing heartily.

The captain made another fast decision. Looking at his watch, he realized the ferry would soon be steaming away. The timing would be close. He quietly opened the office door, reached onto the counter, grabbed his bag, tossed a silver dollar on the counter and yelled, "Buy yourselves a drink of soft stuff on me, boys. I want the hard stuff." He raced out the door while the startled men stood where they were with their mouths open. They then ran after him.

Racing down the station's concrete runway to the dock, he heard the cries of "Hey, you! Stop!" behind him. He saw the chain across the slip and heard the ferry's paddlewheels start to loudly churn. He leaped over the chain and jumped four feet onto the ferry's stern as it started moving away. The three men stopped at the slip chain and shook their fists at him.

"I'll see you in Dublin," O'Brien laughed back. "Not bad for a seventy-two-year-old man." O'Brien ate a very enjoyable dinner, even though he knew the officers left behind would have telephoned ahead to have their men waiting at the San Francisco dock. He knew what they would say: "Watch out for some old fellow on the Oakland Ferry wearing a black derby hat, black overcoat, gold-headed cane, and with a small handbag that has liquor in it. Arrest him!"

He took the bottle out and put it in his overcoat pocket. O'Brien next bought a newspaper, rolled it up, and placed this in the bag. If any officer asked him to open it, the man would find only the newspaper. He noticed three elderly ladies talking together, and their faces "looked friendly." When the ferry docked and passengers were crowded together to leave, he walked up to the ladies and asked them for directions to the St. Francis Hotel, one of the city's finest. While they told him how to get there, he worked his way in between them so he was hidden inside. The ruse worked. No one saw or stopped him.

Thanking the women for their help, O'Brien slowly sauntered to a streetcar and found one that was quite crowded, again so he would blend in. He held the bottle close to his side so that it wouldn't touch any of the standing passengers. When he was within a block of his destination, he asked the conductor to stop the car and stepped off. Although he heard a "kerplop" behind, he began walking quickly over the sidewalk, believing he had made it.

Suddenly he heard shouts directed toward him. O'Brien stopped, thinking he had been caught—and so close to getting away. Turning around, he heard a man shout, "Old man, you lost your bottle!" Several passengers were looking at him with amused faces inside the lighted trolley. Hearing scattered laughter, he hurried back and picked it up. The bottle was intact, as it fell from his pocket and landed on its cork top. In front of the folks, he pulled out the cork and had the "biggest drink I ever took in my life."

Had a policeman been around, O'Brien would have spent at least the night in jail. Hearing the story, some friends questioned him about this. "Why not act your age?" they said. They couldn't believe he would take such risks. But this was pure Dynamite Johnny O'Brien: He lived like there was no tomorrow; he was a rebel with a cause.

All good things, however, must come to an end, and Captain O'Brien's friend, the superintendent of the U.S. Shipping Board, left to take another position. Dynamite Johnny couldn't get along with the newly appointed officer who took his place. The captain resigned and waited for his replacement to show up. A few days later the new superintendent came to him and said, "Your standing with the Shipping Board is one of the highest, and my superiors would like you to remain in charge of the fleet." O'Brien was ready for a change, and turned that down.

* * *

One week after leaving the fleet, O'Brien returned to the sea, this time to command the freighter *Culburra*. The steamer was hauling to Nome a heavy load of twelve- to sixteen-ton dredge equipment for a mining company. The trip was late in the season, the passage was choked with ice and icebergs, a constant sea rolled in, and the loading was done poorly because the charterers had hired cheaper, inexperienced men. Owing to the bad loading, the *Culburra*'s departure was delayed for days, and the heavy deck load needed to be secured again. O'Brien decided to leave with the load still not lashed to his satisfaction because a partner in the venture was a good friend, and the load needed to be delivered on time. "A fairly good salary deceived me into accepting the commission," he wrote later.

On the day the ship sailed, the winds were blowing and torrents of raindrops splattered down. While the vessel worked its way north, the ship occasionally took a steep roll, which caused the "miserably stowed load" on the deck to shift. The crew was forced to work to keep the cargo under control for forty-eight hours straight, with spray and sea constantly covering the decks.

When docked at Nome and unloading, the men complained about their working without extra pay and demanded to be paid overtime. They wouldn't work unless they received the extra money, and time was growing short for every ship in port to leave before the dangerous icebergs and scum ice blocked the way. Times were changing, O'Brien wryly noted. This was the first time he had a crew of sailors demand longshoreman wages for working overtime. He agreed to their terms but "under protest."

The captain discussed the issue "nicely" and gave different reasons why he couldn't accept their demands. He did this so the men would forget the two magic words he had conditioned his approval with. O'Brien stated his protest details in front of the purser and mate and then entered this in the official log, with two officers as witnesses. When the men then asked to be paid the much higher wages after completing the work, the captain answered:

> As for this wage advance, you'll be paid what you are entitled to under the law, or normally one-half of those wages, as I agreed to this "under protest." You men cannot expect me to pay you any money that is contrary to the law.

After the ship was unloaded, it left port but stopped at Dutch Harbor for fuel. From there, the ship had a good run to San Francisco. When the *Culburra* docked at its berth, the question of the overtime and O'Brien's acceptance came up. The U.S. Shipping commissioners stood by his paying "under protest." The seamen received what was due for their work—and not a cent more.

When it came to his job, O'Brien knew either he stood up to the crew or he would be "hauled in on the carpet" and reprimanded or fired on the spot. Still working because he couldn't sit back at home and also needed the money, the older Dynamite Johnny decided to look for another job. Steaming in the Arctic with unseasoned crews and now not liking the cold contributed to his decision.

* * *

Captain O'Brien next turned to piloting ships in the Pacific Northwest, and during this time, he received a telegram in December 1923 that queried his interest in taking the *Buford* with "well heeled" passengers for a cruise in the South Seas. This 5,040-gross-ton ship was built at Belfast, Ireland, in 1890, and it was a long 371 feet, was 44 feet wide, and had one smokestack with two sails. Among other uses, the vessel after the Spanish-American War carried troops to the newly obtained overseas territories. The ship supported relief efforts following the great earthquake at San Francisco, California, and was used as a troopship during and after World War I. The military then sold the *Buford* to this group of investors.

O'Brien was surprised at the offer because he "had words" with one of the owners before leaving on the *Culburra*, but apparently that had been forgotten. Further, he surmised, he had once piloted the *Buford* to Alaska from Puget Sound and had a "familiarity" in sailing the South Seas and the Sandwich Islands. He concluded that "being one of the oldest masters on the Pacific carrying passengers had something to do with my being chosen to command the ship." Arriving in San Francisco, he reported to the owner's office, signed the papers, and headed to the dock to see the ship.

He was aghast at what he found. The ship was in very bad condition, with layers of rust, caked dirt, and splattered bird droppings, and it needed overhauling from trunk to keel. Since he had been on the vessel last, it had fallen into great disrepair. O'Brien hurried back to the office and told them they needed to put a "gang of men" on the ship to make her presentable. In her present condition, they couldn't get a "single soul in San Francisco" to board her. The owners didn't show any surprise at his words and quickly agreed. As they had first thought, O'Brien's experience with the Benicia fleet would certainly come in handy.

While the captain was overhauling and repairing the ship, the company was distributing a cruise brochure that touted the ship's amenities and O'Brien's captaincy. Two months elapsed and he hadn't received any payment for his efforts, as his salary was to start only when passengers were boarding on the ship's departure. He hadn't thought about that tiny detail when signing the papers. As with many aspects of his world then, this would be different today: His services now would be paid starting when he first started working on the company's behalf. O'Brien had left a "good" paying position at $400 per month to take this job because he wanted to sail in his later years in the warm Pacific again and desired a permanent position. He would stick to his goal.

When the ship was in first-class condition, the owners hired the officers and crew to work underneath him. Since O'Brien for years had this responsibility, he wasn't sure about this approach. The owners assured him that they were "first-class" men, however, and this statement mollified him. They also happened to mention that although wealthy passengers had flocked for this cruise, their venture was in financial difficulties. Since the *Buford*'s refurbishment proved more costly than budgeted, "everyone had to work to make this a success."

During the first days at sea, O'Brien was very pleasantly surprised at how well everything seemed to be going. The ship steamed well, and it shone from stem to stern with new railings, fresh paint, replaced decks, and comfortable state-rooms. The food was "excellently" served, the string orchestra played soft music, and time happily passed by. The passengers were indeed upper class, including business owners (Mr. Durant of automobile fame), bank owners (San Francisco's Charles Crocker), writers, and professional athletes. The weather cooperated, and the trip was successfully under way.

They were not long at sea, however, when Dynamite Johnny found out that several of his crew were a "bad lot." He had to discipline the purser and steward later in the voyage, although "out of sight and sound" of the passengers. The chief officer, who was a personal friend of one of the owners, seemed to be "partially insane"; he particularly became a problem when the moon was full. Some crewmembers weren't doing their jobs, but thankfully the passengers hadn't yet picked up on that.

After a stopover in Honolulu in mid-February 1924, the ship made for Hilo on the big island of Hawaii. Along the way, Captain O'Brien noticed the first real sign of trouble among the officers and crew—liquor, "the source of all misery on ships." The purser and steward were under the influence, as they had been partying and drinking nonstop with the passengers. O'Brien grabbed both, shoved them into a room, and gave them a "severe calling down." He ended by warning that if he found them drunk once more, he would strip them of their command.

When the ship stopped at Hilo, the passengers and a few officers were taken to the Kilauea Volcano. Darkness had settled in when the groups approached the seething crater. In a breathtaking experience, they watched the sulfurous vapors through the silvery moonlight rising from the deep cavern and the "seething, spouting, burning" lava at its bottom. Plumes of glowing-red liquefied magma spurted over the black, compacted surface, while solidified lava formed a solid pillar in the middle. O'Brien thought that all of the mean devils from around the world should be brought there and forced to watch the inferno, "hour after hour at night." Any more transgressions and they would become part of the scenery.

On this voyage to the South Pacific, the *Buford* crossed the equator, and the rites of initiation—milder for these passengers—were meted out to those who hadn't crossed the equator before. The jovial rites brought about membership in the esteemed "Solemn Mysteries of the Ancient Order of the Deep," signed properly by Davy Jones, "His "Majesty's scribe," and Neptunus Rex, "the Ruler of the Raging Main," all as evidenced by a heavy lithographed certificate on heavy parchment.

Attended by his court, King Neptune was dressed in his full regalia. At three o'clock in the afternoon, February 26, 1924, Neptune took three steps forward. He raised his scepter high and brought it down with a heavy thud onto the deck. Speaking in a deep voice, the "oakum-bearded" Neptunus Rex ordered all on-board who had not entered his domain before to come forward and be initiated.

The white-uniformed Captain O'Brien left the bridge to welcome King Neptune onto his ship and then gave him the names of thirty people, including crewmembers, who were passing for the first time through the king's domain.

Each man, woman, and child was brought before Neptune, who questioned them as to their merits. The passenger, while seated in a chair, was lifted by the crew and tossed into a large swimming pool, which was created by filling the fore hatch with seawater. The men had another step to go through: They were shaved, but after a lather of soap and tar had been scraped form their faces.

On March first, the ship arrived at Pago Pago in the Samoan islands. The beauty of the South Seas with its white coral reefs, dense green jungles, mountains, tropical trees, multicolored flowers, and turquoise bays brought sweet memories back to O'Brien. From there, the *Buford* sailed to Apia, where Robert Louis Stevenson had lived and died. The ship passed the wreck of another vessel, lost years before in a hurricane, but one that O'Brien remembered when it had sailed magnificently into Hong Kong harbor. With a loud sigh, he watched the hulk pass into the distance while a gentle sea rolled back and forth over her skeleton remains.

Although he was seventy-three years old, Captain O'Brien still had his command moments. The passengers enjoyed their stay at that island port, but it was marred when the crew brought liquor onboard from shore and drank it. The mate wasn't able to control the drunken crew. While in his quarters, O'Brien heard loud cussing and swearing on the saloon deck. He immediately left for the deck and found a large "Russian Finn" seaman annoying the passengers with offensive language. When the sailor was surly to the captain, he grabbed the drunk by the seat of the pants and shoved him over the main deck. The man lay still on the lower deck as O'Brien ran down the closest stairway, thinking he had for sure killed the man.

When Dynamite Johnny raced to the prostrate seaman, the drunk suddenly kicked him in the groin, and O'Brien sank painfully to the deck. His second mate—who had dressed as King Neptune days before—rushed to his rescue and slugged the sailor. Calling for the irons, O'Brien watched the slugfest continue. The Russian pulled himself off the deck and hammered his fists into the second mate. O'Brien ended the fight when he grabbed the irons and strongly snapped one end around one of the man's wrists, then did the same with the other. They subdued the drunk and kept him in lockup for several days.

The problem of the smuggled-in liquor cropped up again. When the captain discovered the quantities of raw liquor smuggled aboard, he had a near mutiny over his confiscation of the brews during these Prohibition days. O'Brien stood up to the crew and disrated the three men who had bought the liquor, and that ended the problem. The ship arrived back in Honolulu two weeks later for supplies and fuel and then sailed away for the principal port of Suva in the Fiji Islands. Once the *Buford* was at anchor, the passengers quickly left to see firsthand the island's magnificent beauty.

He didn't have the chance, however, to revisit the places of his youth. O'Brien was too busy keeping this crew in order, "having several later in the ship's jail, hiring natives in their place, and making those in jail pay for their keep as well as the natives." While at Suva, the owners wired O'Brien that he had to stop by Honolulu again on the return trip to take on a full load of sugar and all of the first-class passengers he could carry. The venture's financial problems were too great.

The ship sailed from Fiji for the Tonga Islands. He kept the news of the extra cargo and more travelers to himself for one week, trying to decide how to best tell his passengers. That they wouldn't be happy would be an understatement. Many were used to being alone in their staterooms, and now new people coming onboard would occupy the spare berth in each one. Two facts were in his favor: No contractual warranties had been made as to those rooms, and the food was first class.

The *Buford* sailed into the port of Nuku'alofa, the Tongan capital that O'Brien knew wasn't an easy harbor to enter without a pilot. Calling on all his instincts, he guided the ship past several reefs, detoured around a particularly bad reef-infested area, and finally anchored off the tiny town. When the passengers returned that evening, however, one couple was missing. He sent out search parties, and seamen discovered the two sunning themselves on a small coral island. The pair had no idea how close they had come to spending a long time on that deserted atoll. Once they were onboard, an eighteen-foot-long shark cruised by the ship, with pilot fish darting ahead. While the passengers milled about the railing in awe, the men baited a long shark hook and dropped that into the ocean. O'Brien wrote:

> Mr. Shark slowly swam to the pork bait, and it acted almost human in nosing the hunk of meat on the large, iron hook, but never opened its mouth to take that fatal bite. Without ever taking the bait, Mr. Shark swam slowly away.

The next morning O'Brien hired a native pilot to guide the ship between the coral reefs to the open sea. Skirting "innumerable reefs" on their way, the ship sailed to its next destination, Lifuka, a village on Haapia, the middle island of the Tongan group. The *Buford* arrived off the island well into the darkening, pink evening, as reefs and coral atolls dotted the ten miles into port. Captain O'Brien then learned his native pilot was now lost. He didn't have a clue as to what course the ship should take in steaming to that desolate port.

The captain took the ship back into his hands and sent two men aloft to spot the sunken reefs. "Never have I had such an anxious time just trying to find an anchorage—which we did after dark," he said later. His stopover at the Vava'u group of islands in the Kingdom of Tonga was also problematic. This was an unspoiled tropical paradise of crystal-clear warm turquoise seas, stunning coral reefs, white sandy beaches, and coconut-fringed islands. The natives crowded the wharf, and the island's royalty came onboard. After insisting that none of the officials serve liquor to his officers or crew, O'Brien watched the numbers of happy passengers disembark to another paradise and evening of fun. He decided to stay onboard and in his cabin, since someone needed to watch over the *Buford* and he wanted to finally enjoy some undisturbed sleep.

The boisterous noises of "bedlam let loose" on the deck awakened him with a start. When he reached topside, he found that "fully two-hundred natives" had taken over his ship. They were roaming through the vacant rooms left by the passengers. "While the natives were ransacking the boat," his crew were nowhere to be seen, as they were on the island having a great time. O'Brien was understandably angered at what he was seeing.

Whether intentionally done or not, the captain ran screaming through the groups with raised fists, yelling "like a Comanche and the poor folks had to think I had become loco." He yelled and swore and threw things as he drove the natives over the side, and "down they went on a line." Many dove off the ship into the blue-green waters, while others scrambled down rope ladders to their outriggers. He ran to the bridge, grabbed the steam whistle cord, and sounded out near staccato blasts until finally the first officer came over the rail with a few crewmembers. When the passengers returned, their question was simply, "Why all the blasts on the steam whistle?"

The trip continued on to Tahiti, stopping along the way at other beautiful South Seas islands. When the ship anchored at Papeete, Captain O'Brien wasn't prepared for the reception he found. While the ship's string orchestra played soft melodies on their approach, the native brass band from ashore performed their booming songs of welcome. The "commodious wharf" was crowded with natives and white people. When the *Buford*'s ladder was lowered, a group of native women—"beautifully dressed in full semi-dress and holding 'lei' garlands of flowers"—boarded the ship's gangway.

O'Brien was struck by the beauty of the island princess with the "queenly bearing," her flower-bedecked retinue following closely behind. She came to the captain and softly placed a lei around his neck, embraced him, and then kissed him. This was the granddaughter of the Tahitian princess whom he had loved nearly fifty years before—the "slim beauty" that had fished with the captain in a beautiful moonstruck lagoon and then swallowed the tiny fish she had caught.

O'Brien looked at the beautiful girl and saw the "black shimmering eyes" he had last seen when in his twenties. "Yes, my dear girl," he answered before she asked the question. "Your grandmother and I were very dear friends." He kissed her with the same feeling of closeness he had with her grandmother. The young princess smiled, bowed, and stepped gracefully away, and the next native girl placed her garland of flowers around his neck, followed by an embrace and a kiss that O'Brien returned; then the next woman did the same, and the next, until fourteen leis were draped around his neck. Seeing this, one of the passengers cried out, "Say, old man, lay off awhile and give some of us other fellows a chance." Meanwhile the string band continued playing its soft, romantic music.

Captain O'Brien asked the granddaughter of his "old Tahitian sweetheart" to bring all of her ladies to the ship's grand saloon. After the "refreshments" of liquor were served, the princess said softly that her grandmother had died four years before. She remembered the queen's stories about her "sailor captain lover." At hearing those words, the captain felt a sadness, one that came from knowing he had lost someone he had cared for, along with those carefree days of youth. O'Brien thought about her beauty and how easily he could have become the son-in-law of the chief, just as King O'Keefe had.

As they walked to the gangway, he kissed the princesses again and gave them a "fond adieu." He left his ship later and walked over to where the old chief's palace had been. He strolled the grounds where the native fire dancers had whirled away in his honor and then visited the graves of his "dear old native friends." He had strange thoughts of love, life, and dance as he viewed "where the dust lay of the lovely girl I had once courted."

With the ship leaving the following morning, Captain O'Brien walked slowly back to his cabin, alone with his memories. He gave strict orders not to be awakened until morning when the *Buford* would sail back to San Francisco. He had already purchased and brought onboard all the spare fuel of coal and oil, paid all the bills, and cleared customs, and the passengers seemed ready to leave.

When the time came and the ship was about to pull away, the bands were playing again their different melodies. The passengers were throwing down serpentine multicolored ribbons to their newfound friends on the wharf. Cheers and salutes and music filled the air. As the foot of the gangway was being pulled up, O'Brien had a long look at the "dear little granddaughter of his native sweetheart of the 'seventies' with her leis and retinue of ladies."

The *Buford* reached Honolulu in the first week of April, and the owners confirmed he was to load all the sugar and first-class passengers that could be taken. After the additional 120 people boarded, the total passengers onboard the ship was now 250—and "dissatisfaction first abounded."

The travelers coming on, however, were well-to-do tourists like those already there, and everyone was ready to return to the United States. The excellent food, string orchestra, new friendships, swimming pool, and other amenities helped to cool the passions. O'Brien was fortunate in that all the passengers seemed to come together in a grand, unexpected party. When the ship approached San Francisco harbor, the passengers presented him with jewelry and a scroll, signed by everyone, that thanked him for his courtesies and the trip. He graciously thanked them in return, and then he sat down to think about his life so many years before.

After unloading the cargo, O'Brien wondered what would be next. Events again played out as if someone had scripted a movie on his life. The famous silent-screen actor Buster Keaton chartered the *Buford* for a thirty-day cruise through the "islands of Southern California." While anchored close to Catalina Island, Keaton made the movie *The Navigator*. As O'Brien wrote:

> That was an enjoyable thirty days. I met the members of the movie cast, and everyone was genial and lovable, especially Buster himself. Many amusing incidents happened while making the picture of *The Navigator*, but as this movie is strung out now [playing], I'll have to confine this to less personal events. When the picture was finished, we were ordered back to San Francisco, where on arrival, all hands were paid off, and the ship was placed out of commission. [A few years later, the *Buford* was scrapped in Japan.]

Said to be Buster Keaton's personal favorite, *The Navigator* is a classic silent comedy and the great comedian's biggest box-office hit. The story tells the tale of two innocent people who were stranded alone on a liner sailing out to sea. The sweetly naive Rollo Treadway (Buster Keaton) is so wealthy that everyone attends to his every need; the girl across the street (Betsy, played by Kathryn McGuire), whom he truly loves, lives an equally sheltered life. Rollo wants to marry Betsy and sail to Honolulu. When she rejects him, he decides to go alone but boards the wrong ship, the *Navigator*, owned by Betsy's father. Unaware of this, Betsy boards the ship to look for her father, whom spies capture before cutting the ship loose. It drifts out to sea. With no one able to help them, the hopeless, helpless couple must learn to fend for themselves until they are finally rescued.

Interestingly enough, the father's name is "John O'Brien." A picture of Buster Keaton and Dynamite Johnny at the time was part of the press package when the movie was released and is included in the photograph insert. Although it isn't known how much of the character of Betsy's father is based on O'Brien's life, he was a consultant on this movie and befriended the actors and actresses during the movie's production.

* * *

The last years of his life were spent as a Pacific Coast pilot. He guided ships over the Columbia River bar, down into the Puget Sound, and through the Alaskan passages. Heading in age toward eighty, O'Brien was still in demand due to his experience, common sense, and intelligence. The malevolent and dangerous Columbia River bar still seemed to give him his most "thrilling adventures," dating back to when he was sailing full-sail ships.

During this time, he piloted a steamer leaving Astoria, Oregon, toward the bar. Upon leaving port, a fresh southeast gale was blowing, and the ship had a seven-degree list. O'Brien turned to the captain and advised him to anchor off the bar until the "blow eased up." The master replied, "This is a chartered ship and she must go to sea."

"With your heavy deck load and list with this gale," O'Brien replied, "you will be lucky if you don't lose it." When the master didn't answer, Dynamite Johnny obeyed the command and started over the bar. When the ship passed buoy eight—heading into the bar's worst sections—the ship's captain finally saw a "real breaking Columbia River bar," and his face showed his fright.

"Can you turn back?" he said in an almost pleading way.

"Of course I can. But I can't vouch for the deck going underwater when she swings into the trough of these lovely old seas." O'Brien could tell that the man was now afraid of this bar, as if seeing for the first time a talked-about ravenous tiger on the prowl in a jungle.

Dynamite Johnny told the engineer they would swing the ship back to anchor and to keep giving a good head of steam. He edged the steamer close to Clatsop Spit so the ship would have plenty of room to turn. He then eased on the engines and watched for an opening in the trough. When this came, he gave the vessel a "hard port helm" and then full-speed ahead.

The ship "came through beautifully," but when she came into the trough of the crest-breaking, rolling sea, it looked for a moment as if the vessel wouldn't recover. The ship listed so far over that crewmen yelped with fright and the captain was speechless. But the ship came back and steamed to its anchorage. During the hours when O'Brien was fighting for the vessel's control, four ships radioed for assistance, as they were swamped or drifting out of control around the deadly bar. This was not an abnormal occurrence.

After twenty-four hours at anchor, the weather moderated. The ship's engineer brought the steam up, and the vessel passed safely over the bar to the sea. When O'Brien was leaving to take a pilot ship back to Astoria, the vessel's captain remarked, "We were lucky not to be out in last night's gale."

Dynamite Johnny took other ships over the Columbia River bar. As he grew older and kept experiencing its awesome power, he began assessing how lucky he had been and how long this could continue. After another close encounter, he vowed he would never again pilot a ship over the "monstrous" Columbia River bar. Age was finally catching up to the "old man."

While in Seattle, he headed out on an errand. O'Brien was walking across a street intersection when he saw fleetingly "the shadow of a shark and then oblivion": A car was speeding, hit him full on, and drove him headfirst into the brick pavement. An ambulance took the unconscious captain to a nearby hospital with a severe brain concussion. In typical O'Brien fashion, he staggered from the hospital and went home, only to collapse on the sofa and need to be taken back. He stayed in the hospital for six weeks.

O'Brien afterwards continued piloting and had close calls again on the Columbia River, despite his previous oath, and in Alaska. It was typical O'Brien. On a voyage in Alaska, the captain didn't take his pilot instructions and the ship grounded on an island, becoming a total loss. Although no lives were lost, a later inquiry held this master to be guilty of negligence, and his certificate was suspended for several months. O'Brien was held not to be at fault and returned to piloting.

Regardless of the weather, stormy or sunny, O'Brien guided ships into Seattle harbor. He loved his work, but—then as ever—he wasn't good with money. If he came upon a check, as M. J. Heney had known so well, Dynamite Johnny spent it. And if he had some "surplus," he still would hit the gambling tables. Life was to experience, not to save for old age. He was too busy living it.

His last journal entry was as follows:

> I resumed my piloting on Puget Sound and although eighty-years old, I am still at it, working for the finest and best company I have ever sailed for, the American-Hawaiian company. I cannot bring myself to think I must seek an anchorage for myself soon—one who has gone through sixty-four years at sea—and only off the payroll some six months in those years. I have had hard crews and mean owners to deal with, but my heart is, and to the last will be, in love with the sea and the dear old sailing ship days. I will leave it, as the old song goes: "My pocket is light; my heart has no pain."

The O'Briens lived at the Spring Apartment Hotel in downtown Seattle. John wanted always to be able to see the harbor and its activities and ships. When O'Brien was in his last illness, passengers on the *Victoria* adopted the following resolution: "As we sail away to the Northland, we want you to know we are wishing the best of everything for an old friend and the best skipper that ever sailed the Alaska waters."

He replied:

> Men of the North, I wish you bon voyage. My old command, the *Victoria*, will see you safely to the land of eternal friendships. I will be on hand to greet you when you return.

He wasn't. Captain "Dynamite Johnny" O'Brien died on August 3, 1931, at the age of eighty in Seattle. Emily, his daughter Kathleen, and his son John were at his side. A nephew, William J. Petrain, a Seattle newspaperman, was also present at the time.

Even in his final hours, he refused to admit to his wife and two grown children that his chances of recovery were slight. When told that his time was due, he laughingly recalled other times when he supposedly had been "due" and had surprised everyone but himself by a string of "comebacks." "I've been through worse storms than this. Just watch me get up and out to sea" was one of the last words he said.

His strong sense of religion as a guiding star was with him to the end. Just three weeks before his death, when he could hardly move, Captain O'Brien attended Mass and received the Sacraments by the priest. O'Brien's reason was that he didn't want any "suspension of his duty to God even for ill health." On his last day, he was holding the rosary in his left hand and the crucifix in his right.

When Captain O'Brien died, newspapers reported that the entire Pacific Northwest and Alaska mourned his passing. Hundreds attended his funeral services at St. James Cathedral, ranging from politicians, wealthy miners, authors, and actors to bankers, shipmasters, sailors, and policemen. As one newspaper wrote: "He died at eighty-three [sic], but lived twice, thrice that long."

Marine Digest (August 8, 1931) editorialized on its front page:

He had a great personality, colorful, vigorous, picturesque, dominating, generous, impulsive, lovable, chivalrous, and buoyant; indeed, his personality had so many qualities, had so many sides, and such depths that it baffles analysis. It had a touch of the magnificent. In the moment of action, in crises, it was overwhelming.

He was always the great sailor. His sea career had spanned sixty-seven years, of which he had been an ocean master for sixty-three years. Captain O'Brien had sailed dangerous waters, skirted treacherous reefs, crept through dense fogs, sailed through terrific storms with the hell of rockbound shores sounding in his ears. He was the master and navigator in the glamorous years of the sailing ship in the China trade and in the trades to Europe, and then later in the steamships that were added to his record. He was the pioneer steamship master of the sensational gold rush to the Klondike and he ran in the Nome gold trade for many years.

He was a great gentleman, equally at home in the roughness of the new mining camp or in the mansions of the powerful. In his quarters aboard ship, he would receive the young, inexperienced, and probably very nervous newspaper reporter with the same courtesy and kindness extended to the famous author. Regardless of position or influence, everyone who went to see him aboard his ship was received as an honored guest.

That same day, *Marine Digest* wrote in a front-page article:

He was probably Seattle's most widely known citizen, his friendships including leading industrial leaders and financiers on all coasts and such famous authors as Rex Beach, the late Jack London, and Emerson Hough [the American author best known for writing westerns]. He was one of the last, if not the last, sailing ship masters who helped make the United States known on the ocean in the great days of canvas.

Esther Birdsall Darling, referred to as the "nationally known writer and poet of Alaska," penned the following:

IN MEMORIAM
(Captain Dynamite Johnny O'Brien)

The Voyage is over, and the anchor dropt
In that fair Port where are no doubts and fears;
"The End" is on his long-book's final page—
The record of his fruitful, splendid years.

He sought, in life, not pleasant sheltered ways.
And lingered not in harbors safe and wide;
But faced the Tropic gale, the Arctic storm,
Dreading no hidden reef, no surging tide.

Not tears and prayers alone, but memories dear,
We of the North, as tribute, bring today
To him, whose genial wit and kindly deed
Are ever, in our hearts, his Wreath of Bay."

Captain O'Brien spanned the eras from full-sail and clipper ships to the large ocean liners we know today. The times have substantially changed, with laws and attorneys now trying to rule the seas—but the ocean cannot be ruled by anyone. The ocean is about survival, whether it involves pirates with their old-fashioned cannons at Nine Pin Rocks or the modern cutthroats off Somalia with their automatic weapons, motorized rafts, and grenades. Hurricanes and typhoons govern, but sailors still—like Captain John A. O'Brien—brave the oceans showing respect and courage. He lived life his way in an age when one could.

SELECTED BIBLIOGRAPHY

"A Poem by M. O'Neill." *The Living Age*, December 2, 1899, vol. 223, 573+.

Andrews, Ralph W., and Harry A. Kirwin. *This Was Seafaring*. Seattle: Superior, 1955.

Beach Comber. "What the Wild Waves Say." *Marine Digest*, August 16, 1930, vol. 8, no. 52, 7.

Betancourt, Marian. "Dynamite Johnny: The Cuban Struggle for Independence and the Remarkable Irishman Who Helped." *Irish America*, December/January 2003, vol. 18, no. 6, 34+.

"Brief Biographies: Captain John A. O'Brien—Noted American Master Who Knows All the Seven Seas." *Marine Digest*, December 15, 1923.

"Capt. J. A. O'Brien Buried Thursday from Cathedral." *Catholic New Progress*, August 7, 1931.

"Capt. J. A. O'Brien Married 50 Years." *Marine Digest*, January 5, 1929.

"Capt. O'Brien, Great Sailor, Passes Away." *Marine Digest*, August 9, 1931, vol. 9, no. 51, 1+.

"Capt. O'Brien Laid to Rest." *Seattle Post-Intelligencer*, August 7, 1931.

"Captain John A. O'Brien, Nestor of American Mariners of the Pacific" (article beginning with these words). *Seattle Railway and Marine News*, August 1924, 24+.

"Captain O'Brien Doggedly Fights Death, But Loses." *Seattle Post-Intelligencer*, August 3, 1931.

"Captain O'Brien's Danger: Precarious Position on Board the Wrecked Whaleback." *Seattle Press-Times*, September 22, 1892.

"Captains of the Pacific: Captain J. A. O'Brien." *Seattle Post-Intelligencer*, March 12, 1907, 16.

"Charlotte Terwilliger Moffett Cartwright." (Oregon Pioneer Biographies, www.rootsweb.com/~orgenweb/bios/ccartwright.html, accessed February 27, 2007).

Clunies, Sandy. "Edward 'Ned' O'Brien." E-mail to author, dated April 21, 2006 (Re: Captain O'Brien's son Ned).

Clunies, Sandy. "New Task (and information)." E-mail to author, dated April 13, 2006 (Re: birthdates, children, wife, and family background).

Clunies, Sandy. "Western Johnny O'Brien." E-mail to author, dated April 22, 2006 (Re: census, family, and background information).

Conover, C. T. "Just Cogitating: Capt. John A. O'Brien Was a Heroic Master Mariner." *Seattle Times*, February 12, 1948.

Conover, C. T. "Just Cogitating: Capt. John O'Brien Was Gallant, Unselfish." *Seattle Times*, May 29, 1955.

Dalby, Milton A. *The Sea Saga of Dynamite Johnny O'Brien*. Seattle: Lowman & Hanford, 1933.

Dana, Richard Henry, Jr. *Two Years before the Mast: A Personal Narrative of Life at Sea*. London: The Folio Society, 1986.

Duncan, Fred B. *Deepwater Family*. New York: Pantheon, 1969.

Editorial. "The curtain descended on a sea career . . ." *Marine Digest*, August 8, 1931, vol. 9, no. 51, 1.

Farrell, Andrew, trans. *John Cameron's Odyssey*. New York: MacMillan, 1928.

"Funeral of O'Brien Is Set for Tomorrow." *Seattle Times*, August 6, 1931.

"Gold! Gold! Gold! Gold!" *Seattle Post-Intelligencer*, July 17, 1897, 1.

Gourlay, R. "The 'Lucky Lieutenant.'" *St. Nicholas*, August 1900, vol. 27, 874–879.

Gowlland, Gladys M. O. *Master of the Moving Sea: The Life of Captain Peter John Riber Mathieson*. Flagstaff, Arizona: Colton, 1959.

Grant, Captain George H. *The Half Deck*. Boston: Little, Brown, 1935.

Harlow, Frederick Pease. *The Making of a Sailor or Sea Life Aboard a Yankee Square-Rigger*. Salem, Massachusetts: Marine Research Society, 1928.

Lampton, William J. "The Cape Nome Gold Fields: Their Remarkable Product and Promise." *McClure's Magazine*, vol. 15, no. 15, 134–142.

London, Charmian. *The Book of Jack London*. New York: Century, 1921.

London, Jack. *John Barleycorn*. New York: Century, 1913.

London, Jack. "Gold Hungers of the North." *Atlantic Monthly*, July 1903, vol. 92, 42–49.

London, Jack. *Smoke Bellew*. New York: Century, 1912.

Lundberg, Murray. "Explore North: Maritime Ghosts of the Klondike." (http://explorenorth.com/library/yafeatures/bl-ghost.htm, accessed January 17, 2007).

Madsen, Charles, with John Scott Douglas. *Arctic Trader*. New York: Dodd, Mead, 1957.

Marshall, Don. *Ship Disasters: Blacklock Point to Tenmile Creek*. Portland, Oregon: Binford & Mort, 1984.

"Master Mariners." *Collier's*, May 23, 1925, vol. 75, 20+.

McSherry, Jack L., III. "Jack London's Klondike Adventure: 1897–1898." (www.arcticwebsite.com/LondonJackKlond.html, accessed September 30, 2009).

Miers, Henry A. "Gold Mining in Klondike." *Popular Science Monthly*, July 1902, vol. 61, 230–240.

Newell, Gordon. *S O S North Pacific: Tales of Shipwrecks off the Washington, British Columbia and Alaska Coasts*. Portland, Oregon: Binford & Mort, 1955.

Newell, Gordon, ed. *The H. W. McCurdy Marine History of the Pacific Northwest*. Seattle: Superior, 1966.

Newell, Gordon, and Joe Williamson, *Pacific Coastal Liners*. Seattle: Superior, 1959.

Nome Convention and Visitors Bureau. "History of Nome." (www.nomealaska.org/vc/history.htm, accessed January 5, 2009).

O'Brian, Patrick. *Master and Commander*. New York and London: Norton, 1970.

O'Brien, John A., and Horace Smith. *A Captain Unafraid: The Strange Adventures of Dynamite Johnny O'Brien*. New York and London: Harper & Brothers, 1912.

"O'Brien Lives Again in Book." *Marine Digest*, April 22, 1933, vol. 11, no. 36, 1+.

Paine, Ralph D. *Roads of Adventure*. Boston and New York: Houghton Mifflin, 1922.

"Parthia I (UK)." (www.parthia.com/ships/parthia_01.htm, accessed October 12, 2009).

"Portrait (Buster Keaton)." *Collier's*, January 16, 1926, vol. 77, 16+.

Quinn, William P. *Shipwrecks Along the Atlantic Coast*. Beverly, Massachusetts: Commonwealth Editions, 1988, 2004.

Reynolds, Stephen. *The Voyage of the New Hazard to the Northwest Coast, Hawaii, and China, 1810–1813*. Fairfield, Washington: Ye Galleon Press, 1970.

Riesenberg, Felix. *Under Sail*. New York: Macmillan, 1918.

Rogers, Stanley. *The Pacific*. New York: Crowell, 1931.

Satterfield, Archie. "Klondike Park: Travels with a Photographer." (www.archiesatterfield.com/work4.htm, accessed January 17, 2007).

"Shipmates and Laymen Attend O'Brien Rites: Father O'Neill Eulogizes Late Mariner as One of Century's Outstanding Characters." *Alaska Weekly*, August 7, 1931.

Slocum, Victor. "The Pilot's Life." *The Outlook*, July 4, 1903, vol. 74, 572–582.

"Soapy Smith, Outlaw Saved Skipper That Day: Captain O'Brien, Pioneer Pilot, Recalls Gold Rush Days in Alaska." *Seattle Times*, March 14, 1930.

"Sunk By Iceberg; Scores Drowned." *New York Times*, August 20, 1901, 3.

Teller, Walter, ed. *Five Sea Captains: Their Own Accounts of Voyages Under Sail*. New York: Atheneum, 1960.

"Veteran of Seas Loses in Valiant Last Fight." *Seattle Times*, August 4, 1931.

"The Victoria." *Marine Digest*, June 19, 1954, 9.

"Victoria Still Dependable as Freight Vessel." *Marine Digest*, December 26, 1953, 7+.

"Victoria Sold; Old Ship May Become Museum." *Marine Digest*, March 13, 1954, 9.

Wakeman, Captain Edgar. *The Log of an Ancient Mariner: Being the Life and Adventure of Captain Edgar Wakeman*, ed. Minnie Wakeman-Curtis. San Francisco: Bancroft, 1878.

Walker, Franklin. *Jack London and the Klondike*. San Marino, California: Huntington Library, 1966, 1994.

Willoughby, Barrett. "Barrett Willoughby, Author, Pays Tribute to O'Brien." *Seattle Times*, August 1, 1931.

Winter, James M. *New York to Alaska Voyage of Steamer "Dolphin" May to July, 1900*. Middletown, New York: Whitlock, 1943.

"Would You Know Him?" *Marine Digest*, April 11, 1925, vol. 3, no. 33, 1+.

INDEX

ABOUT THE AUTHOR

Dennis M. Powers is an established author, frequent media guest, and conference speaker. He was a business law attorney in private practice before joining the faculty and becoming a full professor in the School of Business at Southern Oregon University in Ashland, Oregon. He is a graduate of the University of Colorado, the University of Denver Law School, and Harvard Business School. His interest in the engaging stories about sailors, their lives in the early days, and sea voyages has been ongoing for years.

Since deciding to concentrate on his writing twenty years ago, he has authored ten published nonfiction books, the last five, including *Tales of the Seven Seas*, in maritime history. *The Raging Sea* (2005) chronicles the crushing 1964 tsunami that ravished the U.S. West Coast; *Treasure Ship* (2006) is about the loss, legend, and legacy of the *S.S. Brother Jonathan*, a side-wheel steamer that sank off northern California with millions of dollars of gold—and finally discovered 125 years later; *Sentinel of the Seas* (2007) tells the story of the most remote, dangerous, and expensive lighthouse built in this country's history, St. George Reef Lighthouse; and *Taking the Sea* (2009) tells the sagas of the maritime business of wrecking, or ship salvaging.

He participates at writers' conferences as a workshop leader and speaker, as well as also writing fiction, short stories, and published poetry. Now Professor Emeritus, Mr. Powers resides in Ashland, Oregon, with his wife, Judy, three cats, and libraries of books. More information about the author is available at his website, www.dennispowersbooks.com.